"Challenges to transatlantic relations didn't begin (or end) with the Trump presidency. This book applies historical and contemporary perspectives in addressing an urgent question: How resilient are those relations? Policymakers and researchers striving to understand what the future could bring will find this book helpfully thought-provoking."

Roy Norton, *Balsillie School of International Affairs, Waterloo, Canada*

TRANSATLANTIC RELATIONS

This book explains how and why the transatlantic relationship has remained resilient despite persistent differences in the preferences, approaches, and policies of key member states.

It covers topics ranging from the history of transatlantic relations, North Atlantic Treaty Organization and security issues, trade, human rights, and the cultural sinews of the relationship, to the impacts of COVID-19, climate change, think tanks, the rise of populism, public opinion, and the triangular relationship between the United States (US), Europe, and China. This book also conceptualizes resilience as a quality arising from myriad forms of interdependence. This interdependence helps shed light on the Atlantic partnership's capacity to withstand serious disagreements, such as those that occurred during the Reagan, George W. Bush, and Trump presidencies.

With a principle focus on the US and Europe, the contributors to the volume also employ Canadian case studies to provide a unique and useful corrective. This book will interest all intermediate and senior undergraduate as well as graduate courses on relations between the US and Europe, American foreign policy, and European Union foreign policy. A specialist readership that includes academic and think tank researchers, policy practitioners, and opinion leaders will also benefit from this timely volume.

Donald E. Abelson is Director, Brian Mulroney Institute of Government, Steven K. Hudson Chair in Canada-US Relations, and Professor, Political Science, St. Francis Xavier University.

Stephen Brooks is Professor of Political Science at the University of Windsor and director of the European Union Study Abroad Program, a collaboration of the University of Windsor and Western University.

TRANSATLANTIC RELATIONS

Challenge and Resilience

Edited by Donald E. Abelson and Stephen Brooks

LONDON AND NEW YORK

Cover image: Prime Minister Churchill on board HMS Prince of Wales for his August 1941 Atlantic rendezvous with President Roosevelt

First published 2022
by Routledge
4 Park Square, Milton Park, Abingdon, Oxon OX14 4RN

and by Routledge
605 Third Avenue, New York, NY 10158

Routledge is an imprint of the Taylor & Francis Group, an informa business

© 2022 selection and editorial matter, Donald E. Abelson and Stephen Brooks; individual chapters, the contributors

The right of Donald E. Abelson and Stephen Brooks to be identified as the authors of the editorial material, and of the authors for their individual chapters, has been asserted in accordance with sections 77 and 78 of the Copyright, Designs and Patents Act 1988.

All rights reserved. No part of this book may be reprinted or reproduced or utilised in any form or by any electronic, mechanical, or other means, now known or hereafter invented, including photocopying and recording, or in any information storage or retrieval system, without permission in writing from the publishers.

Trademark notice: Product or corporate names may be trademarks or registered trademarks, and are used only for identification and explanation without intent to infringe.

British Library Cataloguing-in-Publication Data
A catalogue record for this book is available from the British Library

Library of Congress Cataloging-in-Publication Data
A catalog record has been requested for this book

ISBN: 9780367706937 (hbk)
ISBN: 9780367706944 (pbk)
ISBN: 9781003147565 (ebk)

DOI: 10.4324/9781003147565

Typeset in Bembo
by Newgen Publishing UK

CONTENTS

List of Figures ix
List of Tables x
List of Contributors xi
Acknowledgments xiv

Introduction: Sources of Resilience in the Transatlantic
Relationship 1
Donald E. Abelson and Stephen Brooks

PART I
Sensibility, Solidarity, and Stress 27

1 Transatlantic Sensibility and Solidarity: The Distinctive
 Factors of Interpersonal Connection and Shared Historical
 Experience 29
 Alan K. Henrikson

2 The COVID-19 Pandemic as an Incubator of Great Power
 Rivalries 58
 Josef Braml

PART II
Issue Areas and Policies   77

3 Transatlantic Relations and the Challenges of Climate Change and the Environment   79
   Simon Schunz

4 NATO's "Macronian" Peril: Real or Exaggerated?   101
   David G. Haglund

5 What's in My Sandwich? Trade, Values, and the Promise of Deeper Integration   119
   Francesco Duina

6 Human Rights in US and EU Foreign Policies   139
   Joe Renouard

PART III
Broader Determinants of Transatlantic Relations   161

7 Canada–EU–US Relations   163
   Emmanuel Brunet-Jailly

8 The Rise of China and Transatlantic Strategy   184
   Emiliano Alessandri

9 Public and Elite Opinion Relating to the EU–US Relationship   203
   Stephen Brooks

10 Think Tanks and Transatlantic Relations: An Overview   228
    Donald E. Abelson and Christopher J. Rastrick

11 The Rise and Challenge of Populism   248
    Andrea Wagner, Eric Pietrasik, and Dorian Kroqi

Index   *269*

FIGURES

1.1 Prime Minister Churchill on board HMS *Prince of Wales* in Placentia Bay, Newfoundland, Canada, for his August 1941 rendezvous in the Atlantic with President Roosevelt 42
9.1 Confidence in the US president and desirability of US leadership 209
9.2 Ranked importance of relationships with other countries 214

TABLES

11.1 Variations within right-wing populists' perception of the most important 2020–21 US events   258
11.2 Variations within right-wing populists' legitimation and de-legitimation attempts   259
11A.1 Examples of right-wing populist statements and their coding   263

CONTRIBUTORS

Editors

Donald E. Abelson is Director, Brian Mulroney Institute of Government, Steven K. Hudson Chair in Canada-US Relations, and Professor, Political Science, St. Francis Xavier University. He has authored several books including *Handbook on Think Tanks in Public Policy* and *Do Think Tanks Matter? Assessing the Impact of Public Policy Institutes*. He is also a regular commentator on national and international media outlets, discussing think tanks, current events in the US politics, and Canada-US relations.

Stephen Brooks is Professor of Political Science at the University of Windsor and director of the European Union Study Abroad Program, a collaboration of the University of Windsor and Western University. He has taught at various universities on both sides of the Atlantic, including the Katholieke Universiteit Leuven, Sciences Po Lille, the Université de Paris 3, and the University of Michigan. His most recent books focus on public and cultural diplomacy and US foreign policy.

Contributors

Emiliano Alessandri is an international security expert specializing in transatlantic relations. He is a Senior Transatlantic Fellow with the German Marshall Fund of the United States and a non-resident scholar with the Middle East Institute. He also teaches for the College of Europe and Fletcher School's joint Master of Arts in Transatlantic Affairs.

Josef Braml is an expert on the United States and is Secretary General of the German Group of the Trilateral Commission, a global dialogue platform for an exclusive circle of political and economic decision-makers in the US, Europe, and Asia for the cooperative solution of geopolitical, economic, and social problems. He also publishes current analyses via his blog usaexperte.com.

Emmanuel Brunet-Jailly is Professor in the School of Public Administration, University of Victoria, British Columbia, and Jean Monnet Chair in Innovative Governance. He is Director of the Jean Monnet Centre and editor of the journals *Canadian American Public Policy* and *Borders in Globalization Review*. His research areas include comparative and interdisciplinary theorization of cross-border urban regions. Brunet-Jailly's current work focuses on the re-imposition of borders due to Brexit.

Francesco Duina is Professor of Sociology and European Studies at Bates College. His work combines economic and political sociology, international political economy, and cultural sociology to understand how nation-states persist and operate amidst globalization. He writes on themes such as trade policy and competition. His articles have appeared in journals such as *Regulation & Governance* and *Economy and Society*. His books include *The Social Construction of Free Trade* and *Broke and Patriotic*.

David G. Haglund is Professor of Political Studies, Queen's University. His research focuses on transatlantic security. His books include *Latin America and the Transformation of U.S. Strategic Thought, 1936–1940* (1984); *Alliance Within the Alliance? Franco-German Military Cooperation and the European Pillar of Defense* (1991); and *The US "Culture Wars" and the Anglo-American Special Relationship* (2019). His most recent book is on US-French relations and is forthcoming in 2022: *Sister Acts: Strategic Culture and the Franco-American 'Special Relationship.'*

Alan K. Henrikson is the Lee E. Dirks Professor of Diplomatic History Emeritus and founding director of Diplomatic Studies at The Fletcher School of Law and Diplomacy, Tufts University. During 2010–11, he served as Fulbright Schuman Professor at the College of Europe in Bruges. He has written and published widely on the history and current problems of American foreign policy, US-EU relations, and the origins and international role of NATO.

Dorian Kroqi is with Statistics Canada. He completed his PhD in political science at Carleton University, Ottawa, Canada. His research interests lie at the intersection of comparative politics, public policy, and political theory. In particular, he focuses on democratization and grassroots participation at the European and national levels of governance.

Eric Pietrasik is a fourth-year undergraduate at MacEwan University where he is pursuing a Bachelor of Arts (Honours) in Political Science. He is a recipient of the Undergraduate Student Research Initiative Project Grant, which has allowed him to study the rise of contemporary populist movements. Eric's research focuses on the media's framing of populist discourse and its relationship with Euroskepticism.

Christopher J. Rastrick, Chief of Staff, Office of the President of the Treasury Board, received his PhD from Western University in London, Ontario. He has worked for several of Canada's leading think tanks, including the Canada West Foundation. His first book *Think Tanks in the US and EU: The Role of Policy Institutes in Washington and Brussels* was published in 2017, and he co-edited the recent *Handbook on Think Tanks in Public Policy* (2021). His research focuses on think tanks, Canada-EU relations, and skills development policy.

Joe Renouard is Resident Professor of American Studies at the Johns Hopkins University School of Advanced International Studies in Nanjing, China. He specializes in American foreign policy, diplomatic history, human rights, and transatlantic relations. His most recent book is *Human Rights in American Foreign Policy* (2016). His work has also appeared in many edited volumes and in such journals as *American Diplomacy*, the *Journal of Transatlantic Studies*, and *The National Interest*.

Simon Schunz is Professor in the European Union International Relations and Diplomacy Studies Department at the College of Europe and Associate Research Fellow at the UN University Institute on Comparative Regional Integration Studies, Bruges. His research interests include EU external action, especially external climate and environmental policies, and EU relations with major powers. He recently co-edited the volume *The Evolving Relationship Between China, the EU and the USA: A New Global Order?* (2020).

Andrea Wagner is Assistant Professor and Jean Monnet Chair at MacEwan University. Her research focuses on corruption and rent-seeking in the European Union, specifically the importance of Central and Eastern European anti-corruption agencies. In addition, the recent return of the specter of populism in many developed countries has motivated exploration of the connection between populism and Euroskepticism. Her research has been published in multiple journals, including *Comparative European Politics* and *Political Studies*.

ACKNOWLEDGMENTS

Rarely do academics speak with fondness about editing or co-editing scholarly collections. Rather, after struggling for months with contributors to meet deadlines and to heed the advice of those who have read their drafts, editors often throw up their arms and state, "Never again."

Fortunately, this has not been our experience working with a tremendous group of scholars who have produced this incredible collection. From the time Steve and I approached contributors to set aside the time necessary to share their insights on transatlantic relations, they have prioritized this project—a volume that raises important and timely insights about a topic that continues to generate interest and scrutiny from scholars and policymakers on both sides of the Atlantic. We thank those who provided their expertise, shared their wisdom, and gave their time.

We express our profound gratitude to Dr. Anna Zuschlag, the Project/Research Manager at the Brian Mulroney Institute of Government, St. Francis Xavier University, who, with great skill, diplomacy, and tenacity, made this book project not only possible, but also, in so many ways, enjoyable. A seasoned historian and meticulous copy editor, Anna left few stones unturned.

Finally, we would like to thank our colleagues at Routledge who welcomed and encouraged us to pursue this project. It has been an incredibly rewarding experience.

Donald E. Abelson and Stephen Brooks

INTRODUCTION

Sources of Resilience in the Transatlantic Relationship

Donald E. Abelson and Stephen Brooks

Assessments of the transatlantic relationship between Europe and the United States (US) are always in fashion and are bound to attract close and sustained attention among political pundits and scholars. Discussions among these and other stakeholders take many forms but often rest on concerns and dire warnings about the condition and future of the relationship. Indeed, "Periodic angst about the state of trans-Atlantic ties is perhaps as old as the relationship itself" (Kennedy and Bouton 2002, 66). This observation, penned by Kennedy and Bouton (2002), months before the tumultuous War in Iraq and well in advance of the many lesser, but nevertheless significant, causes of friction between the US and the European Union (EU), did not go unnoticed. If anything, they resonated more loudly in the transatlantic policymaking community after the bitterly contested 2016 election of Donald J. Trump. During the four years that America's 45th president was at the helm, predictions about the demise of the transatlantic relationship became banal in their frequency.

These gloomy prognostications were expressed by many respected voices. Former US ambassador to the North Atlantic Treaty Organization (NATO) Nicholas Burns and Anthony Luzzatto Gardner (2020), US ambassador to the EU under President Barack Obama, were among a cadre of former diplomats outspoken in their criticism of the Trump administration's policies toward their European allies. Books and articles with such titles as *Europe and America: The End of the Transatlantic Relationship?* (Bindi 2019), "America's Long Goodbye" (Cohen 2019), "How to Save the Transatlantic Alliance" (Röttgen 2019), "The Pandemic and the Toll of Transatlantic Discord" (Donfried and Ischinger 2020), and innumerable conferences steeped in skepticism about the future of transatlantic relations, including "The End of the Transatlantic Era?" (Chicago Council 2017), "The Crisis in the Transatlantic Relationship" (Kennedy School 2018), and "America First. Europe Alone?" (Brookings-Robert Bosch Foundation 2018) were organized on

DOI:10.4324/9781003147565-1

both sides of the Atlantic. No doubt inspired by the multiplying signs of decline in the state of the transatlantic partnership, in September 2018, the Brookings Institution launched its quarterly Trans-Atlantic Scorecard. The 19 experts polled for the first scorecard gave the transatlantic partnership an overall score of 3.6 out of 10. Two years later, nothing had changed this rather dismal assessment. The 20 experts surveyed concluded that the relationship warranted an overall score of 3.6 out of 10, with only two expressing the view that it was improving (Brookings 2020). The optimism of both these experts was predicated on their expectation that President Trump would lose the 2020 election.

In seeking to explain what most believed to be a deeply troubled relationship, even before Trump's election, commentators provided several explanations that may be grouped into the following five main categories:

- *Asymmetry.* The unequal power relationship between the US and the EU, particularly, but not exclusively, in matters of security and defense, is often seen to be a root cause of stress in their relationship.
- *Global change.* This involves mainly the rise of China and the putative decline of US global influence. More generally, it considers the consequences of major geopolitical transformations and the manner in which they have been refracted through the lens of the politics and institutions of the US and EU, respectively.
- *Drifting apart.* Although there are some important dissents from this view, increasing divergence in the values and beliefs of Americans and Europeans is often argued to be a significant source of conflict between the US and the EU. Some commentators argue that there has been no serious divergence in the *interests* of the transatlantic partners and, indeed, that some actual convergence may have resulted from the actions and goals of China and Russia. However, no one argues that a convergence of values and beliefs has occurred in recent years.
- *Hard and soft power perspectives on the world.* According to this explanation, US political leaders, and not just the current administration in Washington, have tended to approach global politics in a manner that emphasizes their country's hard power attributes. The EU, by this account, prefers to project an image of itself as a "normative" or "civilian" power on the global stage. This leads to important transatlantic differences regarding such matters as the importance of abiding by international law, participating in and resolving conflicts through multilateral institutions and processes, and the willingness to behave in a manner that values and respects norms of shared sovereignty.
- *Donald Trump.* Much of the discord in transatlantic relations in recent years has been ascribed to the ideas, politics, and management—or mismanagement—style of President Trump. Although many observers of the relationship acknowledge that very serious stresses in US-EU relations existed under previous presidents (most openly and intensely during the presidency of George W. Bush), it is undeniable that tensions reached a new and disturbing level

during Trump's term in office. The range of conflicts and strained tone of the relationship, and perhaps even the disinterest and disrespect that President Trump so often showed toward transatlantic allies and the EU in particular, was without precedent. It was, however, a mistake to understand this discord as merely or even principally due to a single, very powerful individual who occupied the White House. Donald Trump was a symptom, not the cause, of the populist–nationalist sentiment that engulfed US politics.

Trump aside, most assessments of the transatlantic relationship emphasize the serious and ongoing divisions and conflicts between the US and its European partners. Moreover, there has been a general consensus that the consequences of this discord have been negative for the US, Europe, global security, and the liberal international order that has been built, largely under US leadership, since World War II. This consensus is shared by many liberal internationalists (Ikenberry 2018) and realists (Kagan 2018) alike.

There are, however, dissenters who seem to fall into three main groups. First, there are those who supported, and who continue to embrace, Trump's rallying cry of "America First" as the US re-evaluates its military alliances, economic partnerships, and behavior toward other nations more generally. They argue that, in playing the role of what some have called "The Great Disrupter,"[1] President Trump achieved trade and security gains for the US that were not achievable under the status quo ante (Dueck 2019; Hanson 2019). Second, some European observers argue that a positive consequence of America's diminished willingness to lead, and of the Trump administration's unprecedentedly aggressive questioning of the relevance of the North Altanic Treaty Organization (NATO), has been to provide the impetus for EU solutions to security challenges that do not rely on US leadership or financial contributions (see, for example, Bindi 2018; *The Economist* 2019; van Ham 2018). Finally, there are those who believe that a decline in US hegemony, including a weakening of US influence in Europe, is a good thing from the standpoint of global security, human rights, and justice, and will perforce lead to a fairer and more just world economic order. These commentators range from those who argue that the US might once have been the "indispensable nation" but that US leadership and certainly American dominance are no longer needed in all cases (Zakaria 2011), to those who argue that the idea of the indispensable nation was always an arrogant delusion and often a cover for exploitation and aggression (Chandra 2008; Reich and Lebow 2014).

Donald Trump's defeat in the 2020 presidential election was, for the most part, celebrated on both sides of the Atlantic among those who study and comment on relations between the US and Europe. Moreover, this collective sigh of relief and elation was shared by all the major foreign policy think tanks inside and beyond the Washington Beltway and in the European capitals of London, Brussels, Paris, and Berlin. The Brookings Trans-Atlantic Scorecard registered a significant uptick in the first months after Joseph R. Biden, Jr.'s election as president, from 3.6 to 4.1 out of 10, with 17 of the 21 experts polled expressing the view that transatlantic relations were trending positive. A guarded bonhomie replaced the gloom that had characterized the previous four years, a change that was evident during US Secretary of State Anthony J. Blinken's well-received visit to Brussels in March 2021. The mood became even better after the June 2021 G7 Summit, the Trans-Atlantic Scorecard average of experts jumping to 6.6 out of 10.

The expectation of better times for relations between the US and Europe provides the backdrop to this book, the aim of which is to provide a sober assessment of the factors that have, in recent times, influenced transatlantic relations. In some cases, these factors were amplified in their impacts during the Trump presidency and are for the most part deeply rooted in developments that have been underway for years. The challenges that have roiled the transatlantic waters are well known and real. Equally real, however, are sources of resilience in the relationship that often have been overlooked, or at least not ascribed sufficient weight. We turn now to these sources of resilience in transatlantic relations.

Resilience and Its Relevance to Transatlantic Relations

Political science and its subfields have a long history of importing, refining, and at times overhauling concepts from other disciplines and adapting them to the analysis of political and governmental affairs. Lasswell (1930) was among a remarkable group of psychologists who borrowed concepts from clinical psychology in developing a typology of personality types in politics. Barber (1972), particularly with respect to predicting presidential performance in the White House, developed his own typology. Easton (1965) borrowed from cybernetics in developing his systems theory of political behavior, a theory later elaborated on by Steinbruner (1974). International relations (IR) theory also has been significantly influenced by concepts imported from other disciplines (Lawson and Shilliam 2010).

Among the more recent of such imported concepts has been *resilience*.[2] The concept is centuries-old and related to the work of Francis Bacon (1627) in the early seventeenth century. In modern discourse, it has come to mean the capacity of a material or structure to withstand or bounce back from unusual and stressful conditions (Gößling-Reisemann, Hellige, and Thier 2018, 4). It has also been used in material sciences since the nineteenth century. For engineers, resilience was, and continues to be, an attribute that can be measured, and whose limits are therefore predictable with the aid of models and mathematical formulae.

Researchers in the study of ecosystems were quick to borrow the concept, applying it to the determination of how well, and under what conditions, plant and animal biosystems could survive either sudden or gradual stress, such as the introduction of previously absent chemicals or non-native species. Although the word "resilience" was not used, or at least as no more than a metaphor, the concept was important in the wave of limits to growth studies that were published in the late 1960s and early 1970s. In the best known of these, the Club of Rome's *Limits to Growth* (Meadows et al. 1972), resilience was understood as the ability of human populations, including their health and prosperity, to withstand various changes in such independent variables as pollution, the supplies of resources needed for industrial production, and stress on agricultural production due to population growth.

Psychology and branches of sociology, including social work, adopted and adapted the concept beginning in the 1970s. Since then, it has been applied to the understanding of the personal attributes and external circumstances that explain why some individuals, families, or other small groups, but particularly individuals, are better able than others to withstand and overcome adverse conditions. Attempts to measure or evaluate such resilience have produced mixed results, and although there is a consensus among those who study individual and small group behavior that resilience matters, there is no agreement on how or even whether it can be measured (Windle, Bennett, and Noyes 2011).

The idea that the resilience of human populations larger than small groups might be measurable, including such geographically limited communities as cities and even national populations was seductive for many social scientists. Scholars in such fields as economics, risk assessment, human geography, and anthropology have attempted to operationalize the concept of resilience for several decades. As the notion that resilience *as a measurable concept* has taken hold across social science disciplines, questions about whether it can in fact be measured when applied to human behavior and populations have continued (Patel et al. 2017).

Political science and the study of IRs were somewhat late in embracing resilience as a potentially measurable concept that might have significant explanatory value. Resilience was the subject of an issue of the *Georgetown Journal of International Affairs* (2012), several articles by, among others, IR theorists Bourbeau (2018a–b; Bourbeau and Ryan 2018) and Chandler (2014), various books including the *Routledge Handbook on Resilience* (Chandler and Coaffee 2017) and *Forward Resilience* (Hamilton 2016), which gave rise in 2018 to the Global Resilience Institute at Northeastern University. The concept's attractiveness is obvious. It appears to explain, or at least seeks to explain, the ability of states, human populations, and economies and other social systems to survive, adapt, and recover from extreme and perhaps unanticipated adversity.

It comes as no surprise, therefore, that resilience very quickly transformed from an academic concern to a goal and sort of mantra among policymakers. Since about 2016 (Juncos 2017), there has been an explosion in the references to resilience as a core concept and policy objective for the EU, NATO, and other international institutions (Korosteleva and Flockhart 2020). This burst of interest in resilience in its application to IR has not produced very much in the way of agreement on how or whether the concept can be operationalized. Much of what has been written on resilience in political science, IR, and security studies does not even attempt to go beyond a rather vague definition of resilience as persistence due to adaptability (Sayers 2011; Vieira 2016). Moreover, no sooner was the concept imported in the fields of politics and governance than it became the target of theoretical and ideological criticism. Such notions as equilibrium, persistence, adaptability, and the management of conflict that are conceptually associated with resilience include, according to critics, unexamined and unexplored premises about the proper functioning of a system (Brassett, Croft, and Vaughn-Williams 2013).

In recent years, transatlantic relations have been examined through the conceptual prism of resilience (Friedrichs, Harnisch, and Thies 2019). The concept, vague and contested as it may be, has a strong intuitive appeal and could conceivably become more prominent in the conversation on IR in general, or more specifically on transatlantic relations. Its "fuzziness" and the fact that it may be closer to metaphor than measurable condition (Carpenter et al. 2001) should not be viewed as reasons to discount the utility of resilience as a framework for understanding these relations. Indeed, as one recent study suggests, it is precisely the "constructive ambiguity" of the concept that is at the heart of its attractiveness to policymakers and scholars (Cusumano and Cooper 2020, 295). Scientifically, however, too much should not be expected of the concept, a warning that is heard even among natural scientists who are otherwise supportive of resilience as a useful concept (Pimm et al. 2019).

This is the spirit in which resilience is used in this chapter and throughout this book. The liberal world order that has been constructed since World War II, and whose buckle has been transatlantic relations is, as Deudney and Ikenberry (2018) argued, a resilient international order. "[I]t is," they wrote, "deeply embedded. Hundreds of millions, if not billions, of people have geared their activities and expectations to the order's institutions and incentives" (Deudney and Ikenberry 2018, 20). The properties that are essential to the resilience of the liberal world order and to transatlantic relations, they argue, include the myriad forms of interdependence among states and between societies. The fact that this order does not require that all its members subscribe to liberal democratic values and the absence of a credible rival to liberal democracy on the global stage gives it more weight.

The sources of resilience that Deudney and Ikenberry (2018) identified include both soft and hard aspects of relations between states. Shared values and the international institutions and rules to which they have given rise, and that embody liberal principles of individual freedom and dignity, are important. But so too are the security, economic, and environmental relations that emerge from the interdependence of states and the societies they govern and whose management requires, more than at any previous moment, cooperation between them.

The optimism that Deudney and Ikenberry expressed for the liberal world order and for the transatlantic relations that underpin it is not, however, universally shared. History may eventually judge the early twenty-first century to have been an inflection point in transatlantic relations and the Trump presidency to have been the tipping point for what Moïsi (2018) has called the "transatlantic rupture." Still, the scale and persistence of the stresses on these relations are well known and must be taken seriously. Some of them predated the Trump presidency and will persist for years. At the same time, however, the gloomy assessments and dire prognoses that have dominated expert and media commentary on the transatlantic relationship over several years may be guilty of what Deudney and Ikenberry (2018) called "a blinding presentism" (20). Such assessments fail to give due attention and weight to those factors that have made the relationship resilient in the past and that can ensure that it remains the linchpin of the liberal world order.

Sources of Resilience in Transatlantic Relations

The sinews of these relations are both hard and soft. In the hard category are ties of trade and investment, defense and security linkages, and physical infrastructure (transportation and communications, energy, shared water management, etc. (Davtyan 2014)). The soft category includes values and beliefs, diplomatic ties and activities, cultural exchanges, and personal and organizational linkages involving elites, interest groups, and other groups in civil society. Between these two categories are international institutions and agreements and the norms associated with them, ranging on a continuum between hard (obligations that are legally binding, precise, and that delegate authority for their interpretation) and soft (where the three dimensions of hard international law are weaker) (Abbott and Snidal 2000, 421–22).

Some of these ties lend greater resilience to transatlantic relations than others. Moreover, there is no a priori rank ordering of their importance. Soft linkages may be more durable than the legalized ties that exist through trade and security agreements. Among the most important of these soft linkages in the transatlantic community have been those associated with shared values, norms, and beliefs, elements that serve as a basis for discussions around the formation of international regimes (Krasner 1983).

Values, Norms, and Beliefs

Sharing fundamental values, norms, and beliefs has long been seen as the cement of the transatlantic relationship. In his famous 1946 "Sinews of Peace" speech, Winston Churchill emphasized their role in what he described as the special relationship between the US and Britain. Churchill argued that, ultimately, the strength of the West would rest on its solidarity behind the liberal democratic principles expressed in the United Nations (UN) Charter (Churchill 1946).

Signs of weakening of the cultural ties across the Atlantic, and particularly those between the US and Western Europe, have always given rise to fears that the transatlantic relationship, including what it stands for globally and its ability to work together to achieve shared goals, is diminished. Such fears have led many to speculate on "the end of the West" (Anderson, Ikenberry, and Risse 2008; Kimmage 2020; Kupchan 2002; Tcherneva 2018; Walt 1998). Not all these speculation points to cultural divergence as the primary cause of a decline in transatlantic unity and in the global influence of values associated with the concept of the West. Nevertheless, it has become common to view culture as something that is as likely to divide as it is to bridge the transatlantic partnership.

This begs two important questions. First, has the transatlantic cultural divide become wider over time and particularly over the past couple of decades? Second, does this matter as much as some commentators claim when it comes to the capacity of the transatlantic community to promote and achieve the security, economic, and political goals that have been associated with the liberal world order?

The first question may be easier to answer or at least it is more amenable to evaluation and measurement. If we begin with the presidency of George W. Bush, when discussion of a transatlantic cultural divide gained serious traction, the opinion of a majority of experts on both sides of the Atlantic seems to have been that the transatlantic values gap—with Canada excluded from this generalization— has widened and that the consequences have been significant (Kohut and Stokes 2006; Micklethwait and Wooldridge 2005; Pew 2011, 2015; Wickett 2018). This tendency to stress cultural divergence abated somewhat during the Obama years but returned with a vengeance after Trump's election.

The evidence for this claim of growing cultural divergence is not; however, as compelling as is often argued. The World Values Survey (WVS) has tracked a wide range of political, social, economic, and moral/religious beliefs for the past four decades. The Inglehart-Welzel cultural maps of the world, generated by each wave of the WVS, have often provided part of the evidential basis for claims that the US is an outlier among affluent democracies (Boucher 2014; Brooks 2014; Karabel and Laurison 2012; Reitz 2018). Americans have occupied a location on this map that is in the same broad cluster of transatlantic societies that share a Christian and Western heritage. But the location of American society on this map, with regard to the traditional vs. secular–rational values axis, has been closer to many less-developed and non-Western countries than to many European countries. This outlier status has, however, diminished over the 40 years of the WVS. Moreover, there is no evidence that it has increased since the 1990s, although religion continues to distinguish less secular Americans from what are, on the whole, more secular European societies.

This conclusion is based on a set of seven questions that are widely acknowledged to be valid measures of attitudes and beliefs relating to important aspects of equality, personal freedom, and the role of democratic government.[3] In only one case does the transatlantic values gap increase over the four rounds of the WVS carried out between 1995 and 1999 and between 2017 and 2020. This involves the proper balance between protecting the environment versus the economic growth and the protection of jobs, where the gap between Americans and the populations of the western European countries for which there are data over these four rounds of the WVS increases somewhat. Value convergence, although far from dramatic in the case of most of the response items, appears to be the most reasonable conclusion to be drawn from what is an admittedly limited set of questions and countries.

In the absence of strong, or at least unequivocal, evidence that a sort of continental drift in values is pushing apart the transatlantic partners, the question of how cultural divergence undermines this relationship is moot. Some observers, including Baldwin (2009) in *The Narcissism of Minor Differences*, argued that not only has there not been convergence, but also the value differences between American and European societies tend not to be very large and are probably smaller than the range of values found across European countries and within the US.

Nevertheless, the belief that there is a transatlantic values gap that may have grown wider in recent years and that has a direct and negative impact on economic and security relations between the US and Europe (and between the US and Canada too), remains strong. The George W. Bush years were widely seen as a time when the rightward drift of US politics under a president with strong support from social conservatives and evangelicals, combined with geopolitical circumstances to encourage unilateralism in foreign policy and to a kind of moral crusade on the world stage (den Dulk and Rozell 2011; Judis 2005). Likewise, the Trump presidency was widely interpreted as a turn toward authoritarian populism in US politics, the foreign policy implications of which were summed up in a slogan he borrowed from Ronald Reagan in the 1980 presidential campaign, "Make America Great Again" and "America First," which was repeated several times in Trump's inaugural address. This ascendance of right-wing populism in America (Inglehart and Norris 2016; Löfflmann 2019), it is argued, widened the transatlantic values gap and was an important driver of the strained relations that existed during these years between the US government and both NATO and the EU.

That these relations were strained is undeniable. Causal attribution, however, is often trickier than may at first appear. Right-wing populism has been on the rise over the past several years in many EU countries too and has achieved notable electoral and policy successes in the United Kingdom (UK), Poland, Hungary, and Austria. As of 2020, right-wing populist parties were also part of coalition governments in 11 of 33 European countries (Timbro 2019). In fact, the Timbro populism index reveals that support for populist policies and beliefs is no higher in the US than in several European countries (Timbro 2019). Some Canadian surveys also suggest that populist sentiment in that country is not significantly less than in the US (Morris J. Wosk Centre 2019).

In the end, the evidence that a widening cultural gap has been an important driver of strains in the transatlantic relationship over the past couple of decades is not especially convincing, at least at the level of mass populations. This issue is revisited in Chapter 9 on public opinion and the transatlantic relationship.

People, Associations, and Networks

In explaining the fact that the values systems of transatlantic countries have been and continue to be more similar than they are to those of populations in other regions of the world, shared ancestry is generally thought to be an important contributing factor. Until the 1970s, the majority of the tens of millions of people who immigrated to the US and Canada were of European ancestry. Permanent relocation in the other direction represented only a very small fraction of this immigration. In recent decades, the majority of Americans and Canadians who emigrate have often done so temporarily for reasons of work or study, going mainly to European countries and Australia (Dumont and Lemaître 2005).[4]

For roughly 20 years, there has been serious speculation about whether and how demographic change in North America and Europe might affect transatlantic relations (Dunn 2009, 7–9). This literature has ignored Canada, focusing on demographic developments in the US and Europe, and how these are thought to affect their respective domestic and foreign policies and, ultimately, transatlantic relations. The arguments regarding changing population characteristics may be summarized as follows.

- *Kith and kin matter.* One-half century ago, roughly 85 percent of the American population and 96 percent of the Canadian population had European ancestry. Today, the shares are about 70 percent in both countries.[5] Ties of ethnicity and the cultural bonds that accompanied them ensured that Europe was more personally relevant for more Americans and Canadians than other parts of the world. As both the US and Canada have become less European in terms of their ethnic mix, and as persons from other regions of the world and from non-European cultures have come to comprise an ever-growing share of their respective populations, the geopolitical relevance accorded to Europe and the affective ties toward it have diminished.
- *Diasporas and their influence.* A corollary of the preceding argument is that large or otherwise influential diasporas of European populations have acted as lobbies from within, advocating for policies that are believed to be in the interests of their homeland and their ancestral people. The best-known case of this argument does not involve a European country or people but rather Israel and the influence on US foreign policy that Jewish-Americans and organizations that represent them are thought to have had, and continue to have, on shaping US foreign policy in the Middle East (Mearsheimer and Walt 2006). A prominent European illustration of the diaspora influence involves Irish Americans. Although not always as successful as they might have wished in overcoming what historically has been the special relationship between the US and the UK, there is little doubt that the large Irish diaspora in the US has been a factor in attracting more attention and sympathy in Congress. It also appears to have been a factor under some American presidents for the Republic of Ireland and the preferences of Irish Catholics in Northern Ireland than would otherwise have been the case (Haglund and Stein 2020; Kenny 2003).
- *Other demographic characteristics.* Among these, the age profile of populations on both sides of the Atlantic has attracted the most attention. Some observers argue that the fact that Europe's population having become older than those of the US and Canada, and that this age gap is projected to continue, has fiscal and policy consequences that ultimately affect foreign policy. "An ageing population," wrote Wickett (2018), "[…] increases the costs of social services and other entitlements, leaving fewer resources for other priorities (especially those that are central to foreign policy, such as military spending and foreign aid)" (see also, Linn 2004, 6–7). A second influence attributed to population aging as such is that the historical memory of those events that contributed to the special nature and importance of the transatlantic relationship is fading over time. In particular, the relevance of the Cold War and military threats to Europe may

not be so apparent to younger generations on both sides of the Atlantic and, relatedly, the role of NATO and the need to maintain past levels of defense spending and American bases and troops in Europe may seem unconvincing.

At the same time, however, one should not be too quick to interpret these demographic trends as portents of decline in transatlantic relations. Studies of the impact of ethnic minorities on US foreign policy appear to indicate that the independent impact of ethnicity neither depend on the size of the minority ethnic group, nor that it exists except in the case of some well-mobilized groups (Hastings Dunn 2009, 9; Rubenzer and Redd 2010). Regular surveys by the Pew Center and the Chicago Council on Global Affairs of Americans' foreign policy attitudes have found correlations between race and such attitudes. However, these surveys have not asked about respondents' ethnicity. Moreover, while there is some evidence that diaspora populations have influenced US foreign policy, there is also no shortage of historical cases where a large ethnic population has not achieved this sort of influence (Haglund and McNeil 2011). At best, such influence appears to be episodic.

Visiting, for a While

Much of the movement of persons between countries is for purposes other than permanent relocation. Tourists, businesspeople, students, government officials, professionals of various sorts, and people visiting family may contribute to the resilience of the transatlantic relationship. The sheer number of those involved in such back-and-forth movement of persons is quite massive and far eclipses travel between the transatlantic community and other regions of the world. The COVID-19 pandemic that began in 2020 brought most of this movement to a temporary halt, not simply across the Atlantic, but between regions across the world. It may be that the international movement of people will not recover to pre-COVID-19 levels, or at least not soon. Assuming some significant rebound, however, this should continue to be an important source of resilience in the transatlantic relationship.

In the case of tourism, the US has long been a major destination for European travelers, and vice versa. In 2018, about 16.4 million Americans traveled to European destinations, about four out of five on vacation and/or to visit family. In the other direction, about 15.5 million Europeans visited the US, roughly 80 percent of whom were tourists (US Department of Commerce 2020). European destinations account for about half of all outbound overseas travel (not including Canada and Mexico) by Americans. Canada and Mexico are the main sources of travelers to the US, but Europe follows them and continues to be well ahead of Asia as a source of both tourists and business visitors.

For their part, Canadians, like Americans, travel mainly to contiguous regions of the world with Mexico, the US, and the Caribbean being Canadians' favorite tourism destinations. After the "near neighborhood," Europe is the next most popular destination with roughly 3 million visits in 2019 compared to about 3.5 million to Mexico and the Caribbean. Travelers from Europe took 3.2 million trips to Canada in 2019, representing about 43 percent of all overseas visitors compared to about 34 percent from Asia (Statistics Canada 2020).

Students represent another link in this chain of people that spans the Atlantic. It was once the case that Europe, along with Canada, represented the major source of foreign students studying in the US. This is no longer the case. Asia, principally China and India, had become the main sources of the 1.1 million foreign students in the US, accounting for slightly more than half of all foreign students when COVID-19 caused almost all international movement of students to grind to a halt. Europe continued to be the most popular destination for the roughly 342,000 US students studying abroad, accounting for about 55 percent of the total, compared to under 10 percent in Asian countries (US Department of State 2020).

In the case of Canada, at the time of the COVID-19 outbreak in early 2020, over half of the roughly 600,000 foreign students in the country were from China and India. Asian countries as a whole accounted for about six-of-ten foreign students. Students from Europe accounted for only about 8 percent of all foreign students. If Canadians studying in the US are excluded (well over half of all Canadians studying abroad are at US universities), the profile of Canadian students' study abroad choices is roughly similar to that for the US. About half study in Europe, with France, the UK, and Germany, in that order, being the most popular choices (Canadian Bureau for International Education 2019).

Data on the number of Americans living abroad temporarily for reasons related to work or some reason that does not involve study or permanent relocation are notoriously difficult to find, and their reliability is uncertain. The category of expatriates includes such people. What is known with some certainty, even if the numbers are not precisely known, is that the largest number of US expatriates live in Mexico, followed by Canada. An often-cited State Department figure for 2016 indicated that about 8.7 million Americans lived abroad.[6] A previous State Department estimate from 2011 indicated that about one-quarter of those living abroad at that time were in Europe.

Data from host countries provide some picture of the number of Americans residing in Europe. A 2017 report published by a UK government agency put the number at about 138,000. A German state agency placed the number of US citizens in 2018 at 120,000. In both cases, these numbers exclude those in the US military. But a 2016 Federal Voting Assistance Program report calculated that the number of voting-age Americans in that year was 329,274 in the UK, 97,777 in Germany, 169,037 in France, and quite significant in some other European countries (Federal Voting Assistance Program 2018). A 2018 Pew Research Center study found that about 690,000 American-born persons were living in Western Europe (Pew 2020). A survey by the Swiss bank HSBC reported that about one-quarter of all American expatriates live in Europe (HSBC 2018). Uncertainty aside, it is clear that the US expatriate community in Europe is large and that much of it consists of people who are living in Europe for employment reasons. Moreover, as anyone familiar with the large number of US voluntary organizations in Europe can attest—such groups as Republicans Overseas, Democrats Abroad, and the large number of American clubs in cities throughout Europe—many of these individuals are highly educated, civically active, and tend to think fondly of their time in Europe.

The number of Europeans living in the US, including those working there, is likewise imprecise but nonetheless significant. The HSBC survey mentioned above estimated that 58 percent of all expatriates in the US are from Europe. A study by the Pew Research Center found that, as of 2018, over 4.8 million people born in Europe were living in the US (Pew 2020). Of course, not all these European-born people came to the US to work or are still there with the intention of returning to their home countries. Many have become permanent residents. It is clear from data compiled by the US Bureau of Labor Statistics that the vast majority of the 28.4 million foreign-born workers in the US are Hispanic, followed by Asians. Together they comprise about three-quarters of all foreign-born workers. This has been the case for quite some time. In 2000, Asian and Latin American foreign workers comprised about 76 percent of the foreign-born labor force in the US, compared to about 15 percent from Europe (Mosisa 2002). Nevertheless, available data indicate that European-born workers continue to be more educated and to have higher incomes than foreign-born workers from other regions of the world (with the exception of Canada).

It is no less tricky to estimate the number of Europeans working in Canada. The data are scarce and fragmentary, and there is a wide range between estimates. Figures on the size of the Canadian expatriate community are somewhat easier to find, but here too, the estimates are extremely variable. The UN Department of Economic and Social Affairs placed the number for 2013 at about 1.3 million expatriates, a category that includes many more than just those who are abroad for reasons of work. But a University of Toronto study arrived at a much higher number of just under 3 million expatriates (Chouikh et al. 2015). The largest share by far, over half of all expatriates, were in the US. Nevertheless, Europe (defined to include the UK) followed, with the estimated number ranging between about 250,000 and 500,000 people (Chouikh et al. 2015, 5). The UK accounts for the largest number of such people (Statistics Canada 2014). What Statistics Canada says about Canadian expatriates in the UK, based on data that admittedly is not very recent, is very likely true of the majority of those who live in Europe:

> The bulk of the Canadian-born population residing in the UK were of prime working age, that is between ages 25 and 54. Employment opportunities are often strong motivating factors in the decision to migrate abroad. According to UK Census data from 2001, 78% of working-age Canadian-born residents of the UK were employed and 3% were looking for work.
>
> *Statistics Canada 2014*

Whether they are working and will eventually return to Canada or will live out the rest of their lives in the European countries where these expatriates reside, the fact remains that the transatlantic relationship is more likely to be more important to them than relations with other parts of the world.

All of this underscores the significance of an unorchestrated form of cultural diplomacy. Visiting as a student, a tourist, a businessperson, or in some other capacity, provides no guarantee that empathy and understanding will result. Nevertheless, on balance, it almost certainly contributes more to a mutual understanding about societies on the other side of the Atlantic than would otherwise exist.

Institutions, Organizations, and Networks

The personal ties that help bridge what would otherwise be a wider transatlantic gap often occur within a framework that is structured and ongoing. Professional and scientific associations, research institutions, and the activities of non-governmental organizations (NGOs) and international organizations (IOs) that bring together public officials institutionalize these personal connections in ways that focus on shared interests and concerns. Empirical research on the consequences of such institutionalized networks began with the Correlates of War Project and the work of Russett and others on democratic peace theory (Gartzke and Schneider 2013). Although findings regarding the effects of IOs on the likelihood that conflicts between member states will be amicably resolved are mixed, it appears that their capacity to make such a contribution is greater when the states are democracies (Pevehouse 2005).

Some of these institutionalized networks are specifically transatlantic, as in the case of the EU-US summits that date from the Transatlantic Declaration in 1990, and the various dialogues and working groups that exist under the EU-US Declaration on Enhancing Transatlantic Economic Integration and Growth and the Transatlantic Economic Council (TEC 2019). The ongoing importance of the transatlantic partnership, even during periods of unusual stress in the relationship, is evident in the fact that visits by top EU officials to the US during the period 2014–19 far outnumbered those to any other country and surpassed those to China, Japan, and Turkey combined (Lehne and Siccardi 2020). From the US side, State Department data reveal that Europe continues to be a major destination for official visits. During John Kerry's tenure as secretary of state, 43 percent (150) of his 353 separate official meetings abroad were in European countries. This excludes meetings in Russia and Turkey. Europe dropped off somewhat as a destination for official visits of the secretary during the Trump administration. Nevertheless, 28 percent of the 160 official visits abroad by secretaries Rex Tillerson and Michael Pompeo (up to 5 December 2019) were to Europe (US Department of State 2020). It is certainly true that some of these meetings highlighted stresses and differences in the transatlantic partnership rather than cooperation. However, it is facile and incorrect to conclude that the edifice of institutional ties built over the years since 1953, when the first US observers to the European Defense Community and the European Coal and Steel Community were appointed, has been abandoned or otherwise rendered inactive.

"To act together," wrote Moïsi (2003), "Europe and the US do not need to think the same way, *but they must understand the other's way of doing things* [emphasis added]" (71). Moïsi argued that in addition to intergovernmental linkages, connections at the level of civil society can make an important contribution to this mutual understanding and to resilience in the partnership. This appears to be supported by the findings of Paar-Jakli (2014) in her study of the extensive transatlantic networks that exist in the areas of science and technology. These networks are largely virtual in nature, created and maintained through the web of communications that take place between their members. "While state actors are not invisible [in these networks]," she observed, "they are not predominant actors" (Paar-Jakli 2014, 178). IOs and NGOs, including think tanks, are the predominant actors in these transatlantic networks of information and knowledge exchange. They perform the role of "communicative linchpins" in transatlantic relations (Paar-Jakli 2014, 179).

Understandably, state-to-state relations, and particularly the meetings of heads of state and other senior government officials, dominate media coverage of the transatlantic relationship. Seldom mentioned, but potentially significant as a source of resilience in turbulent times, are the regular meetings of the Transatlantic Legislators' Dialogue (TLD). Created in 1999, its roots go back to 1972 when members of the US House of Representatives and the European Parliament created the US-European Community Interparliamentary Group, providing a forum for the representation of lawmakers and the exchange of views (Archick and Morelli 2013, 2). Meetings of the TLD typically take place twice per year. Although its significance should not be exaggerated, along with the British-American Parliamentary Group, the NATO Parliamentary Assembly, and the Canada-Europe Parliamentary Association, these organizations represent institutional bridges between legislative elites from both sides of the Atlantic.

Another institutional linkage that would seem to have the potential to play a stabilizing role in transatlantic relations is the Trans-Atlantic Business Council (TABC), whose roots go back to 1995 when the European-American Business Council was created. The TABC is recognized by the US Department of Commerce and the European Commission as the official forum for exchange between business leaders on both sides of the Atlantic and for the communication of business views on matters of trade and investment. Together with the British-American Business Council, the American Chamber of Commerce to the EU in Brussels and its counterpart in New York, the European-American Chamber of Commerce, and the many bilateral European-American business organizations, these business associations serve as forums for the development and communication of transatlantic positions on trade, investment, regulatory, and other matters. They were extremely active during the Transatlantic Trade and Investment Partnership negotiations, and their influence is judged by some observers to be significant (Dür and Lechner 2015; Serfati 2015).

These business organizations were not silent during the Trump presidency, but many of their voices were distinctly out of tune with the pronouncements and actions of that administration. This might seem to suggest that the ability of business elites to attenuate stresses in the transatlantic relationship is weak. In fact, however, their influence has usually been significant in drawing the US and the EU toward some convergence of policy positions. Even when circumstances diminish the influence of these transatlantic business groups, the dialogue and linkages that are sustained through their activities may serve as something of a buffer in the face of political headwinds.

Economics

In recent years, economics has often been thought of as a major source of conflict and weakness in transatlantic relations. Trade disputes between the EU- and the US-dominated media coverage of these relations during President Trump's time in office. No aspect of America's relationship with Europe—defense was a close second—was subjected to as much criticism from the Trump administration as what the president repeatedly characterized as the grossly unfair terms of trade that the US suffered. Canada has had its own trade issues with the EU during long negotiations that culminated in the Canada-EU Comprehensive Economic and Trade Agreement, which provisionally came into force in 2017.

Much more will be said about the transatlantic trade relationship in Chapter 7. For now, however, some pushback against the idea that the economic relationship between the US and Europe is chiefly a source of conflict is in order. This aspect of the relationship involves more than trade. It includes the employment and other consequences of investment, regulatory standards and coordination, and the agreements and forums for conflict resolution in which the transatlantic economic partners jointly participate. On balance, the overall economic relationship provides serious ballast rather than being a destabilizing factor in relations between Europe and the US.

The dramatic growth of trade between both the US and Europe, on the one hand, and China on the other hand, has obscured the fact that the trade and investment relationship between the US and Europe continues to be significantly greater than the relationship that either one has with China. The total value of trade in goods between the US and the EU-27, plus the UK in 2019, was roughly US$984 billion compared to US$557 billion in trade with China. During the COVID-19 pandemic year of 2020, the gap shrank but remained large at US$755 billion and US$559 billion, respectively (US Census n.d.). It may well be that, in time, trade with China and other Asian economies will become more important for the prosperity of transatlantic economies than is currently the case. Some experts certainly believe that this day is not far off. A major US bank estimates that by 2050 China's share of global GDP (measured by PPPs) will reach 20 percent, India will be at roughly 15 percent, the US will fall to 12 percent, and the EU to only 9 percent (PwC 2017). Such a restructuring of the global economic order would be accompanied by a dramatic decline in both the transatlantic economies' share of all world trade and in the importance of their trading relations with one another.

Projections of this sort, though by no means accepted by everyone who studies the world economy (see Dollar, Huang, and Yao 2020), are not uncommon. While it could be that the assumptions on which predictions of a sharp decline in the importance of transatlantic trade are based are sound, there also exist considerable reasons for skepticism. Moreover, the current gap between the importance of transatlantic trade and that with China and other Asian markets is so great that it is very unlikely to disappear for quite some time.

Trade is only part of the economic relations that stitch together the transatlantic community. Indeed, as recent annual reports on the transatlantic economy published by Johns Hopkins University and the American Chamber of Commerce highlight, there is much more to these relations than is revealed by trade statistics (Hamilton and Quinlan 2020). Although accounting for about 11 percent of the global population, the combined personal consumption of Canada, Europe, and the US amounts to slightly more than half of the global total between them. China and India account for about one-seventh of global personal consumption. Consumer spending is the major catalyst of economic activity and employment in all developed economies, a fact that was driven home with a vengeance during the COVID-19 pandemic. This is another gap that, while narrower than in the past, is not likely to close dramatically in the near future.

When it comes to foreign direct investment (FDI), about 60 percent of US FDI is in Europe, about three times the amount invested in all of Asia (Hamilton and Quinlan 2020). Almost 70 percent of all European FDI is in the US, or about seven times the amount invested by European companies in Asian economies. The web of corporate affiliate activities that this generates includes millions of jobs on each side of the Atlantic: Almost 5 million in Europe and just slightly less in the US as of 2018 (Hamilton and Quinlan 2020). In that same year, 48 of the 50 American states exported more to Europe than to China (Hamilton and Quinlan 2020). These sturdy facts tended to be obscured by the trade skirmishes that figured so prominently in transatlantic relations during the Trump presidency. Far from being a weak point in the transatlantic relationship, economic ties continue to be, on balance, an important source of resilience.

Security

For a brief moment after the terrorist attacks of 11 September 2001, the security interests of the transatlantic community experienced a degree of alignment not seen since the Cold War. Article 5 of the North Atlantic Treaty on the common defense obligations of NATO member states was invoked for the first and only time in the history of that security alliance. The NATO mission to oust the Taliban regime from Afghanistan originally included troops from 14 of the alliance's member states. The threat of international terrorism acted as a unifying agent in a way that the wars in the former Yugoslavia during 1991–95 and the war in Kosovo in 1998–99 had failed to do.

The months after the 9/11 attacks proved, however, to be a fleeting moment. Since then, under a series of US presidents, transatlantic security relations appear to have been more often a cause of rancor and disagreement than of solidarity. On the face of it, much of this disagreement has had to do with American complaints—complaints that go back to the presidency of George H.W. Bush—that the majority of NATO's European members (and Canada) do not pull their weight when it comes to defense spending. On the eve of his resignation as secretary of defense under President Obama, Robert Gates put the matter bluntly at a 2011 NATO meeting in Brussels:

> In the past, I've worried openly about NATO turning into a two-tiered alliance: Between members who specialize in 'soft' humanitarian, development, peacekeeping, and talking tasks, and those conducting the 'hard' combat missions. Between those willing and able to pay the price and bear the burdens of alliance commitments, and those who enjoy the benefits of NATO membership—be they security guarantees or headquarters billets—but don't want to share the risks and the costs. This is no longer a hypothetical worry. We are there today. And it is unacceptable.
>
> *US Department of Defense 2011*

Under President Trump, this long-standing American complaint was expressed often and with less courtesy. Following in a long line of predecessors, Secretary of State Blinken voiced this same complaint, albeit more politely than his immediate predecessors, on his first visit to NATO's Brussels headquarters in March 2021.

The rift between the US and its European security partners (and Canada) is not just, or even primarily, about who contributes how much, and in what form, to the collective defense of the transatlantic community and to global security. More fundamentally, it is about the nature of the perceived threats to global security and how to manage them, and to the values and institutions associated with the liberal world order. Agreement on these matters has often been elusive, to say the least. The wide division among NATO allies over the 2003 invasion of Iraq was the most striking of these disagreements, a topic that continues to generate widespread interest (Draper 2020). President Trump's 2018 decision to abrogate the Iran nuclear deal that had been signed by President Obama, and that has been an important line of division between the Republican and Democratic parties, also demonstrates the wide gulf that has occasionally existed between transatlantic allies when it comes to determining an appropriate response to global security. And on a range of other issues, including those relating to human rights that were raised during the Bush administration's War on Terror, the sharp escalation in the use of drones to kill suspected terrorists during the Obama presidency, how to respond to the challenge of growing Chinese economic and military influence, and even the existential question of NATO's future, Washington, or at least part of the American political establishment, has regularly found itself at odds with at least some of its European allies.

After several decades during which shared security interests, embodied in NATO, mostly served as a major source of resilience in the transatlantic relationship, a new reality has been unfolding. At the top of the drivers of divergence between NATO partners are different views of the security threat posed by China (Ford and Goldgeier 2021), followed by differences between member states regarding the proper response to Russia on several fronts (Rumer and Weiss 2021). There is no reason to expect that a consensus among member states of the alliance on these challenges will develop anytime soon. The one certainty is that NATO continues to be, even if *faute de mieux*, an indispensable part of any coordinated and effective response to these challenges and thus a key contributor to resilience in the security relationship between the transatlantic partners.

Conclusion

By any standard, the Trump years were a serious test of the transatlantic partnership. It is not clear, however, that this test was of a nature and scale greater than had been faced by the transatlantic partners between 2003 and 2008, and particularly during the first few years after the invasion of Iraq. Indeed, the partnership has known a handful of moments that were, at the time, believed to be fraught with the potential to seriously, and perhaps even irreparably, damage the relationship. The Suez Crisis was the first such moment, followed by the Vietnam War, and then the rift between the Reagan administration and some of America's most important European partners over Cold War strategy. The Trump years were the latest in a long history punctuated by moments of doubt and serious questioning about the future of the transatlantic relationship.

The main goal of this book is the identification and explanation of the sources of resilience in transatlantic relations that have enabled the relationship to survive wide and persistent differences in preferences, approaches, and policies. To this end, the chapters that follow address such questions as the following:

- On balance, is the transatlantic relationship mainly cooperative or confrontational? Do common interests, ideas, and policies predominate or is conflict the overriding condition of the relationship in the subject area examined by a contributor?
- What are the sources of divergence and/or convergence in these interests, ideas, and policies? When and why did they develop and how have they evolved since the 1990s?
- Are the factors that have in the past and that currently affect transatlantic relations exogenous or endogenous? Relatedly, to what degree are they manageable by the governments of the US, Canada, the EU, and the governments of the EU's most influential member states?
- What are the sources of resilience in the relationship between, in particular, the US and Europe? Are they strong enough to withstand whatever forces of divergence may exist and conflicts that have and, to one degree or another, doubtless will continue to arise?

Notes

1 Although there is uncertainty over who was first to christen Trump the "Great Disruptor," it may have been political writer Peggy Noonan (2016) in a piece that she wrote for the *Wall Street Journal* early in the 2016 Republican primaries. It subsequently was used by many commentators, sometimes approvingly and other times not.
2 "The use of the word resilience has a long history replete with diverse meanings ranging from bouncing, leaping, and rebounding, to human resourcefulness, to elasticity and resistance properties in materials including steel, yarn, and woven fabrics" (Olsson et al. 2015, 1).
3 The questions from the seventh round of the WVS are Q48, Q108, Q109, Q110, Q111, Q240, and Q241. Details, including tables and graphs showing change over time, may be requested from Stephen Brooks at brooks3@uwindsor.ca.
4 The US government does not collect official statistics on emigration. Nevertheless, based on Internal Revenue Service data on tax returns and other sources, it appears that Mexico is probably the main destination for American emigrants, returning to their country of origin, followed by the EU and Canada. In these latter two cases, the reasons for emigration have to do mainly with employment and study. The measurement of Canadian emigration is equally difficult. It is clear, however, that the majority of emigrants, both short- and long-term, have gone to the US (Bérard-Chagnon 2018).
5 Precise shares of the population by ethnic origins are difficult to determine, particularly in the US. This is partly due to changes in census definitions over time but also because, in the US, the census did not ask a particular question about ancestry or ethnic origins until 1980. White is generally used as a surrogate marker for European origins among Americans. In Canada, the latest census found that 57 percent of Canadians reported some European ancestry. But about 17 percentage given only "Canadian" as their ethnic origin, and these respondents are more likely to be persons from long-established, mainly European ancestral groups. The numbers provided here are based on Statistics Canada data and data from Poston and Sáenz (2019).
6 This figure and its source are often cited, but no information on the actual document in which this number is provided can be found. It cannot be found at the State Department's website.

References

Abbott, Kenneth W., and Duncan Snidal. 2000. "Hard and Soft Law in International Governance." *International Organization* 54 (3): 421–56. https://doi.org/10.1162/002081800551280.

Anderson, Jeffrey J., G. John Ikenberry, and Thomas Risse, eds. 2008. *The End of the West: Crisis and Change in the Atlantic Order*. Ithaca, NY: Cornell University Press.

Archick, Kristin, and Vincent Morelli. 2013. *The U.S. Congress and the European Parliament: Evolving Transatlantic Legislative Cooperation*. Congressional Research Service (CRS).

Bacon, Francis. 1627. *Sylva Sylvarum: or a Naturall Historie in Ten Centuries*. London: William Rawley.

Baldwin, Peter. 2009. *The Narcissism of Minor Differences: How America and Europe Are Alike*. New York: Oxford University Press.

Barber, James David. 1972. *The Presidential Character: Predicting Performance in the White House*. New Jersey: Prentice-Hall.

Bérard-Chagnon, Julien. 2018. "Measuring Emigration in Canada: Review of Available Data Sources and Methods." Statistics Canada. www150.statcan.gc.ca/n1/pub/91f0015m/91f0015m2018001-eng.htm.

Bindi, Federiga. 2018. "Why Trump and Brexit Will Lead to a Stronger Europe." Carnegie Endowment for International Peace. 26 November. https://carnegieendowment.org/2018/11/26/why-trump-and-brexit-will-lead-to-stronger-eu-security-pub-77775.

———. 2019. *Europe and America: The End of the Transatlantic Relationship?* Washington, DC: Brookings Institution Press.

Boucher, Christian. 2014. "Canada-US Values: Distinct, Inevitably Carbon Copy, or Narcissism of Small Differences?" *Horizons*, June.

Bourbeau, Philippe. 2018a. "A Genealogy of Resilience." *International Political Sociology* 12 (1): 19–35.

———. 2018b. *On Resilience: Genealogy, Logic, and World Politics.* Cambridge, UK: Cambridge University Press.

Bourbeau, Philippe, and Caitlin Ryan. 2018. "Resilience, Resistance, Infrapolitics, and Enmeshment." *European Journal of International Relations* 24 (1): 221–39.

Brassett, James, Stuart Croft, and Nick Vaughan-Williams. 2013. "Introduction: An Agenda for Resilience Research in Politics and International Relations." *Politics* 33 (4): 221–28. https://doi.org/10.1111/1467-9256.12032.

Brookings Institution. 2020. "Trans-Atlantic Scorecard." October. www.brookings.edu/research/trans-atlantic-scorecard-october-2020/.

Brookings-Robert Bosch Foundation. 2018. "America First. Europe Alone?" Panel presentation, Brookings Institution, Washington, DC. 24 May. www.brookings.edu/events/america-first-europe-alone/.

Brooks, Stephen. 2014. *American Exceptionalism in the Age of Obama.* New York: Routledge.

Canadian Bureau for International Education. 2019. "Facts and Figures." https://cbie.ca/media/facts-and-figures/.

Carpenter, Steve, Brian Walker, J. Marty Anderies, and Nick Abel. 2001. "From Metaphor to Measurement: Resilience of What to What?" *Ecosystems* 4, 765–81. https://doi.org/10.1007/s10021-001-0045-9

Chandler, David. 2014. *Resilience: The Governance of Complexity.* London: Routledge.

Chandler, David, and Jon Coaffee, eds. 2017. *The Routledge Handbook of International Resilience.* London: Routledge.

Chandra, Chari, ed. 2008. *War, Peace and Hegemony in a Globalized World: The Changing Balance of Power in the 21st Century.* London: Routledge.

Chicago Council on Global Affairs and Chatham House. 2017. "The End of the Transatlantic Era?" Panel presentation. Chicago, 5 October. www.chathamhouse.org/events/all/corporate-members-event/end-transatlantic-era?utm_medium=feed&utm_source=feedburner.

Chouikh, Malek, Allison McHugh, Neil Peet, Caroline Senini, and Sahl Syed. 2015. *Canada's Expatriates.* March. https://munkschool.utoronto.ca/mga/files/2019/11/Capstone-Final-Report-Canadians-Abroad.pdf.

Churchill, Winston. 1946. "Sinews of Peace." International Churchill Society. https://winstonchurchill.org/resources/speeches/1946-1963-elder-statesman/the-sinews-of-peace/.

Cohen, Eliot A. 2019. "America's Long Goodbye: The Real Crisis of the Trump Era." *Foreign Affairs* (January/February). www.foreignaffairs.com/articles/united-states/long-term-disaster-trump-foreign-policy.

Cusumano Eugenio, and Nathan Cooper. 2020. "Conclusions." In *Projecting Resilience Across the Mediterranean*, edited by Eugenio Cusumano and Stefan Hofmaier, 295–314. London: Palgrave Macmillan.
Davtyan, Erik. 2014. "The Role of Infrastructure in International Relations: The Case of South Caucasus." *International Journal of Social Sciences* 3 (4): 22–38.
den Dulk, Kevin R., and Mark J. Rozell. 2011. "George W. Bush, Religion, and Foreign Policy: Personal, Global, and Domestic Contexts." *The Review of Faith and International Affairs* 9 (4): 71–82.
Deudney, Daniel, and John Ikenberry. 2018. "The Liberal World: The Resilient Order." *Foreign Affairs* 97 (4): 16–24.
Dollar, David, Yiping Huang, and Yang Yao. 2020. *China 2049: Economic Challenges of a Rising Global Power*. Washington: Brookings Institution Press.
Donfried, Karen, and Wolfgang Ischinger. 2020. "The Pandemic and the Toll of Transatlantic Discord." *Foreign Affairs*, 20 April. www.foreignaffairs.com/articles/united-states/2020-04-18/pandemic-and-toll-transatlantic-discord.
Draper, Robert. 2020. *To Start a War: How the Bush Administration Took America into Iraq*. New York: Penguin.
Dueck, Colin. 2019. *Age of Iron*. New York: Oxford University Press.
Dumont, Jean-Christophe, and Georges Lemaître. 2005. *Counting Immigrants and Expatriates in OECD Countries: A New Perspective*. OECD Social, Employment and Migration Working Papers No. 25. Paris: Organisation for Economic Co-operation and Development.
Dunn, David Hastings. 2009. "Assessing the Debate, Assessing the Damage: Transatlantic Relations After Bush." *British Journal of Politics and International Relations* 11 (1): 4–24.
Dür, Andreas, and Lisa Lechner. 2015. "Business Interests and the Transatlantic Trade and Investment Partnership." In *The Politics of Transatlantic Trade Negotiations*, edited by Jean-Frederic Morin, Tereza Novotná, Frederik Ponjaert, and Mario Telò, 69–80. New York: Routledge.
Easton, David. 1965. *A Systems Analysis of Political Life*. New York: Wiley.
The Economist. 2019. "Emmanuel Macron Warns Europe: NATO Is Becoming Brain-Dead." 7 November 2019. www.economist.com/europe/2019/11/07/emmanuel-macron-warns-europe-nato-is-becoming-brain-dead.
Federal Voting Assistance Program. 2018. 2016 Overseas Citizen Population Analysis. www.fvap.gov/uploads/FVAP/Reports/FVAP-2016-OCPA-FINAL-Report.pdf.
Ford, Lindsey W., and James Goldgeier. 2021. "Retooling America's Alliances to Manage the China Challenge." Brookings Institution. January. www.brookings.edu/research/retooling-americas-alliances-to-manage-the-china-challenge/.
Friedrichs, Gordon, Sebastian Harnisch, and Cameron G. Thies. 2019. *The Politics of Resilience and Transatlantic Order: Enduring Crisis?* London: Routledge.
Gardner, Anthony Luzzatto. 2020. *Stars With Stripes: The Essential Partnership Between the European Union and the United States*. London: Palgrave.
Gartzke, Erik, and Christina Schneider. 2013. "Data Sets and Quantitative Research in the Study of Intergovernmental Organizations." In *Routledge Handbook of International Organization*, edited by Bob Reinalda, 41–53. London: Routledge.
Georgetown Journal of International Affairs. 2012. Resilience, special issue. Vol. 12, no. 2. www.georgetownjournalofinternationalaffairs.org/online-edition/12-2-resilience.
Gößling-Reisemann, Stefan, Hans Dieter Hellige, and Pablo Thier. 2018. "The Resilience Concept: From Its Historical Roots to Theoretical Framework for Critical Infrastructure Design." Forschungszentrum Nachhaltigkeit Working Paper No. 217. June. Universität

Bremen. www.uni-bremen.de/fileadmin/user_upload/sites/artec/Publikationen/artec_Paper/217_paper.pdf.

Haglund, David, and Elizabeth Stein. 2020. "Ethnic Diasporas and U.S. Foreign Policy." *Oxford Bibiliographies*. doi: 10.1093/OBO/9780199756223-0069

Haglund, David, and Tyson McNeil. 2011. "The 'Germany Lobby' and US Foreign Policy: What, if Anything, Does It Tell Us about the Debate over the 'Israel Lobby'?" *Ethnopolitics* 10 (3–4): 321–44.

Hamilton, Daniel S., ed. 2016. *Forward Resilience: Protecting Society in an Interconnected World*. Washington, DC: Center for Transatlantic Relations. https://archive.transatlanticrelations.org/wp-content/uploads/2017/02/Forward_Resilience_Full-Book.pdf.

Hamilton, Daniel S., and Joseph Quinlan. 2020. *The Transatlantic Economy 2020: Annual Survey of Jobs, Trade and Investment between the United States and Europe*. Johns Hopkins University and the American Chamber of Commerce for the European Union.

Hanson, Victor Davis. 2019. *The Case for Trump*. New York: Basic Books.

Hastings Dunn, David. 2009. "Assessing the Debate, Assessing the Damage: Transatlantic Relations after Bush." *The British Journal of Politics and International Relations* 11 (1): 4–24. https://doi.org/10.1111/j.1467-856x.2008.00348.x.

HSBC. 2018. *Expat Explorer Survey 2018*. https://expatexplorer.hsbc.com/survey/files/pdfs/country-reports/US.pdf.

Inglehart, Ronald, and Pippa Norris. 2016. "Trump, Brexit, and the Rise of Populism: Economic Have-Nots and Cultural Backlash." Faculty Research Working Paper Series, John F. Kennedy School of Government, Harvard University.

Ikenberry, John. 2018. "The End of Liberal International Order." *International Affairs* 94 (1): 7–23. doi: 10.1093/ia/iix241.

Judis, John. 2005. *The Chosen Nation: The Influence of Religion on U.S. Foreign Policy*. Carnegie Endowment for International Peace. March. https://carnegieendowment.org/files/PB37.judis.FINAL.pdf.

Juncos, Ana E. 2017. "Resilience as the New EU Foreign Policy Paradigm: A Pragmatist Turn?" *European Security* 26 (1): 1–18. doi: 10.1080/09662839.2016.1247809.

Kagan, Robert. 2018. *The Jungle Grows Back: America and Our Imperiled World*. New York: Penguin.

Karabel, Jerome, and Daniel Laurison. 2012. "An Exceptional Nation? American Political Values in Comparative Perspective." Institute for Research on Labor and Employment Working Paper No. 136-12. December. www.irle.berkeley.edu/files/2012/An-Exceptional-Nation.pdf.

Kennedy, Craig, and Marshall M. Bouton. 2002. "The Real Transatlantic Gap." *Foreign Policy* (November–December), 66–74.

Kennedy School, Institute of Politics. 2018. "The Crisis in the Transatlantic Relationship." Panel presentation, Harvard University, Boston, 6 October. https://iop.harvard.edu/forum/crisis-transatlantic-relationship.

Kenny, Kevin. 2003. "Diaspora and Comparison: The Global Irish as a Case Study." *Journal of American History* 90 (June): 134–62.

Kimmage, Michael. 2020. *The Abandonment of the West: The History of an Idea in American Foreign Policy*. New York: Basic Books.

Kohut, Andrew, and Bruce Stokes. 2006. *America Against the World: How We Are Different and Why We Are Disliked*. New York: Times Books.

Korosteleva, Elena A., and Trine Flockhart. 2020. "Resilience in EU and International Institutions: Redefining Local Ownership in a New Global Governance Agenda." *Contemporary Security Policy* 41 (2): 153–75. doi: 10.1080/13523260.2020.1723973.

Krasner, Stephen D., ed. 1983. *International Regimes*. Ithaca, NY: Cornell University Press.
Kupchan, Charles. 2002. "The End of the West?" *The Atlantic* (November). www.theatlantic.com/magazine/archive/2002/11/the-end-of-the-west/302617/.
Lasswell, Harold. 1930. *Psychopathology and Politics*. Chicago: University of Chicago Press.
Lawson, George, and Robbie Shilliam. 2010. "Sociology and International Relations: Legacies and Prospects." *Cambridge Review of International Affairs* 23 (1): 69–86.
Lehne, Stefan, and Francesco Siccardi. 2020. "Where in the World Is the EU Now?" Carnegie Europe. 29 April. https://carnegieeurope.eu/2020/04/29/where-in-world-is-eu-now-pub-81658.
Linn, Johannes F. 2004. "Trends and Prospects of Transatlantic Economic Relations the Glue That Cements a Fraying Partnership?" Brookings Institution. 28 April.
Löfflmann, Georg. 2019. "America First and the Populist Impact on US Foreign Policy." *Survival* 61 (6): 115–38.
Meadows, Donella, Dennis Meadows, Jørgen Randers, and William W. Behrens, III. 1972. *The Limits to Growth*. New York: Universe Books.
Mearsheimer, John J., and Stephen M. Walt. 2006. "The Israel Lobby and U.S. Foreign Policy." *Middle East Policy* 18 (3): 29–87.
Micklethwait, John, and Adrian Wooldridge. 2005. *The Right Nation: Conservative Power in America*. New York: Penguin.
Moïsi, Dominique. 2003. "Reinventing the West." *Foreign Affairs*, November–December. www.foreignaffairs.com/articles/united-states/2003-11-01/reinventing-west.
———. 2018. "The Transatlantic Rupture." *The Strategist*, 30 June. www.aspistrategist.org.au/the-transatlantic-rupture/.
Morris J. Wosk Centre for Dialogue. 2019. *Canadians' Views on Democracy*. Report 1: State of Democracy & Appeal of Populism. Simon Fraser University. August. https://drive.google.com/file/d/0By898SGRhY2cQlQtN1BnU21KVExCTDlvMWhJMzM0M1F5TnZR/view.
Mosisa, Abraham T. 2002. "The Role of Foreign-Born Workers in the U.S. Economy." *Monthly Labor Review* 125 (5): 3–14.
Noonan, Peggy. 2016. "The GOP Establishment's Civil War." *Wall Street Journal*, 8 January 2016. www.wsj.com/articles/the-gop-establishments-civil-war-1452212775.
Olsson, Lennart, Anne Jerneck, Henrik Thoren, Johannes Persson, and David O'Byrne. 2015. "Why Resilience Is Unappealing to Social Science: Theoretical and Empirical Investigations of the Scientific Use of Resilience." *Science Advances* 1 (4): e1400217. doi: 10.1126/sciadv.1400217.
Paar-Jakli, Gabriella. 2014. *Networked Governance and Transatlantic Relations: Building Bridges through Science Diplomacy*. New York: Routledge.
Patel, Sonny S., M. Brook Rogers, Richard Amlôt, and G. James Rubin. 2017. "What Do We Mean by 'Community Resilience'? A Systematic Literature Review of How It Is Defined in the Literature." *PLoS Currents*, 9, ecurrents.dis.db775aff25efc5ac4f0660ad9c9f7db2.https://doi.org/10.1371/currents.dis.db775aff25efc5ac4f0660ad9c9f7db2.
Pevehouse, John C. 2005. *Democracy From Above: Regional Organizations and Democratization*. Cambridge: Cambridge University Press.
Pew Research Center. 2011. "The American-Western European Values Gap." 17 November. www.pewresearch.org/global/2011/11/17/the-american-western-european-values-gap/.
———. 2015. "How Do Americans Stand Out From the Rest of the World?" 12 March. www.pewresearch.org/fact-tank/2015/03/12/how-do-americans-stand-out-from-the-rest-of-the-world/.

———. 2020. "Facts on US Immigrants, 2018", 20 August. www.pewresearch.org/hispanic/2020/08/20/facts-on-u-s-immigrants-current-data/.
Pimm, Stuart L., Ian Donohue, José M. Montoya, and Michel Loreau. 2019. "Measuring Resilience Is Essential to Understand It." *Nature Sustainability* 2: 895–97.
Poston, Dudley L., Jr., and Rogelio Sáenz. 2019. "The US White Majority Will Soon Disappear Forever." *The Conversation*, 30 April. https://theconversation.com/the-us-white-majority-will-soon-disappear-forever-115894.
PwC. 2017. *The Long View: How will the global economic order change by 2050?* www.pwc.com/gx/en/world-2050/assets/pwc-the-world-in-2050-full-report-feb-2017.pdf.
Reich, Simon, and Richard Ned Lebow. 2014. *Good-Bye Hegemony! Power and Influence in the Global System*. Princeton, NJ: Princeton University Press.
Reitz, Kevin. 2018. *American Exceptionalism in Crime and Punishment*. New York: Oxford University Press.
Röttgen, Norbert. 2019. "How to Save the Transatlantic Alliance: Waiting Out Trump Won't Be Enough." *Foreign Affairs*, 17 June 2019. www.foreignaffairs.com/articles/europe/2019-06-17/how-save-transatlantic-alliance.
Rubenzer, Trevor, and Steven B. Redd. 2010. "Ethnic Minority Groups and US Foreign Policy: Examining Congressional Decision Making and Economic Sanctions." *International Studies Quarterly* 54 (3): 755–77.
Rumer, Eugene, and Andrew S. Weiss. 2021. "Back to Basics on Russia Policy." Carnegie Endowment for International Peace. March. https://carnegieendowment.org/files/202 103-WeissRumerBasics.pdf.
Sayers, Brian. 2011. "The North Atlantic Treaty Organization: A Study in Institutional Resilience." *Georgetown Journal of International Affairs* 12 (2): 48–55.
Serfati, Claudio. 2015. "The Transatlantic Bloc of States and the Political Economy of the Transatlantic Trade and Investment Partnership (TTIP)." *Work Organisation, Labour & Globalisation* 9 (1): 7–37.
Statistics Canada. 2014. "Canadians Abroad." *Canadian Social Trends*. www150.statcan.gc.ca/n1/pub/11-008-x/2008001/article/10517-eng.htm.
———. 2020. *Travel Between Canada and Other Countries, December 2019*. www150.statcan.gc.ca/n1/daily-quotidien/200221/dq200221b-eng.htm.
Steinbruner, John D. 1974. *The Cybernetic Theory of Decision: New Dimensions of Political Analysis*. Princeton: Princeton University Press.
Tcherneva, Vessela. 2018. "The End of the Concept of the West?" Heinrich Böll Foundation. Brussels. https://eu.boell.org/en/2018/03/12/end-concept-west.
Timbro. 2019. Authoritarian Populism Index. https://populismindex.com/.
Transatlantic Economic Council (TEC). 2019. "About Us." www.state.gov/transatlantic-economic-council/.
US Census. n.d. "Foreign Trade: Trade Goods With China." www.census.gov/foreign-trade/balance/c5700.html.
US Department of Commerce. 2020. Foreign Direct Investment (FDI). www.selectusa.gov/servlet/servlet.FileDownload?file=015t0000000LKSn.
US Department of Defense. 2011. "The Security and Defense Agenda (Future of NATO)." Speech by Secretary of Defense Robert Gates. Brussels. 10 June.
US Department of State. 2020. Bureau of Educational and Cultural Affairs. https://eca.state.gov/impact/open-doors-reports.
van Ham, Peter. 2018. *Trump's Impact on European Security Policy Options in a Post-Western World*. Netherlands Institute of International Relations. www.clingendael.org/sites/default/files/2018-01/Report_Trumps_Impact_on_European_Security.pdf.

Vieira, Marco A. 2016. "Understanding Resilience in International Relations: The Non-Aligned Movement and Ontological Security." *International Studies Review* 18 (2): 290–311. https://doi.org/10.1093/isr/viw002.

Walt, Stephen M. 1998. "The Ties That Fray: Why Europe and America are Drifting Apart." *The National Interest*. December. https://nationalinterest.org/article/the-ties-that-fray-why-europe-and-america-are-drifting-apart-900.

Wickett, Xenia. 2018. *Transatlantic Relations: Converging or Diverging?* London: Chatham House. https://reader.chathamhouse.org/transatlantic-relations-converging-or-diverging#introduction.

Windle, Gill, Kate M. Bennett, and Jane Noyes. 2011. "A Methodological Review of Resilience Measurement Scales." *Health and Quality of Life Outcomes* 9, 8. https://doi.org/10.1186/1477-7525-9-8.

Zakaria, Fareed. 2011. *The Post-American World*. New York: W.W. Norton.

PART I
Sensibility, Solidarity, and Stress

1
TRANSATLANTIC SENSIBILITY AND SOLIDARITY

The Distinctive Factors of Interpersonal Connection and Shared Historical Experience

Alan K. Henrikson

Introduction: The Role of "Allies" and Their Generations in the Atlantic Partnership

The resilience of the United States of America (US) under its federal Constitution has been tested many times, most recently on 6 January 2021, by the incitement of mob action by President Donald J. Trump against the Capitol Building to prevent the US Congress from certifying the recent election—properly conducted—of the country's next chief executive. With the inauguration of Joseph R. Biden, Jr., as the US president on 20 January came a notable change, certainly in tone and prospectively also in substance, in the relationship between the US and Europe. Speaking soon after his inauguration to other participants at a virtual Munich Security Conference (MSC), President Biden, who had attended MSC meetings in person many times before, and as a private citizen two years earlier had then promised, "We will be back," now declared officially: "America is back." Not only that, he also said, "The transatlantic alliance is back" (White House 2021a). Not surprisingly, given the disruption of the Trump years, Europeans could not be easily reassured (Erlanger 2021).

On what foundations are these assertions—personal ones by the current US president about the recovery of US political and Atlantic solidarity and, by implication, also the alliance's resilience meeting future challenges—based? "The alliance" in this chapter is interpreted broadly, and in a somewhat unusual way, with a focus on the *interpersonal relations* of members of the Atlantic community, particularly its political leaders and their close associates as well as diplomatic agents and civil servants, and the bonds they have formed as "allies" in the process of conducting their nations' affairs—in normal times and during crises. This highlighting of personal relationships does not minimize the importance of the structural relationships that exist between the North American countries—the US

DOI:10.4324/9781003147565-3

and Canada—and the countries of Europe, connected formally through common membership in the North Atlantic Treaty Organization (NATO) and also through explicit cooperative arrangements with the European Union (EU). These are the legal-political frameworks within which transatlantic policy decisions are made. Without them, agreements arrived at might be less binding. However, without the informal relationships of the political leaders, diplomats, and others who achieved the agreements, and may even have created the organizational structures within which the agreements were negotiated, the political connection that exists across the Atlantic surely would be weaker.

The intellectual and moral content of the connection itself is largely the product of history—the legacy of the European and North American past and the collective lineage of the many generations of participants in transatlantic exchange. This includes far more than an "elite"—that is, an identifiable group of influential individuals, either members of government or those with influence over governments, who in a somewhat exclusive way have "served as a bridge connecting the allies' values and interests," as University of Toronto historian Timothy Andrews Sayle (2019) has epitomized the idea (5). The values and interests of the Atlantic nations are socially profound. They are deeply embedded in, and engendered by, their general populations, significant portions of which have interacted transatlantically—as immigrants and refugees, businesspeople and professionals, military personnel and diplomats, students and tourists, and, increasingly, just as "netizens." The basic policy positions taken by President Biden, for example, in support of "democracy," are expressions of well-known and widely communicated social beliefs and cultural practices. They need not be especially "bridged" across the Atlantic by those at or very near the top. Nonetheless, there exists a commonality of outlook among those who are engaged, formally and informally, in transatlantic relations at the political level, and this matters—as do the *connections* they form through personal contact, conversation, and, especially, collaboration. "I know we make foreign policy out to be this great, great skill," President Biden said during his trip to Europe for a series of meetings in June 2021. Actually, "all foreign policy is [...] a logical extension of personal relationships" (White House 2021b). Such relationships in themselves, of course, do not constitute connections, which have a functional potential. Connections require more, including the building of trust, the development of mutual reliance, and also a reciprocal understanding of the other as an available resource—a possible "ally."

There is, in addition to this intimate—interpersonal—factor that contributes to the cohesiveness of the transatlantic relationship, the factor of history, particularly that of shared *generational experience* (Henrikson 1998). "Allies," considered not just as states, or as governments, but also as individual members of transatlantically affiliated national societies, are also, as persons situated chronologically, members of historical generations, formed by the events they have actively participated in, or just lived through. What President Biden and others refer to as the "transatlantic partnership," the strength and resilience of which is the main subject of this volume, has not only a profound human dimension but also an experiential dimension. It is a product of people in their place and their time. Generations are not continuously formed. There are "breaks" between them, owing mainly to differences in the historical events that shaped them. Transitions occur. Successions are necessary. Partnerships are not eternal. The "transatlantic partnership," like others, needs renewal.

American and Canadian Relationships With Europe: The Historical Background

Historically, the values and interests of North American and European countries, separated by 3,000 miles of ocean and situated on physically very different continents, have not always coincided. The Atlantic perspectives of the US, owing to its Revolution, and of Canada, which resisted involvement in that conflict, have differed markedly. As Brebner has written, the US "attained nationhood by rebellion against Great Britain" and Canada did so "by gradual growth within the British Empire." As a result, "not only were their responses to the mother country usually sharply contrasted, but their understandings of each other were habitually warped" (Brebner 1945, xi). Although both were "North American," their geopolitical horizons were different.

The US defined itself against Europe, with which it nonetheless still had to deal. "The great rule of conduct for us in regard to foreign nations is in extending our commercial relations to have with them as little political connection as possible," President George Washington stated in his 1796 Farewell Address. He continued,

> So far as we have already formed engagements, let them be fulfilled with perfect good faith. Here let us stop. Europe has a set of primary interests which to us have none; or a very remote relation. Hence she must be engaged in frequent controversies, the causes of which are essentially foreign to our concerns. Hence, therefore, it must be unwise in us to implicate ourselves by artificial ties in the ordinary vicissitudes of her politics, or the ordinary combinations and collisions of her friendships or enmities.
>
> *Washington 1796*

There is a residue of this belief—the non-entanglement tradition—in US policy toward Europe to this day. Although not any longer in any sense "isolationist," the US retains a unilateralist proclivity—a preference for ad hoc, goal-oriented, and temporary "coalitions of the willing," rather than permanent organizational commitments.

By contrast, Canada, long dependent on Great Britain for its security as well as its identity, was, indirectly, a part of the European system through the extension of the balance of power to North America (Bourne 1967) and through its monarchical attachment. Canada was invaded by US forces during the War of 1812—an event not forgotten by Canadians and their political leaders. John A. Macdonald, in his Confederation speech of February 1865, acknowledged the precariousness of

Canada's position between Great Britain and the US, where the Civil War appeared likely to end with a decisive victory by the North. "If we are not blind to our present position," Macdonald warned,

> we must see the hazardous situation in which all the great interests of Canada stand in respect to the United States. I am not an alarmist. I do not believe in the prospect of immediate war. I believe that the common sense of the two nations will prevent war; still we cannot trust to probabilities.
>
> *Macdonald 1865*

Although Canada still had a place in Britain's imperial defenses, with the prospect of Confederation there needed to be "a united, a concerted, and uniform system of defense" for Canadians themselves. Macdonald, who would become the first prime minister of a British Dominion, then promised: "We will have one system of defense and be one people, acting together alike in peace and in war" (Macdonald 1865). For Canada, domestic political unity and imperial defense unity have not always coincided, which is a reason for its multilateralist tradition, which encompasses involvement in both the English-speaking Commonwealth and the Organisation Internationale de la Francophonie as well as the broader United Nations (UN) organization.

The structures of government that the US established with the Constitution of 1787 and that Canada established with the British North American Act of 1867 historically have been powerful forces of political coherence. So, too, have been the more recent structures formed in the Atlantic world following World War II: NATO and other post-war bodies, including the European Coal and Steel Community (ECSC) and the Organisation for European Economic Co-operation which, in 1961, with the inclusion of the US and Canada, became the Organisation for Economic Co-operation and Development. From a practical start with the ECSC, the European Communities (EC) further evolved into the EU. All these entities were based on the World War II experience, a devastating ordeal, which no one wanted to risk ever repeating. That wish—to make war between Atlantic nations no longer possible, or even thinkable—was a common cause (Kissinger 2001, 25). In political-scientific terms, the Atlantic sphere could become, in the phrase of Karl W. Deutsch, a "pluralistic security-community" (Deutsch et al. 1957, 5–9, 200).

These institutions were brought about as a result of consultation and cooperation—through "jointness" of thought and action. For Americans, even beyond only those steeped in its military tradition, this has a particular resonance. President Washington in his Farewell Address, as a consideration that would appeal to the "sensibility," as he termed it, of his countrymen in support of their national Union, stated: "You have in a common cause fought and triumphed together; the independence and liberty you possess are the work of joint counsels, and joint efforts of common dangers, sufferings and successes" (Washington 1796). The joint counsels and joint efforts of World War II, in the form of the inter-allied military, economic, and political coordination that occurred then, also have been influential, not only as a memory but also as a model (Rosen 1951). The pattern of Atlantic community formation in the following years thus was not completely novel. Leaders and officials from both North American countries as well as the allied countries in Europe were inspired by the example of wartime cooperation. Major personalities in Washington, DC, and Ottawa, as well as those in London, Paris, Brussels, and other European capitals, were involved in this replicative *and* creative process of collaboration.

The "Atlanticists": The Founding Generation

Close personal ties were formed during the remarkable period of transatlantic construction. The best-known of the participants, in Secretary of State Dean Acheson's phrase "present at the creation" (Acheson 1968), were no less "founding fathers"—of the transatlantic relationship—than were Benjamin Franklin and George Washington, along with Alexander Hamilton, John Adams, Thomas Jefferson, James Madison, and notable European figures including the Marquis de Lafayette, were of the American political community (Ferreiro 2007; Morris 1965, 1973). Also, there were remarkable "founding mothers," including Abigail Adams, Sarah Livingston Jay, and Dolley Madison, who raised the nation (Roberts 2004). Among Canadians, Sir John A. Macdonald and others, including George Brown and Sir George-Étienne Cartier, are similarly regarded as "fathers" of Canadian nationhood (Creighton 1965). In the US, victory in World War II was secured under the presidential leadership and Atlanticist global vision of Franklin Roosevelt, aided by Henry Stimson, George Marshall, Dwight Eisenhower, and others. The presidential administration of Harry Truman and its many Europe-oriented officials included Acheson, George F. Kennan, and most of their State Department colleagues. In Canada, Lester B. Pearson and Escott Reid come prominently to mind. On the European side, there are, of course, Winston Churchill, Jean Monnet, Robert Schuman, Paul-Henri Spaak, Ernest Bevin, Konrad Adenauer, Alcide De Gasperi, and other leaders from the smaller and larger European countries (Griffiths 2012). As an extended "group," they were but a segment of a larger entity: an entire "generation" including the mass of citizenry—soldiers and civilians, men, and women—of whole Atlantic populations inspired and led by their leaders in situations of both triumph and defeat. The peoples of the vanquished countries were generationally bound too.

With the passage of time, personal recollections fade. Memories of large-scale and challenging events, however, become embedded in recorded history and become social legacies—to be passed on, for the "lessons" they contain (May 1973), to succeeding generations. The experiences of the officials and soldiers who served in World War II, some of whom remained in government afterward, were the historical memory-base of the post-war liberal international order they worked to construct during the late 1940s. In their book *The Wise Men*, Isaacson and Thomas (1986) observed of the group of American post-war statesmen whose relationships they studied, "They were internationalists, and more specifically Atlanticists, an outlook that resulted in a certain willingness to make sweeping American commitments. They viewed America's leadership role, as their own, as part of a moral destiny" (29–30). Regarding essentially the same group of "distinguished men," whom he characterized as "an aristocracy" dedicated to the US "on behalf of principles beyond partisanship," Henry Kissinger (1979) wrote in *White House Years*: "Free peoples owe them gratitude for their achievement: Presidents and Secretaries of State have been sustained by their matter-of-fact patriotism and freely tendered wisdom" (22). When Kissinger came into office as national security adviser, they were all in their seventies. "As the older group leaves public office," he lamented, "they take with them one of the steadying and guiding factors in our foreign policy" (22).

Canada has had a similar group of influential "wise men"—the legendary Mandarins. They were the senior civil servants formed in the tradition of O. D. Skelton who, advising Pearson and other cabinet ministers, shaped post-war Canadian public policy, including foreign policy. The country's relations with the US, Britain, and other members of the Commonwealth, and continental Europe as well, bore the mark of "The Ottawa Men," as Granatstein called them (Granatstein 1998). Nationalistic in their emphasis on Canada's ability to act independently, they were mostly also traditional Atlanticists. Pearson and Reid (1977), a close colleague in the Department of External Affairs, explicitly advocated an "Atlantic community."

In Europe after the war, there were, of course, many sets of national statesmen and officials working in capitals focused on their respective countries' particular problems. However, there were also groups of individuals, notably the economic planner Monnet with his intimate "team" of men and women in Paris who were thinking in larger, Europe-wide terms (Monnet 2015). Overcoming the continent's history of internecine rivalry through European integration was their goal. Some, including Monnet himself, had personal experience and close working relationships in the US. There were outright "Atlanticists" in Europe as well, not only among the British for whom transatlantic relationship had been a wartime lifeline. The 1939–45 experience demonstrated Europe's dependence on US power. Especially as relations with the Soviet Union worsened, and Eastern Europe fell under Soviet sway, with even access to Berlin in occupied Germany under threat, fear mounted. "There was," as Dutch statesman Dirk Stikker remembered,

> but one reaction: to resist together, since it was plain that no nation on its own could achieve either recovery or security. But this resistance was also hopeless if we were not to be joined by the United States and Canada.
>
> *Stikker 1966, 281*

The existence of the Atlantic community as a geostrategic reality was increasingly recognized—on both sides of the ocean. Journalist Walter Lippmann (1943) had argued during World War I, and again during World War II, that even the US with its strength, size, and resources could not defend its territory and protect its interests entirely by itself. It needed access and allies in the Atlantic, both large and small.

Atlantic Crises, Their "Lessons," and Their Management: The Consultative Variable

The history of the transatlantic alliance, like that of European unification, has been described as a story of a series of "crises," for the most part successfully overcome. The Atlantic story can be seen as part of a broader pattern. In *A Study of History*, Arnold Toynbee (1934–51) explained the rise and fall of civilizations—on the list of which the "Atlantic civilization" dating from the eighteenth century (Kraus 1949) may be included—in terms of "challenge" and "response." By the former, Toynbee meant factors or events, mostly unpredictable, that pose threats to the ways people live their lives and earn their livelihoods. By the latter, he meant action (or failure thereof) by a civilization's leadership capable of meeting such threats and creating the basis for long-term survival. "Response," in contrast with "challenge," was a matter of volition, the exercise of will. It required something further: vision—both hindsight and foresight—along with decisiveness and action.

The capacity to survive depends also on deep systemic factors, inherent in the "civilization" itself. One of the binding factors of a civilization—a source of its tensile strength, so to speak—is as the very word suggests, its "civility." This includes its habits of communication. An international community such as that surrounding the Atlantic has been defined scientifically by Deutsch et al. (1957) as a communication sphere. Its range is empirically determinable: People within it communicate more often, more intensely, and about a wider range of subjects than they do with others, outside of it (Deutsch et al. 1957). The manner of this communication is a reflection of the sociocultural conditions, including the institutional influences, of what Bourdieu (1977) termed *habitus*, the normalized practice of a community. In transatlantic diplomacy, the measure as well as the means of community is *consultation*.

The history of the larger Atlantic community, or "civilization," as well as the interrelated North American and European communities within it, since World War II, which President Roosevelt once suggested calling "the Survival War" (Kluckhohn 1942), has indeed been marked by serious crises. All have been resolved by consultation. A number of these crises have been existential in the Toynbeean sense, affecting life and livelihood—potentially or actually. The Cuban Missile Crisis of October 1962 surely is one. In its widespread economic consequences, the 2007–8 Financial Crisis is another. More recently, the continuing COVID-19 pandemic also must qualify. The most significant crises have not merely punctuated the flow of events but have also been historical moments that have endured in time and have occasioned continuing reflection. As long-time NATO official and historical scholar Jamie Shea has observed, between "the invocation of the past" and "obsession with an anxious present," there are events that bridge the two. "The definition of a significant event is not only that it had a deep and lasting impact at the time but also that it continues to be a trove of lessons for our own time" (Shea 2016).

A recurrent lesson from the crises, major and minor, that have seized the attention of the Atlantic world for longer or shorter periods of time has been the need, often publicly expressed, for consultation. The frequency and adequacy of it have varied considerably. "Consultation" is a concept of international relations that is not well understood, partly because of the disparities that have existed in the power of the parties involved, particularly between the US and its Atlantic partners. While consultation does not need to be based on equality of strength or resources, it does imply an equality of regard. That in turn entails, beyond openness to another's point of view, a readiness to accept advice, to entertain new ideas, and to modify preconceived designs. The process of deliberation should be truly reciprocal, with give-and-take occurring freely. Furthermore, it should occur in a timely fashion, and with no presentation of *faits accomplis* or, worse, surprise moves. Consultation within an international partnership, ideally, should be "joint." Decisions should be *arrived at* together even if, ultimately, *taken* separately, by national authorities of sovereign and independent countries as those of the Atlantic community are. Optimally, the end result of a consultative process should be "consensus," itself a concept of some complexity (Henrikson 1986). While implying general agreement, on the substance of issues as well as procedures to be followed, consensual decision-making does allow for "silent" dissent as well as assent, for reservations to be held without necessarily blocking action by the overall body, be it a formal international organization or a group of states associated in "partnership."

Frameworks of Transatlantic Consultation Between Europe and the US and Canada

Within the NATO context, consultation is a formal requirement. Article 4 of the North Atlantic Treaty signed in Washington on 4 April 1949, states: "The Parties will consult together whenever, in the opinion of any of them, the territorial integrity, political independence or security of any of the Parties is threatened" (NATO 2019). It is not widely known, even today, that the parties to the Washington Treaty in a set of confidential "agreed minutes of interpretation" recorded their common understanding that "Article 4 is applicable in the event of a threat in any part of the world," including a threat to the "overseas territories" of any of the parties (Henderson 1983, 103–4). NATO has further defined and gradually elaborated its "consultation process" with a set of procedures, the essence of which, however, remains: "All NATO decisions are made by consensus, after discussion and consultation among member countries. Consultation between member states is therefore at the heart of NATO since Allies are able to exchange views and information prior to reaching agreement and taking action" (NATO 2020). It should be noted that, despite the normative "consensus" requirement, individual NATO members either alone or grouped as "Allies" occasionally have acted in place of the "Alliance"

(Stikker 1966). The US particularly, with its "global" role, was reluctant to be bound by the NATO consultation constraint.

The North Atlantic Council (NAC), in recognition of NATO's perceived consultative deficiency, in April 1954 adopted a resolution put forward by Canada stating that "all members should bear constantly in mind the desirability of bringing to the attention of the Council information on international political developments whenever they are of concern to other members of the Council or to the Organization as a whole." Moreover, "the Council in permanent session should from time to time consider what specific subject might be suitable for political consultation at one of its subsequent meetings when its members should be in a position to express the views of their governments on the subject." The resolution, which was immediately approved, nonetheless provoked a "reaction" by the American representative, Secretary of State John Foster Dulles. The US, as his position was recorded,

> supported the Canadian resolution on the understanding that consultation would be limited within the bounds of common sense. Countries like his own with world-wide interests might find it difficult to consult other NATO governments in every case. For a sudden emergency, it was more important to take action than to discuss the emergency. In other words, consultation should be regarded as a means to an end, rather than the end itself.
>
> *NATO 2020*

In the transatlantic relations of the EU with the US and with Canada consultation has not been a legally based requirement. Nonetheless, it occurs, and it increasingly has become an expectation. Declaratory agreements have almost mandated it, without the assurance, however, that it will actually happen—or be meaningful. During the implementation of the Marshall Plan, to which not only the US but also Canada contributed, there was detailed discussion within and between Washington, Ottawa, Paris, and other European capitals of the economic support that would be needed, including the supply of food, equipment, and raw materials. This was made possible in significant part by the provision of US dollars which, it was agreed as a result of the efforts of Ambassador Hume Wrong and other Canadian officials, could be applied by Europeans to the "offshore" purchase of exports from Canada as well as from the US (Granatstein and Cuff 1977). Marshall Plan coordination engendered lasting goodwill and a generation of human contact, even though it did not directly establish a permanent structure of transatlantic economic cooperation and consultation. Neither did NATO develop that way. Despite the Canadian government's hope that, through the Washington Treaty's Article 2 (the "Canadian article") provision on "promoting conditions of stability and well-being," by which the signatories were to "seek to eliminate conflict in their international economic policies" and to "encourage economic collaboration between any or all of them," NATO did not develop as an instrument for economic collaboration, except in limited areas such as arms production and procurement and scientific research cooperation (Campbell 1985; NATO 2019).

North American communication with the EU began in the 1950s with its forerunner, the ECSC. The US government sent a special representative, David K. E. Bruce, to the High Authority of the ECSC in Luxembourg as an observer in 1953, and formally opened a US Mission to it in 1956. Bruce had been US ambassador in France where he oversaw the work in Europe of the Economic Cooperation Administration (ECA), the implementation arm of the Marshall Plan. While there for understanding issues related to efforts to unify Europe, Bruce was expected to be a kind of "roving ambassador." He had become friendly with the ECSC High Authority's president Jean Monnet, who had successfully recommended his appointment to Secretary Dulles and the Eisenhower administration. In 1954, the ECSC opened an Information Service Office in Washington. Its director was an American, Leonard Tennyson, recruited by Monnet on the recommendation of his longtime legal adviser in the US, George W. Ball (European Commission 2014, 345).

After the signing of the Treaties of Rome on 25 March 1957, which created the European Economic Community (EEC) and the European Atomic Energy Community (Euratom). In 1958, Euratom sent Curt Heidenreich to Washington as head of a liaison office, incorporated subsequently into an EC Commission liaison office. That same year the US government accredited a diplomat, Walton Butterworth, as its representative to the EEC and Euratom. The influence of his mission was quickly felt. As Francesco Fresi, a young Italian official involved in these events at the time, recalled, "we didn't say so or weren't aware of it at our level. We did, however, begin to feel US pressure for Great Britain to successfully catalyse all this renewal in Europe into forms that were not hostile to US policy" (European Commission 2014, 347)

Canada was also establishing itself with the newly unifying Europe. "Our relationship," the Government of Canada (n.d.) proudly notes, "is the EU's oldest formal relationship with any industrialised country, officially dating back to 1959 when we signed the Agreement for Cooperation in the Peaceful Uses of Atomic Energy." It soon followed the US when, in 1960, it opened a Canadian mission to the EEC. In 1976, it negotiated a Framework Agreement for commercial and economic cooperation with the EC—a "privileged" position the US government did not have (Henrikson 1993b, 176–77). On the basis of the 1976 Framework Agreement, and in light of European movement to form an internally integrated market and the possibility that the US might become its exclusive partner, early in 1990, the Canadian government began discussions with the European Community regarding a joint declaration. Among the key figures participating were Secretary of State for External Affairs Joe Clark, the Canadian ambassador in Washington Derek Burney, and Under-Secretary of State for External Affairs de Montigny Marchand. Their preferred policy option was a bilateral Canada-EC Free Trade Agreement or, even better, a multilateral Atlantic Trade Association. The fact that the US government under President George H. W. Bush had begun discussions with the Mexican presidential administration of Carlos Salinas de Gortari about a possible US-Mexico trade pact, despite the recently launched Canada-US Free Trade Agreement, indicated a disturbing US tendency toward bilateralism. A counter to this trend would be a *transatlantic* trade pact—a revival of an older "NAFTA," a North Atlantic Free Trade Area idea (Henrikson 1993b, 178–79).

Encouragement was no doubt given by the German foreign minister, Hans-Dietrich Genscher, who on a visit to Ottawa said in an address to the Canadian Parliament that the two North American democracies should consider it useful "to give our relationship a new quality in addition to our membership in NATO, and to have a new declaration concerning the common challenges we face in the political, economic, technological, and ecological fields." In saying this, Genscher himself was influenced by his US counterpart James A. Baker's remarks before the Berlin Press Club on 12 December 1989, having envisioned "a new Atlanticism for a new era." In his address, Baker had proposed ways in which NATO as well as the EC and the Conference on Security and Cooperation in Europe (CSCE) could collectively respond to the challenging international situation following the dramatic fall of the Berlin Wall the month before (Baker 1995, 172–73). "It was not the German foreign minister," Genscher pointed out, "it was the American foreign minister who for the first time, when he presented his speech in Berlin, spoke of the more political character of the alliance—and I think Jim Baker is totally right in saying this" (Henrikson 1993b, 179).

The two foreign ministers, who were to become fast friends, actually "wanted a treaty" to formalize the closer transatlantic relationship they both were contemplating, with the European Community to be the formal partner. Baker, however, knew how long and difficult the US ratification process would be, and they wanted something tangible to show in time for a historic summit meeting of the CSCE to take place in Paris in November 1990. They, therefore, settled upon the idea of a declaration. It would be made by the US with the EC. This would be paralleled by a similar Canadian declaration with it. The declarations would be the EC-US/EC-Canada counterpart to what became the CSCE's "Charter of Paris for a New Europe" (Henrikson 1993b, 179–80).

The results were the "DECLARATION ON EC-US RELATIONS," of 23 November signed in Paris on the margins of the Paris CSCE Summit of Heads of State or Government, and on the day before, in Rome, a parallel—though not quite identical—"DECLARATION ON EC-CANADA RELATIONS." The two Transatlantic Declarations—or TADs, as they are sometimes called—may be considered the first formal expression of the New Atlanticism. Both documents contain statements of "common goals" and "principles of partnership." They propose cooperation in economic, scientific, cultural, and educational areas, and also in meeting "trans-national challenges." Interestingly, the designated official framework for "security" cooperation is the CSCE rather than NATO. There is in the texts, however, a "firm commitment" by the US, Canada, and "the EC member states *concerned*" to the "North Atlantic *Alliance*" [emphases added]. Implicitly, the EC member states that are not NATO members or participants in the Alliance's integrated military structure, as France then was not, were not so tightly bound. For Canada, whose government even then was contemplating withdrawal of Canadian troops from the European theater, the wording could prove to be significant. The EC-Canada text, it may be noted, refers to the "historic" role played by transatlantic solidarity. The EC-US text describes that solidarity as "essential."

From an operational perspective, by far the most important section of both the US and Canadian TADs with the EC was the section that contained, under the heading "Institutional Framework for Consultation," some proposed linkage between the parties—but only that. The EC-US text, in fact, speaks of making full use of and further strengthening of "existing procedures"—not creating new ones. These procedures, however, were, for the first time, formalized. The listed procedures include, at the top level, biannual consultations to be held, in the US and in Europe, between the US president and the European Council's president together with the EC Commission's president. The text of EC-Canada Declaration, in significant contrast, provides only for "regular" meetings—between the Canadian prime minister and the EC Council and Commission presidents (Henrikson 1993b, 183, 186).

For the US, the Transatlantic Declaration of 1990 was the beginning of a consultative relationship with the EC—after the 1993 Maastricht Treaty, the EU—that has gained programmatic content, though not formal treaty status. The New Transatlantic Agenda (NTA) was signed at the EU-US Madrid Summit in 1995. As Anthony Gardner, then serving as director for European Affairs on the staff of the National Security Council, has written, the NTA "called for the US-EU relationship to evolve from joint consultation to joint action in a number of areas by specific target dates." It expressed the determination to create a New Transatlantic Marketplace—"essentially a transatlantic free trade agreement." The "core purpose" of the NTA, Gardner (2020) explained, was "to enhance structured foreign policy cooperation—specifically the promotion of peace, democracy, and prosperity around the world" (37–38). An accompanying Joint Action Plan identified the regions and the problems to be addressed. The 1998 London US-EU Summit, which was focused on trade and investment, saw the Transatlantic Economic Partnership agreed upon. In support of the US-EU official process, and in coordination with it, the relevant interests of the business and other sectors were to be brought to bear. Under the NTA subheading, "Building Bridges Across the Atlantic," a number of "people-to-people dialogues" were organized. After the preexisting TransAtlantic Business Dialogue, there came the Transatlantic Consumer Dialogue, the Transatlantic Environment Dialogue, and the Transatlantic Legislators' Dialogue. Within the US House of Representatives, a bipartisan Congressional EU Caucus was brought together to "strengthen our partnerships with our allies in the EU, to make the world a safer place, promoting peace through strength" (European Parliament n.d.). The Transatlantic Policy Network, composed of leaders in politics and business across the US and Europe and with representation also from think tanks, civil society, and academe, intends to "keep the two administrations focused on the indispensable goal of a strengthened Transatlantic Partnership" (Transatlantic

Policy Network n.d.). At the US-EU Summit in Washington in 2007, on the basis of the 2005 Summit Declaration on the Initiative to Enhance Transatlantic Economic Integration and Growth, the Transatlantic Economic Council (TEC) was established. The TEC remains today "the primary plenary forum for economic dialogue between the United States and the European Union" (US Department of State n.d.).

For Canada, the 1990 Transatlantic Declaration was followed by a Joint Political Declaration (1996), on the basis of which it was decided at a 2002 summit in Ottawa to launch a comprehensive review of EU-Canada relations. The product was the EU-Canada Partnership Agenda of 18 March 2004. The text identified, distinctively, as fundamental to their relationship, along with "common values" and "close historical and cultural ties," a shared "respect for multilateralism"—indicated by the "increasing frequency with which we vote together" within the UN and other international and regional organizations (EEAS 2004).

Atlantic Generations and Their Succession, Decades of Interaction, and Consolidation

Transatlantic connections, whatever the structures such as those described above within which they may have been formed, are ultimately a *human* texture. They are results of the weaving of personal relationships between individual leaders and officials, who have met, conferred, and most importantly, worked together. They are a distinguishing element—and also a major source of strength—in the overall international relationships of the US and Canada, with each other, and with the nations of Europe during more than a half century of recent history. Some may consider this a "soft" factor as opposed to the "hard" factors of trade, defense, technology, etc. However, it is just these acquaintances, often resulting in enduring friendships, that, in some of the most challenging situations that the Atlantic community has faced over past decades, have maintained the cohesion of and contributed to policy advances that have strengthened the transatlantic relationship, transforming it into a "partnership." The fabric of connection was woven gradually, from decade to decade, with sensitivity and sometimes insensitivity. The result of this political and diplomatic *tissage* is a statesmanly configured Atlantic tapestry which may be considered to have begun with Winston Churchill's voyage to meet Franklin Roosevelt off the coast of Newfoundland (see Figure 1.1)—the occasion and origin of the Atlantic Charter, 14 August 1941 (Wilson 1969).

In the 1940s, it was the military and political relationship between the wartime allies, carried over well into the post-war period, that helped to establish a historically unprecedented transatlantic security organization, NATO. The 1949 Washington Treaty, the alliance's fundamental text, was for Americans their first formal transatlantic defense commitment since the Revolutionary War–era defensive pact with France, which was abrogated in 1800 (Henrikson 1982; Kaplan 1984). During World War II, as Sayle pointed out, Dwight Eisenhower as supreme allied commander of the Allied Expeditionary Force served (and planned the D-Day

FIGURE 1.1 Prime Minister Churchill on board HMS *Prince of Wales* in Placentia Bay, Newfoundland, Canada, for his August 1941 rendezvous in the Atlantic with President Roosevelt

invasion) alongside his British counterpart, Bernard Montgomery. They again worked "side by side" in 1951, as, respectively, supreme commander and deputy supreme commander of NATO forces. "The only real difference," said a retired British officer who observed them working together, "is that the shooting war in Normandy has been replaced by the cold war in the East" (Sayle 2019, 6).

In the area of transatlantic economic relations, the example of Monnet and his American friends is illustrative. As a business entrepreneur in the interwar period, Monnet had traveled to the US many times and had established a "network of contacts" among men in whom he knew President Roosevelt had confidence (Monnet 2015, 123). His connections served him well when he was made Franco-British arms supply coordinator in Washington. After the war, as head of Le Commissariat général du Plan in France, he worked closely with Ambassador Bruce in implementing the Marshall Plan and, most notably, in devising the Schuman Plan that led to the creation of the ECSC. Bruce, who saw the importance of the Schuman Plan which was perceived by some as a "cartel," flew to London where he met the initially skeptical secretary of state, Dean Acheson, and convinced him that it was imperative that the US react positively to the Plan (Winand 1995, 114–15). Without an American official blessing, or at least polite acceptance, this major step toward European integration would have been more difficult. Monnet continued to use his American ties until he passed away in 1979.

In the 1950s, the most significant event in the transatlantic context was the Suez Crisis, coinciding with the revolt of Hungarians against their Soviet occupiers, in 1956. This was a test of NATO, its cohesion as well as its capability. The US administration under President Eisenhower did not share the preoccupation of the British and French governments with preserving their former imperial positions in the Middle East. The Eisenhower administration was more concerned about maintaining political stability there and the military balance in Europe against the Soviet Union and the forces of the Warsaw Pact. Nonetheless, such was the tie, going back to the war, between the leadership of the US and especially the United Kingdom (UK), that it was awkward for US government, as a NATO ally, to openly oppose the action against the Nasser regime in Egypt that London and Paris seemed intent on taking. Eisenhower, drawing on their wartime friendship, wrote to Prime Minister Anthony Eden:

> Whenever, on any international question, I find myself differing even slightly from you, I feel a deep compulsion to re-examine my position instantly and carefully. But permit me to suggest that when you use phrases in connection with the Suez affair like 'ignoble end to our long history' […] you are making of Nasser a much more important figure than he is.
>
> *Thomas 1967, 71*

Despite Eisenhower's warning, the British and French governments, ostensibly to separate Israeli and Egyptian forces in the region, invaded the Canal zone. "They ran an operation against us," angrily commented Andrew Goodpaster (1986), Eisenhower's military assistant at the time, years later.

For Canada, concerned about Commonwealth unity and NATO solidarity, the Suez Crisis was a turning point. Pearson, Canada's External Affairs Minister and then serving as president of the UN General Assembly, at the urging of Prime Minister Louis St. Laurent proposed what became the first UN Emergency Force, UNEF (Anderson 2015). This marked the beginning of Canada's focus on peace-keeping under UN auspices and, while remaining in NATO, a gradual lessening of its interest in maintaining a conventional military presence in Germany. NATO, its unity badly shaken by the failure of consultation, heightened the attention being given to a Committee on Non-Military Cooperation ("Committee of Three") it had appointed. The Committee members were Pearson, Gaetano Martino from Italy, and Halvard Lange from Norway. The "Report of the Three Wise Men" resulted in significant new procedures for political consultation with the Alliance, including an enhanced role for the secretary general (Shea 2016).

In the 1960s, the subject of transatlantic unity was given prominence when a new American president with youthful experience in Europe, John F. Kennedy, envisioned a "Grand Design" (Kraft 1962; Schlesinger 1965, 842–66). The basic concept, of a US-European relationship of "two separate but equally powerful entities," was being promoted by Monnet's Action Committee for a United States of Europe. Kennedy's proposal was further prompted by Britain's 1961 decision to seek entry into the Common Market. This created the possibility of "a united Europe" with which, as Kennedy said in Philadelphia on 4 July 1962, the US, which was "ready for a declaration of interdependence," would be "prepared to discuss the ways and means of forming a concrete Atlantic partnership" (Kleiman 1964, 12–14, 35). The Grand Design failed to materialize, not least because French President Charles de Gaulle vetoed the bid of the Harold Macmillan government for British entry into the European Community (achieved later by Prime Minister Edward Heath in 1973). The French leader also opposed British-American nuclear cooperation and the US government's interest in negotiating with the Soviet Union over the Berlin problem. Nonetheless, in the most serious crisis of the decade, concerning the Soviet missiles in Cuba, de Gaulle was a stalwart. Former Secretary of State Acheson, sent during the crisis by President Kennedy to Paris with photographic evidence of the threat, was received by the French president in the Palais d'Elysée. "I understand that you have come not to consult me but to inform me," de Gaulle said. Yet, whatever his sense of indignation, with a wave of his arm he assured Acheson, "Your president's word is enough" (Mahan 2002, 128).

Differences over Indochina, a former French colony, roiled not only France but also the entire Atlantic world as the US, with almost no support from Europe, became deeply involved in the Vietnam War. Particularly, youth—the Generation of 1968—in both Europe and North America became exercised about the conflict, which intersected with issues of racial and other kinds of injustice at home and abroad (Horn 2007; Mead 1970). The "Vietnam generation" broadened the human connection that henceforward would shape the thinking, if not the action, of Western governments regarding military intervention. Within NATO and the support network of Atlantic Councils, serious efforts were made, including the Harmel Exercise with its dual-track emphasis on dialogue along with defense, to form a Successor Generation (Atlantic Council n.d.; Sayle 2019, 154–60; Scott-Smith 2013).

In the 1970s, extrication from Vietnam was the dominant preoccupation of US policy as conducted by President Richard Nixon and Henry Kissinger, his national security adviser and later the secretary of state. A withdrawal agreement, growing out of talks in Paris, finally was reached on 27 January 1973. In combination with the "triangular diplomacy" of their historic trips the two had made to Beijing and Moscow, the apparent settlement of the Vietnam conflict contributed to a widespread belief in the arrival of an era of global détente. In this context of reduced tension, Kissinger, with the thought of revitalizing the Atlantic alliance, launched the "Year of Europe" in a speech, with the programmatic suggestion of a "new Atlantic Charter." In retrospect, he considered this "one of the worst mistakes" he had made, for rather than transcending US-European trade and other issues and elevating the Atlantic dialogue, it turned into what seemed an almost adversarial negotiation used by Europeans to assert their own separate identity. Kissinger, who supposedly once had asked, "What is the phone number of Europe?" was offended when the Europeans designated as their point person for negotiating the "declaration" with the US the chair of the committee of European foreign ministers—Danish foreign minister Knud Børge Andersen (Kissinger 1982, 151–62, 192–94, 700–7; Sayle 2019, 178–80; Schwartz 2019).

A fundamental, although less noted, purpose of the "Year of Europe" for the Nixon administration was reshaping NATO in order to better counter Soviet pressures against Europe (Sayle 2019, 178–83). Within the US, there was a serious questioning of need for keeping a large number of troops there, notably by Senate Majority leader Mike Mansfield (D-Montana). His amendment to a selective security bill would cut the number of US personnel in Europe roughly in half, to approximately 150,000. Only an organized effort by the administration, including the enlistment by Kissinger of "the Old Guard" of Atlantic-oriented elders—Acheson, Bruce, John J. McCloy, and other venerables—to stand and speak publicly against the Mansfield Amendment, stopped its momentum (Kissinger 1979, 938–49; Williams 1985, 169–204). The Mutual and Balanced Force Reduction (MBFR) talks were in part a response to this domestic legislative pressure. In Europe, where there was concern about a possible strategic "decoupling" by the US, which could rely on its nuclear retaliatory capability. Transatlantically, the MBFR talks were a reassurance—for allies joined in them. They "accomplished two things," as Weisbrode insightfully pointed out. "They trained a generation of conventional arms controllers, and they advanced Allied unity, particularly among the British, Germans, Dutch, and Canadians, which underscored the important role of NATO's Senior Political Committee" (Weisbrode 2015, 190).

In the 1980s, with the election to the US presidency of Ronald Reagan, a conservative Republican from California with a North American continental outlook and a doctrinaire faith in American private enterprise and technological progress, but little personal or political connection to Europe except through Hollywood, the future of the Atlantic relationship was highly uncertain. To Canada and Mexico, Reagan proposed a "North American accord," which ultimately developed into the North American Free Trade Agreement (Henrikson 1993a). There was, again, thought of a North Atlantic free trade agreement as well—an idea periodically proposed by Canadian economists and politicians and during this period by Reagan's British ideological counterpart, Prime Minister Margaret Thatcher. It was the Strategic Defense Initiative, popularly referred to as "Star Wars," which Reagan outlined in a speech on 23 March 1983, that most caught the attention of Europeans, for it raised the specter of "Fortress America" and US nuclear disengagement as well as posed a technological challenge to the Russians. That the president, almost as an afterthought, indicated that NATO allies could be covered and even offered participation in the strategic defensive system, when it was developed, to the Soviet Union hardly was reassuring (Hiebert 1986). Canadian participation, incorrectly, was almost assumed. When Reagan met Soviet President Mikhail Gorbachev in Reykjavík in October, it was clear that the transition from offensive to defensive weaponry would be difficult. Not least of the problems was how to reassure US allies in Europe that they would be protected if nuclear missiles there were withdrawn. "Chancellor Helmut Kohl had fought the battle of his political life to get Pershing II missiles deployed in West Germany," recognized Secretary of State George Shultz (Shultz 1993, 767).

Canada's prime minister, Pierre Elliot Trudeau, who long had been opposed to reliance on nuclear weapons, had announced during a speech on East–West relations in October 1983 that he would travel to consult with the heads of the five nuclear powers and others on ways "to persuade all five nuclear-weapons states to engage in negotiations aimed at establishing global limits on their strategic nuclear arsenals," ways to improve European security "through the raising of the nuclear threshold" and re-energizing the Vienna MBFR talks, and ways to "arrest the proliferation among other states" (Trudeau 1983). When Trudeau met with Reagan in Washington, where predictably there was, among realists, sharp criticism of his "peace initiative," the president himself was, surprisingly to many, sympathetic. He wished him "Godspeed" on his mission (English 2009, 596–602). For the Canadian leader, whose international position in Europe and elsewhere had been enhanced by the country's inclusion (along with Italy) in the Group of Seven (G7) in 1976, owing to support from Kissinger and from his friend, Germany's Chancellor Helmut Schmidt (English 2009, 270–71), the peace initiative was a personal success. He had achieved a hearing but not a breakthrough. That came with President Reagan's meetings with Soviet leader Mikhail Gorbachev in Geneva and in Reykjavík, and subsequently in Moscow and in Washington, with agreement in December 1987 on the Intermediate-Range Nuclear Forces (INF) Treaty.

In the 1990s, after the Berlin Wall fell on 9 November 1989, the Cold War in Europe gradually came to an end. The succession of Vice President George H. W. Bush, who had been director of the Central Intelligence Agency and also permanent representative to the UN, to the US presidency suggested a combination of realism and internationalism. When Iraq's leader Saddam Hussein invaded Kuwait on 1–2 August 1990, Bush drew on his experience and also his many diplomatic and political associations. Having just seen Thatcher in Aspen, he sought the advice of Canadian Prime Minister Brian Mulroney, a good friend whom he asked to come down to Washington. Mulroney suggested going to the UN Security Council and that he also reach out to France's president, François Mitterrand, whom Bush promptly telephoned (Hampson 2018, 195–97, 224). This and other high-level Bush telephone calls and Secretary of State James Baker's travels to key foreign capitals resulted in an unprecedented series of UN Security Council resolutions, passed with Soviet support (and Chinese abstention), that ultimately authorized "all necessary means" to force Iraq's withdrawal. Under UNSC Resolution 678, a coalition of 35 countries led by the US expelled the Iraqi invaders. Collective security remarkably had worked, and what President Bush described as a "new world order" seemed to be at hand (Bush and Scowcroft 1998, 370, 400).

This included even the reunification of Germany, which was a transatlantic achievement as well as a European one. Bush and Baker, with Mulroney interceding with the deeply skeptical Thatcher and Mitterrand, produced, along with the Russians and the Germans, the final, resolving 2+4 formula. Among those publicly thanked by Chancellor Helmut Kohl was Brian Mulroney (Baker 1995,

208–16; Hampson 2018, 224, Newman 2005, 320). The enlargement of NATO to include even countries of the former Warsaw Pact was also an Atlantic-wide effort, involving many countries. The personal rapport that US President Bill Clinton, of the "Baby Boomer" generation, formed with Gorbachev's successor, Boris Yeltsin, was a key to NATO enlargement's acceptance by Russia at that time (Talbott 2002). Noteworthy in this period also was the growing participation of women in Atlantic decision-making, with Secretary of State Madeleine Albright playing a particularly prominent, as well as gender-inclusive, role (Albright 2003). For Secretary Albright, the immigrant daughter of a diplomat from Czechoslovakia, the US was itself "a European power"—a provocative notion advanced also by Richard Holbrooke, negotiator of the 1995 Dayton Peace Accords that ended the war in Bosnia-Herzegovina (Albright 1997; Holbrooke 1995, 1999).

In the 2000s, the salient world event was 11 September 2001, the coordinated attack by al-Qaeda on the World Trade Center in New York and on the Pentagon, which precipitated what the new presidential administration under George W. Bush quickly termed the "Global War on Terror." Expressions of solidarity within the Atlantic community were immediate. The French paper *Le Monde* declared: "*Nous sommes tous américains*" (We are all Americans), a statement filled with symbolism (Henrikson 2003). For the first time in its history, NAC invoked Article 5, the alliance's mutual-defense article, and authorized the use of AWACS surveillance aircraft to supplement North American coverage. The suggestion to use Article 5 came from Canadian Ambassador David Wright, dean of the Council; it was enthusiastically supported by Secretary General Lord Robertson (Buckley 2006). Secretary of State Colin Powell, while expressing gratitude for this unprecedented allied gesture, indicated that the US was prepared to act unilaterally. In "building a coalition," Powell (2001) said, "we will not be constrained by the fact that we are working with others as well," emphasizing that, "There may be some things that the United States has to do alone, and we will always reserve the right to do that." Rather than rely on cooperation within NATO or any other organization, the Bush administration preferred an ad hoc solution. As Deputy Secretary of Defense Paul Wolfowitz (2002) stated, its operational doctrine was "the mission must determine the coalition." The UK's leader Tony Blair, determined to stand "shoulder to shoulder" with the US, threw himself into rallying international support for military action. When the Bush administration subsequently shifted its focus from Afghanistan to Iraq, intent upon overthrowing Saddam Hussein, the British government at the UN, through its representative Sir Jeremy Greenstock, sought diplomatically to steer the US toward at least allowing completion of the inspections for Iraq's possible possession of weapons of mass destruction—before the administration of "consequences." There was strong opposition to military action against Iraq from France as well as Germany and from many other countries in Europe where, however, differences were seen to be emerging between what Secretary of Defense Donald Rumsfeld labeled "old Europe" in contrast with NATO's "new members" in the post-communist east, which were "with the United States" (Baker 2003).

Unanimity within NAC, as in the UN Security Council, clearly was not obtainable. Nevertheless, in March 2003, the US, acting together with only Britain, Australia, and Poland, and with Italy, the Netherlands, and Spain giving support, launched Operation Iraqi Freedom. In the *post*-invasion phase of the Iraq War more than 40 nations, including many from Europe, participated in some fashion. Canada—its government under Prime Minister Jean Chrétien having made clear its refusal to join in using force without UN sanction—did not (Cellucci 2005, especially chs. 6–8).

Of serious common concern to all the countries of the Atlantic community, and indeed around the globe, was the financial crisis that began in the US during 2007–8 with the drop in mortgage-backed mortgage values and the bankruptcy of Lehman Brothers. In Europe, with the revelation of the size of Greece's debt in 2009 and the collapse of several commercial banks in Iceland, there was profound anxiety. Bailouts of troubled financial institutions became necessary. The US Federal Reserve System, the Bank of England, and the European Central Bank—led by Benjamin Bernanke, Mervyn King, and Jean-Claude Trichet—coordinated efforts in trying to contain the damage and to restore stability (Irwin 2013).

In the 2010s, with Barack Obama now US president, the challenge of dealing with the continuing financial crisis, and stimulating the American economy, was foremost. His foreign policy perspective was not traditional. His staff were from a younger generation (Obama 2020, 311–12). He promised a "new beginning" in relations with the Muslim world and, with adversaries including Iran, he expressed a readiness to "engage" (Henrikson 2018, 278–87). He did allow support for NATO action in Libya, "leading from behind" it was said, but he resisted intervention in Syria. As promised during his campaign, President Obama resumed the interrupted effort against al-Qaeda, and on 1 May 2001, Navy SEALs found and killed its leader, Osama bin Laden. His relationship with Europe was perceived initially as being cool, owing partly to his having grown up in the Pacific. As president, Obama approved a "pivot" of US interest toward East Asia. Members of his administration, however, worked closely with Europeans in negotiating the nuclear deal—the Joint Comprehensive Plan of Action (JCPOA)—with Iran in 2015 and the Paris Climate Agreement in 2016.

Obama's own relationships with European leaders developed an intimacy, as indicated by the regular consultations he had, sometimes virtually, with other members of the "Quint"—François Mitterrand, Angela Merkel, Matteo Renzi, and David Cameron. Revelation of its existence prompted recollection of de Gaulle's desire for an Atlantic big-power *"directoire"* (Gegout 2002). Within NATO itself, coordination was close. The International Security Assistance Force, established by the UN Security Council in December 2001 and led by NATO, demonstrated remarkable allied solidarity, with national forces rotating in and out. Canada contributed early, undertaking major responsibility in Kandahar Province (Stein and Lang 2008). US partnership with the EU also deepened with Hillary Clinton as secretary of state working closely with Lady Catherine Ashton, EU high representative for Foreign Affairs and Security Policy, collaborated on various matters ranging from overseas crisis management to peace in the Balkans and the advancement of women's rights (Clinton 2014, 222–23).

The inauguration of Donald Trump as US president in January 2017 badly shook the sense of Atlantic solidity. Trump's blunt espousal of "American First," his questioning of the relevance of NATO, his son-in-law Jared Kushner's description of the EU as the enemy," his own conspicuous support for Britain's withdrawal from the EU, and his abrupt departure from the G7 summit hosted by Prime Minister Justin Trudeau at La Malbaie, Québec, challenged even the comity of transatlantic relationship. More serious was his announcement of US withdrawal from the Paris Climate Agreement, followed by US withdrawal from the nuclear agreement with Iran, and the re-imposition of economic sanctions against it (Daalder and Lindsay 2018). His puzzling refusal to criticize the aggressive behavior of Russian President Vladimir Putin coincided, oddly, with his administration's joining in a NATO decision to enhance deterrence by shifting forces closer to front lines in the east and also its announcement that the US would pull out of the INF Treaty owing to Russian noncompliance (Bugos 2019). Trump, having punitively ordered a severe reduction of the US troop presence in Germany as the Germans were "not paying their bills," allowed his Defense Secretary Mark Esper to reposition some American troops to the Black Sea region and to send some to the Baltic states on temporary rotation (Stewart and Ali 2020). These contradictions and mixed signals, evident within the administration of the US government itself, were confounding to observers. There seemed no certain connection between the US and Europe. If America ever was "a European power," that seemed no longer the case (Shea 2020). Even communication with Washington was uncertain. As Federica Mogherini, Ashton's successor as high representative who subsequently became rector of the College of Europe, commented, even "telephone numbers" are not there (Carnegie Endowment 2021; Mogherini 2021).

Conclusion: Bouncing Back (Newer)?: The Personal Factor, Generational Awareness, and Restoration or a Renovation of the Transatlantic Alliance?

With the constitutionally assured prospect of Joe Biden assuming the US presidency (and of Kamala Harris its vice presidency), on 2 December 2020, the EU took the initiative in putting forward "[a] new transatlantic agenda for global change." It was presented as a "once-in-a-generation opportunity" for a working together on a design for *global* not just European-American cooperation. "The transatlantic alliance is based on shared values and history, but also interests: building a stronger, more peaceful and more prosperous world," European Commission President Ursula von der Leyen stated. "When the transatlantic partnership is strong, the EU and the US are both stronger. It is time to reconnect with a new agenda for transatlantic and global cooperation for the world of today." Her argument was echoed by Josep Borrell, the EU high representative and a Commission vice-president.

> With our concrete proposals for cooperation under the future Biden administration, we are sending strong messages to our US friends and allies. Let's look forward, not back. Let's *rejuvenate* our relationship. Let's build a partnership that delivers prosperity, stability, peace and security for citizens across our continents and around the world. There is no time to wait—let's get to work [emphasis added].
>
> *European Commission 2020*

Within NATO, also, the arrival of the Biden administration, with the experience it offered, was welcomed. NATO's perspective, however, was not only on the future but also on difficulties of the present, including the military, political, and economic, and also moral problem of NATO's departure from Afghanistan. Many of the allies individually had doubts, fearing the consequences of withdrawal. They were in favor of retaining a presence there but realized that, after President Biden's 14 April definitive statement that all American troops would be out by 11 September 2021 (the 20th anniversary of 9/11), continued NATO involvement would be impossible without the US. When NATO Secretary General Jens Stoltenberg (NATO 2021) then welcomed Secretary of State Antony J. Blinken and Secretary of Defense Lloyd J. Austin III at a meeting with their counterparts at NATO headquarters in Brussels, he recognized the interpersonal character of the alliance and the importance of consultation when difficult decisions had to be made.

> So Tony and Lloyd, I am very grateful for your personal, strong commitment to NATO, to our transatlantic bond. Your presence here today is a continued demonstration of the importance of the transatlantic bond. And the United States' commitment to consulting with its NATO allies,

Stoltenberg said.

> Today, we decided together on the future of our presence in Afghanistan. We have been in Afghanistan for almost 20 years. After we invoked Article 5 of our founding treaty for the first time, in support of the United States after the horrific 9/11 terrorist attacks.

The "drawdown" of NATO's Resolute Support Mission would begin shortly. Stoltenberg continued, "We went into Afghanistan together. We have adjusted our posture together. And we are united in leaving together" (NATO 2021).

President Biden, soon after taking office, had already taken steps to solidify the Atlantic community by rejoining the Paris Climate Agreement, re-engaging diplomatically in Geneva with Iran and other signatories of the JCPOA, and canceling the Trump cutback, as well as increasing the US troop commitment in Germany in a coordinated effort to bolster Ukraine in the face of Russian military buildup along its border (Erlanger, Eddy, and Cooper 2021). He affirmed the transatlantic connection personally by traveling to Europe for a series of meetings. His itinerary included a G7 gathering in Cornwall, a NATO summit, and a US-EU summit in Brussels, and also a bilateral meeting with Russian Federation President Putin in Geneva. Face-to-face diplomacy seemed back on track. "Call it the much-welcomed death of Zoom diplomacy," correspondents of the *New York Times* observed (Shear and Sanger 2021).

Biden explained the trip's purpose in advance. "In this moment of global uncertainty, as the world still grapples with a once-in-a-century pandemic, this trip is about realizing America's renewed commitment to our allies and partners, and demonstrating the capacity of democracies to both meet the challenges and deter the threats of this new age" (Biden 2021). With France, where doubts about US reliability under Trump had encouraged its president, Emmanuel Macron, to recommend European "strategic autonomy," the return of the US was welcome. "I think it's great to have the U.S. president part of the club, and very willing to cooperate," said Macron, sitting next to Biden at the G7 meeting. "What you demonstrate is that leadership is partnership" (Leonard 2021).

For Canada, too, the Biden trip was a reaffirmation. At NATO, the new president said Article 5 (the mutual-defense commitment covering the European allies as well as Canada and Turkey) was "a sacred obligation" (Emmott, Holland, and Siebold 2021). When together in Cornwall, he and Justin Trudeau, with whom he had met only virtually since becoming president, spoke about further relaxing COVID-related restrictions on traffic across the US-Canada border (Ljunggren 2021). More than three years earlier, Biden and Trudeau had bonded, continuing what Biden had jokingly called the "bromance" of Obama and Trudeau. The bonding happened at a state dinner presciently given in December 2016 by the Canadian leader in honor of then Vice President Biden after Trump's surprise election victory. Guests for the event, held in the Sir John A. Macdonald Building in Ottawa, included former prime ministers Mulroney and Chrétien. Trudeau's father, Pierre, was present in memory. "I watched your father. I watched everything he did," Biden said to his host. "He was a man of great integrity" (Blatchford and Allen 2020).

These and comparable recollections are the emotional and political cement of the transatlantic alliance. Whether they contribute significantly to the resilience, as well as only to the stability, of the transatlantic relationship is, however, uncertain. "Resilience" is a *forward*-looking concept, requiring new thought, the widening of horizons, and a readiness for unforeseen circumstances (Hamilton 2016). Much depends both on the fresh transmission of historical memory and on the constant renewal of association through in-person consultation and conferencing which, in the circumstances of the COVID-19 pandemic and the impetus this has given to digital diplomacy and other networking, may not so often take place. The "bounce back" of relationships across the Atlantic also requires governments, institutions, and enterprises that promote innovation and growth as well as personally connected individuals, both leaders and followers, who envision a future world that is generated, but not dominated, by the present and past. Crucially, it must be noted, as George Washington recognized, the "sensibility" that arises from and is nurtured by the personal relationships that knit together national and international communities, and build solidarity, involves actual collaboration—"the work of joint counsels, and joint efforts" (Washington 1796). Transatlantic solidarity depends on cooperative synergy as well as on diplomacy.

References

Acheson, Dean. 1968. *Present at the Creation: My Years in the State Department.* New York: W.W. Norton.

Albright, Madeleine K. 1997. Prepared Statement Before the Senate Foreign Relations Committee. Washington, DC. 8 January. https://1997-2001.state.gov/statements/970108a.html.

———. 2003. *Madam Secretary.* New York: Miramax Books.

Anderson, Anthony. 2015. *The Diplomat: Lester Pearson and the Suez Crisis.* Fredericton, NB: Goose Lane Editions.

Atlantic Council. n.d. History. www.atlanticcouncil.org/about/history/.

Baker, James A., III. 1995. *The Politics of Diplomacy: Revolution, War and Peace, 1989–1992.* New York: Putnam.

Baker, Mark. 2003. "U.S.: Rumsfeld's 'Old' and 'New' Europe Touches on Uneasy Divide." *Radio Free Europe/Radio Liberty.* www.rferl.org/a/1102012.htmlw.rferl.org/a/1102012.html.

Biden, Joe. 2021. "Joe Biden: My Trip to Europe Is About America Rallying the World's Democracies." *The Washington Post,* 5 June 2021.

Blatchford, Andy, and Sue Allen. 2020. "Can Joe Biden Pick Up Where Trudeau-Obama Left Off? *Politico,* 3 November. www.politico.com/news/2020/11/03/biden-trudeau-canada-relationship-obama-433983.

Bourdieu, Pierre. 1977. *Outline of a Theory of Practice.* Vol. 6. Cambridge: Cambridge University Press.

Bourne, Kenneth. 1967. *Britain and the Balance of Power in North America, 1815–1908.* Berkeley: University of California Press.

Brebner, John Bartlett. 1945. *North Atlantic Triangle: The Interplay of Canada, the United States, and Great Britain.* New Haven: Yale University Press.

Buckley, Edgar. 2006. "Invoking Article 5." *NATO Review,* 1 June. www.nato.int/docu/review/articles/2006/06/01/invoking-article-5/index.html.

Bugos, Shannon. 2019. "U.S. Completes INF Withdrawal." *Arms Control Today.* www.armscontrol.org/act/2019-09/news/us-completes-inf-treaty-withdrawal.

Bush, George, and Brent Scowcroft. 1998. *A World Transformed.* New York: Knopf Doubleday Publishing Group.

Campbell, Edwina S. 1985. *Consultation and Consensus in NATO: Implementing the Canadian Article.* Lanham, MD: University Press of America.

Carnegie Endowment for International Peace. 2021. "Reinventing the Transatlantic Relationship." 28 January. https://carnegieendowment.org/2021/01/28/reinventing-leadership-in-transatlantic-relationship-event-7527.

Cellucci, Paul. 2005. *Unquiet Diplomacy.* Toronto: Key Porter Books.

Clinton, Hillary. 2014. *Hard Choices.* New York: Simon & Schuster.

Creighton, Donald. 1965. *The Road to Confederation: The Emergence of Canada, 1863–1867*. Toronto: Macmillan.

Daalder, Ivo H., and James M. Lindsay. 2018. *The Empty Throne: America's Abdication of Global Leadership*. New York: Public Affairs.

Deutsch, Karl W., Sidney A. Burrell, Robert A. Kann, Maurice Lee, Martin Lichterman, Raymond e. Lindgren, Francis L. Loewenheim, and Richard W. Van Wagenen. 1957. *Political Community and the North Atlantic Area: International Organization in the Light of Historical Experience*. Princeton, NJ: Princeton University Press.

Erlanger, Steven. 2021. "U.S. Says 'We're Back,' But Europe Still Recalls Trauma of Trump Years." *The New York Times*, 8 June 2021.

Erlanger, Steven, Melissa Eddy, and Helene Cooper. 2021. "More Troops to Germany as U.S. Bolsters Ukraine." *The New York Times*, 14 April 2021.

Emmott, Robin, Steve Holland, and Sabine Siebold. 2021. "At NATO, Biden Says Defence of Europe, Canada Is 'Sacred Trust' for U.S." *National Post*, 14 June. https://nationalpost.com/news/world/at-nato-biden-says-defence-of-europe-canada-is-sacred-obligation-for-u-s.

English, John. 2009. *Just Watch Me, The Life of Pierre Elliott Trudeau*, Volume Two: 1968–2000. Toronto: Penguin Random House.

European Commission. 2014. *The European Commission 1958–72: History and Memories of an Institution*. Brussels.

———. 2020. *EU-US: A New Transatlantic Agenda for Global Change*. Press Release. December. Brussels.

European External Action Service (EEAS). 2004. EU-CANADA PARTNERSHIP AGENDA. EU-Canada Summit, Ottawa, 18 March. https://eeas.europa.eu/archives/docs/canada/docs/partnership_agenda_en.pdf.

European Parliament. n.d. "EU-US Relations." European Parliament Liaison Office in Washington DC. www.europarl.europa.eu/unitedstates/en/eu-us-relations.

Ferreiro, Larrie D. 2007. *Brothers at Arms: American Independence and the Men of France and Spain Who Saved It*. New York: Vintage Books.

Gardner, Anthony Luzzatto. 2020. *Stars With Stripes: The Essential Partnership Between the European Union and the United States*. London: Palgrave Macmillan.

Gegout, Catherine. 2002. "The Quint: Acknowledging the Existence of a Big Four-US Directoire at the Heart of the European Union's Foreign Policy Decision-Making Process." *Journal of Common Market Studies* 40 (2): 331–34.

Goodpaster, Andrew. 1986. Conversation with the author, 6 June, at The Fletcher School of Law and Diplomacy, Tufts University, Medford, MA.

Government of Canada. n.d. "Canada and the European Union: Canada-EU Relations." www.international.gc.ca/world-monde/international_relations-relations_internationales/eu-ue/index.aspx?lang=eng.

Granatstein, J. L. 1998. *The Ottawa Men: The Civil Servant Mandarins, 1935–1957*. Toronto: University of Toronto Press.

Granatstein, J. L., and R. D. Cuff. 1977. "Canada and The Marshall Plan, June–December 1947." *Historical Papers/Communications historiques* 12 (1). https://doi.org/10.7202/030828ar.

Griffiths, Richard T. 2012. "The Founding Fathers." In *The Oxford Handbook of the European Union*, edited by Eric Jones, Anand Menon, and Stephen Weatherill, 181–92. Oxford: Oxford University Press.

Hamilton, Daniel S., ed. 2016. *Forward Resilience: Protecting Society in an Interconnected World*. Center for Transatlantic Relations, Paul H. Nitze School of Advanced International

Studies, Johns Hopkins University. https://archive.transatlanticrelations.org/publication/forward-resilience-protecting-society-interconnected-world/.

Hampson, Fen Osler. 2018. *Master of Persuasion: Brian Mulroney's Global Legacy*. Toronto: McClellan & Stewart.

Henderson, Nicholas. 1983. *The Birth of NATO*. Boulder, CO: Westview Press.

Henrikson, Alan K. 1982. "The Creation of the North Atlantic Alliance." In *American Defense Policy*, edited by John F. Reichart and Steven R. Sturm, 296–320. 5th ed. Baltimore: Johns Hopkins University Press.

———. 1986. "The Global Foundations for a Diplomacy of Consensus." In *Negotiating World Order: The Artisanship and Architecture of Global Diplomacy*, edited by Alan K. Henrikson, 217–44. Wilmington, DE: Scholarly Resources Inc.

———. 1993a. "A North American Community: 'From the Yukon to the Yucatan.'" In *The Diplomatic Record, 1991*–1992, edited by Hans Binnendijk and Mary Locke, 69–95. Boulder, CO: Westview Press.

———. 1993b. "The New Atlanticism: Western Partnership for Global Leadership." *Revue d'intégration européenne/Journal of European Integration* 16 (2–3): 165–91.

———. 1998. "The Role of Generations and 'Lessons' of History in American Planning During the Persian Gulf Crisis." In *Rethinking International Relations: Ernest R. May and the Study of World Affairs*, edited by Akira Iriye, 389–95. Chicago: Imprint Publications.

———. 2003. "The Iconography and Circulation of the Atlantic Community." *Ekistics/ ΟΙΚΙΣΤΙΚΗ: The Problems and Science of Human Settlements*. Part 3, *In the Steps of Jean Gottmann* 70 (418/419): 270–94. [Published in 2005. Calogero Muscarà (guest ed.) and Panayis C. Psomopoulos (ed.)]

———. 2018. "United States Contemporary Diplomacy: Implementing a Foreign Policy of 'Engagement.'" In *Diplomacy in a Globalizing World: Theories and Practices*, edited by Pauline Kerr and Geoffrey Wiseman, 269–88. 2d ed. New York: Oxford University Press.

Hiebert, Timothy H. 1986. "Reagan's Strategic Defense Initiative: The U.S. Presentation and the European Response." *The Fletcher Forum of World Affairs* 10 (1): 51–64.

Holbrooke, Richard C. 1995. "America, A European Power." *Foreign Affairs* 74 (2): 38–57.

———. 1999. *To End a War*. New York: Modern Library.

Horn, Gerd-Rainer. 2007. *The Spirit of '68: Rebellion in Western Europe and North America, 1956–1976*. New York: Oxford University Press.

Irwin, Neal. 2013. *The Alchemists: Three Central Bankers and a World on Fire*. New York: The Penguin Press.

Isaacson, Walter, and Evan Thomas. 1986. *The Wise Men: Six Friends and the World They Made: Acheson, Bohlen, Harriman, Kennan, Lovett, McCloy*. New York: Simon & Schuster.

Kaplan, Lawrence S. 1984. *The United States and NATO: The Formative Years*. Lexington: The University Press of Kentucky.

Kissinger, Henry. 1979. *White House Years*. Little, Brown.

———. 1982. *Years of Upheaval*. Boston: Little, Brown.

———. 2001. *Does America Need a Foreign Policy? Toward a Diplomacy for the 21st Century*. New York: Simon & Schuster.

Kleiman, Robert. 1964. *Atlantic Crisis: American Diplomacy Confronts a Resurgent Europe*. New York: W.W. Norton & Company.

Kluckhohn, Frank. 1942. "President Sees 2 or 3 Years' War Until We Are Certain of Survival." *The New York Times*, 15 April 1942.

Kraft, Joseph. 1962. *The Grand Design: From Common Market to Atlantic Partnership*. New York: Harper.

Kraus, Michael. 1949. *The Atlantic Civilization: Eighteen-Century Origins*. Ithaca, NY: Cornell University Press.

Leonard, Ben. 2021. "Macron: Biden Has 'Definitely' Convinced Allies That U.S. Is Back." *Politico*, 12 June 2021. www.politico.com/news/2021/06/12/biden-emmanuel-macron-g7-493724.

Lippmann, Walter. 1943. *U.S. Foreign Policy: Shield of the Republic*. Boston: Little, Brown and Co.

Ljunggren, David. 2021. "Canada's Trudeau Says He Discussed Border With Biden, But No Deal." *Reuters*, 13 June 2021. www.reuters.com/world/us/canadas-trudeau-says-he-discussed-border-with-biden-no-deal-2021-06-13/.

Macdonald, Sir John A. 1865. Sir John A. Macdonald, Speech in the Confederation Debates – February 6, 1865. The Macdonald-Laurier Institute. https://macdonaldlaurier.ca/18745/.

Mahan, Erin R. 2002. *Kennedy, de Gaulle, and Western Europe*. New York: Palgrave Macmillan.

May, Ernest R. 1973. *"Lessons of the Past": The Use and Misuse of History in American Foreign Policy*. New York: Oxford University Press.

Mead, Margaret. 1970. *Culture and Commitment: A Study of the Generation Gap*. Garden City, NY: Natural History/Doubleday & Company, Inc.

Mogherini, Federica. 2021. "America Is Back, Diplomacy Is Back: Perspectives and Challenges for a Renewed Transatlantic Partnership." Webinar. Belfer Center for Science and International Affairs, Harvard Kennedy School, Harvard University, 8 March. https://hks.harvard.edu/events/america-back-diplomacy-back-perspectives-and-challenges-renewed-transatlantic-partnership.

Monnet, Jean. 2015. *Memoirs*. Translated by Richard Mayne. London: Third Millennium Publishing.

Morris, Richard B. 1965. *The Peacemakers: The Great Powers and American Independence*. New York: Harper & Row.

———. 1973. *Seven Who Shaped Our Destiny: The Founding Fathers as Revolutionaries*. New York: Harper & Row.

Newman, Peter C. 2005. *The Secret Mulroney Tapes: Unguarded Confessions of a Prime Minister*. Toronto: Random House Canada.

North Atlantic Treaty Organization (NATO). 2019. The North Atlantic Treaty. Washington D.C. – 4 April 1949. www.nato.int/cps/en/natolive/official_texts_17120.htm.

———. 2020. "The Consultation Process and Article 4." 28 February. www.nato.int/cps/en/natohq/topics_49187.htm.

———. 2021. Joint Press Point by NATO Secretary General Jens Stoltenberg, US Secretary of State Antony Blinken and US Secretary of Defense Lloyd J. Austin III. 14 April. www.nato.int/cps/en/natohq/opinions_183061.htm.

Obama, Barack. 2020. *A Promised Land*. New York: Crown.

Powell, Colin. 2001. "September 11, 2001: Attack on America: Secretary Colin L. Powell Remarks to the Press." The Avalon Project, Yale Law School. 13 September. https://avalon.law.yale.edu/sept11/powell_brief01.asp.

Reid, Escott. 1977. *Time of Fear and Hope: The Making of the North Atlantic Treaty, 1947–1949*. Toronto: McClelland & Stewart.

Roberts, Cokie. 2004. *Founding Mothers: The Women Who Raised Our Nation*. New York: William Morrow.

Rosen, S. McKee. 1951. *The Combined Boards of the Second World War: An Experiment in International Administration*. New York: Columbia University Press.

Sayle, Timothy Andrews. 2019. *Enduring Alliance: A History of NATO and the Postwar Global Order*. Ithaca, NY: Cornell University Press.

Schlesinger, Arthur M., Jr. 1965. *A Thousand Days: John F. Kennedy in the White House*. Boston: Houghton Mifflin Company.

Schwartz, Thomas Alan. 2019. "'A Frankenstein Monster': Henry Kissinger, Richard Nixon, and the Year of Europe." *Journal of Transatlantic Studies* 17 (1): 110–28.
Scott-Smith, Giles. 2013. "Reviving the Transatlantic Community? The Successor Generation Concept in U.S. Foreign Affairs, 1960s-1980s." In *European Integration and the Atlantic Community*, edited by Kiren Klaus Patel and Kenneth Weisbrode, 201–25. Cambridge: Cambridge University Press.
Shea, Jamie. 2016. "What Can We Learn Today From the 'Three Wise Men'?" *NATO Review*, 5 December. www.nato.int/docu/review/articles/2016/12/05/what-can-we-learn-today-from-the-three-wise-men/index.html.
———. 2020. "America: A European Power?" *Friends of Europe*, 2 October. www.friendsofeurope.org/insights/america-as-a-european-power/
Shear, Michael D., and David E. Sanger. 2021. "Face-to-Face Meeting Is a Welcome Return of Staged Diplomacy." *The New York Times*, 12 June 2021.
Shultz, George P. 1993. *Turmoil and Triumph: My Years as Secretary of State*. New York: Charles Scribner's Sons.
Stein, Janice Gross, and Eugene Lang. 2008. *The Unexpected War: Canada in Kandahar*. Toronto: Penguin.
Stewart, Phil, and Idrees Ali. 2020. "U.S. to Withdraw About 12,000 troops From Germany But Nearly Half to Stay in Europe." *Reuters*, 29 July 2020. www.reuters.com/article/us-usa-trump-germany-military/u-s-to-withdraw-about-12000-troops-from-germany-but-nearly-half-to-stay-in-europe-idUSKCN24U20L.
Stikker, Dirk U. 1966. *Men of Responsibility: A Memoir*. New York: Harper & Row.
Talbott, Strobe. 2002. *The Russia Hand: A Memoir of Presidential Diplomacy*. New York: Random House.
Thomas, Hugh. 1967. *Suez*. New York: Harper & Row.
Toynbee, Arnold. 1934–51. *A Study of History*. 12 vols. London: Royal Institute of International Affairs.
Transatlantic Policy Network. n. d. "Building Tomorrow's Partnership Today." www.tpnonline.org/.
Trudeau, Pierre E. 1983. "Reflections on Peace and Security." Address at the University of Guelph. 27 October. www.speeches-usa.com/Transcripts/pierre_trudeau-peace.html.
US Department of State. n.d. Transatlantic Economic Council, Bureau of European and Eurasian Affairs. www.state.gov/transatlantic-economic-council/.
Washington, George. 1796. Washington's Farewell Address 1796. The Avalon Project, Yale Law School. https://avalon.law.yale.edu/18th_century/washing.asp.
Weisbrode, Kenneth. 2015. *The Atlanticists: A Story of American Diplomacy*. Santa Ana, CA: Nortia Press.
White House. 2021a. Remarks by President Biden at the 2021 Virtual Munich Security Conference. 19 February. www.whitehouse.gov/briefing-room/speeches-remarks/2021/02/19/remarks-by-president-biden-at-the-2021-virtual-munich-security-conference/.
———. 2021b. Remarks by President Biden in Press Conference. Hôtel du Parc des Eaux-Vives, Geneva, Switzerland. 16 June. www.whitehouse.gov/briefing-room/speeches-remarks/2021/06/16/remarks-by-president-biden-in-press-conference-4/.
Williams, Phil. 1985. *The Senate and U.S. Troops in Europe*. London: Macmillan.
Wilson, Theodore A. 1969. *The First Summit: Roosevelt and Churchill at Placentia Bay, 1941*. Boston: Houghton Mifflin.

Winand, Pascaline. 1995. "Eisenhower, Dulles, Monnet and the Uniting of Europe." In *Monnet and the Americans: The Father of a United Europe and His American Supporters*, edited by Clifford P. Hackett, 103–39, Washington, DC: The Jean Monnet Council.

Wolfowitz, Paul. 2002. Remarks at the 38th Verkunde Conference on Security Policy. Munich, Germany. 2 February. *American Rhetoric Online Speech Bank*. www.americanrhetoric.com/speeches/wariniraq/paulwolfowitzmunichconference.htm.

2
THE COVID-19 PANDEMIC AS AN INCUBATOR OF GREAT POWER RIVALRIES

Josef Braml

Introduction

China's Communist Party has been put in danger above all by the immediate effects of the COVID-19 pandemic, which is why it suppressed the debate about the virus at home and distracted from it with an aggressive foreign policy (Walter Russell Mead as quoted in Sauerbrey 2020). To be true, China's lack of transparency in the onset of the pandemic and Europe's awareness of its own over-reliance on Chinese medical supplies have damaged China's reputation in Europe and brought Europe's stance closer to the tougher position held by the United States (US). Yet, the US government's handling of the coronavirus pandemic has also disillusioned hopes that, given a life-threatening situation, transatlantic cooperation would at least be improved.

Confrontation Instead of Cooperation

The COVID-19 pandemic and the global economic crisis it triggered have not led to global cooperation but have intensified existing geoeconomic rivalries, especially between the US and China, and have also affected Europe in the process. Although cooperative behavior by the most important states would be essential to combat the global pandemic—and the global economic crisis it precipitated—then-US President Donald J. Trump intensified the previous confrontation with China and attacked the World Health Organization. Trump set up scapegoats to distract from his own failure in the crisis and the serious socioeconomic consequences in his country that threatened his re-election. With sharp rhetoric, the Trump administration blamed China for the spread and drastic socioeconomic consequences of the pandemic in the US. According to Trump, the "China virus," the origin of which the White House suspected to be created in Chinese laboratories (and pushed this narrative in the media), was an "attack" that was worse than Japan's attack on Pearl Harbor in World War II or the 9/11 terrorist attacks (*BBC News* 2020). By apportioning blame, the Trump administration justified an even tougher approach on China. The cross-party critical stance was represented on both sides in the 2020 presidential election campaign (Silver, Devlin, and Huang 2020). Both Trump and his Democratic challenger, Joseph R. Biden, Jr., made China a central campaign issue. The two opponents tried to outdo each other with their criticism on China (Riechmann and Lemire 2020).

German and European decision-makers should expect a tougher approach by the US toward China under the new Biden administration. This will also affect Europe's economy and foreign policy. Meanwhile, the leaders of the Democratic and Republican parties are articulating, with ever sharper words, the noticeably more negative attitudes of their voters toward China (Silver, Devlin, and Huang 2020).

Wolf Krug, of the Hanns-Seidel-Stiftung, summed up the situation for *Die Welt* in the lead up to the US presidential election: We have already been in the midst of an "era of economic and political great power rivalries" for some time, which "not only results in new trade conflicts, but also a changed geostrategic role for the Federal Republic and Europe" (Krug 2020). So far, Europe has only been a spectator in this showdown, but in the event of the worst-case scenario, it will become the collateral damage of history if it does not quickly become capable of making decisions, acting, and defending its interests.

The Irony of History

In love with the self-image of their noble value orientation, however, the representatives of Europe and especially the decision-makers of the Berlin Republic still remain in the zeitgeist of German reunification and, despite retrograde steps in the meantime, continue to trust the "world spirit" of history in their belief in progress. However, the "end of history" (Fukuyama 1992)—the worldwide victory of liberal-democratic rule and a free-market economy—celebrated by the Western value community after the downfall of the system rival, the Soviet Union, was ironically refuted by history: Trump's authoritarian challenge to US democracy and his nationalist economic policy were clear signs of a new system of competition between the US, an ailing world power, and the increasingly self-confident China. Although the US was busy with the Trump administration retreating economically into the nationalist shell and alienating its allies, China's comprehensive "One Belt, One Road" (OBOR) initiative did not shy away from diplomatic initiatives and economic investments to reorder world trade on its terms.

Significantly, it is US political scientist, Francis Fukuyama, who rashly predicted the final victory of liberal democracies and free-market economies in 1992, today diagnoses elementary democratic deficits in Western leadership. These US shortcomings are all the more problematic because a new competitor—China—is preparing to export its counter-model. So, the story goes on because Fukuyama now sees a new "historic contest" in progress focused on the fate of Eurasia and between the US and its Western partners and China (Fukuyama 2016).

Finally gone is the time when US strategists benevolently accompanied China's economic development. According to Washington's original plans, China was to be integrated as a "responsible stakeholder" in the US-dominated Western world (economic) order, as then Deputy US Secretary of State Robert Zoellick put it in 2005. Economic liberalization, it was thought, would sooner or later also make China's political system more democratic and fit into the US-led community of market economies and democratic systems.

System Competition and Great Power Rivalry

Although the fall of the Soviet Union initially unleashed an economic surge in globalization and, above all, enabled political liberalization for a number of countries of the former Eastern Bloc, many autocratic regimes have, so far, proven to be very resistant. They have survived several waves of democratization, color revolutions (such as Ukraine's Orange Revolution and the Green Movement in Iran), and seasonal changes, such as the "Arab Spring" (Braml, Merkel, and Sandschneider 2014).

China's Communist Party has seen these upheavals as warning signs. Liberal ideas are also attractive in China, especially for younger Chinese, who are often educated in the US and Europe. But for now, good economic development serves the regime as a pillar of its stability and a bulwark against subversive developments—especially when comparisons to Western socioeconomic problems are sought.

The economic and financial crisis of 2007/8, which emanated from the West, did the rest. The global financial crisis shook faith in the far-reaching self-regulation of the markets and the creditworthiness of the US state. The "Washington Consensus," that has encouraged other countries around the world to liberalize and "Americanize" their political systems and economic systems, has lost credibility.

State-controlled economies, above all the authoritarian capitalism of the People's Republic of China, were also affected but were able to master the crisis better than the US and its value community. Authoritarian great powers, such as China, are today regarded even beyond East Asia as "serious counter-designs to liberal democracy" (Köllner 2008, 17–31). China's economic rise is already associated with the decline of the West (Sandschneider 2011); some experts already praise the "Beijing Consensus" as forward-looking (Halper 2010).

Even if only a few countries take the Chinese system of government as a model, more and more appreciate trade with the rising world economic power. About two-thirds of the world's 190 countries today trade more with China than with the US, with about 90 countries trading more than twice as much with China as with the US, according to Australia's Lowy Institute (2021).

For some time, China has been involved in breaking away from interdependence with the US, thereby reducing its vulnerability. Alternately, new dependencies have been created in which China is sitting at the longer lever. By providing public goods such as infrastructure, trade, and information routes around the world,

China is slowly but surely expanding its supremacy. With its OBOR initiative, the Middle Kingdom wants to connect its economy with its neighbors in the region, with West Asia, Africa, and Europe by land and sea. By defining its national interests more broadly as a wise power and allowing others to benefit as well, China can claim leadership and expect allegiance. Proof of this is Beijing's success—despite great counter-pressure from the US—in winning over European partners, such as the United Kingdom (UK), France, and Germany, for its Asian Infrastructure Investment Bank.

While the American state lacks money to renew the dilapidated roads, bridges, and airports even in its own country, China finances infrastructure worldwide, develops new sales markets, and can thus emancipate itself from its trading partner, the US, to which it had previously lent large quantities of money so that it could buy Chinese products. If China no longer makes its cheap goods and currency reserves available to the US, then this will not only affect US citizens who are being torn from their illusion of prosperity but also the American state, which has also been living beyond its means for a long time. China is no longer prepared to use its foreign exchange reserves to the extent that it has up until now to finance the US state budget, which is largely used to arm the world power militarily and in terms of security against China. These changes are alarming the US military industry as well as Wall Street.

The thought leaders of US think tanks, such as General James Mattis, who forged ideas in the Hoover Institution before his assignment as secretary of defense (2017–19) in the Trump's administration, are calling for a new "grand strategy" (Mattis 2015). They, too, are targeting China. Instead of the previous patchwork of individual strategies toward various countries and in certain policy areas (security, trade, or energy policy), the US should again pursue a global, cross-thematic orientation, namely a grand strategy, in order to curb China's rise and large-scale activities. In the eyes of the geostrategists in Washington, the Middle Kingdom now forms a counter-power that must be pushed back in the sense of a "rollback."

In July 2020, then-US Secretary of State Michael Pompeo dashed the last hopes of many Europeans that the US might still be able to come to terms with China's economic and military rise in the future. While at a symbolic location, the Richard Nixon Presidential Library, Pompeo made it clear that the strategy of rapprochement heralded in 1972 by President Nixon and his national security adviser Henry Kissinger had proved to be an epochal mistake. In his speech, which recalled the Cold War against the Soviet Union, Pompeo used Ronald Reagan's religious vocabulary in the best manner to make his compatriots aware of the system and value differences with China. Pompeo spoke of the Chinese Communist Party's rule as a tyranny that not only oppresses the Chinese people but also threatens the "free nations" of the world. This was the more secular message to US allies. The deep ideological gap between the democratic and liberal West on the one hand and the Marxist-Leninist and totalitarian regime of China on the other is insurmountable. In order to avert the danger posed by the Middle Kingdom, Western market economies would also have to "decouple" from the Chinese planned economy.

Pompeo called on US allies in Europe and Asia to jointly set standards and form a new group of like-minded nations to counter the Chinese threat (Pompeo 2020).

While Trump and his comrade-in-arms Pompeo are (for the time being) history, the self-praise for US democracy after the 6 January 2021 storming of the Capitol in the course of certifying the outcome of the presidential election has been somewhat subdued. But there is now no hope, even among representatives of the Biden administration, that China will also democratize its political system through economic liberalization. This also removed the basic assumption from the previous Western "engagement" policy that China would fit into the Western order dominated by the US as a "responsible stakeholder." The US now uses every means to contain or even to curb China's rise. "Containment" or "rollback" are now the buzzwords in the strategy debate. In this geoeconomic competition, (free) markets are no longer the end but the means to the geostrategic end. The economy is used as a weapon, so to speak, as a "non-military instrument of statecraft" (see, generally, Blackwill and Harris 2016; Stuhlberg 2005, 1–25).

Geoeconomics: Economics as a Weapon

In the increasingly dominant geoeconomic thinking of the world powers, economic interdependence and the worldwide division of labor are no longer necessarily guarantors of prosperity and peace. Instead, they become a risk, as imbalances in interdependence can be exploited. Value chains and trade relations have become "weaponizable": They are becoming the object of geostrategic ambitions. Interdependence today invites attacks.

Conflicts of interest, especially between the US and China, are (still) fought below the threshold of direct military confrontation by geoeconomic means. Trade, technology, or financial policies are used as instruments to achieve geostrategic objectives. Today's dynamic geoeconomic thinking is about the control of flows, particularly energy, armaments, industrial goods, financial, and data flows. The game of forces in free markets is politically undermined and manipulated.

The game of forces on so-called free markets recedes even more into the background and is only accepted by the US as long as it serves the political goal of geostrategic dominance. Thus, the modern liberal basic idea of free-market economies, the win-win thinking, is abandoned in favor of pre-industrial, mercantilist zero-sum thinking: One wins at the expense of the other.

This attitude, which Trump and his economic and security advisers freely expressed (and is basically being continued by the Biden administration) is also compatible with the neorealistic thinking of international relations, according to which national economic power is one of the basic prerequisites for military "hard power." Conversely, the "hard power" can be used to achieve economic advantages: The "invisible hand" of the market works better with the often already easily visible fist in the pocket.

Although the new Biden administration is rhetorically striving for more "values" and the "community of democracies," the US is still essentially concerned with safeguarding its national interests with all its cores. US "allies" in Europe are also to be forced to obtain more "freedom gas" from the US instead of cheaper Russian gas and to pay for the infrastructure necessary for transport, such as liquefied natural gas terminals. Even those Europeans who expected business in Iran had underestimated the military and economic power of the US. The US government also openly threatened to stop giving Germany intelligence and to sanction German companies that continue to do business with the Chinese supplier Huawei.

The competition between the US and China for the resources of the future is in full swing and is being conducted with increasing severity. Germany and Europe are caught between the fronts. According to the request of the US, the Western "protecting power," strategic rival China must no longer be helped by economic exchange to rise economically and technologically. Rather, everything possible must be done to prevent China from overtaking the US in key technological areas.

There have long been concerns in Washington that China could benefit from American technology and use it against the US. In 2012, then-Secretary of Defense Leon Panetta warned of a "cyber Pearl Harbor" threat from China and other countries (Bumiller and Shanker 2012). Fears that the US could fall behind China technologically and thus be threatened have grown all the more since China's President Xi Jingping confidently announced his goal of taking over global technology leadership by 2049 (*China Daily* 2016; Zhou and Wang 2019). China's technological capabilities and "big data" are already causing a shock in Washington similar to the launch of the first artificial satellite, Sputnik 1, by the Soviet Union in 1957.

The transatlantic dispute over Huawei's 5G technology is just the tip of the iceberg of fundamental rivalries in the geotechnology space. "Big data" and the ability to use large amounts of data with artificial intelligence (AI) for economic development as well as political and military power are the real "game changers." For they will determine who will lead in future economic and military competition and then also determine the rules of the game, the world (economic) order, in their interest. On the 5G/Huawei conflict issue, the US will therefore remain intransigent toward its allies.

In order to curb China's economic and military modernization, the US is pushing for a strategy of economic "decoupling" instead of the previous policy of inclusion and integration. The US corporate sector will have to second its administration and also promote "decoupling." More and more US companies are trying to gain more "resilience" at the expense of "efficiency," such as the previous internationally networked "just-in-time" production. This "nearshoring," "reshoring," or "localization" means that Western companies are relocating their supply chains from China back home. Some industries, particularly in the technology and health sectors, will come under all the more pressure from the US government to do the same. With the eyes of Argus, Washington is particularly keen to ensure that the supply chains that are important for its strategic industries become less dependent on China. With its "Economic Prosperity Network," the US is trying to persuade an alliance of "trusted partners" worldwide to relocate its value chains from China (Pamuk and Shalal 2020).

There should be fear that the US will continue on this uncompromising course against China because it also has less to lose than other countries. While global trade now accounts for about 60 percent of global value-added, the US gross domestic product (GDP) is only a quarter dependent on trade with other countries (World Bank 2021). In particular, the economic costs of a confrontation with China are lower for the US than for many other countries. Thus, President Biden can continue the trade war with China, which was started by his predecessor, especially since there is little domestic political resistance to it and this course has bipartisan support in Congress.

However, the growing antagonism between the US and China will have significant negative side effects for other countries, as bilateral decoupling creates a broader process of de-globalization. Thus, the political calculations of German representatives, who are being pushed by the Biden administration to become part of its anti-China coalition, are different. The Chinese market is particularly important for large German companies, especially the export-oriented automotive groups BMW, Mercedes, and Volkswagen. Unlike in the US, those responsible in Germany do not see an existential threat from China, so that the US security argument is not useful as a means of exerting pressure to abandon economic interests.

By contrast, Japan, which sees itself as a neighbor and directly threatened by the Middle Kingdom because of its territorial conflicts with China, is more willing to pay tribute to US protection. In early 2020, in addition to its extensive direct payments for US military protection, Japan's government also provided over US$2 billion in additional funds to subsidize Japanese companies and their suppliers who want to leave China and move their production back home or to Southeast Asia (Tajitsu, Yamazaki, and Shimizu 2020).

The US's Future Region: Asia

The Southeast Asia region could become one of the winners of this reorientation, especially since it also has a trade framework with the Comprehensive and Progressive Agreement for the Trans-Pacific Partnership (TPP) of 2018, finalized under Japan's leadership, which gives companies from the 11 participating member countries of Asia and the Americas involved further incentives to relocate their production chains (Ward 2020).

It is probably only a matter of time before the US under President Biden again assumes the leadership of this (China-excluding) TPP, which it previously refused in the Trump era. The Biden administration will make further efforts in the Asia-Pacific region—also as a way to restore confidence in the protecting power, the US, which was severely damaged by the previous administration. After all, the US administration under Trump had made a radical change of course in foreign policy and had also let the Asian allies stand in the rain, who had previously decided in favor of the US and against their economic interests with China, not least due to pressure from the Obama administration. To the dismay of his allies, Trump announced, in one of his first acts in office in January 2017, the withdrawal of US participation in the TPP. In doing so, the Trump administration unsettled the allies all the more on the existentially important question of whether the US would continue to provide for their protection.

For the strongest argument of the US under President Barack Obama, with which they were able to persuade countries like Japan to decide against their economic interests with China and to join the US initiative, was the protective shield of the US. With its TPP initiative, which was explicitly not aimed at China, the US responded to its efforts to integrate the Asia region into an economic community.

China, in turn, responded to US attempts at exclusion by creating an Asia-Pacific forum, the Regional Comprehensive Economic Partnership (RCEP), which left the US out in the margins. In the meantime, China has succeeded in completing its RCEP initiative. The RCEP was signed at a virtual Association of Southeast Asian Nations (ASEAN) summit on 15 November 2020. In addition to the ten ASEAN countries (Brunei, Myanmar, Cambodia, Indonesia, Laos, Malaysia, the Philippines, Singapore, Thailand, and Vietnam), China's RCEP initiative also includes Australia, Japan, South Korea, and New Zealand but not the US. The RCEP agreement makes it clear that even the US's Asia-Pacific allies are skeptical of Washington's demands to "decouple" technologically and economically from China. The RCEP, which is being pushed by China and comprises 2.2 billion people and about one-third of global economic output, will reduce tariffs, set trade rules and, last but not least, strengthen the trend toward regional value chains in the growth region of Asia-Pacific.

But the US, under Biden, will once again exert more attraction and, if necessary, pressure on the US's allies in Asia and take over the leadership of the Comprehensive and Progressive Agreement for Trans-Pacific Partnership (CPTPP), which Japan has taken over in the meantime. For the TPP was intended by the then Obama/Biden administration to underpin the centerpiece of the US's much noticed but, in Asia at the time, already doubted "Pivot to Asia." According to Michael Froman, then US trade representative and previous deputy national security adviser on economic affairs, it was not only about "economic" but also "strategic" goals that need to be pursued in the Asia-Pacific region:

> Economically, TPP would bind together a group that represents 40 percent of global GDP and about a third of world trade. Strategically, TPP is the avenue through which the United States, working with nearly a dozen other countries (and another half dozen waiting in the wings), is playing a leading role in writing the rules of the road for a critical region in flux.
>
> *Froman 2014*

Then-US Secretary of Defense Ashton Carter positioned even heavier rhetorical guns: For him, the TPP agreement was "as important to me as another aircraft carrier" (Ashton Carter as quoted in Perlez 2015).

The Asia-Pacific region is vital to US security and economic interests. In any case, Washington wants to prevent a possible rival from contesting the US's maritime or air sovereignty in the Eurasian region—the most populous and economically interesting area on earth—and prevent the exclusion of US economic activities or denying them access to resources. Although this has rarely been openly stated, US military operations and diplomatic activity over the past decades have precisely pursued this central goal—according to the analysis of the Congressional Research Service, congressional scientific service (O'Rourke 2015, 8).

The US and China are maneuvering themselves more and more into a security dilemma: the individual striving of the two protagonists for more security ultimately creates more uncertainty on both sides. US security strategists' long-held fear that China wants to establish an exclusive sphere of influence in East Asia is fueled by China's growing drive for expansion: Its increasingly aggressive activities to establish a security zone and to undermine America's ability to intervene.

In order to secure the vital Indo-Pacific sea lanes that are important for China's economy—and political stability—Beijing is building up its so-called blue-water navy, which are naval units suitable for the high seas and intended to enable a global power projection at sea in addition to coastal defense. In the course of this "active defense," the area within the "first island chain" is to be controlled, which includes the Yellow Sea bounded by Korea and Japan, the western part of the East China Sea with Taiwan, and the South China Sea. The expanded area, the "second chain of islands," extends further east from the Kuril Islands via Japan and southeastwards via the Bonin Islands and the Mariana Islands to the Caroline Islands (Paul and Overhaus 2020, 24).

China's large-scale activities are of particular concern to its regional neighbors and are an impetus for them to cooperate in the Indo-Pacific region—not least with the protecting power, the US. China's more aggressive stance in the region has already led to the reactivation of the Quadrilateral Security Dialogue (Quad) between Australia, India, Japan, and the US. The Quad is a previously informal security dialogue established to counter growing Chinese influence in the Indian and Pacific Oceans.

While the US has long maintained closer security relations with Japan and Australia, India has so far sought equidistance from the two great powers, the US and China, to preserve its independence and not to strain its relations with China. But recent tensions between China and India—with which China's leaders also tried to distract from domestic political difficulties in the COVID crisis (Walter Russell Mead as quoted in Sauerbrey 2020)—have prompted "the world's largest democracy," India, to move closer to the "oldest democracy," the US, economically and militarily. India and Australia also want to strengthen their economic and defense relations (Flournoy 2020).

Europe's Turn to Asia

In light of the economic and geopolitical prospects in the growth region of Asia-Pacific, the "Old Continent" and the transatlantic free trade talks, namely the Transatlantic Trade and Investment Partnership (TTIP), are falling even further behind with the Europeans. The US's "pivot to Asia" course, already taken under the Obama/Biden administration, is expected to be continued by the Biden/Harris administration and still at the expense of TTIP and European interests. Even before, for President Obama and Vice President Biden, and to the dismay of the Europeans, the TPP initiative was more important and through which they intended to contain China's trade policy and inflict economic tolls on its allies.

Rising Sino-US tensions will have a divisive effect on the global economic order through regional trade agreements but will also have a significant impact on "dual-option" countries like Germany, which have strong national security ties with the US, but also extensive economic ties with the US and China. The costs of this dual strategy will increase in the future, as is already evident in the technology sector. In the struggle for techno-political spheres of influence, in which future economic and military dominance is at stake, Washington will increase pressure on third countries such as Germany and their companies, giving them the choice of either abandoning business with China or the US. The result is a world divided into Chinese and American standards and systems.

In this intensified geoeconomic rivalry, Germany and Europe have fallen into a quandary because China is also involved in minimizing interdependence with the US by taking its currency reserves out of the so-called dollar trap, diversifying its sales markets, grasping geopolitical space, and creating new dependencies—not least in Europe.

In order to arm itself against an economic decoupling promoted by Washington, China has finally given in to the seven-year negotiations with Europe and agreed to an investment partnership at the end of 2020. In the future, investment conditions are to be improved both here and there because they will be made fairer—as soon as Europe's decision-makers have agreed to this deal, whose details have yet to be negotiated.

Despite this temporary "success," Europe's relations with China will remain ambivalent for the foreseeable future, including with regard to transatlantic relations. In a strategy document from March 2019 entitled "EU-China—A Strategic Outlook," the European Commission and the then high representative of the European Union (EU) for Foreign Affairs and Security Policy, Federica Mogherini, identified four levels in the EU's relationship with China. In some policy areas, such as climate protection, China is a cooperation partner and in others, a negotiating partner with which a balance of interests can be found. However, China is also seen as a competitor when it comes to technological innovation and infrastructure, for example, and even as a systemic rival pursuing an alternative global governance model (European Commission and High Representative of the Union for Foreign Affairs and Security Policy 2019).

China's OBOR initiative, which has long been overlooked or not taken seriously in Brussels and European capitals, is now also seen as a geoeconomic threat on the "Old Continent." After all, China's infrastructure investments in well over 100 countries do not stop at Europe's borders and are now even undermining Europe's unity and ability to act in an intensifying system rivalry.

So far, there is also no common position of European states toward the request of the Chinese tech giant Huawei to integrate its 5G technology into the network infrastructures of European countries—and to make them, which Washington especially fears, open to China's influence and possible industrial espionage. Germany, whose economic interests with China are particularly extensive, can deepen or help overcome the division within the European Union—and in transatlantic relations—through its decisions.

Not least due to the massive pressure from the US, it has now also become clearer in the German debate that the pending decision for or against Chinese supplier Huawei is not only an economic but also a geoeconomic and security policy question for the future. The stakes are high: If China succeeds in implementing its own authoritarian digital model across parts of Asia and Africa worldwide, it would not only undermine European (and transatlantic) efforts to develop common global standards for emerging technologies and AI, but it also would encourage authoritarian temptations from governments, even democratic regimes. China's export of surveillance technology and social control techniques helps not only repressive regimes, but also spread illiberal notions of governance and society. Last but not least, China is establishing new international forums and organizations that correspond to its own values and concepts of order.

China's disinformation campaigns, and its COVID-19 diplomacy to win hearts and minds in the confusion and uncertainty that surrounded the virus (especially in order to make the Western COVID fight look bad and to put its own response in a good light), cyberattacks as well as its territorial claims and aggression in the South China Sea could give EU leaders all the more reason for serious thinking in terms of security policy. Further food for European thought was provided by a Congressional report from the Senate Foreign Relations Committee, entitled "The United States and Europe: A Concrete Agenda for Transatlantic Cooperation on China" (US Senate Committee on Foreign Relations 2020).

Europe Must Show Its Colors

Although the transatlantic economic and security community could also be put to another acid test by the Biden administration, which French President Emmanuel Macron fears above all, equidistance between the US and China or even a stronger rapprochement with China would in no case be sensible options, if only because of the distance between democratic values and China's authoritarianism and Europe's dependence on the US in terms of security policy.

Nevertheless, Europe's decision-makers should be prepared for the US's tougher market-power conditions, which have already been pushed under President Trump. The US, even under Biden's leadership, will use its economic and military power as a competitive advantage; this is reinforced in the case of countries in need of protection in Europe. In future, the US will demand more economic compensation for military and security protection in negotiations.

However, Europeans could also be more assertive on security issues by showing those responsible in Washington that the US has been able to afford its exorbitant armament for decades only because foreign lenders have been willing to forego their own consumption and investment, in return for financing the increasing indebtedness of private and public households in the US. For a long time, these were mainly China and Japan and, since the financial crisis of 2007/8, increasingly also the Gulf and EU states. Ten years later, in 2019, the US net capital account was still US$6.244 billion. Although the capital account fluctuated greatly from 2000 to 2018, the flow of capital to the US has tended to continue to increase (IMF 2021).

In this broader economic view, the criticism of Germany's foreign trade surplus, which has been intensified since the Obama/Biden administration, and of its unwillingness to spend more money—specifically the North Atlantic Treaty Organization (NATO) target of two percent of economic output—on (US) armaments resembles a "milk boy's bill." For it is only thanks to European renunciation of consumption and investment, and their willingness to invest in the "deep" markets of the US, that Europeans can help the superpower to enable its life, economies, and ability to invest.

When financial journalists euphemistically talk about "deep" markets, thereby praising the US's "ability" to get into debt without end, unlike Europe, they overlook the fact that these could once again be abysmal markets. After all, the total US debt has been out of control for a long time. It has quadrupled since the economic and financial crises of 2007/8 to currently (2020) US$21 trillion dollars—not counting the debt of individual states and municipalities (CBO and OMB 2021). The federal government debt (i.e., "debt held by the public") financed by government bonds on the financial markets alone already exceeds the country's economic output (GDP) at 100.1 percent today (2020). By historical standards—roughly the average (about 40 percent) of the past 50 years—the US debt was already worrisome five years ago at three-quarters (74 percent) of economic output, the Congressional Budget Office (CBO) (2016, 6) warned. According to the CBO's calculations, which have now been updated to include the effects of the Trump era and the COVID-19 pandemic, the historic high of 106 percent of GDP reached in World War II is expected to be surpassed as early as 2031 and then reach all the more dizzying heights at a rapid pace: In 2051, a further doubling of the public debt burden alone (i.e., financed by the financial markets) would occur to 200 percent of GDP (!) if the US's previous fiscal debt course is continued and not slowed down by tax increases or savings.

The non-partisan CBO (2016), which advises the US Congress on budgetary matters, has been warning for some time that the debt burden poses "substantial risks" for the country, threatens financial collapse, and could seriously paralyze the state's ability to act (9). Since the COVID-19 pandemic and the country's fight against it cut tax revenues as massively as it dramatically increased spending, the mountain of debt financed by the markets has grown noticeably in just one year, from 79 (2019) to 100 percent of GDP in the fiscal year 2020. In its recent March

2021 report, the CBO already warned of the worst: "A growing debt burden could increase the risk of a fiscal crisis and higher inflation as well as undermine confidence in the U.S. dollar, making it more costly to finance public and private activity in international markets" (2021, 5).

The US debt has not been a major problem as long as foreign countries are willing or can be coerced into forgoing their own consumption and investment and accepting the risk of continuing to lend to the US. Above all, Japan and China are financing US$1.3 and US$1.1 trillion dollars respectively, and not least, a number of European countries are financing the American dream of unlimited consumption on credit and are acquiring US government bonds (Department of the Treasury and Federal Reserve Board 2021). The US's lack of savings and exorbitant debt will result in the US running a trade deficit for the foreseeable future. As long as the US lives beyond its means, it will need other countries with strong production and exports and will continue to force them to give the foreign-exchange reserves generated by export business to the US as loans to finance its debts.

In addition to financing the US state and thus military budget, Washington's request is that the Europeans should then spend even more money (keyword: "two percent") on US armaments and thus remain militarily and technologically dependent. This logic of interests becomes particularly clear when it comes to the retrofitting of German Panavia Tornado fighter jets, which Washington deliberately links to the power question of so-called nuclear participation. So far, the German armaments industry has been able to prevent a decision for the F-35 Lightning II stealth multipurpose fighter aircraft of the US manufacturer Lockheed Martin, an investment that would also have undermined a planned European armaments project from a strategic point of view.

Nevertheless, the US arms industry will at least be given a chance in the form of an interim solution because the Eurofighter, which is being built by a consortium of Airbus, BAE Systems and Leonardo, is not currently certified for the use of US nuclear weapons. While it would be possible to technically adapt the Eurofighter, it would take more time and money to do so, giving the US (and its defense industry) quite comprehensive insights into the aircraft systems. To enable a seamless transition, Germany will have to opt for a mixed fleet solution: On the one hand, to procure American (and thus easier and faster certifiable) Boeing F/A-18F Super Hornet and EA-18G Growler, and on the other hand, to procure Eurofighter aircraft (Giegerich and Terhalle 2021). This compromise solution will make it possible to grant nuclear participation and to maintain the prospect of the Future Combat Air System (FCAS), a future German-French project as well as technical and industrial know-how in Europe.

To refute the pressing demands on the allies for higher military spending and to ensure their own security, which are becoming increasingly clear across party lines in the US, European governments should increase the European Defence Fund (EDF), which has existed since 2017. The armament efforts made possible by the EDF were thus to be expanded—also in cooperation with US companies. In this way, the fears in Washington could be dissipated that Europe discriminates against the US in awarding contracts, duplicates the capabilities of the US, and thus wants to emancipate itself from the protecting power in terms of security policy. These fears have been cherished in Washington since the late 1990s and have increased since 2017 as a result of increased European cooperation on defense issues.

In return, the Europeans should also demand security guarantees. For European and Asian allies to continue to be prepared, from a strategic point of view, to surrender their economic interests, especially with China, to continue to receive protection from the US, the protecting power will have to ensure that the Pax Americana becomes more credible and reliable again in the eyes of the Allies.

This could once again call on NATO—and repeatedly call for it to adapt to the new security conditions of the twenty-first century. After Trump mistreated the alliance with scorn and also threatened to destroy it in the eyes of many other US observers, new president Biden still sees alliances as a useful tool for increasing US power—and burden sharing (Biden 2020, 73). In addition to a clear (mutual) commitment to a possibly expanding, global NATO, a so-called alliance of democracies (Daalder and Lindsay 2004), the admission of European states to the hitherto exclusive club of the "Five Eyes" would also be conceivable, in the intelligence alliance, which so far only includes Australia, Canada, New Zealand, the UK, and the US.

However, the Europeans should not rely solely on the protecting power, the US. Empty words such as "strategic independence" or "autonomy" have so far only concealed the EU's lack of decision-making and ability to act, which is urgently needed to adapt to the new world order shaped by the Sino-US major conflict.

European countries need a common stance on Huawei's request to integrate its 5G technology into the network infrastructures of European countries. A European solution (suppliers such as Ericsson in Sweden and Nokia in Finland) would help to overcome the divisions within the EU and in the transatlantic relationship.

The US administration is calling for Europeans to coordinate more closely with the US in future on investment screening and export controls. To strengthen their regulatory power in high-tech sectors vis-à-vis China, Brussels, and Washington want to work more closely together in a "Transatlantic Trade and Technology Council" to develop technical standards and norms for new technologies, especially in the digital sector. With her call for the US to join Europe's rules for the digital market, EU Commission President Ursula von der Leyen confidently claimed a European leadership role in questions of internet governance (von der Leyen 2021).

To lend weight to their words and not to fall into the predicament of Sino-US rivalry, Europeans should strengthen their ability to make sovereign decisions based on their own values and rules. In particular, the dominant business model of US online platforms endangers the prosperity, security, and democratic quality of Europe. European competition watchdogs are therefore called upon to limit the power of the large US and Chinese digital companies, at least in Europe.

It would also be in the interests of Europe as a whole to take joint action against the power-politically underpinned market power of large US and Chinese corporations in the expansion of the internet infrastructure in Europe's neighborhood. Who owns underwater cables and which routes they take have become questions of power in an increasingly fierce geoeconomic competition between the US and China, in which Europe has so far lost out. Underwater cables play a decisive role in economic development and security: Companies and states can access information and financial data that are transmitted via the digital cables they manage. Thus, the US owes its economic and military dominance to the mastery of the civil and military use of new forms of communication, including radio, television, satellites, and the internet (Mead 2015).

That is why Europeans should support Macron's demand that Europe should control its maritime, energy, and digital infrastructure itself and also sovereignly set the standards that are imposed on European companies to guarantee Europe's collective security and ability to act. Above all, independence in the technology sector is "the core of our sovereignty" and the "ability to act autonomously" (Macron 2020).

In order to strengthen Europe's technological independence and its ability to anticipate future strategic changes, an autonomous and competitive industrial base is needed. This requires massive efforts at the European level to innovate as well as the control of security technologies and defense exports. Without further political leadership from Paris and Berlin and pan-European cooperation incentives (especially of a financial nature) for the respective armament industries of the participating countries, however, a failure of the FCAS project cannot be ruled out.

As early as the mid-1980s, there was an unsuccessful attempt to implement Rafale as a joint project, with German and British participation, among others. Only a few months after the contract was signed at the end of 1984, the project failed because of a dispute over the equipment and work shares and because of the question of who called the shots. While France ousted and from then on developed its Rafale single-handedly, the other contractual partners agreed on the competing product, the Eurofighter. According to Delphine Deschaux-Dutard, who conducts research on German-French armaments cooperation at the Université Grenoble, budget constraints caused not least by the COVID-19 pandemic today speak against another French solo effort:

> Technically, this would probably be feasible [...] We could develop such an aircraft ourselves, but it is very expensive. And the question is: are French taxpayers prepared to have such a fighter aircraft developed, with the corresponding consequences for the state budget? I believe that this financial aspect carries a great deal of weight in the project.
>
> *Deschaux-Dutard as quoted in Remme and Noll 2021*

What the "Grande Nation" of France, despite all the budget constraints, does not lack, however, is geostrategic foresight:

> What we want is a system that gives our military superiority in the air and the ability to intervene first wherever we want it. And this is made possible

by the interaction of all the planned elements in this project: satellites, drones, fighter aircraft, reconnaissance modules and all other systems that are grouped around them,

said Natalia Pouzyreff from the presidential party La République en Marche! explaining the strategic importance of the FCAS project (Pouzyreff as quoted in Remme and Noll 2021). As an engineer who worked in the industry for many years, she is familiar with the technology and also knows the political levers. After consultations with her colleagues from the Defense Committee of the Bundestag, she noted a strategic rethinking on the German side:

> During my talks in Berlin, I got the impression that the Germans do not want to be dependent on technologies that do not come from Europe either. After all, we do not know what the future holds. And from a political point of view, without these developments, we Europeans would probably find it difficult to continue to make our voice heard among the major powers on the international stage.
>
> *Pouzyreff as quoted in Remme and Noll 2021*

Conclusion: A Strategic Culture Needed

The basic prerequisite for all these instruments of European sovereignty is a strategic culture oriented toward common interests. Until now, the inability of Europeans to reflect and work together on their sovereign interests has given other powers the opportunity to divide and weaken Europe. Only a comprehensive strategic understanding will enable the EU to bundle the interests of its member states and thus also to develop more economic and foreign policy weight in a "new" world order that has so far been determined by the interests of others.

The EU is particularly vulnerable to the divide and conquer strategies of the major powers, namely China and the US. To overcome its political vulnerability, improve its ability to act and become capable of geopolitics, the EU should move from the illusion of unanimity to a more realistic consensus-building in the form of qualified majority voting in foreign and security policy. Admittedly, this would be a rather dramatic change for member-states' roles in EU decision-making. Yet the alternative would be devastating, since Europe caught in the pincers of the great power rivalry seems likely to continue in the foreseeable future. Only a decision-making European association guarantees market power and options for action, so that Europe's countries can continue to operate and live independently.

References

BBC News. 2020. "Trump Says Coronavirus Worse 'Attack' Than Pearl Harbor." 7 May 2020. www.bbc.com/news/world-us-canada-52568405.

Biden, Joseph R. 2020. "Why America Must Lead Again: Rescuing U.S. Foreign Policy After Trump." *Foreign Affairs* 99 (2): 64–76.

Blackwill, Robert D., and Jennifer M. Harris. 2016. *War by Other Means: Geoeconomics and Statecraft*. Cambridge, Mass.: Belknap Press.

Braml, Josef, Wolfgang Merkel, and Eberhard Sandschneider, eds. 2014. "Außenpolitik mit Autokratien" [Foreign Policy vis-à-vis Autocracies]. *Jahrbuch Internationale Politik* [Yearbook International Relations]. Band 30, München.

Bumiller, Elisabeth, and Thom Shanker. 2012. "Panetta Warns of Dire Threat of Cyberattack on U.S." *New York Times*, 12 October 2012. www.nytimes.com/2012/10/12/world/panetta-warns-of-dire-threat-of-cyberattack.html.

China Daily. 2016. "Xi Sets Targets for China's Science, Technology Progress." 5 May 2016. www.chinadaily.com.cn/china/2016-05/30/content_25540484.htm.

Congressional Budget Office (CBO). 2016. *The 2016 Long-Term Budget Outlook*. Washington, DC. 7 December.

———. 2021. *The 2021 Long-Term Budget Outlook*. Washington, DC. March 2021.

Congressional Budget Office and Office of Management and Budget (CBO and OMB). 2021. *The Budget and Economic Outlook: 2021 to 2031*. www.cbo.gov/publication/56970.

Daalder, Ivo, and James Lindsay. 2004. "An Alliance of Democracies. Our Way or the Highway." *Financial Times*, 11 June 2004.

Department of the Treasury and Federal Reserve Board. 2021. Major Foreign Holders of Treasury Securities. Washington, DC. 15 April. https://ticdata.treasury.gov/Publish/mfh.txt.

European Commission and High Representative of the Union for Foreign Affairs and Security Policy. 2019. EU-China – A Strategic Outlook, Joint Communication to the European Parliament, The European Council and the Council. Strasbourg. 3 December.

Flournoy, Michèle. 2020. "Treat China's Border Clash With India as a Clarion Call." *Financial Times*, 19 June 2020.

Froman, Michael. 2014. "The Strategic Logic of Trade." Remarks by Ambassador Froman at the Council on Foreign Relations. New York. 16 June.

Fukuyama, Francis. 1992. *The End of History and the Last Man*. New York: Free Press.

———. 2016. "Exporting the Chinese Model." *Project Syndicate*, 12 January 2016. www.project-syndicate.org/onpoint/china-one-belt-one-road-strategy-by-francis-fukuyama-2016-01?barrier=true.

Giegerich, Bastian, and Maximilian Terhalle. 2021. *The Responsibility to Defend. Rethinking Germany's Strategic Culture*. International Institute for Strategic Studies (IISS). London: IISS Adelphi Books.

Halper, Stefan. 2010. *The Beijing Consensus: How China's Authoritarian Model Will Dominate the Twenty-First Century*. New York: Basic Books.

International Monetary Fund (IMF). 2021. Balance of Payments Statistics Yearbook and Data Files, Net Capital Account (BoP, current US$) – United States. https://data.worldbank.org/indicator/BN.TRF.KOGT.CD?locations=US.

Köllner, Patrick. 2008. "Autoritäre Regime – keine weltweit aussterbende Gattung, sondern eine wachsende Herausforderung" [Authoritarian Regime – Not a Species Dying Out in the World, But a Growing Challenge]. GIGA Focus (German Institute of Global and Area Studies) No. 6 (2008).

Krug, Wolf. 2020. "Deutsches Versteckspiel" [German Game of Hide-and-Seek]. *Die Welt*, 2 December 2020. www.welt.de/print/die_welt/debatte/article205790213/Gastkommentar-Deutsches-Versteckspiel.html.

Lowy Institute. 2021. *The US-China Trade War. Who Dominates Global Trade?* https://interactives.lowyinstitute.org/charts/china-us-trade-dominance/us-china-competition/.

Macron, Emmanuel. 2020. Speech of the President of the Republic on the Defense and Deterrence Strategy. Paris. 7 February. www.elysee.fr/en/emmanuel-macron/2020/02/07/speech-of-the-president-of-the-republic-on-the-defense-and-deterrence-strategy.

Mattis, Jim. 2015. *A New American Grand Strategy*. Stanford, CA: Hoover Institution.
Mead, Walter Russell. 2015. "Global Challenges and Grand Strategy." Testimony Delivered to the US Senate Committee on Armed Services. Washington, DC. 22 October. www.the-american-interest.com/2015/10/22/global-challenges-and-grand-strategy/.
O'Rourke, Ronald. 2015. A Shift in the International Security Environment. Potential Implications for Defense – Issues for Congress. Congressional Research Service (CRS), CRS Report for Congress. Washington, DC. 14 July.
Paul, Michael, and Marco Overhaus. 2020. "Sicherheit und Sicherheitsdilemmata in den chinesisch-amerikanischen Beziehungen" [Security and Security Dilemmas in Sino-American Relations]. In *Strategische Rivalität zwischen USA und China* [Strategic Rivalry Between the US and China], edited by Barbara Lippert and Volker Perthes, 22–26. SWP Berlin, February.
Pamuk, Humeyra, and Andrea Shalal. 2020. "Trump Administration Pushing to Rip Global Supply Chains From China: Officials." *Reuters*, 4 May 2020. https://uk.reuters.com/article/us-health-coronavirus-usa-china/trump-administrationpushing-to-rip-global-supply-chains-from-china-officialsidUKKBN22G0BZ.
Perlez, Jane. 2015. "US Allies See Trans-Pacific Partnership as a Check on China." *New York Times*, 6 October 2015.
Pompeo, Michael R. 2020. "Communist China and the Free World's Future." Secretary Michael R. Pompeo Remarks at the Richard Nixon Presidential Library and Museum. 23 July. https://sv.usembassy.gov/secretary-michael-r-pompeo-remarks-at-the-richard-nixon-presidential-library-and-museum-communist-china-and-the-free-worlds-future/.
Remme, Klaus, and Andreas Noll. 2021. "Rüstungsprojekt FCAS. Das zähe Ringen um Europas neue Kampfflugzeuge" [Armaments Project FCAS. The Tough Struggle for Europe's New Fighter Jets]. *Deutschlandfunk*, 23 April 2021. www.deutschlandfunk.de/ruestungsprojekt-fcas-das-zaehe-ringen-um-europas-neue.724.de.html?dram:article_id=496201.
Riechmann, Deb, and Jonathan Lemire. 2020. "Trump, Biden Try to Outdo Each Other On Tough Talk on China." *Associated Press*, 12 July 2020. https://apnews.com/article/025d0fea834a4c0c60b33fe56e632758.
Sandschneider, Eberhard. 2011. *Der erfolgreiche Abstieg Europas* [Europe's Succesful Descent]. Munich: Hansa.
Sauerbrey, Anna. 2020. "Trump's Path to Re-election Leads Through Beijing." *Tagesspiegel*, 2 May 2020.
Silver, Laura, Kat Devlin, and Christine Huang. 2020. "Republicans See China More Negatively Than Democrats, Even as Criticism Rises in Both Parties." Pew Research Center. 30 July.
Stuhlberg, Adam N. 2005. "Moving Beyond the Great Game: The Geoeconomics of Russia's Influence in the Caspian Energy Bonanza." *Geopolitics* 10 (1): 1–25.
Tajitsu, Naomi, Makiko Yamazaki, Ritsuko Shimizu. 2020. "Japan Wants Manufacturing Back From China, But Breaking Up Supply Chains Is Hard to Do." *Reuters*, 8 June 2020. https://uk.reuters.com/article/us-health-coronavirus-japan-production-a/japanwants-manufacturing-back-from-china-but-breaking-upsupply-chains-is-hard-to-do-idUKKBN23F2ZO.
US Senate Committee on Foreign Relations. 2020. *The United States and Europe: A Concrete Agenda for Transatlantic Cooperation on China*. Majority Report. Washington, DC. November.
von der Leyen, Ursula. 2021. Address by President von der Leyen at the Davos Agenda Week. European Commission. Brussels. 26 January. https://ec.europa.eu/commission/presscorner/detail/de/speech_21_221.

Ward, Robert. 2020. "The Geo-economic Implications of COVID-19." In *The Strategic and Geo-economic Implications of the COVID-19 Pandemic*, chapter two. IISS (International Institute for Strategic Studies) Manama Dialogue 2020 Special Publication. London.

World Bank. 2021. Trade (% of GDP). https://data.worldbank.org/indicator/NE.TRD.GNFS.ZS.

Zhou, Laura, and Orange Wang. 2019. "How 'Made in China 2025' Became a Lightning Rod in 'War Over China's National Destiny." *South China Morning Post*, 18 January 2019. www.scmp.com/news/china/diplomacy/article/2182441/how-made-china-2025-became-lightning-rod-war-over-chinas.

PART II
Issue Areas and Policies

3
TRANSATLANTIC RELATIONS AND THE CHALLENGES OF CLIMATE CHANGE AND THE ENVIRONMENT

Simon Schunz

Introduction: The Environment in the Transatlantic Space

Climate change and environmental degradation processes—from biodiversity loss and deforestation to air, soil, and water pollution—represent major, human-induced challenges to the "Earth system" in a geological epoch that is increasingly characterized as the "Anthropocene" (Rockström, Klum, and Miller 2015). They are indicative of humanity's exceeding of "planetary boundaries," which causes local challenges (e.g., water scarcity) and acts as a global "threat multiplier" requiring collective responses. A striking recent example of the consequences of humanity's disrespect for planetary boundaries is the COVID-19 pandemic caused by a virus (SARS-CoV-2) that most probably migrated from a non-human host to humans. COVID-19 exemplifies the risks of excessive "conversion of natural habitats to human use" (Ostfeld and Keesing 2020).

It is not just the conversion of natural habitat, however, but also various production and consumption patterns—among others related to chemicals, fossil fuels, or plastics—that place a strain on the Earth system. Central to these problematic patterns is the transatlantic space. Inhabited by merely 11 percent of the global population, "the combined personal consumption of Canada, Europe, and the US [i.e., the transatlantic space] amounts to slightly more than half of the global total" (see this volume's introduction). Where these consumption patterns provide commonality and tie across the Atlantic, the patterns also attribute a strong historical responsibility for environmental degradation processes to the United States (US), Canada, and the European Union (EU)—alongside a moral obligation for individually and collectively contributing to their reversal.

The US, Canada, and the EU have responded to this responsibility in different ways and in varying degrees across time. Individually, during the 1970s and 1980s, the US was the uncontested global environmental leader, setting regulatory measures domestically and heavily influencing multilateral responses such as—together with Canada—during the negotiations on the regime protecting the ozone layer. However, as of the 1990s, the US and the EU "traded places": The EU strengthened its domestic legislative acquis and became a global green leader while an increased reluctance to environmental regulation turned the US into a laggard (Kelemen and Vogel 2010). Across this entire period, the US and the EU entertained a complex bilateral relationship, with alternating periods of cooperation and contestation that had significant repercussions for global environmental politics.[1]

To discuss the contemporary transatlantic relations around the challenges of climate change and environmental degradation, this chapter starts from the assumption that—given their interdependence, their contribution to the problems and their capacity to be central to their solution—it is indispensable that the EU and the US work together to ensure the respect for planetary boundaries. It asks *which factors condition US-EU cooperation on climate and environmental matters?* From among the sources of "resilience" of transatlantic relations identified in this volume's introduction, emphasis is placed on the soft factors, that is, values, norms and beliefs, diplomatic ties and activities, and personal/organizational linkages involving elites and civil society. This chapter argues that a profound transatlantic normative disconnect relating to precaution in the face of risk is periodically overcome through pragmatic transatlantic bargains based on political will, interest convergence, and relying on cross-Atlantic civil society networks. Although there has not been a stable pattern of transatlantic cooperation, the environment-specific political ties between the two sides of the Atlantic add up to a tighter and more consequential relationship than either the US (with the exception of its relations with Canada) or the EU have had with any other major player on the planet. Following the end of the Trump presidency, and with growing cross-Atlantic public demand for decisive environmental action, the 2020s may well become the time to stabilize transatlantic sustainability cooperation and provide durable co-leadership.

To develop this argument, this chapter offers a discussion of the transatlantic climate and environmental relationship from three analytical perspectives. It starts with a comparison of domestic policies that serves to highlight commonalities and differences in the values underpinning environmental policies in the US and the EU. The chapter then examines the US-EU bilateral relationship around environmental matters. Finally, it discusses how the transatlantic relationship plays out in the context of global environmental politics. Each perspective pays due attention to historical contexts to avoid the "blinding presentism" that so often impairs debates about transatlantic relations (Deudney and Ikenberry 2018, 20). Illustrative examples are—centrally—climate change as today's quintessential problem alongside other environmental challenges (e.g., e-waste). The chapter concludes with an outlook into the future by discussing the potential of the most recent climate/environmental strategies proposed in the US (President Joseph R. Biden, Jr.'s Plan for a Clean Energy Revolution and Environmental Justice) and the EU (the European Commission's European Green Deal (EGD)) for fostering a joint transatlantic approach to tackling the challenges posed by the Anthropocene.

Contrasting US and EU Domestic Approaches and Policies on Climate and Environmental Risks

Both the US and individual countries in Europe, followed later by the EU, have gradually developed comprehensive regulatory frameworks to address environmental degradation processes. Their approaches are, however, characterized by diverging regulatory logics that translate into a "persistent coexistence of different rules" (Biedenkopf and Walker 2018, 308). Before reviewing key US and EU environmental policies, this section discusses the root causes of these differing approaches.

US and EU Diverging Attitudes Toward Precaution

Diverse reasons have been offered to explain the transatlantic discrepancy. They include differing domestic institutional setups and degrees of openness of the political systems to lobbying (Skjærseth, Bang, and Schreurs 2013), varying interests—with cost-benefit calculations influenced by the different geographies of the US and the EU—and the role of public opinion (Kelemen and Vogel 2010). It is argued here that not so much institutions and interests but ideas—the public's and elites' attitudes on the environment—centrally determine policymakers' choices. These attitudes are, in turn, primarily shaped by values, that is, standards in a society about what is "right." Hence, value differences across the Atlantic, notably when it comes to assessing environmental risk, hold strong explanatory power, especially for the period since the 1990s (Smith 2012; Vogel 2012). The diverging "directions of [...] environmental regulation in the United States and the EU" are rooted in "systematic differences in societal willingness to tolerate risk" (Smith 2012, 1–2). A key indicator for the variation in the tolerance of risk, risk assessment, and risk management practices are US and European attitudes to precaution. To explain why the US and the EU have domestically and—by consequence—internationally followed different environmental policy paths, and to understand their propensity to cooperate around environmental matters, emphasis thus needs to be placed on this fundamental value gap.

In the environmental domain, the precautionary principle emerged in international law debates in the 1980s and made it into the 1992 Rio Declaration on Environment and Development: "[W]here there are threats of serious or irreversible damage, lack of full scientific certainty shall not be used as a reason for postponing cost-effective measures to prevent environmental degradation" (UNEP 1992). The US and the EU reacted differently to this rise to prominence of precaution, particularly regarding the use of science to assess and address risk.

The US operates with a "liberal science-based approach" to environmental risk (Kleinman, Kinchy, and Autry 2009). Often referred to as a "sound science" approach, it holds that in the absence of proven harm, no restrictions should be imposed on economic activities. In the area of genetically modified organisms (GMOs), for instance, "without scientific evidence of risk to human health, animal health, or the environment, permission to experiment with, and ultimately commercialize" biotechnological products must be granted (Kleinman, Kinchy, and Autry 2009, 363). Scientific analysis is thus only deployed to demonstrate harm *a posteriori*. Only if such a review detects problems, regulation is considered necessary. This liberal approach, ultimately eschewing *pre*-caution, has permeated US domestic environmental legislation and influenced its stance on global environmental affairs, particularly since the 1990s.

In contrast to the US, the EU took up the initial global discussions on precaution by enshrining the principle in Article 130r.2 of the 1992 Maastricht Treaty on European Community (TEC) (today's Article 191.2 Treaty on the Functioning of the EU). The European Commission clarified in 2000 that "[r]ecourse to the precautionary principle presupposes that potentially dangerous effects deriving from a phenomenon, product or process have been identified, and that scientific evaluation does not allow the risk to be determined with sufficient certainty." In the EU's "precautionary science-based approach," science is used to assess risks and an *a priori* "evidence of an absence of harm" is required across various policy areas, such as GMOs, or else regulation ensues—up to the point of not authorizing an economic activity or product (Kleinman, Kinchy, and Autry 2009, 363). Seen as indispensable for attaining sustainable development, precaution has, since the 1990s, become a major driver of EU internal and external climate and environmental policies (Kelemen and Vogel 2010; Van Schaik and Schunz 2012).

A review of US and EU domestic legislation on key environmental challenges illustrates how this transatlantic value gap related to environmental risk and precaution plays out in practice.

US and EU Domestic Climate and Environmental Policies

Global trends in environmental regulation have been heavily influenced by developments in the US and Europe (for historical overviews of environmental policies in the US and the EU, see Andrews 2012; Knill and Liefferink 2013). This section briefly retraces the historical trajectories of US and EU environmental action before discussing their contemporary regulation of major policy domains.

Historical paths: From convergence to divergence

In the 1970s, the US was a pioneer and "the clear global leader in environmental policy [...] and many countries copied its policy initiatives," including in Europe (Dryzek 2003, 160). By the late 1960s, an environmental movement involving "many previously disparate groups advocating for environmental health protection, ecological conservation, and nature preservation" had emerged (Andrews 2012, 33). Its pressure contributed to the enactment of the 1969 National Environmental Policy Act (NEPA), which outlined US environmental policies and goals, establishing provisions for federal agencies to enforce such policies, and led to a series of regulatory measures. Such early regulation included the 1963 Clean Air Act, the first federal piece of legislation regarding air pollution control, and its

1970 amendment, the 1972 Clean Water Act, as well as multiple laws on solid and hazardous waste. Regulatory activity went hand-in-hand with the institutionalization of environmental matters, notably through the creation, in 1970, of the Environmental Protection Agency (EPA). The various regulations "directed the EPA to set technology-based standards for pollutant discharges to air, water, or land, respectively, for each industrial sector and for municipalities," while delegating their implementation and enforcement to the states (Andrews 2012, 34). These policies helped to "more safely and professionally manage" risks related to the pollutants, "but they were far less than fully successful in improving ambient air and water quality" (Andrews 2012, 34). For instance, reduced pollution through more stringent emission standards were offset by an increase in vehicle sales.

In Europe, an environmental movement had equally emerged in the 1960s and influenced policies in individual member states of the European Communities (EC) such as Denmark (which joined the EC in 1973), Germany, and the Netherlands. Quickly, these countries pushed for EU-level measures, enhancing levels of protection and "regulatory requirements for European environmental policies" (Knill and Liefferink 2013, 19). Initial developments of EU policies were enacted via the Environmental Action Programmes (EAP). The first EAP (1973–76) focused, similarly to the US, on "action to reduce [air and water] pollution and nuisances," setting out key environmental principles (e.g., prevention at the source). In parallel, environmental affairs were institutionalized at the EU level. In 1973, the first Environment Council meeting was held, bringing together the member states' ministers in charge of environmental matters, whereas the Commission created the first unit on environmental issues within its Directorate-General for Industry (Delreux and Happaerts 2016, 17–23).

Where EU environmental policy had initially been mostly a market-flanking policy aimed at the harmonization of standards (e.g., regarding the lead content of petrol), which had been less progressive than the US on matters such as ozone-depleting substances, this would gradually change as of the late 1980s. In the conclusions of its December 1988 meeting in Rhodes, the European Council (1988, Annex I) emphasized that "the Community and the Member States are determined to play a leading role in the action needed to protect the world's environment." This leadership bid was followed by additional domestic (and external) initiatives during the subsequent period. Each treaty reform strengthened EU primary law: The 1992 Maastricht Treaty made precaution into a key principle and the environment into a shared competence, whereas the 1997 Treaty of Amsterdam stipulated environmental mainstreaming ("environmental policy integration principle"). In parallel, the EU put precaution into action by adopting numerous, oftentimes ambitious legislative proposals across the entire spectrum of environmental degradation challenges, gradually developing into the "most comprehensive regional environmental protection regime in the world" (Axelrod and Schreurs 2015, 168). Its strong legislative acquis implies that in the 2010s more than 80 percent of the environmental legislation in vigor in its member states emanated from the EU level, pointing to high levels of "communtarization" (Vogler 2011, 352). After a persistent implementation deficit had been addressed and a brief period of regulatory stagnation (Zito, Burns, and Lenschow 2019) overcome, the Commission's adoption of the EGD in December 2019 promised to further reinforce the EU's acquis by turning climate change and the environment into the Union's top priorities for the period 2019 to 2024.

The dynamism that characterized EU environmental policymaking since the late 1980s was not matched by the US: Environmental policies went into an opposite direction under Presidents Ronald Reagan (1981–89), George H.W. Bush (1989–93), and George W. Bush (2001–9),[2] as Republicans "reframed" environmental issues and "campaign[ed] against them as excesses of 'big government'" (Andrews 2012, 37; Kelemen and Vogel 2010, 439). The Republicans' attitude was equally felt in Congress, where right-wing majorities and an increasing polarization around climate and environmental policies hampered possible advances—for instance, regarding the Kyoto Protocol adoption in the late 1990s or ambitious domestic climate legislation in the late 2000s—during the Democratic presidencies of Bill Clinton (1993–2001) and Barack Obama (2009–16). Further polarization ensued when a populist wave swept Republican Donald J. Trump into office. By 2020, his administration had all but dismantled the EPA by cutting funding and appointing former fossil fuel lobbyists as its lead administrators, while rolling back almost 100 environmental laws, including many of those enacted during Obama's tenure (Gross 2020). A telling example was Trump's initiative to revoke and water down the Corporate Average Fuel Economy standards, set in 2012, which were aimed at significantly increasing fuel economy (Gross 2020). Additionally, the Trump administration invested heavily in polluting coal, oil, and gas industries, authorizing drilling in hitherto protected areas onshore and offshore.

Where the historical trajectories of US and EU environmental policies started out similarly, the two have thus increasingly parted ways during the post-Cold War era (Vogel 2012). This trend has been attributed to the value gap discussed above and the fact that as "the American electorate had become satisfied with the regulatory status quo," "the influence of environmental lobbies in the United States steadily weakened beginning in the early 1990s" and taking full effect during George W. Bush's presidency in the 2000s, whereas "the opposite occurred in Europe" (Kelemen and Vogel 2010, 441). To further examine the differences and their practical relevance, it can be helpful to compare US and EU contemporary policies on climate change and other key environmental challenges.

Contemporary US and EU domestic climate and environmental policies

On climate change, the differences between US and EU domestic legislations "are real and are telling" (Carlarne 2010, 239). Climate change policy debates in the US really only began following the ratification of the 1992 United Nations Framework Convention on Climate Change (UNFCCC) and with the Clinton administration. Yet, until the start of Obama's first term, it was fair to argue that while "the US federal government does have an official climate change policy, [it] lacks substantive legal content" (Carlarne 2010, 35). Even since then—and despite Obama's progressive climate agenda—partisanship in Congress has prevented the emergence of comprehensive and solid federal climate legislation (Ellerman 2014, 50). Attempts to pass a cap-and-trade bill (see below) failed in the Senate during Obama's first term. During his second term, he followed up on earlier announcements and resorted to regulating through executive orders that were grounded in existing legislation, notably the Clean Air Act (Ellerman 2014, 52). The centerpiece of these efforts was the EPA's 2015 Clean Power Plan, which set a carbon-reduction goal for each state but flexibly allowed them to reach that goal via the most cost-effective means (EPA 2017). If a state refused to act, the EPA could directly regulate power plants in that state. This was estimated to reduce emissions from electricity generation by 32 percent from 2005 levels until 2030. Where such executive action has the advantage of enabling "to announce bold regulatory initiatives," it faces "subsequent guerrilla fighting through the underbrush of administrative procedures, regulatory rulings, litigation, and, finally, judicial decisions" (Ellerman 2014, 50). This has precisely been the fate of the Obama administration's rules, especially during the Trump presidency (Mehling and Vihma 2017). Some of the resistance to Trump's rollback of Obama's measures came from subfederal action, but even if such "subnational actions are laudable [...] many states fail[ed] to act at all. Interest group opponents and partisan polarization [were] impeding progress at the subnational level" (Stokes and Breetz 2020, 289).

In contrast to the US, the EU has been acting in line with a more stringently precautionary approach to climate change. Since 1996, it has argued for keeping global temperature increase below 2°C above pre-industrial levels (Council of the European Union 1996). Policies have been driven by the European Commission and leading member states in the Council. Despite this ambition, initial attempts to design an internal climate regime were limited. The proposal of an EU-level carbon tax in the early 1990s failed, and only a few policies related to energy efficiency and renewable energy were put in place: "[I]solated measures [which] could not be considered a comprehensive set of climate policies" (Delreux and Happerts 2016, 207). This changed in the wake of the adoption of the Kyoto Protocol, which led to the first series of EU climate measures. Central to these was the European Union Emissions Trading System (EU ETS), a cap-and-trade policy creating a "carbon market," which began its pilot phase in 2005. Additional policies included energy efficiency and renewable energy measures as well as a "burden-sharing agreement" that assigned targets for the member states to meet the EU's Kyoto "bubble target" of -8 percent from 1990 levels over the period between 2008 and 2012 (Delreux and Happaerts 2016, 210–25). The second wave of legislative acts further communitarizing EU climate policies was adopted in preparation for the 2009 Copenhagen Summit with the Climate and Energy Package of 2008/9. It advanced the EU's "20-20-20" targets: 20 percent emissions reductions from 1990 levels, a 20 percent share of renewable energy in energy consumption, and 20 percent energy efficiency gains by 2020. These targets have been largely met (EEA 2019). Finally, in 2014, the EU adopted its 2030 Climate and Energy Framework, including its target proposal of 40 percent reductions of 1990 emissions by 2030 alongside 27 percent targets for renewables and energy efficiency. This served as its position for the negotiations on what would later become the Paris Agreement (PA). Since the adoption of the PA, the EU has undertaken further efforts to enhance what is now its "nationally determined contribution" (NDC). The renewables and energy efficiency targets were stepped up to 32 percent and 32.5 percent respectively, whereas the 2019 EGD provided a new impetus for enhancing the EU's NDCs from 40 percent to 55 percent by 2030 in order to attain net-zero emissions by 2050 (European Commission 2020). Comparing the US and EU approaches, one can thus detect solid differences in approach, which in Europe is more consequential, to a larger extent legally binding and—for the moment—successful.

Equal levels of differences can be detected in the regulation of other environmental challenges such as chemicals, a key source of pollution that was at the origins of the environmental movement across the transatlantic space. In this domain, the first major piece of legislation was the 1976 US Toxic Substances Control Act (TSCA). Under the TSCA, the EPA had to demonstrate that a chemical presented an "unreasonable risk," had to "choose the least burdensome regulation and verify that the regulatory benefits outweigh the costs to industry"—this led de facto to few restrictions on producers (Biedenkopf 2016, 64). Initially, the TSCA "contributed to the 1979 decision of the [EU] to both harmonize and strengthen its chemicals regulations" (Vogel 2012, 153). However, in the 2000s, the EU surpassed the US when reforming its chemicals laws with the 2006 Registration, Evaluation, Authorisation and Restriction of Chemicals (REACH) regulation—despite heavy lobbying aimed at preventing it from doing so, most notably by the US "government, working closely with the American chemical industry" (Vogel 2012, 162). REACH has been considered as a "pioneering piece of legislation that goes beyond prior EU and global chemicals regulation by addressing chemicals management [...] in a comprehensive and systematic way," enshrining precaution (Biedenkopf 2016, 65). Producers and importers must register chemicals with the European Chemicals Agency (ECHA) before these can be placed on the EU's market. In this process, they must prove that they procure no harm. This information is evaluated, and in cases of "very high concern" about a chemical, its authorization can be conditional or restricted. The innovative nature of REACH lies in the shift of the burden of proof from the regulatory agency—which before REACH had to prove that a substance is harmful to be able to regulate it—to the producer. This latter now has to demonstrate that a substance provides no harm to the environment or human health. This "privatization of risk identification and assessment" goes hand-in-hand with "extremely low thresholds for regulatory intervention," providing a major difference with the US approach to chemicals regulation (Heyvaert 2009, 115). In the US, the TSCA was not reformed until 2016. The reform made it easier for the EPA to collect data from industry on a "substance-by-substance" basis but did not privatize risk assessment. It is also less strict and precautionary than REACH: Contrary to the comprehensive approach taken by the latter, under TSCA 2.0, the EPA can focus its action on "safety assessments for a maximum of only a few dozen substances over the next several years" (Botos, Graham, and Illés 2019, 1193).

GMOs provide yet another illustration of transatlantic differences. US biotechnology policy relies on the above-mentioned "sound science" approach and is *product-focused*. If a regulator considers a product as "equivalent" to a conventionally produced product, it is subject to the same regulation ("principle of substantial equivalence"). GMOs are thus viewed as a mere extension of traditional plant breeding, which can be treated through existing regulations (Stephan 2015). This approach contrasts strongly with the GMO rules of the EU, which constitute a prime example of the application of precaution (Falkner 2007). The EU's *process-focused* approach imposes that as soon as biotechnology is used in a production process, there is a risk of uncertainty, and the product must be assessed. This institutionalization of precaution implies that restrictions are always possible, even if there is no unequivocal scientific evidence for harm. Hence, the

> burden of proof is the mirror-reverse across the Atlantic. In the EU, it needs to be proven that genetically modified varieties do not pose a risk, while in the USA the standard assumption is that genetically modified varieties do not pose a risk until proven otherwise.
>
> *Biedenkopf and Walker 2018, 306*

Other domains in which differences exist include hazardous waste and waste export policies (Dreher and Pulver 2008), as well as nanotechnology, an area in which "the EU introduced an official definition of nanotechnology and created several new […] regulations […] whereas the United States has followed more of a 'wait and see' policy" (Rodine-Hardy 2016, 89). The two parties' diverging domestic attitudes and policies have strong repercussions for their ability and willingness to cooperate as well as the forms and intensity of their interaction bilaterally and in multilateral contexts.

US-EU Bilateral Relations on Climate Change and the Environment

This section discusses the dynamics of the US-EU bilateral relationship by considering formal and informal institutional ties before contemplating several policy examples.

Formal and Informal Institutional Links

Over time there have been numerous attempts to formally institutionalize the bilateral climate and environmental relations between the US (government) and the EU (institutions) (for a detailed overview, see Biedenkopf and Walker 2018, 301–5). Milestones were the 1990 Transatlantic Declaration, followed by the 1995 New Transatlantic Agenda (NTA) and a Joint EU/US Action Plan, which formally institutionalized US-EU relations (United States Mission to the European Union 2020). Both the Declaration and the NTA referred to the environment as a key transnational challenge to be jointly tackled. To this end, annual dialogues at various levels of seniority were established. Particularly noteworthy were the creations, in 1999, of the Transatlantic Environmental Dialogue aimed at fostering exchanges between the environmental communities across the Atlantic and of the Transatlantic Legislators' Dialogue involving members of Congress and the European Parliament (Biedenkopf and Walker 2018, 304–5; European Parliament 2020). In 2002, an EU-US High Level Dialogue on Climate Change was launched with the objective of keeping the channels of communication on the subject open despite the US withdrawal from the Kyoto Protocol ratification process. In 2009, this Dialogue was superseded by the EU-US Energy Council, which met once a year during the Obama presidency (and only once during the Trump presidency) and included discussions on climate matters. While these institutionalizations of bilateral climate and environmental relations certainly testify to the desire of US and EU policymakers to jointly address sustainability matters, their practical relevance beyond a continuity of dialogue (largely interrupted during the Trump presidency) has, however, remained limited.

US-EU interaction beyond the sphere of government-to-government exchanges has arguably been more prolific. Especially in periods of discontent at the highest political level, such as during George W. Bush's and Trump's tenures, transnational cooperation was booming. Examples during the 2000s included regulatory cooperation between the EU and individual US states with progressive environmental agendas, in particular California, around matters such as carbon trading (Vogel and Swinnen 2011). Under Trump, such cooperation has even extended into tripartite arrangements involving California, China, and the EU (Voice of America 2017). More than with the EU per se, however, states like California have been cooperating with EU members (e.g., France, Germany, and Sweden) or their regions (Scotland) (California Energy Commission 2020). Other instances of transnational, cross-Atlantic cooperation also involve city cooperation, for instance, via the Global Covenant of Mayors for Climate and Energy, the "largest global alliance for city climate leadership" and an EU-driven extension of the European Covenant of Mayors (Global Covenant of Mayors 2020). Its membership is predominantly transatlantic, and its board is co-chaired by the European Commissioner in charge of the Green Deal, Frans Timmermans, and former New York City mayor Michael Bloomberg (Global Covenant of Mayors 2020). Bloomberg is also one of the driving forces behind America's Pledge on Climate Change, which—in coalition with the We Are Still In Coalition (2020)—mobilizes US "states, cities, businesses, universities, and citizens [accounting for 51 percent of US emissions] to ensure the United States remains a global leader in reducing emissions and delivers the country's ambitious climate goals of the Paris Agreement" (America's Pledge 2020). These initiatives have grown into vibrant transnational networks that not only proposed progressive policies domestically but also projected an alternative image of the US during the Trump presidency. Spokespersons of these initiatives attended global climate summits and fostered multiple informal ties with European policymakers and civil society actors, which may form the basis for stronger re-engagement under the

Biden administration (Steinhauer 2018). Added to this can be major interconnected young-generation grassroots movements that are increasingly global but have a transatlantic core, such as Fridays for Future, Extinction Rebellion, and the (US-focused) Sunrise Movement.

While institutional ties are key to transatlantic relations by providing factors of resilience, in the environmental domain the relevance of informal links between European actors and US subfederal and non-state actors exceeds that of formal ties. Even more significant, however, are the issue-specific forms of interaction and the cooperation and cross-fertilization around concrete environmental challenges.

Bilateral Interaction in Practice: Climate Change and Other Environmental Policies

The bilateral transatlantic interaction around climate change and other environmental policies has been characterized by mutual influences, for example, via the diffusion of ideas and policies, and periods of close cooperation, alternating with phases of greater distance.

Historically the world's leading greenhouse gas emitters, the US and EU were central players in international climate politics ever since climate change first emerged on the global agenda in the 1990s. Initially, their bilateral interaction around the matter was then also embedded into the international negotiations of the UNFCCC (1991–92, see below). More structured bilateral dialogues about climate change, as discussed above, emerged only in the late 1990s and 2000s.

A first major instance of (attempted) policy diffusion could be observed during the Kyoto Protocol negotiations (1995–97): The EU had been reluctant to accept the US call for "flexible mechanisms," including emissions trading, only to become a champion of this market-based policy tool soon thereafter (Schunz 2014, 104). In the design of its ETS, the EU took inspiration from the US experience with the sulfur dioxide trading system created under the 1990s Acid Rain Program. It also sought the exchange with players in the US who were experimenting with similar policy tools, such as California and the participants in the Regional Greenhouse Gas Initiative, a carbon market involving nine north-eastern states, and the Western Climate Initiative of five US states and four Canadian provinces, notably via the EU-initiated International Carbon Action Partnership (ICAP 2020).

Moreover, and although US-EU climate cooperation during Bush, Jr.'s presidency was generally limited, in 2008, the ETS provided the grounds for exchanges when it served as an inspiration for the (failed) bipartisan attempt to adopt cap-and-trade legislation via the US Climate Security Act (Lieberman-Warner Bill) (Schunz 2014, 142). During the first term of the Obama administration, the dialogue around the ETS was further intensified (Schunz 2010). Obama's climate agenda initially foresaw the adoption of ambitious climate legislation, including another attempt at passing a cap-and-trade bill. The American Clean Energy and Security Act (Waxman-Markey Bill) passed the House of Representatives in June 2009 but was never submitted for a vote in the Senate given Republican resistance. In the run-up to drafting these legislative proposals, US lawmakers actively sought to learn from the EU's experience (including about aspects that had not worked with the EU's ETS during its pilot phase) by exchanging with Commission and member state officials as well as EU parliamentarians (Schunz 2010, 83). The short-lived history of US federal-level cap-and-trade legislation represented thus an—ultimately unsuccessful—attempt of transatlantic cross-fertilization. During the Trump presidency, formal US-EU bilateral climate relations were very limited.

Other examples of environmental policies in which bilateral exchanges are frequent include the areas of chemicals and electronic waste. On chemicals, the EU initially took its cues from the US TSCA before adopting the precautionary stance embodied in the 2006 REACH reform. During the REACH negotiations as well as since its entry into force, the US and the EU extensively exchanged about chemicals regulation (Biedenkopf 2016; Vogel 2012). The EU attempted to diffuse its rules to the US, not in the least through a 2010 Statement of Intent about technical cooperation and sharing best practices between the ECHA and the EPA. However, given the two parties' diverging regulatory philosophies, the EU's impact on the 2016 TSCA reform remained limited. Just as in the case of cap and trade, the "EU's attempt to export [the] REACH regulation failed […] as the U.S. Congress did not reform TSCA based on the REACH model" (Botos, Graham, and Illés 2019, 1187). Similar patterns of interaction can be detected in the regulation of electronic waste, on which the EU implements restrictive measures and the US adopted weaker ones at the federal level. In this case, however, "U.S. state and non-state actors learned from and emulated EU policy" to a certain extent (Biedenkopf 2013, 209).

Across these and other policies, US-EU bilateral relations cannot be considered in isolation from the global, multilateral context into which they are embedded.

US and EU Climate and Environmental Diplomacies in a Multilateral Context

The US-EU bilateral relations in the climate and environmental domains are inseparably linked to the multilateral negotiations on major environmental challenges. The global regimes that have been created around "multilateral environmental agreements" in areas such as biodiversity and biosafety, climate change, chemicals, or waste, have, in almost all cases, been strongly shaped by transatlantic bargains.

The US and the EU were the most significant players in these contexts during the 1980s and 1990s (flipping leadership roles in the 1990s), in part because they were *the* key polluters. Since then, the external context has significantly changed, altering also their respective roles in global environmental politics. Since the mid-2000s and the rise of the emerging countries as major polluters and powerhouses cooperating in the BASIC Group (Brazil, South Africa, India, and China), global climate and environmental politics are conducted through an interminable series of negotiations characterized by forms of "multiple bilateralism" (Belis et al. 2018), that is, a multitude of bilateral relationships between major polluters determines the shape that multilateral political bargains take. While still at the heart of these political processes, both the US and the EU are arguably less central now, notably because their ecological footprints are in relative decline.

Climate change and other environmental issues illustrate these dynamics (for broader historical reviews, see Gardner 2020, 385–403; Vogel and Kelemen 2010).

The US, the EU, and the Global Climate Regime: Negotiating the Paris Agreement

In the global climate arena, the US and the EU have historically played central roles (Schunz 2016). The negotiations on the creation and development of the UN climate regime were regularly key sites of transatlantic deals: While the 1992 UNFCCC was the fruit of a US-EC compromise around the emerging regime's ultimate objective facilitated by the special relationship between the US and the UK (Schunz 2014, 60–61), the bargain around the 1997 Kyoto Protocol, which also involved Japan as the summit host and third-largest emitter at the time, centered around the magnitude of the emissions reduction targets and the means of achieving them. On the targets, the US had entered the Kyoto Summit with the suggestion to stabilize greenhouse gas emissions (+/- 0 percent) at their 1990 level over the period 2008–2012, whereas the EU had proposed a 15 percent reduction from the 1990 level by 2010. On the means, the US had supported "flexible mechanisms" (including emissions trading), whereas the EU had favored command-and-control measures. The outcomes were transatlantic compromises: On emission reductions, the key to the EU's position, the US met the Union in the middle (-8 percent for the EU and -7 percent for the US over the period 2008–12) (Schunz 2014, 107–8). As a concession, the EU had to cave in regarding the flexible mechanisms.

Hopes for a similar transatlantic bargain were disappointed in the next big round of climate negotiations: The post-2012 regime reform attempt that should have been adopted at the 2009 Copenhagen Summit fell well short of its aspiration. Against the EU's desire for a legally binding, profoundly new treaty with ambitious targets, the US (during Obama's first year in office) and the BASIC Group settled for a minimal, two-and-a-half-page political declaration of intent, paired to very limited "nationally appropriate mitigation actions" (Van Schaik and Schunz 2012). It took the parties two years to collectively recover from what was perceived as a failure of multilateralism and to begin new reform negotiations for the post-2020 period.

This new process, kicked off with the 2011 Durban Platform for Enhanced Action, was successfully completed at the 2015 Paris Summit. The adoption of the PA benefited from the crucial input of many players, with the US and the EU— alongside China and the French Presidency of the Conference of the Parties 21— playing leading roles. Despite ambitious intentions, the Obama administration had not been fully prepared for wide-reaching commitments in the late 2000s. This was, in part, because domestic climate policy initiatives had been unsuccessful (see previous section). During the PA negotiations, the US president, therefore, desired to show stronger leadership. This leadership was exerted primarily by bringing on board major emitters, notably China and India (Parker and Karlsson 2018, 526). The "major breakthrough for the post-2020 talks" was a November 2014 US-China deal in "which they promised each other comparatively ambitious targets and the respect for national sovereignty" in the future climate regime (Schunz 2016, 442).

Around this entente between the two top emitters, other relationships between major emitters developed in what has been depicted as an arena of multiple bilateralisms (Belis et al. 2018). Next to the bilateral China-US relations, US-India, China-India, China-EU, EU-India as well as US-EU relations paved the way for the multilateral outcome reached in Paris. Bilateral exchanges "served trust-building and the identification of 'landing zones'" for the final agreement, rooted in better mutual understanding (Belis et al. 2018, 97). In this context, US-EU relations were one piece in a broader puzzle. They were less central than in the negotiations before Copenhagen, but the Paris Summit would prove that the US and the EU had engaged in an "implicit division of labour. There was no joint transatlantic strategy but instead loose cooperation, frequent information exchange" based on a joint willingness to reach a meaningful deal (Biedenkopf and Walker 2018, 308). This came together in a way that made some observers claim that "the Paris Agreement stands as a monument to what the US and EU can do to advance important global priorities when they work together [… as] they […] were critical actors in getting global participation" (Gardner 2020, 412).

The dynamics of the Paris Summit indeed support the conclusion that "the US and the EU jointly exercised leadership" (Gardner 2020, 385) but in a rather improvised, co-creative process that also involved several other key players (Schunz 2016). Beyond their desire for a meaningful agreement bringing in all—developed, emerging, and developing—countries, their positions had little common ground. On the crunch issue regarding the nature of the outcome and shape of the future climate regime, the US and the EU were in diametrically opposed camps: The US (and China) wanted a "bottom-up" architecture with targets that were legally binding in national law, whereas the EU negotiated for a legally binding "top-down" solution with strong globally set targets. On this matter, a transatlantic compromise thus had to be found. The US (together with its Chinese and Indian partners) "clearly exercised […] asymmetric influence in shaping the institutional design of […] the Paris Agreement" (Parker and Karlsson 2018, 535). The US preference in terms of the legal outcome and the bottom-up setting of NDCs became the essential new feature of the climate regime. This was only possible, however, by conceding a top-down target to the EU and its partners, including many small-island and least developed countries from the so-called High Ambition Coalition for Nature and People. The target is now enshrined in the PA's Articles 2 and 4 aimed at keeping global warming "well below 2°C above pre-industrial levels and to pursue efforts to limit the temperature increase to 1.5°C" and achieving net-zero emissions by 2050. Both the US and the EU had thus indeed managed to mobilize different party groups to enable the package deal sealed by the French COP 21 Presidency.

This pattern of multiple bilateralism also proved important in the aftermath of the Paris Summit when the US and China simultaneously ratified the PA, closely followed by the EU. Since President Trump announced the US withdrawal from the Agreement in June 2017, the EU has sought to co-lead the implementation process with other partners, most notably China and Canada, while engaging with US subfederal actors (Steinhauer 2018, 20–21).

Beyond the Climate Regime: Unstable Patterns of US-EU Environmental Cooperation

Like the US-EU interaction in the climate regime, the patterns of cooperation tend to also be unstable in other environmental domains. During the 1970s and 1980s, US global environmental leadership was particularly pronounced regarding the design of the ozone regime with the adoption of the 1987 Montreal Protocol on Substances that Deplete the Ozone Layer, an international treaty that filled the 1985 Vienna Convention for the Protection of the Ozone Layer with life (Kelemen and Vogel 2010, 428). This created one of the few successful environmental regimes. Where the EU was undoubtedly a laggard in this negotiation process, its leadership in global environmental politics emerged particularly in the areas of biodiversity (1992 Convention on Biological Diversity, 2010 Nagoya Protocol) and biosafety (2000 Cartagena Protocol on Biosafety), chemicals (2001 Stockholm Convention on Persistent Organic Pollutants), and waste (1989 Basel Convention on Hazardous Waste Disposal).

In the global negotiations on many of these treaties, the EU and the US were antagonists rather than partners, with the US deliberately playing either very limited or obstructive roles. Whenever the US was largely absent from a negotiation setting and/or clearly signaled its intent not to ratify a treaty, the EU could regularly—thanks to its overarching power, weight as a polluter, and negotiation capacities—strongly influence the final outcomes. The EU's vision of precaution permeated the Cartagena Protocol on Biosafety, and the Nagoya Protocol on Access and Benefit-Sharing was also "very much in line with" EU positions (Oberthür and Rabitz 2014). Also on chemicals, the EU—driven by the intra-EU entrepreneurship of Sweden—became "a driving force for many international […] agreements," strongly influencing their content as the world's biggest chemicals market in the absence of the US (Biedenkopf 2016, 66). On chemicals as on waste, the EU has also unilaterally adopted measures that transcend what has been decided and ratified internationally (Biedenkopf 2013; 2016, 63).

Beyond those domains of discontent, there are, however, also—often less prominent—examples of areas in which the US and the EU have successfully cooperated. At the intersection of climate change and ozone, the two parties were instrumental in pushing through the 2016 Kigali Amendment to the Montreal Protocol aimed at the reduction of hydrofluorocarbons (Gardner 2020, 387), which was initially not ratified by the US during the Trump presidency. Long-lasting cooperation has also been noted within the framework of the 1973 Convention on International Trade in Endangered Species of Wild Fauna and Flora, whereas, more recently, US-EU cooperation has placed the protection of the oceans on the agenda of global policymakers (Gardner 2020, 418–21).

Overall, the US-EU relationship has been central to global multilateral efforts to deal with climate change and the environment more generally—cases in which the two were joint protagonists alternate with examples of antagonism. The concluding section discusses whether the most pronounced antagonism that existed during the Trump presidency can be overcome under President Biden.

Conclusion: The Future of Transatlantic Sustainability Relations

Ever since environmental degradation made it on political agendas across the planet, the transatlantic space has been at the heart of global climate and environmental politics. Not only have the US and the EU been major polluters, but they have also been among the pioneers in taking regulatory action. Starting in the 1960s, they have each developed a comprehensive set of policies and have interchanged in multiple ways bilaterally and multilaterally. While the build-up of domestic policies started from a shared concern and has benefited from cross-fertilizations, the two parties increasingly parted ways in the 1990s. As the EU embraced precaution and the US adopted a stronger risk-taking attitude, their regulatory philosophies regarding environmental risks drifted further apart.

This has resulted in unstable patterns of bilateral and multilateral transatlantic cooperation. Many key environmental regimes, such as those on ozone and climate change, benefited strongly from transatlantic bargains. An overarching shared desire for designing global agreements on environmental matters often brought the two players to the negotiation table and helped them compromise despite opposing ideas on how to deal concretely with these challenges. In other areas of global environmental politics, however, most notably chemicals, GMOs, and hazardous waste, discontent rendered such bargains impossible, primarily due to US reluctance. Even in cases where US-EU bargains had allowed for striking a deal, and where US administrations under Democratic presidents had strongly influenced global outcomes—such as the 1997 Kyoto Protocol and the 2015 PA—cooperation patterns became unsteady when Republican-led administrations withdrew from these agreements.

The factors that enabled transatlantic sustainability cooperation were regularly converging ideas on the general necessity of global collective action. In the absence of such ideational convergence, the resilience of transatlantic relations in the environmental domain has frequently come from informal ties between European players and US subfederal actors and civil society. This is also the case at the start of the 2020s. As the US power transition after four years of Trumpian anti-environmentalism is under way, progressive actors are yearning to engage in stronger environmental policy cooperation globally with the EU, Canada, and other players.

The trust that has been eroded might be rebuilt if the US and the EU manage to converge around a common sustainability project, as increasingly demanded by their citizens. Policymakers on both sides of the Atlantic have developed wide-reaching policy proposals to this end. In the US, the 2019 Resolution for a Green New Deal adopted in the House had called for "meeting 100 percent of the power demand in the United States through clean, renewable, and zero-emission energy sources" (US Congress 2019). During his campaign, Biden revived large portions of this proposal to appeal to young voters. Biden's Plan for a Clean Energy Revolution and Environmental Justice foresaw "a 100% clean energy economy and net-zero emissions no later than 2050," which involves decarbonization of the electric sector by 2035 (Biden 2020). This was to be achieved through the setting of an ambitious new US NDC by the end of Biden's (first) term, large-scale green investments into research, and "clean energy innovations" (Biden 2020). This major effort was to be flanked by policies aimed at "environmental justice" that focus on attenuating socio-economic hardships of "workers impacted by the energy transition" and pay special attention to "People of Color and Low-Income Communities [...] at Especially High Risk" from environmental degradation (Biden 2020). It was also supported by a commitment to global climate leadership. Once in office, Biden immediately delivered on his promises: On the day of his inauguration, he signed an executive order that allowed the US to re-join the PA. In April 2021, his administration introduced an ambitious novel national emissions reduction target of 50–52 percent from 2005 levels by 2030, underpinned by a US$2.25 trillion infrastructure and clean energy plan. The announcement of these domestic plans coincided with the organization of a global leaders summit by Biden's US special envoy for climate, John Kerry. It brought together 40 heads of state from major emitting and vulnerable countries and resulted in public commitments to enhanced climate action by, among others, Brazil, Canada, and Japan (Newburger 2021). It had benefited from multiple bilateral meetings between Kerry and his third-party counterparts, notably EU Commissioner Timmermans.

The European Commission's December 2019 EGD proposal represents "a new growth strategy that aims to transform the EU into a fair and prosperous society, with a modern, resource-efficient and competitive economy," equally for the purpose of attaining the PA's 2050 net-zero emissions target, which was to be enshrined in a "European Climate Law" (in force since July 2021) (European Commission 2019, 2). It offers a holistic vision of setting the EU on a sustainable path via a "set of deeply transformative policies" across a variety of sectors, from agricultural to transportation policies (European Commission 2019, 2, 4). Similar to Biden's plan, the EGD comes with a detailed roadmap and strong social as well as external dimensions: It aims to be "just and inclusive" so as to "leave no one behind" when transforming European societies and involving "the public and [...]

all stakeholders" in its implementation (European Commission 2019, 2, 16, 22); it also foresees an elaborate "Green Deal diplomacy." Just like the US, the EU had also, already in September 2020, pledged to enhance its 2030 target from 40 to 55 percent emissions reductions from 1990 levels.

The two projects thus display clear commonalities, but also differ, most notably in scope: Biden's plan concentrates on a "clean energy" transition, whereas the EGD broadly aims at a profound transformation addressing production and consumption patterns that shape environmental degradation. The proposals also face distinct implementation challenges. In the US, a polarized society and divided Congress render environmental legislation relying on bipartisanship very intricate. In the EU, aligning all member states around common targets may involve major but solvable distributive disputes requiring concessions from the most and the least progressive countries.

If implementing each of them is proving to be challenging, the two projects do offer the platform for exchange, which has intensified significantly under Biden, and mutual learning. Bringing them together into a joint "transatlantic Green Deal" may be daunting (Schunz 2020). Yet, in an interdependent global setting, responding to the erosion of planetary boundaries represents a challenge that may help reconstruct a strong transatlantic bond, as other players demand US-EU co-leadership. The key to a successful domestic implementation and cross-Atlantic cooperation may lie in tying environmental to social measures. That is what the notion of a "deal" is primarily about: The proposed energy and/or ecological transition can only work if it is couched in a broader socioeconomic and sociocultural narrative in which long-term structural transformations are understood as necessary but positive for people's well-being, not as a threat to their prosperity. How fair and inclusive the US and the EU manage to make the envisaged "just transition" may thus well be the make-it-or-break-it issue. On this matter, the two sides of the Atlantic may be able to learn most from each other (Schunz 2020). If their projects succeed, this could serve as *the* example to follow in other parts of the (developed) world. This could mark the beginning of a transatlantic renaissance that may not be based on shared regulatory philosophies but on a common desire in keeping this planet viable through policies that work for citizens.

If the nucleus of reinvigorated transatlantic sustainability cooperation is thus domestic, their impact passes by cooperative global action: Domestic transformations provide credibility and the grounds to engage with other major polluters around climate change, biodiversity loss, and—not in the least—the significant global health crisis resulting from an overstepping of planetary boundaries that is COVID-19.

Notes

1 Given space constraints, this chapter focuses on US-EU relations. References to Canada are made where Canadian policies or diplomacy are of particular relevance. Generally, due to its geographical proximity that comes with comparable environmental

challenges and its close commercial ties with the US, Canada's climate and environmental policy objectives have regularly been similar to those of the US. The two also cooperate extensively bilaterally and are part of the same coalition (Umbrella Group) in global climate negotiations (EPA 2020). Periods of Canada-US discontent, however, such as during the Trump presidency, have regularly seen rapprochement between Canada and the EU.

2 George H. W. Bush represented the partial exception to this rule. During his presidency, the Acid Rain Program was adopted and bilateral and multilateral treaties like the Air Quality Agreement with Canada and the UNFCCC were negotiated and signed.

References

America's Pledge. 2020. www.americaspledgeonclimate.com/.
Andrews, Richard. 2012. "Environmental Politics and Policy in Historical Perspective." In *The Oxford Handbook of U.S. Environmental Policy*, edited by Michael Kraft and Sheldon Kamieniecki, 24–47. Oxford: Oxford University Press.
Axelrod, Regina, and Miranda Schreurs. 2015. "Environmental Policy Making and Global Leadership in the European Union." In *The Global Environment – Institutions, Law, and Policy*, edited by Regina Axelrod and Stacy VanDeveer, 157–86. 4th ed. Washington: CQ Press.
Belis, David, Simon Schunz, Dhanasree Jayaram, and Tao Wang. 2018. "Climate Diplomacy and the Rise of 'Multiple Bilateralism' between China, India and the EU." *Carbon and Climate Law Review* 12 (2): 85–97.
Biden, Joseph. 2020. "Biden Plan for a Clean Energy Revolution and Environmental Justice." https://joebiden.com/climate-plan/#.
Biedenkopf, Katja. 2013. "The Multilevel Dynamics of EU and U.S. Environmental Policy: A Case Study of Electronic Waste." In *L'Union Européenne et les Etats-Unis: Processus, Politiques et Projets* [The European Union and the United States: Process, Politics and Projects], edited by Yann Echinard, Albane Geslin, Michel Gueldry, and Fabien Terpan, 189–210. Brussels: Larcier.
Biedenkopf, Katja. 2016. "The EU in Global Chemicals Governance." In *The European Union's Foreign Policy in Comparative Perspective: Beyond the 'Actorness and Power' Debate*, 61–79. Abingdon: Routledge.
Biedenkopf, Katja, and Hayley Walker. 2018. "USA: Oscillating Between Cooperation, Conflict and Coexistence." In *European Union External Environmental Policy*, edited by Camilla Adelle, Katja Biedenkopf, and Diarmuid Torney, 297–315. Basingstoke: Palgrave Macmillan.
Botos, Ágnes, John Graham, and Zoltán Illés. 2019. "Industrial Chemical Regulation in the European Union and the United States: A Comparison of REACH and the Amended TSCA." *Journal of Risk Research* 22 (10): 1187–1204.
California Energy Commission. 2020. "Climate Change Partnerships." www.energy.ca.gov/about/campaigns/international-cooperation/climate-change-partnerships.
Carlarne, Cinnamon. 2010. *Climate Change Law and Policy: EU and US Approaches*. Oxford: Oxford University Press.
Council of the European Union. 1996. "Council Conclusions." June. Brussels. www.consilium.europa.eu/uedocs/cms_data/docs/pressdata/en/envir/011a0006.htm.
Delreux, Tom, and Sander Happaerts. 2016. *Environmental Policy and Politics in the European Union*. Basingstoke: Palgrave Macmillan.
Deudney, Daniel, and John Ikenberry. 2018. "Liberal World: The Resilient Order." *Foreign Affairs* 97 (4): 16–24.

Dreher, Kelly, and Simone Pulver. 2008. "Environment as 'High Politics'? Explaining Divergence in US and EU Hazardous Waste Export Policies." *Review of European Community & International Environmental Law* 17 (3): 306–18.

Dryzek, John. 2003. *Green States and Social Movements: Environmentalism in the United States, United Kingdom, Germany, and Norway*. Oxford: Oxford University Press.

Ellerman, Denny. 2014. "The Shifting Locus of Global Climate Policy Leadership." In *The EU, the US and Global Climate Governance*, edited by Cristine Bakker and Francesco Francioni, 41–57. Farnham: Ashgate.

Environmental Protection Agency (EPA). 2017. "Clean Power Plan." https://archive.epa.gov/epa/cleanpowerplan/fact-sheet-overview-clean-power-plan.html.

———. 2020. *EPA Collaboration With Canada*. www.epa.gov/international-cooperation/epa-collaboration-canada.

European Commission. 2019. *The European Green Deal*. COM(2019) 640 final. 11 December. Brussels.

———. 2020. "2030 Climate and Energy Framework." https://ec.europa.eu/clima/policies/strategies/2030_en.

European Council. 1988. "Conclusions of the Presidency." 2–3 December. Rhodes.

European Environment Agency (EEA). 2019. *Trends and Projections in Europe 2019*. Report No 15/2019. Copenhagen: European Environment Agency.

European Parliament. 2020. "Delegation for Relations with the United States." www.europarl.europa.eu/delegations/en/d-us/about/introduction.

Falkner, Robert. 2007. "The Political Economy of 'Normative Power' Europe: EU Environmental Leadership in International Biotechnology Regulation." *Journal of European Public Policy* 14 (4): 507–26.

Gardner, Anthony. 2020. *Stars With Stripes: The Essential Partnership Between the European Union and the United States*. Basingstoke: Palgrave Macmillan.

Global Covenant of Mayors. 2020. www.globalcovenantofmayors.org/.

Gross, Samantha. 2020. *What Is the Trump Administration's Track Record on the Environment?* Washington, DC: Brookings Institution. www.brookings.edu/policy2020/.

Heyvaert, Veerle. 2009. "Globalizing Regulation: Reaching Beyond the Borders of Chemical Safety." *Journal of Law and Society* 36 (1): 110–28.

International Carbon Action Partnership (ICAP). 2020. https://icapcarbonaction.com/.

Kelemen, Daniel, and David Vogel. 2010. "Trading Places: The Role of the United States and the European Union in International Environmental Politics." *Comparative Political Studies* 43 (4): 427–56.

Kleinman, Daniel, Abby Kinchy, and Robyn Autry. 2009. "Local Variation or Global Convergence in Agricultural Biotechnology Policy? A Comparative Analysis." *Science and Public Policy* 36 (5): 361–71.

Knill, Christoph, and Duncan Liefferink. 2013. "The Establishment of EU Environmental Policy." In *Environmental Policy in the EU: Actors, Institutions and Processes*, edited by Andrew Jordan and Camilla Adelle, 13–31. 3rd ed. Abingdon: Earthscan from Routledge.

Mehling, Michael, and Antto Vihma. 2017. *'Mourning for America' – Donald Trump's Climate Change Policy*. Helsinki: Finnish Institute of International Affairs.

Newburger, Emma. 2021. "Here's What Countries Pledged on Climate Change at Biden's Global Summit." CNBC, 22 April 2021. www.cnbc.com/2021/04/22/biden-climate-summit-2021-what-brazil-japan-canada-others-pledged.html.

Oberthür, Sebastian, and Florian Rabitz. 2014. "On the EU's Performance and Leadership in Global Environmental Governance: The Case of the Nagoya Protocol." *Journal of European Public Policy* 21 (1): 39–57.

Ostfeld, Richard, and Felicia Keesing. 2020. "Species That Can Make Us Ill Thrive in Human Habitats." *Nature*, 5 August 2020. www.nature.com/articles/d41586-020-02189-5.

Parker, Charles, and Christer Karlsson. 2018. "The UN Climate Change Negotiations and the Role of the United States: Assessing American Leadership from Copenhagen to Paris." *Environmental Politics* 27 (3): 519–40.

Rockström, Johan, Mattias Klum, with Peter Miller. 2015. *Big World, Small Planet: Abundance Within Planetary Boundaries*. New Haven: Yale University Press.

Rodine-Hardy, Kirsten. 2016. "Nanotechnology and Global Environmental Politics: Transatlantic Divergence." *Global Environmental Politics* 16 (3): 89–105.

Schunz, Simon. 2010. "Moving Closer or Drifting Further Apart? The European Union, the United States and the Struggle for a Post-2012 Climate Change Agreement." In *European Union, United States and Global Governance – Major Trends and Challenges*, edited by Jan Wouters and Steven Sterkx, 76–88. Leuven: Leuven Centre for Global Governance Studies.

Schunz, Simon. 2014. *European Union Foreign Policy and the Global Climate Regime*. Brussels: Peter Lang.

Schunz, Simon. 2016. "The Prospects for Transatlantic Leadership in an Evolving Multipolar World." *European Foreign Affairs Review* 21 (3): 431–48.

Schunz, Simon. 2020. "Towards a 'Transatlantic Green Deal'? How the EU Can Re-engage the US on Climate Change." *College of Europe Policy Brief*, No. 8/2020, December.

Smith, Mitchell P. 2012. *Environmental and Health Regulation in the United States and the European Union*. Basingstoke: Palgrave Macmillan.

Skjærseth, Jon, Guri Bang, and Miranda Schreurs. 2013. "Explaining Growing Climate Policy Differences Between the European Union and the United States." *Global Environmental Politics* 13 (4): 61–80.

Steinhauer, Valentin. 2018. "Leaving the Paris Agreement: An Analysis of the United States' Disengagement From the Global Climate Regime and Its Impact on EU Climate Diplomacy." *EU Diplomacy Papers*, No. 4/2018. Bruges: College of Europe.

Stephan, Hannes. 2015. *Cultural Politics and the Transatlantic Divide Over GMOs*. Basingstoke: Palgrave Macmillan.

Stokes, Leah, and Hanna Breetz. 2020. "States of Crisis: Subnational Inaction on Climate Change in the United States." In *Handbook of U.S. Environmental Policy*, edited by David Konisky, 289–301. Cheltenham: Edward Elgar.

United Nations Energy Programme (UNEP). 1992. *Rio Declaration on Environment and Development*. June. Rio de Janeiro.

US Congress. 2019. H. RES. 109 "Recognizing the Duty of the Federal Government to Create a Green New Deal." 7 February. Washington, DC.

United States Mission to the European Union. 2020. "History of the U.S. and the EU." https://useu.usmission.gov/our-relationship/policy-history/io/.

Van Schaik, Louise, and Simon Schunz. 2012. "Explaining EU Activism and Impact in Global Climate Politics: Is the Union a Norm- or Interest-Driven Actor?" *Journal of Common Market Studies* 50 (1): 169–86.

Vogel, David. 2012. *The Politics of Precaution: Regulating Health, Safety, and Environmental Risks in Europe and the United States*. Princeton, NJ: Princeton University Press.

Vogel, David, and Jo Swinnen, eds. 2011. *Transatlantic Regulatory Cooperation: The Shifting Roles of the EU, the US and California*. Cheltenham: Edward Elgar.

Vogler, John. 2011. "The Challenge of the Environment, Energy, and Climate Change." In *International Relations and the European Union*, edited by Christopher Hill and Michael Smith, 349–79. 2nd ed. Oxford: Oxford University Press.

Voice of America. 2017. "California to Collaborate with EU, China on Carbon Markets." 7 November 2017. www.voanews.com/usa/california-collaborate-eu-china-carbon-markets.

We Are Still In Coalition. 2020. www.wearestillin.com/.

Zito, Anthony, Charlotte Burns, and Andrea Lenschow. 2019. "Is the Trajectory of European Union Environmental Policy Less Certain?" *Environmental Politics* 28 (1): 187–207.

4
NATO'S "MACRONIAN" PERIL

Real or Exaggerated?

David G. Haglund

Introduction: The (Brain) Death of NATO?

In November 2019, France's president, Emmanuel Macron, granted an interview to the British journal, *The Economist*. That last pre-COVID-19 autumn was a season in which many Western leaders' thoughts were on the future of the transatlantic alliance, seen by quite a few of them to be experiencing more than its usual amount of turmoil. There were four reasons for this heightened alliance angst (discussed below), so there could be nothing terribly surprising about the French president giving voice to what was thought to be wrong with the North Atlantic Treaty Organization (NATO). Nor was there anything surprising about the media outlet to which he unburdened himself. *The Economist* had been Macron's biggest cheerleader since his surprise election some two years earlier. Indeed, such was his rockstar appeal to the magazine's editorial team that they had accorded the youthful president no fewer than three cover-page appearances during the second half of 2017 alone.[1]

Macron was hailed by *The Economist*'s "small-l" liberal editorialists as a breath of *air frais*. For he was regarded as being one of those rare French leaders who had a reputation as an atlanticist who is "fully committed to NATO and knows that the United States is France's and Europe's natural ally" (Tiersky 2018, 94).[2] Moreover, he was known to be a reformer who would brook no nonsense from those in France bent on nourishing the sacred cows pasturing in the overly protectionist and *dirigiste* French political paddock, one where liberals had long been routinely taken to task for being the closest thing this secular republic could have to devil worshippers (see Julienne 2001; Leterre 2000). What Macron happened to be thinking meshed well with what *The Economist*'s editorialists were thinking: All agreed that when thoughts turned to the current state and future prospects of the venerable transatlantic alliance, there was ample cause for worry.

DOI:10.4324/9781003147565-7

Even though COVID-19 had already begun its sinister spread from its epicenter in Wuhan, China, no one had an inkling of what was to come in the very near term. Instead, leaders could vent their anxiety about other matters, which, in light of what was shortly to befall their countries, can now seem almost quaint. What so upset Macron, judging from his remarks in the interview, was the perception of grave danger facing a Europe whose integrative juices had been steadily desiccated by a myriad of economic, political, and demographic challenges that had arisen over the past decade. The challenges were such as to lead some analysts to fear that the European Union (EU) itself was in danger of falling apart (Kirchick 2018). Brexit was an obvious portent, but the problem was far more serious than just the British exit that *The Economist* and Macron had both deplored. Something far worse loomed: Europe itself risked being left to its own devices by a United States (US) that had, since World War II, installed itself as an omnipresent fixture in its regional security but was now, under President Donald J. Trump, showing signs of wanting to decamp from the Old Continent.

It was in this context that Macron commented on NATO's geopolitical health that will go down in history as among the "frankest" things ever said about the alliance by a leader of one of its member states. NATO, asserted the French president, was suffering from "brain-death." He coupled this lugubrious diagnosis with an equally dramatic call to action from Europeans, who now, more than ever, would have to set about "autonomously" erecting their own security and defense structures because, as Macron put to his interviewer, Europe was sitting "on the edge of a precipice" and needed, above all, to "reassess the reality of what NATO is in light of the commitment of the United States" (as quoted in *The Economist* 2019, 9).

Many of France's European allies, otherwise in reasonably general accord that the consequences limned by Macron could be dire, nevertheless were shocked by the blunt diagnosis delivered by the good doctor. Brain death equals death, whether for individuals or institutions, and for most allies, a world from which NATO had disappeared was not a comforting place in which to be living. Germany's chancellor, Angela Merkel, was particularly unsettled by what she took to be this gratuitously astringent description of NATO's current status because, for Germans, it can still be said that the alliance remains the "indispensable guarantor of German, European, and transatlantic security" (Schmidt 2019, 17).[3] It was reported that Merkel had become "uncharacteristically furious" with her French counterpart, a reaction that a few commentators alarmingly (if prematurely) took as heralding an unstoppable deterioration in the level of Franco-German cooperation (Erlanger 2019, 8). Elsewhere in the alliance, others grumbled about Macron's choice of imagery. Even Trump, who had himself earlier in his mandate never shied away from heaping dispraise upon an alliance he liked to claim was "obsolete," saw fit to use Macron's word choice as an opportunity to *defend* NATO! Not only had the alliance ceased being obsolete—thanks to, as the president saw it, his own enlightened leadership—but it now "serves a great purpose," and thus it was being unfairly slimed with the "very, very nasty" term of opprobrium Macron had hurled in its direction (as quoted in Wintour and Sabbagh 2019).

As we will see, Trump was obviously one of the reasons for Macron's (and other allied leaders') trepidation. Indeed, it might be tempting to conclude that now with Joe Biden dwelling at 1600 Pennsylvania Avenue, all will be well once more in the transatlantic alliance. No doubt, there is something to this tempting thought, for NATO has unquestionably demonstrated a remarkable degree of "resilience" in the past, leading to the assumption that it will muster enough of this same quality in the future to sustain itself as the preeminent institutional feature of transatlantic defense and security affairs. Still, the alliance does, these days, face a set of real challenges, most of which would exist even if Trump had never come to power in January 2017. Those challenges are fourfold and will be discussed in the following sections of this chapter.

The first of these concerns the ability of the US, no matter by whom led, to continue to support the globalized economic and security order—call it the "Liberal International Order" (LIO)—to anything like the same extent as it had in the years since that order's creation in the aftermath of World War II. The second challenge concerns the long-running saga regarding the prospects and consequences of the European "autonomy" aspiration touted by Macron and some other Europeans (most but not all of them French) over the decades. The third challenge is associated with the evident rise of "illiberalism" in many NATO states, carrying with it the risk that a growing values divergence will redound negatively for interest-based cooperation between the allies. And the fourth, and perhaps most intriguing, challenge will be how NATO positions itself in respect to the return of great-power competition as the principal menace to international peace, a question addressed in this chapter's concluding section.

The Trump Experience: Cause or Symptom?

The biggest question in transatlantic security over the past several years has involved the US's ability or desire (or both) to continue to function as a central—indeed, *the* central—organizer of European security affairs, working through NATO. A facile judgment regarding this question would hold that it received its definitive answer in the November 2020 US presidential election when the US electorate fired Trump. Some believe that with Joe Biden now at the helm of foreign policy, the US will live up to its (or his) promise to be "back" and that it will recommit to bolstering the LIO and the Western alliance by resuming the mantle of leadership of the community of like-minded states, at whose core has been, since 1949, the transatlantic alliance. It is far too early for anyone to know the extent to which it will be "back to business as usual" for NATO. Partly, of course, this is merely to say that none of us are preternaturally gifted when it comes to discerning the outlines of even the near-term future, which despite what some like to call it, is hardly ever a "foreseeable" one; if the pandemic has taught us nothing else, then surely it has taught us this. However, our inability to fathom NATO's future also inheres in our amnesia about its *past*.

Simply put, it is not clear what, in the NATO context, "back to business" would mean. The best we can do is to say what it does *not* mean. It does not imply returning to a blissful time when all the allies sang from the same hymn book, and the unison of their voices was sweet harmony, indeed. Such a construe would overlook just how much chronic squabbling has *always* taken place among the Western allies, with France and the US never being too far from the center of the rhetorical action, hence the sobriquet given to them two-dozen years ago, the "feuding hillbillies" of the West (Grantham 1998, 58).

Perhaps an anecdote from the Cold War best illustrates the fundamental difficulty with romanticizing NATO's past. The anecdote involves a comment made during the Carter administration by the secretary of defense, Harold Brown, as recounted a decade or so later by a French analyst, François Heisbourg. At the time of Heisbourg's retelling in 1987, NATO was witnessing another spike in intra-alliance bickering, this round of carping being over the merits of the recently signed Intermediate-Range Nuclear Forces Treaty between Washington and Moscow, which some in Europe feared would "de-couple" US and European security. In this heated environment, Heisbourg did well to instruct his readers on the "same-old, same-old" quality of alliance debates, drawing their attention back to an afternoon, ten years previously, when a breathless aide burst into Brown's office to convey the distressing news that NATO had just fallen into disarray, only to be met with this nonchalant response from the defense secretary: "Tell me," Brown calmly asked, "when has NATO ever been in *array*? [emphasis in original]" (as quoted in Heisbourg 1987, 111–12).

For the US, one constant source of this lack of array has involved "burden sharing," taken to mean, with some rare exceptions, that Washington was growing fed up with European allies (and Canada) not spending enough on defense. Trump did not invent this US grievance. It has a lengthy pedigree, having upset Democratic as well as Republican presidents alike, dating back almost to the very origins of the Atlantic alliance. The first public staging of the burden-sharing drama occurred with the alliance's Lisbon Summit in 1952, when the Truman administration called on the allies to so step up their contributions to the alliance's conventional defenses as to be able to, within two years, field 98 divisions and 7,000 combat aircraft for the European theater (Ratti 2017, 52)! Needless to say, the allies showed themselves incapable of meeting this ambitious conventional-force goal. Yet, the alliance proved resilient and, in the short run, was able to benefit from a decision by the Eisenhower administration to prioritize nuclear rather than conventional deterrence with its "New Look" strategy. In the longer run, alliance resiliency was mightily boosted by the fortuitous ending of the Cold War, followed by the demise of the Soviet Union itself (see Schwartz 1983).

The old burden-sharing disquiet would prove, like NATO itself, to have remarkable survival skills, managing to outlive the ending of the Cold War. The alliance's gradual assumption of new security obligations outside of its traditional "area," starting in the Balkans in the 1990s and continuing in the "greater" Middle East in the early twenty-first century, witnessed a ramping up in the volume of the traditional refrain, as US presidents, no matter their names or their parties, implored allies to do more, with the metric for assessing "more" typically being the percentage share of gross domestic product allocated to their respective defense budgets. In the event, 2 percent has come to be the magic figure that attests to an ally's doing "enough" to carry its share of the burden, but it is not a metric that flatters most alliance members, with only a third of them managing to have hit that target before the arrival of the pandemic, which will certainly put further strains on the capacity of member states to increase spending on the military (Webber, Sperling, and Smith 2021, 71).

Before Trump, presidential finger-wagging was just that. Few "underspenders" really sensed there to be much if any downside risk of their choosing to allocate relatively larger shares of public finances to budgetary envelopes other than defense. In the words of three eminent alliance watchers, what Trump did was "criticize NATO in a manner unparalleled among previous American presidents" (Webber, Sperling, and Smith 2021, 3). In so doing, he injected a new and disturbing element into their calculations, predicated upon the thought that perhaps he was serious when he warned that unless they spent more, the US *itself* might leave NATO. Although no ally has ever seriously entertained the option of invoking Article 13 of the Washington Treaty and exiting the alliance—not even France in 1966, when Charles de Gaulle kicked NATO's headquarters out of his country and pulled France's forces out of its integrated command structures—with Trump, there spread a suspicion that the US's commitment to the alliance it had created and sustained could no longer be taken for granted.

Trump certainly managed to elevate the tension associated with this eternal dispute by debasing the quality of debate, resorting to his hallmark trait of insulting, and demeaning those with whom he happened to disagree. Not surprisingly, many allies (though not all) responded by elevating their criticism of the US president. This resulted in stirring up anew the old "anti-American" bogey that always seems to sleep with one eye open within the confines of the transatlantic region, a phenomenon that one analyst, writing a decade and a half ago, astutely labeled "friendly-fire" anti-Americanism (Sweig 2006).[4] Between 2017 and 2021, the fire was coming fast and furiously, as attested to by survey data that measured Trump's (and by implication, his country's) favorability in the reckoning of allies.[5]

Lost in the emotionally charged atmosphere of the Trump years, though, was an *attitudinal* change afoot in the US, one for which Trump served much more as consequence than cause. The conviction was growing that the multilateral international order, the LIO, that had for so many years been the cynosure of US grand strategy, was no longer working in the US's interests. Many drew the alarmist conclusion that if the US was retreating from the LIO, it might also step back from NATO. Although the US public still seems supportive of the latter, there can be no question that the belief in an all-virtuous LIO has suffered a reversal in wide swaths of public opinion and has important champions in the Biden coalition, many of whose members believe (perhaps correctly) that today's LIO has been built on illusions. One of those illusions concerned the relative painlessness of globalized free trade, such that in increasing overall global wealth (which it did), it could also ensure that the fruits of greater prosperity could be more ethically and equitably shared (which it did not). Another of those illusions was that a liberal power of such vast capacity—in the event, the US—could be counted upon to understand that as it was the principal beneficiary of the multilateral order, it must fall to it to become *and to remain* the order's leading champion. Quite a few analysts have been moved to suggest that for the US, the appropriate role to adopt had to be that of "hegemon," even if it remained unclear what the concept of hegemony was actually supposed to mean in practice (see Foot, MacFarlane, and Mastanduno 2003; Ikenberry 2020).[6] However, whatever it might have meant, the "h-word" (Anderson 2017) implied one certainty: There could be no "Amerexit" from the task of overseeing the liberal international order.[7] Or so it was thought.

One astute critic of US foreign policy has given this post-Cold War mindset a metaphorical label, the "Emerald City consensus." Andrew J. Bacevich (2020), retired US Army colonel-turned-university professor, and a self-declared conservative, invoked this trope to identify that magical place to which the yellow brick road led in *The Wizard of Oz*—a place where everyone's dreams could come true. For Bacevich, this post-1991 consensus rested upon three core assumptions, all of them critically dependent upon US superintendence. These assumptions were (1) that "unfettered" capitalism worked best for Americans and everyone else; (2) that "unabashed" American military domination of the system worked best for Americans and everyone else; and (3) that the purpose of life after the Cold War had become, for Americans and everyone else, to enjoy to the fullest individual liberty while taking on as few as possible civic responsibilities.

In light of this trio of assumptions, Bacevich found it easy to understand the Americans' defection from the liberal multilateral order: They simply ceased to believe that it continued to work to promote their interests. Instead, it had become a menace to those interests. Bacevich and former president Trump, with whom he stood in fundamental disagreement on many issues, did share at least one important quality: Membership in the same—Baby Boom—generation:

> During the period stretching from the mid-1940s through the 1980s, as [Donald Trump] and I passed from infancy and childhood into adolescence and then manhood, most Americans most of the time nurtured the conviction that the three versions of postwar freedom to which they subscribed could coexist in rough equipoise. That their nation could be simultaneously virtuous *and* powerful *and* deliriously affluent seemed not only plausible, but also essential [emphasis in original].
>
> Bacevich 2020, 15–16, 88

Somewhere along the road, however, the wheels began to fall off the cart that was supposed to lead to Emerald City.

One clear implication of this has been a greater reluctance than in previous decades for Americans to, in the words of John F. Kennedy, "pay any price, and bear any burden" for the defense of freedom (Kennedy 1961). We have seen already, with the Biden administration's decision to put a quick end to the experiment with nation-building in Afghanistan, one immediate consequence of the abandonment of the Emerald City vision. This does not mean, as some want rashly to conclude, that the US is returning to "isolationism," for it is very unlikely to do this, as I discuss below. However, it does mean that observers in the alliance who have been querying the US's willingness to backstop their security have some reason to be anxious, as they sense an implicit identification between supporting the LIO and supporting NATO. This anxiety will have obvious implications for the alliance; in the first instance by reinforcing, in some allies' imagination, the perennial yearning for a more "autonomous" European security and defense capability.

"Huntingtonianism" Revisited

It is of more than passing interest that Macron should have been intoning the mantra of "autonomy" in his many addresses and other interventions on security and defense topics in the past three years. For autonomy has represented, in France, what elsewhere in the alliance can often be considered, at best, a will-o'-the wisp, and in some places can be regarded as downright suicidal. Thus, if US resolve constitutes one important challenge to NATO, the prospect of a French-led autonomy drive that "widens" the Atlantic is a second. Importantly, the two problems are interrelated, as we discover in this section. And once again, neither can be said to have come into existence because of Donald Trump. Nor will either vanish because of Joe Biden.

In fact, it was while Biden was serving as vice president to the popular (among public opinion in Europe and North America) Barack Obama that French security and defense analysts resuscitated what had been a familiar concern about the US's perceived willingness to stay committed to Europe, one that long predated Charles de Gaulle's decade in the Élysée, having its roots in France's feeling of abandonment during the interwar era (Martin 1999; Nelson 1975). French analysts considered Obama to be too fixated on parts of the world other than Europe, or simply too fixated on "nation-building" at home, to be counted upon.[8] As one of these commentators observed, apropos the growing disenchantment of Americans with international leadership so evident during the 2016 campaign, there was a common thread linking such otherwise disparate members of the US's political class as Trump, Ted Cruz, Bernie Sanders—and yes, even Barack Obama: All had been promoting the idea that the US's role in the world needed to be reduced (Kandel 2018, 174–75).

If this indeed was the problem—if a US defection was considered possible—then it behooved Europeans to think more constructively about their collective defense than they had been accustomed to doing. Failure to step up their game, some feared, would soon result in their confronting serious threats to their security they would be incapable of handling. Of course, most European countries did not share this French pessimism regarding US staying power as a fixture of the Old Continent's security. Still, the French critique was worrisome, representing as it did the latest instantiation of an older worry that we might refer to as "Huntingtonianism."

The above eponym is a reference to the late Harvard professor and well-known commentator on foreign policy, Samuel Huntington. So fecund was this scholar that it is possible to associate his name with any number of policy orientations, and it is probably the case that he is mainly recalled for his celebrated and much-debated "clash of civilizations" thesis from a quarter-century ago. Early in the first post-Cold War decade, indeed as an integral part of his "clash" thesis, Huntington had waxed enthusiastically about the ability of the civilizational grouping whose roots were "Euro-American" to withstand the challenges of a new era in which cultural identity would come to supplant political ideology as the dominant cleavage in global politics. He was positively upbeat about this prospect, sure that, in moments of crisis, the Western allies would find it within themselves to engage in successful "civilization rallying." His optimism about Western resilience compelled him to debunk the rising tide of skepticism regarding the alliance's survivability during the immediate aftermath of the Cold War's end, which left the allies bereft of a Soviet enemy around which to coalesce. To the growing legion of NATO critics in those early post-Cold War years, Huntington offered the rebuttal that

> if North America and Europe renew their moral life, build on their cultural commonality, and develop close forms of economic and political integration to supplement their security collaboration in NATO, they could generate a third Euroamerican phase of Western economic affluence and political influence.
>
> *Huntington 1996, 308*

By the late 1990s, and continuing into the following decade, his mood would darken, as he sensed a looming conflict *within* the West itself, fueled by a French-led desire to effect greater autonomy for the US's European allies. Nor was he alone in having this sense of foreboding.[9] Hence, my invocation of Huntingtonianism in this section's heading; for what would come to consume Huntington's fears was the suspicion that France had defected from universalistic Western undertakings it had once espoused and henceforth was going to throw itself wholly into the project of building an exclusionary Europe. This Europe, once constructed, would be bound to widen the Atlantic—not in any geographic sense, obviously, but certainly in an affective one, and likely even a strategic one.

As a result, just a few short years after expressing himself so exuberantly through the clash thesis, Huntington now saw the solidity of Western civilization to be under dire threat; only this time, it was not the "rest" from beyond the pale who were the problem. Far worse, the source of the trouble was internal. All the evidence, according to Huntington, pointed in France's direction. The French, he claimed, were determined to forge an "antihegemonic" coalition intended to balance US power. Whether they would succeed in this objective depended upon their ability to entice Germany to slip from its traditional pro-NATO, pro-Washington, moorings. The stakes could not be higher, Huntington warned. The future of world order depended upon which way "Europe" would lean, for, at a time when it was still possible to miss the geostrategic significance of China's rise, only Europe was said to be capable of making or breaking that dispensation some knew as US hegemony. The latter, to function, required others to want to follow US leadership—exactly the thing that a rebarbative France was contesting. Thus, to Huntington, the way to preserve hegemony, and thereby stave off the loneliness of the US's "superpowerdom," was obvious. France would have to be blocked from winning Germany over to its side because "given the pro- and anti-American outlooks of Britain and France, respectively, America's relations with Germany are central to its relations with Europe" (Huntington 1999, 48).

Much would happen over the years since Huntington expressed himself in such a worried manner. For the alliance, there was for a time good news on the autonomy front, associated with France's "return" to NATO in 2009, under Nicolas Sarkozy (see Bozo 2008). It seemed to some as if the risk of transatlantic rupture had well and truly been put to rest, with NATO and the EU apparently developing into mutual admiration societies, committed to working together in as seamless a manner possible. Yet, the old autonomy itch never did, or could, disappear, such that one impact of the Trump presidency, revealed in recent Macronian initiatives to rally Europe, was to set some policymakers once more to scratching furiously.

Ironically, the French response to Trump, while not exactly a welcoming one, was less hostile than was the response of other allied publics. The so-called anti-American French actually thought better—or to phrase it more accurately, "less worse"—of Trump than did publics in many other Western allied countries. The main reason for this was that, in France, it was possible to see him as facilitating that which many elsewhere in Europe (and in Canada) feared might well happen: The attainment of greater (as in *genuine*) European autonomy in security and defense policy. This is why Alain Frachon, perhaps tongue in cheek, could scold Europeans on the manner in which they had treated the 45th president. Shortly after Biden's victory, Frachon, an editorialist in the Parisian daily, *Le Monde*, called Europe's numerous Trump-haters a bunch of "ingrates," who did not understand the remarkable gift that the defeated president had bestowed upon them. For he had given Europeans the impetus needed to complete the job of building that "more perfect" Europe that continually gets touted as an obviously necessary policy goal. Trump accomplished this, wrote Frachon, by showing the Europeans the "world as it is." Force is the ultimate ratio in that world, and Trump's gift consisted in demonstrating to the Europeans that they needed to enhance their own military capabilities. For doing this, he deserved to be acknowledged as the "obstetrician" (*accoucheur*) facilitating the birth of that new, and autonomous, Europe (Frachon 2020).

The Rise of Illiberalism

If there was something familiar about the first two challenges facing NATO, the third challenge really did manifest itself in something new, as undesirable as it was novel. It is the challenge subsumed under the label of democratic "backsliding," otherwise known as the rise of illiberalism within countries thought to be established liberal democracies (see Levitsky and Ziblatt 2018). NATO has been conceptualized over the years in different ways. At one extreme can be found those who regard it as a collective-defense entity conceived *solely* to safeguard its members from the threat of great-power aggression. At the other extreme are those who see it as something truly new under the global security sun, that is, a community of like-minded states held together far more by shared liberal-democratic values than by traditional security worries. According to this second way of looking at things, NATO has always been much more than a marriage of security convenience between partners possessed of interest-based reasons for cooperation; it is a community of shared values, the foremost of which are human rights, the rule of law, and especially, democratic governance.

This is why, once the end of the Cold War removed (temporarily, as it turned out) concerns about Russia as a threat, some analysts could be confident that NATO was not destined to go out of existence, for as one of them put it at the start of the 1990s, "it is a fair bet that the values engendered in Western cooperation in security affairs will be maintained in the years ahead, based on the assumption that these values have become internalized in the systems of Western alliance nations" (see Boyer 1993). Now, it has always been true that the community-of-values argument needed to be taken with a grain of salt, given the charter membership in the alliance of António de Oliveira Salazar's Portugal, to say nothing of the occasional democratic "lapses" experienced during the Cold War by the first pair of new members, Turkey and Greece. But *la nécessité oblige*, and sometimes during the Cold War, it was imperative to overlook a bit of value "straying" for the greater sake of security against the Soviets.

What was *not* so easily acceptable is what came as a result of NATO's great post-Cold War experiment with enlargement. That experiment was intended to contribute to spreading the democratic "zone of peace" eastward in Europe; in the first instance (in 1999), by the incorporation into alliance ranks of three former Soviet allies: Poland, Hungary, and the Czech Republic. Subsequently, 11 other new members were added, between 2004 and 2020, so that today's NATO is made up of 30 member states. If what was intended was to spread liberal values, the experiment has been a bust, nowhere more so than with respect to two members of the expansion class of 1999, Poland and Hungary (the court is still out on the third, the Czech Republic).

Despite what so many today, and not just in Russia, seem to want to believe about NATO's expansion, initial enthusiasm for it had *far* less to do with containing Russia than it did with spreading liberal democracy. That latter objective was obviously valued in and of itself, but it was also intended to serve as a means to another end. Many advocates of enlargement saw that end as being the safeguarding of NATO's very existence, on the good logic that for the alliance to remain viable in an era when the "threat" of yore had disappeared, it needed other ambitious projects to keep it from lapsing into irrelevance. At its inception, enlargement was the most important of those projects, one that was a political experiment more than it was a strategic one (see Asmus 2002; Goldgeier 1999; Maddox and Rachwald 2001; Sayle 2019; von Hlatky and Fortmann 2020).[10]

And herein arises the contemporary irony. There is today, in many (though not all) of the earlier NATO member countries, a growing sense of disquiet regarding what some construe as the unintended consequences of the alliance's decision to enlarge a generation ago—disquiet reflected in a February 2019 report written by two former US ambassadors to NATO, Douglas Lute and Nicholas Burns, who did not mince words in underscoring what they called "a potentially cancerous threat from within." The threat, they said, arose from three particular allies, two of the members of the first enlargement class of the post-Cold War NATO and the third a member of the first enlargement class of the *Cold War* NATO:[11]

> Three allied governments—Poland, Hungary and Turkey—have undermined their own democracies in varying degrees by suppressing free speech and a free press and limiting the independence of the courts. As NATO is, first and foremost, an alliance of democracies, the actions of these governments threaten the core values—democracy, individual liberty and the rule of law—to which each ally is committed in the North Atlantic Treaty.
>
> *Lute and Burns 2019, 4*[12]

The ex-ambassadors' commentary reflected a general mood among alliance-watchers, troubled by the retreat from liberal democracy appearing to gather momentum within the alliance—and not just among its newest members (see Krastev and Holmes 2020; Larsen 2019; Sloan 2018; Wallander 2018). This somber mood was reflected in early April 2019, when NATO held a subdued ceremony in Washington to mark its 70th anniversary, at the site of its founding. One European attendee quipped that the ersatz celebration resembled a wake more than a birthday party, such was the current funk enveloping the transatlantic community, a malaise with several causes, not least of which is the worry that allies who once had been Soviet client states were busily "turning authoritarian" (McDougall 2019; Sanger 2019).

Conclusion: Back to the Future?

If one of the big surprises between the ending of the Cold War and today has been the retreat of liberal democracy in so many alliance member-states, another surprise has been the *return* of great-power competition as the central issue in international security. It had seemed as if it was just yesterday that such competition had been authoritatively declared "obsolete."[13] And now it had come roaring back, with anxieties being fueled by the deeds and declarations of two particular countries.

The first of these was the traditional NATO adversary, Russia, which, under Vladimir Putin, has made earlier visions of working "cooperatively" with Moscow through a variety of NATO institutional mechanisms seem like pipe dreams.[14] The debate over just who or what "lost" Russia to the prospect of cooperation with Western countries can be expected to continue, but few imagine, especially after Russia's seizure of Crimea from Ukraine in 2014 and its continued meddling in the eastern portion of that former Soviet republic, a return any time soon to a good working relationship with the Russians. But, so long as Russia does not aggress against any of the current NATO membership, its recent bellicosity can be, and has been, regarded as providing a boost to NATO's resilience, by reminding the allies—old and new alike—what it was that led to the original formation of the alliance. In that sense, we are reminded once again of the truth in the apothegm of that remarkable English proverbialist of the sixteenth century, John Heywood, about "an ill wind that bloweth no man to good" (quoted in Bartlett 1968, 185b).

If some can clearly discern the good that might come from the alliance's being forced to retrench from its post-Cold War "overstretch" and concentrate once more on its core objective of providing collective defense within the transatlantic community, less obvious is what the implications might be for NATO of the emergence of a new cold war between the US and China. Delusionary, in retrospect, as the earlier visions of spreading liberal democracy in Central and Eastern Europe through institutional enlargement of NATO (and the EU) may have been, even more delusionary were those early assumptions about China's being brought within the embrace of liberal democracy as a result of its deepening ties with the Western capitalist world (see Wright 2017). China's economy did in so many ways become capitalist, but in no way, shape, or form has the Chinese polity evolved in a liberal-democratic direction. Just the opposite has occurred, making us wonder today how anyone could possibly have thought "engagement" was going to be an important first step leading to China's eventual democratization. Instead, it has represented an essential component in China's growth into a peer competitor of the US.

Interdependence between the West and China has served as the equivalent of the Western countries giving China the rope from which they, rather than it, would someday find themselves dangling. For in making China richer and more powerful, globalization and the engagement mindset that accompanied it have combined to foster, more than anything else has done, the return of what its erstwhile champions once thought it could prevent—great-power competition. This is a worry that has been especially pronounced among analysts who take seriously the supposedly ineluctable implications embedded in what is called "power-transition theory" (PTT), among whose most celebrated recent adherents has been Graham Allison (Allison 2017). But PTT scholars are far from the only experts who foresee trouble ahead between the US and China. Nearly everyone does, though the trouble need not take the form of military conflict between the two.

Nevertheless, China's well-commented "rise" of recent years may turn out to provide a tonic for US-European ties, strange as the thought might otherwise seem on first encounter. This is because of two trends. The first is that, in the US, China is one of the few issues in foreign policy (indeed, it may be the only one) capable of engendering a semblance of bipartisanship (see Sanger et al. 2021). It is hard to detect much difference between the China-averse Republicans and the similarly inclined Democrats. The second trend is the recognition that is setting in in the US, namely that allies might just be useful things to have vis-à-vis China. And, with respect to the latter, in US thinking, nothing tops the utility of NATO allies.[15]

The question that cannot be answered, and the one on which this chapter concludes, is whether China will prove a unifying or divisive force within the transatlantic community. It used to be argued by some European policy intellectuals that, unlike the US, "Europe doesn't do China" (Danchev 2005, 433). Recently, however, there is evidence that Europeans themselves are growing aware that if they do not "do" China, then China may well "do" them.[16]

In the end, there is some irony in the quondam pessimist John Mearsheimer's speculation that China may yet prove to be the allies' *deus ex machina*, quieting their fear about an American defection from European security and defense. This concluding section's title is an obvious allusion to Mearsheimer's (1990) very pessimistic (and very inaccurate) prognosis about NATO's resilience at the beginning of the post-Cold War decade when the Chicago professor worried about the resurgence of a German challenge (!) to Western security. Thus, it is fitting to leave the last words to him, as, this time, he may possibly get it right.

For Mearsheimer, the demise of the LIO need not lead to the demise of NATO and likely will not do so. Instead, what will replace the LIO will be two fairly strong but "bounded" orders, one managed by the US and the other by China. (There will also be a weaker, global, order for dealing with second-order concerns.) Mearsheimer foresaw most European states adhering to the US-led order, "although they are unlikely to play a serious military role in containing China." That is not what the US wants from them, in any case. Instead, what it seeks is to "keep European countries from selling dual-use technologies to China and to help put economic pressure on Beijing when necessary." That will be the European allies' side of the evolving arrangement. As for the US, its commitment to the Europeans will be militarily to

> remain in Europe, keeping NATO alive and continuing to serve as the pacifier in that region. Given that virtually every European leader would like to see that happen, the threat of leaving should give the United States significant leverage in getting the Europeans to cooperate on the economic front against China.
>
> *Mearsheimer 2019, 48–49*

This, in a nutshell, may be the shape of a new, to use Harlan Cleveland's well-known term from the late 1960s, "transatlantic bargain" (as quoted in Sloan 2020, ch. 1) one that keeps the US interested in Europe, if only because it is so interested in China. In other words, those in France and elsewhere who worried that the US's ballyhooed "pivot to Asia," starting in the Obama administration, signaled a retreat from the Old Continent, may not have considered fully the implications of China's emergence as a peer-competitor of the US.

Notes

1 The first appearance came in the 17 June issue, which featured a picture of Macron walking on water, in support of its editorial "Europe's Saviour?" The second was on 30 September with Macron's visage advertising a special nine-page report on France bearing the hopeful title "Regeneration." The third appearance came in the year-ending double issue, which lauded France as the "Formidable Nation."
2 Also favorably taking the measure of the French president is Drozdiak (2020).
3 Also see, on Franco-German differences over transatlantic and European security, Meimeth and Schmidt (forthcoming) and Vincze (2021).
4 Also see, for that era's wave of criticism of US foreign policy, Katzenstein and Keohane (2007).
5 A useful metric for gauging the quality of ties between the US and its European allies is the "transatlantic scorecard" published quarterly by the Brookings Institution's Center on the United States and Europe as part of a transatlantic initiative it co-sponsors with the Robert Bosch Stiftung in Germany. Recent quarterly scorecards all attest to the consensus view that transatlantic relations could benefit greatly from an upgrade. These quarterly scorecards are available at www.brookings.edu/research/trans-atlantic-scorecard-april-2020/?utm_campaign=Brookings%20Brief&utm_source=hs_email&utm_medium=email&utm_content=86981260.
6 For a caution regarding potential misuse of this ill-defined term, see Wilkinson (1999).
7 As argued forcefully in Kagan (2018).
8 For reflections of this concern, exacerbated by worry about an Obama "pivot to Asia" redounding negatively for European interests, see Leparmentier and Lesnes (2010, 1, 6); Quessard and Kandel (2017); and Quessard, Heurtebize, and Gagnon (2020). For sure, it has not only been French defense intellectuals who have worried about recent US foreign policy signaling a lack of commitment to allies. Many US voices were getting raised, even prior to the Trump administration, about excessive strategic diffidence. See, for instance, the sarcastically titled critique penned by former Obama supporter Vali Nasr, *The Dispensable Nation: American Foreign Policy in Retreat* (2013). The sarcasm inherent in Nasr's paraphrase of Madeleine Albright's well-known assertion about American exceptionalism, made while the secretary of state was being interviewed on NBC's *Today Show* in February 1998, some ten months before Operation Desert Fox was unleashed against Saddam Hussein's Iraq: "[I]f we have to use force, it is because we are America; we are the indispensable nation. We stand tall and we see further than other countries into the future, and we see the danger here to all of us." In fact, Albright was merely repeating a phrase used by President Bill Clinton the year before in his second inaugural address in January 1997: "America stands alone as the world's indispensable nation" (as quoted in Lieber 2012, 67).
9 Others included Pfaff (1998/99); Kupchan (2002); Glucksmann (2003); and Habermas (2006). And for an otherwise decidedly *non*-"Habermasian" perspective, see Buchanan (2002).
10 Also see Mearsheimer (2019). "NATO expansion into Eastern Europe," wrote the prominent realist theoretician,

> is a good example of the United States and its allies working to turn the bounded Western order into a liberal international order. One might think that moving NATO eastward was part of a classic deterrence strategy aimed at containing a potentially aggressive Russia. But it was not, as the West's strategy was geared toward liberal ends.
>
> *Mearsheimer 2019, 23*

11 Turkey joined the alliance in 1952, at the same time as Greece. Some analysts hold Turkey to be far more of a problem than either Hungary or Poland—or the two Visegrád delinquents combined. For one sharply worded criticism of the nominal "ally" Turkey, said to have embarked on a determined campaign to challenge the US, and to act generally as the "troll under the bridge to hell using his geographical position to blackmail the West," see Lévy (2019, 147–48, 164). Also see the more restrained critique by Yegin (2019).
12 Sharing this downcast view is Flockhart (2019).
13 Most memorably by Mueller (1990). Testifying to the current "retreat" from this optimistic perspective are Loong (2020) and Layne (2020).
14 Those mechanisms were the Permanent Joint Council, set up in 1997 but undone by tensions resulting from the 1999 Kosovo War, and its successor, the NATO-Russia Council, created in the aftermath of 9/11 but rendered ineffective after the Russia-Georgia conflict in 2008. Webber, Sperling, and Smith (2021, ch. 4).
15 Stressing the value of allies as a "force maximizer" for the US, are Brooks and Wohlforth (2016).
16 For reactions to Chinese influence-attempts in Central and Eastern Europe, see Karásková et al. (2021).

References

Allison, Graham. 2017. *Destined for War: Can America and China Escape Thucydides's Trap?* Boston: Houghton Mifflin Harcourt.
Anderson, Perry. 2017. *The H-Word: The Peripeteia of Hegemony.* London: Verso.
Asmus, Ronald D. 2002. *Opening NATO's Door: How the Alliance Remade Itself for a New Era.* New York: Columbia University Press.
Bacevich, Andrew J. 2020. *The Age of Illusions: How America Squandered Its Cold War Victory.* New York: Metropolitan Books.
Bartlett, John. (1882) 1968. *Familiar Quotations: A Collection of Passages, Phrases and Proverbs Traced to Their Sources in Ancient and Modern Literature.* Edited by Emily Morison Back. 14th ed. Boston: Little, Brown.
Boyer, Mark A. 1993. *International Cooperation and Public Goods: Opportunities for the Western Alliance.* Baltimore: Johns Hopkins University Press.
Bozo, Frédéric. 2008. "France and NATO Under Sarkozy: End of the French Exception?" Fondation pour l'Innovation Politique [Foundation for Political Innovation] Working Paper. Paris. March.
Brooks, Stephen G., and William C. Wohlforth. 2016. "The Once and Future Superpower: Why China Won't Overtake the United States." *Foreign Affairs* 95: 91–104.
Buchanan, Patrick. 2002. *The Death of the West: How Dying Populations and Immigrant Invasions Imperil Our Country and Civilization.* New York: Thomas Dunne.
Danchev, Alex. 2005. "Shared Values in the Transatlantic Relationship." *British Journal of Politics and International Relations* 7: 429–36.
Drozdiak, William. 2020. *The Last President of Europe: Emmanuel Macron's Race to Revive France and Save the World.* New York: Public Affairs/Hachette.
The Economist. 2019. "A Continent in Peril." 9 November 2019.
Erlanger, Steven. 2019. "NATO Differences Stoke a Franco-German Feud." *New York Times,* 24 November 2019.
Flockhart, Trine. 2019. "A Fractured Alliance in Good Shape? NATO at 70." *Atlantisch perspectief* [Atlantic Perspective] 43 (2): 10–14.

Foot, Rosemary, S. Neil MacFarlane, and Michael Mastanduno, eds. 2003. *US Hegemony and International Organizations*. Oxford: Oxford University Press.
Frachon, Alain. 2020. "Donald Trump a révélé aux Européens le monde tel qu'il est: une affaire de rapports de force" [Donald Trump Revealed to Europeans the World as It Is: A Matter of a Balance of Power]. *Le Monde*, 17 December 2020.
Glucksmann, André. 2003. *Ouest contre Ouest* [West Against West]. Paris: Plon.
Goldgeier, James M. 1999. *Not Whether But When: The U.S. Decision to Enlarge NATO*. Washington: Brookings Institution Press.
Grantham, Bill. 1998. "America the Menace: France's Feud with Hollywood." *World Policy Journal* 15: 58–65.
Habermas, Jürgen. 2006. *The Divided West*. Translated by Ciaran Cronin. Cambridge: Polity.
Heisbourg, François. 1987. «Europe/États-Unis: le couplage stratégique menacé» [Europe-United States: The Endangered Strategic Coupling]. *Politique étrangère* [Foreign Policy] 52: 111–27.
Huntington, Samuel P. 1996. *The Clash of Civilizations and the Remaking of World Order*. New York: Simon & Schuster.
———. 1999. "The Lonely Superpower." *Foreign Affairs* 78: 35–49.
Ikenberry, G. John. 2020. "American Decline, Liberal Hegemony, and the Transformation of World Politics." In *Coping with Geopolitical Decline: The United States in European Perspective*, edited by Frédéric Mérand, 222–50. Montreal and Kingston: McGill-Queen's University Press.
Julienne, Christian. 2001. *Le Diable est-il libéral?* [Is the Devil Liberal?]. Paris: Les Belles Lettres.
Kagan, Robert. 2018. *The Jungle Grows Back: America and Our Imperiled World*. New York: Alfred A. Knopf.
Kandel, Maya. 2018. *Les États-Unis et le monde, de George Washington à Donald Trump* [The United States and the World: From George Washington to Donald Trump]. Paris: Perrin.
Karásková, Ivana, Alicja Bachulska, Tamás Matura, and Matej Šimalčík. 2021. *Careful or Careless? Debating Chinese Investment and 5G Technology in Central Europe*. Prague: Association for International Affairs. May. https://mapinfluence.eu/wp-content/uplo ads/2021/05/Mapinfluence_policy-paper_careful-or-careless_A4_web_05-4.pdf.
Katzenstein, Peter J., and Robert O. Keohane, eds. 2007. *Anti-Americanisms in World Politics*. Ithaca: Cornell University Press.
Kennedy, John F. 1961. Transcript of John F. Kennedy's Inaugural Address. *Our Documents*. www.ourdocuments.gov/doc.php?flash=false&doc=91&page=transcript.
Kirchick, James. 2018. *The End of Europe: Dictators, Demagogues, and the Coming Dark Age*. New Haven: Yale University Press.
Krastev, Ivan, and Stephen Holmes. 2020. *The Light that Failed: A Reckoning*. London: Penguin.
Kupchan, Charles A. 2002. "The End of the West." *Atlantic Monthly* 290: 42–44.
Larsen, Henrik B. L. 2019. *NATO's Democratic Retrenchment: Hegemony After the Return of History*. London: Routledge.
Layne, Christopher. 2020. "Coming Storms: The Return of Great-Power War." *Foreign Affairs* 99 (6): 42–48.
Leparmentier, Arnaud, and Corine Lesnes. 2010. «Les Européens ébranlés par l'indifférence d'Obama» [The Europeans Shaken by Obama's Indifference]. *Le Monde*, 4 February 2010.
Leterre, Thierry. 2000. *La Gauche et la peur libérale* [The Left and the Liberal Peril]. Paris: Presse de SciencesPo.
Levitsky, Steven, and Daniel Ziblatt. 2018. *How Democracies Die*. New York: Crown.
Lévy, Bernard-Henri. 2019. *The Empire and the Five Kings: America's Abdication and the Fate of the World*. Translated by Steven B. Kennedy. New York: Henry Holt.

Lieber, Robert J. 2012. *Power and Willpower in the American Future: Why the United States Is Not Destined to Decline*. Cambridge: Cambridge University Press.

Loong, Lee Hsien. 2020. "The Endangered Asian Century: America, China, and the Perils of Confrontation." *Foreign Affairs* 99 (4): 52–64.

Lute, Douglas, and Nicholas Burns. 2019. *NATO at Seventy: An Alliance in Crisis*. Report of the Project on Europe and the Transatlantic Relationship. Cambridge, MA: Harvard University Kennedy School, Belfer Center for Science and International Affairs. February.

Maddox, Gale A., and Arthur R. Rachwald, eds. 2001. *Enlarging NATO: The National Debates* Boulder, CO: Lynne Rienner.

Martin, Benjamin F. 1999. *France and the Après Guerre, 1918–1924: Illusions and Disillusionment*. Baton Rouge: Louisiana State University Press.

McDougall, Walter A. 2019. "NATO at Three Score and Ten: An Anticipatory Elegy." *Law & Liberty Forum*, 1 April 2019. https://lawliberty.org/forum/nato-at-three-score-and-ten-an-anticipatory-elegy/.

Mearsheimer, John J. 1990. "Back to the Future: Instability in Europe After the Cold War." *International Security* 15: 5–56.

———. 2019. "Bound to Fail: The Rise and Fall of the Liberal International Order." *International Security* 43: 7–50.

Meimeth, Michael, and Peter Schmidt. Forthcoming. "France, Germany and European Security: 'Building Castles in the Sky'?" In *Beyond Unification: Germany's Liberal Democracy Thirty Years Hence*, edited by John D. Robertson and Michael Oswald. Basingstoke: Palgrave Macmillan.

Mueller, John. 1990. *Retreat From Doomsday: The Obsolescence of Major War*. New York: Basic Books.

Nasr, Vali. 2013. *The Dispensable Nation: American Foreign Policy in Retreat*. New York: Doubleday.

Nelson, Keith. 1975. *Victors Divided: America and the Allies in Germany, 1918–1923*. Berkeley: University of California Press.

Pfaff, William. 1998/99. "The Coming Clash of Europe With America." *World Policy Journal* 15: 1–9.

Quessard, Maud, and Maya Kandel, eds. 2017. *Les États-Unis et la fin de la grande stratégie? Un bilan de la politique étrangère d'Obama* [The United States and the End of Grand Strategy? An Assessment of Obama's Foreign Policy]. Paris: Institut de Recherche Stratégique de l'École Militaire [Institute of Strategic Research, Military School].

Quessard, Maud, Frédéric Heurtebize, and Frédérick Gagnon, eds. 2020. *Alliances and Power Politics in the Trump Era: America in Retreat?* New York: Palgrave Macmillan.

Ratti, Luca. 2017. *A Not-So-Special Relationship: The US, the UK and German Unification, 1945–1990*. Edinburgh: Edinburgh University Press.

Sanger, David E. 2019. "As NATO Envoys Celebrate, Signs of Fracturing From Within." *New York Times*, 4 April 2019. www.nytimes.com/2019/04/04/us/politics/nato-anniversary.html?emc=edit_th_190405&nl=todaysheadlines&nlid=621718380405.

Sanger, David E., Catie Edmondson, David McCabe, and Thomas Kaplan. 2021. "Senate Poised to Pass Huge Industrial Policy Bill to Counter China." *New York Times*, 7 June 2021. www.nytimes.com/2021/06/07/us/politics/senate-china-semiconductors.html?campaign_id=2&emc=edit_th_20210607&instance_id=32417&nl=todays headlines&regi_id=62171838&segment_id=60059&user_id=23a0e0df85dc5b50fc649e ea833dabd0.

Sayle, Timothy Andrews. 2019. *Enduring Alliance: A History of NATO and the Postwar Global Order*. Ithaca: Cornell University Press.

Schmidt, Peter. 2019. «La conception allemande de la défense européenne» [The German Conception of European Defense]. *Défense & Stratégie* 44: 1–18.

Schwartz, David N. 1983. *NATO's Nuclear Dilemmas*. Washington: Brookings Institution.

Sloan, Stanley R. 2018. *Transatlantic Traumas: Has Illiberalism Brought the West to the Brink of Collapse?* Manchester: Manchester University Press.

———. 2020. *Defense of the West: Transatlantic Security from Truman to Trump*. 2nd ed. Manchester: Manchester University Press.

Sweig, Julia E. 2006. *Friendly Fire: Losing Friends and Making Enemies in the Anti-American Century*. New York: Public Affairs.

Tiersky, Ronald. 2018. "Macron's World: How the New President Is Remaking France." *Foreign Affairs* 97: 87–96.

Vincze, Hajnalka. 2021. "Germany's Transatlantic Ambiguities." Foreign Policy Research Institute. 5 March. www.fpri.org/article/2021/03/germanys-transatlantic-ambiguities/?utm_source.

von Hlatky, Stéfanie, and Michel Fortmann. 2020. "NATO Enlargement and the Failure of the Cooperative Security Mindset." *International Politics*, 8 May. https://doi.org/10.1057/s41311-020-00240-w.

Wallander, Celeste A. "NATO's Enemies Within: How Democratic Decline Could Destroy the Alliance." *Foreign Affairs* 97: 70–81.

Webber, Mark, James Sperling, and Martin A. Smith. 2021. *What's Wrong With NATO and How to Fix It*. Cambridge: Polity Press.

Wilkinson, David. 1999. "Unipolarity Without Hegemony." *International Studies Review* 1: 141–72.

Wintour, Patrick, and Dan Sabbagh. 2019. "Trump Blasts Macron Over 'Brain Dead' Nato Remarks." *The Guardian*, 3 December 2019. www.theguardian.com/world/2019/dec/03/trump-macron-brain-dead-nato-remarks.

Wright, Thomas J. 2017. *All Measures Short of War: The Contest for the Twenty-First Century and the Future of American Power*. New Haven: Yale University Press.

Yegin, Mehmet. 2019. "Turkey Between NATO and Russia: The Failed Balance." *SWP* [*Stiftung Wissenschaft und Politik* (Science and Politics Foundation)] *Comment* No. 30 (June). doi:10.18449/2019C30.

5
WHAT'S IN MY SANDWICH?

Trade, Values, and the Promise of Deeper Integration

Francesco Duina

Introduction

Trade is a major dimension of the transatlantic relationship. The United States (US) and the European Union (EU) have been close trading partners for decades. This is so even if we take into account the "banana wars" of the 1990s, the recent US steel and aluminum tariffs and EU countermeasures, and the long conflict over EU subsidies to the aviation industry. The relationship rests on solid and shared economic, legal, and political principles. In most cases, the two partners trade based on the World Trade Organization's (WTO) most-favored-nation regime, which has translated into low tariffs for many products. Much the same can be said about the EU-Canada trade relationship: Ties have been close and firmly grounded in shared guiding principles.

The recent negotiations over the Transatlantic Trade and Investment Partnership (TTIP) have shown, however, that major obstacles stand in the way of deeper integration. Begun in the 1990s and restarted in 2007, the negotiations suffered setbacks. They were relaunched in 2013. In 2017, after 15 rounds of efforts, they were finally abandoned. Similar observations apply to the Comprehensive Economic and Trade Agreement (CETA) between the EU and Canada: It suffered major setbacks along the way. Eventually signed in 2016, it is still awaiting ratification by 12 of the 27 EU national legislatures as of mid-2021. The outcome is far from guaranteed.

What have been the major obstacles? What do they say about the main challenges the partners will encounter moving forward? In addition, what steps should policymakers on both sides of the Atlantic take to preserve and deepen their relationship?

TTIP and CETA were pursued as part of a new generation of EU trade agreements across the world. Rather than aiming primarily for tariff reductions,

DOI:10.4324/9781003147565-8

those agreements seek substantive regulatory alignment around a wide variety of major and sensitive issues including food standards, consumer health, and investor rights. Such an alignment inevitably involves values. It therefore can acquire great symbolic and even moral significance. In the cases of TTIP and CETA, a variety of actors—from interest groups to citizen associations—mobilized in unprecedented fashion and presented demands. Their fierce opposition led to the collapse of TTIP and significant adjustments to CETA.

The lessons from TTIP and CETA are clear. Regulatory alignment will be a major challenge for the transatlantic partners moving forward. With that in mind, meaningful progress will depend on at least three factors. First, the Biden administration and the EU will need to resume talks on a comprehensive trade agreement or a set of more targeted agreements. These should, from the start, take into account the positions of EU civil and other actors on sensitive issues and grant those actors input from the outset. It might, of course, also mean choosing not to pursue deeper integration in certain sectors. Whether the US Congress will be interested in ratifying what may result from this remains an open question.

Second, any future agreement will need to cover key elements of the digital economy—a complex matter with tensions already mounting over the taxation of US companies, data protection, and consumer rights. It is important to note that on all these fronts it will be helpful for post-Brexit United Kingdom (UK) to reach compatible agreements—something that already seems likely to happen with Canada, as the two countries appear set to continue trading based on CETA. Third, competition from China and Asia more generally might provide the necessary incentives for the partners to make significant progress. The transatlantic relationship will inevitably evolve, in part at least, in reference to the rise of China and other countries.

This chapter is organized as follows: the first section describes the transatlantic trade relationship over the recent decades; the second section examines the EU's recent shift toward regulatory alignment with partners across the world and how this, inevitably, has involved values and thus the potential for significant public opposition; the third section considers the travailed histories of TTIP and CETA; and the final section reflects on the factors that are likely to shape the future of the transatlantic trade relationship, considering along the way the initiatives already taken by the Biden administration in the first half of 2021.

Strong and Growing: Transatlantic Trade Over Time

The US-EU trade relationship is the largest in the world. In 2019, the US represented the top export destination for EU goods: 18 percent of those exports, or €384 billion. The US in turn exported to the EU-27 €232 billion worth of goods.[1] If the UK is added to the EU-27 figures, the Office of the United States Trade Representative (USTR) reports the total for 2018 to be US$318 billion.[2] This made the EU the primary destination of US exports.[3] The EU is, in turn, Canada's second largest trading partner after the US (Hübner, Deman, and Balik

2017, 846), although Canada is, primarily because of its size, not a top-ten destination for EU products.

As to services, the USTR estimates that, in 2019, the total amount traded (imports and exports) with the EU-27 was US$346 billion, with the US running a surplus of US$54 billion.[4] The European Commission reports that the EU invests in the US eight times what it invests in India and China together.[5]

These impressive figures have been steadily increasing over time. If we take 2008 as a starting point, EU-28 exports of goods to the US increased by over 60 percent by 2018, while the US's exports to the EU-28 increased by approximately 35 percent.[6] While some of this growth may be attributable to national economies gaining in size, an environment of very low tariffs has also certainly had a significant impact. As the cost of trading has decreased, the volume of trade has grown.

The content of that trade also points to significant interdependencies. It is highly diversified across many industry sectors.[7] It includes both finished and component products—consistent with the fact that 70 percent of international trade in the world involves global value chains rather than complete products (OECD n.d.). Data indicate that the EU's participation in global value chains has increased greatly in recent years, and analysis by the International Monetary Fund points to the US as one of its major destinations (Huidrom et al. 2019, 12).

Of course, not everything has been smooth. Several trade disputes have been publicized over time. Although some have been between Canada and the EU, the more substantial ones have involved the US and the EU. Ultimately, however, the latter have concerned only about 2 percent of what is being traded.[8] Some readers may recall the "banana wars" of the 1990s and 2000s in which the US won its case at the WTO that the EU's favorable import terms for bananas from Caribbean countries were illegal (Barkham 1999). The EU aimed to help producers from those countries—mostly former colonies—export even if they faced more efficient competition from Latin American countries where US multinationals were able to produce bananas at lower costs. The US imposed hefty tariffs on the EU when it claimed the latter had not adjusted its approach. It took 20 years for the matter to be resolved (*BBC News* 2012).

More recently, tensions rose mostly as a result of the Trump administration's aggressive measures toward the EU. The US imposed tariffs on steel; the EU responded with countermeasures targeted at swing states and associated companies, such as Harley-Davidson (Blenkinsop 2020). The US also decided to impose tariffs on various goods (from aviation to food items) in response to the WTO's finding in 2019—after a 15-year dispute—that European countries illegally subsidized Airbus. The first tariffs came late that year, with the US announcing that it would rotate them across product lines to maximize their impact (Sardana 2020). In August 2020, the tariffs were further confirmed, despite EU officials' demands that they be dropped (Shalal and Shepardson 2020). Then, in October 2020, the WTO ruled that the EU had the right to impose US$4 billion of tariffs on US goods in response to subsidies to Boeing—something it proceeded to do the following month (*BBC News* 2020).

These are real disputes, but they remain minor in the context of the overall picture and often they are accompanied by announcements of positive news. Indeed, starting in August 2020, for the first time in more than 20 years, the US and the EU announced tariff reductions for hundreds of millions of dollars in exports. This included the elimination of EU tariffs on US live and frozen lobster products and a 50 percent reduction of US tariffs on products from prepared meals to propellant powders (European Commission 2020). Regarding retaliatory tariffs related to the airline industry, the new Biden administration (after announcing that it would seek to amend the US's relationship with the EU) made immediate progress: In June 2021, European Commission President Ursula von der Leyen announced, after meeting with President Joseph R. Biden, Jr., that tariffs would be suspended for five years, and a new Working Group on Aircraft would be formed to find a lasting solution (*CNBC* 2021). Earlier in December 2020, the UK announced that it would simply drop those tariffs (Jolly 2020).

Underpinning the relationship have been commitments to basic market and rule-of-law principles. The US, Canada, and the EU have been core supporters of the WTO. Even as the EU's 2006 "Global Europe" initiative heralded a new era of bilateral deals (consistent, of course, with WTO guidelines), the EU Commission made clear that the "EU is totally committed to the WTO and the multilateral trading system as its first priority" (European Commission 2006).

Over time, moreover, the three partners have promoted the so-called Washington consensus on free markets, open borders, and limited state intervention. The US drove all eight rounds of the General Agreement on Tariffs and Trade talks (the WTO's predecessor). Indeed, since the 1960s, open markets and trade liberalization have become centerpieces of US trade policy—albeit not always coherently—both at the global level and in the case of bilateral and regional agreements (Feinberg 2003, 1021–22). The same may be said of the EU: Its paramount position has been in favor of free trade (De Ville and Siles-Brügge 2018).

Politically, the partners have shared a commitment to democratic principles, human rights, and the protection of private property. They are stable democracies with limited corruption, high levels of transparency,[9] and relatively minor internal political tensions. They thus offer favorable climates for investments and long-term exchanges. Consistent with that, they rely on the international system of dispute settlement mechanisms—primarily in the WTO—to resolve differences with partners across the world. Indeed, the EU, the US, and Canada are the three parties that have launched the most cases through its adjudication system (they are also among the most active respondents),[10] although here we should also note the US's recent undermining of its appellate body, followed in any case by workarounds by the EU and Canada along with Norway (*Washington Post* 2019).

Simply put, then, the transatlantic relationship stands on solid grounds and is resilient. Internal tensions may seem at times to undermine it. Yet, on the whole, those are minor issues. At the same time, if the aim is to further deepen that partnership, serious challenges await. The subsequent sections expand on this point.

The Shift Toward Regulatory Alignment

During the last 20 years, the WTO appears to have gradually lost its usefulness for trade promotion. In part, this may have been a function of its own success at reducing tariffs across the world: From a weighted average of nearly 9 percent in the mid-1990s, when the WTO was launched, to below 3 percent in 2018.[11] The WTO noted that from 1996 to 2013 most member states greatly reduced or outright eliminated tariffs. Meanwhile, trade has substantially increased (WTO 2015). A primary objective has therefore been achieved and little more can be accomplished by way of tariff reductions.

The WTO also attempted, unsuccessfully, to pursue further integration when it launched the Doha Round in 2001. The spotlight turned to the remaining obstacles to trade, that is, quotas, subsidies, and disparate regulatory environments. Doha stalled multiple times and is, at the time of writing, essentially suspended. The primary reason has been a major conflict between developing countries and the richer economies of the Global North. The former refuse to open their markets as long as the latter subsidize their farmers and industries. Those subsidies, the argument has been, would destroy countless livelihoods in developing countries that cannot compete with the resulting lower prices that producers from richer countries can afford to sell their goods for.

In response, and also as part of a broader post-Cold War turn to neoliberal and open-market agendas, countries have sought to strike bilateral and regional trade deals. From around 28 in force in 1991, those deals numbered over 300 in 2020.[12] Many have reached beyond tariff reduction and include regulatory harmonization in selected areas (Bown 2017). As Young (2017) put it, starting especially in 2000, "trade governance" has shifted in both "form and substance" and has become "more about addressing the adverse effects of domestic policies, such as regulations, than about reducing traditional, at-the-border trade barriers, such as tariffs. Rather than 'shallow' agreements focused on at-the-border measures, economic integration became 'deeper,' tackling measures behind the border" (454).

The EU has been among the most active players in this new environment (Laursen and Roederer-Rynning 2017; Young 2016). It has embarked on negotiations with countries and trading blocs across the world—from India to Australia, ASEAN, Japan, New Zealand, Morocco, Mercosur, and Chile. The EU Commission lists nearly 80 such agreements in place at the time of writing—65 of which were completed from 2000 onward—and especially after 2006 and the launch of the Global Europe initiative. Dozens of others are being negotiated or ratified for adoption.[13]

The EU has justified tackling non-tariff barriers in many of these deals by stressing not only the economic benefits of wider market access but, crucially, the protection of its domestic approaches in sensitive areas such as the environment, labor rights, social rights, consumer health, and quality standards. Ideally, for the EU, deeper integration, in other words, means the "upping" of standards by the other parties to match its own standards. With this objective in mind, the 2009 Lisbon

Treaty—the major international agreement amending the constitutional basis of the EU—explicitly subjected the EU trade agreements to several higher-order principles—including human rights, natural resources sustainability, and environmental protection (Treaty on the Functioning of the European Union Article 207 and Treaty on European Union Article 21(2)).

Logically, this impressive wave of EU activity has attracted attention. Some scholars have described it as a novel way of striking international agreements (Wouters et al. 2015). Others have sought to understand with more precision the EU's motivations (see, for instance, Bossuyt 2009), including its desire to project power onto the world through regulation (Meunier and Nicolaïdis 2006). Yet others have questioned whether these agreements have had the desired effects on the EU's partners (see, for instance, Harrison et al. 2019). These have all been valuable contributions. What they have so far missed, however, is an appreciation for what we may call the cultural implications of this regulatory turn (for a partial exception, see DeVille and Siles-Brügge 2017, 1496) and thus the difficulties and opposition it can face. We can turn to economic sociology to delve deeper into this point.

As economic sociologists argue, market exchanges never occur in a void but are instead "embedded" in cultural contexts (Duina 2011; Granovetter 1985). Goods and services reflect and assert shared understandings of the world: There is always "more" to them than technical specifications. Histories, consumption patterns and rituals, advertisers, and other forces infuse them with a range of attributes, such as "good," "healthy," "environmentally sustainable," "risky," or "traditional" (Beardsworth and Bryman 1999; Brown 2011; Fourcade and Healy 2007). We may say that goods and services belong to wider webs of significance.

Market regulations from this perspective reify in formal ways many of the attributes of those goods and services. In so doing, they facilitate—rather than undermine, as sometimes economists believe—exchanges. Those regulations assert in binding ways what participants in a given marketplace believe in. Thus, particular cheeses must be produced in certain ways to receive certain denominations, doctors must undergo specialized training to become such, cars must have certain safety features, and advertisers cannot present consumers with false information. Understood this way, regulations are at once technical *and* cultural material: They affirm the values of a society. We may even say that market regulations have a moral quality—and that, in the last analysis, they are reflections of market participants' identities.

If so, the pursuit of regulatory alignment in bilateral trade deals logically has the potential to pivot around very sensitive matters. At stake are not only technical but also culturally salient issues. Alignment means harmonization and thus the elimination of differences: Gaps must be closed by having one or both parties depart from what in many cases has been established over a long period of time. The possibilities for opposition from public actors, and of course from impacted economic players, are great.

To be clear, this does not mean that all agreements will inevitably face difficulties. In some cases, highly sensitive matters are intentionally left off the table. With New

Zealand, for instance, the EU has opted for expediency and preemptively removed certain products from the negotiations. The US has taken a similar approach in its bilateral efforts. In other cases, the regulatory gap around sensitive areas is quite small—as with the EU and Japan, for instance, especially around food. In yet other cases, difficulties can be avoided when one of the partners is willing or expected to make most of the adjustments. Here, the case of South America's MERCOSUR, and its openness to EU rules, comes to mind.

However, some trade agreements will run into major difficulties. In this regard, TTIP and CETA are the two most clear and consequential examples. The problems with TTIP became so intractable that it was abandoned. CETA was eventually secured but not without great tensions and adjustments made in response to public pressures. The gaps were too large, the parties and their constituents too entrenched, and what was at stake was too important for alignment to occur. Civil society organizations, interest groups, and others mobilized in unprecedented fashion to oppose both deals (Duina 2019; Meunier and Czesana 2019).

The TTIP and CETA negotiations, of course, have been closely examined by scholars and observers alike. For the most part, however, explanations for the outcomes have been primarily technical. They have pointed to factors such as the institutional changes introduced by the Lisbon Treaty that have increased the likelihood of public scrutiny of EU trade initiatives, national parliamentary opposition, and resistance from the European Parliament (EP) (Grande and Hutter 2016; Gstöhl 2013, 6; Hübner, Deman, and Balik 2017, 845–48; Richardson 2012, 17). While valid, these accounts are not enough to explain TTIP's and CETA's suffered fates. Indeed, they suggest that major difficulties should be expected for *all* the EU's recent trade agreements across the world. In fact, only TTIP and CETA have encountered major problems. The following section explains why.

TTIP and CETA: A Clash of Values

The TTIP and CETA experiences point to the sorts of challenges from civil society organizations, economic actors, and interest groups that the partners can face when seeking to go beyond tariff reductions. The focus is on regulatory matters and, with those, the resulting clash of values. Attention turns to the most sensitive issue—food. In the case of CETA, however, an additional concern arose: The rights of international investors to challenge domestic regulations in areas such as the environment and labor rights. We proceed first by examining the differences in food regulatory frameworks between the transatlantic partners ahead of TTIP and CETA. These differences set the two sides on a collision course.

GMOs and Hormone Beef: Historical Divergences

In the two decades leading to TTIP and CETA, the EU developed an approach to GMOs and hormone beef that prioritized consumer and environmental health and traditional views on food over corporate interests (Acuti 2009). The EU followed the "precautionary" principle: A product should not be allowed into the marketplace unless there is scientific agreement on its safety. By contrast, the US and Canada developed essentially opposite regulatory stances. More risk-tolerant and business-oriented (Dudek 2015), they allowed products in the marketplace unless proof of their harmfulness could be rendered.

The EU's approach was shaped by the 1989 mad cow crisis. Hormone beef was then banned from the food supply chain,[14] while GMO products were effectively banned unless positive scientific proof could be given about their safety. In addition, the member states retained the ability to restrict the cultivation and sale of permitted GMOs. In 1999, a moratorium on all new GMOs was introduced. This was later replaced by a very restrictive approval process (Viju, Yeung, and Kerr 2012). To be sure, the EU's position did not emerge from seamless consensus among the member states. Countries such as France and Italy favored it, but others such as the Netherlands and the UK, more neoliberal and with less historical attachment to traditional agricultural and food methods, resisted it (Bernauer 2003, 45; Scholderer 2005). Thus, the EU itself had to undergo an internal process of confrontation and alignment.

During the same time period, the US and Canada developed liberal regimes. They allowed hormones and set low approval thresholds. Six could be used in the food production systems of both countries.[15] In turn, the US Food and Drug Administration classified GMOs as "generally recognized as safe" and treated them like any other food product, thus requiring no pre-market approval or special labeling.[16] Canadian regulators adopted a similar approach. The result was a marked contrast to the EU: Permissive and open and requiring evidence from those arguing that something should not enter the food chain.

Not surprisingly, tensions sparked repeatedly between the EU and its transatlantic counterparts in the years preceding TTIP and CETA (Dudek 2015). In the 2000s, Canada and the US argued at the WTO that the EU's GMO moratorium violated trade rules. This forced the EU to end the moratorium—although this meant only adopting a slightly less restrictive alternative (US Library of Congress 2015a). As for hormone beef, in 1989, the US imposed a US$93 million tariff on EU imports to protest its import ban. In 1996, the WTO ruled that the US and Canada had the right to impose sanctions on various EU products. In 2004, the EU challenged those sanctions. The WTO found all parties at fault (US Library of Congress 2015b). After the US raised tariffs again in 2009, the three parties signed memoranda of understanding foregoing sanctions on unrelated foods.[17] With that stalemate reached, the EU went into TTIP negotiations with a ban on hormone beef.

Conflicts and Failures

As the TTIP and CETA negotiations began, European civil society groups, small businesses, and farming associations feared that the EU Commission might open up the EU market to GMOs and hormone beef. The secrecy surrounding the negotiations intensified tensions. The public reaction was unprecedented and intensely set against both agreements.[18]

With TTIP, civil society groups set out early by requesting access to position papers, meeting lists, and correspondence (Gheyle and De Ville 2017). When negotiations restarted in 2013, "more than 80 organizations from the EU and the US wrote to the then Presidents Barack Obama, José Manuel Barroso and Herman Van Rompuy" demanding more transparency (Gheyle and De Ville 2017, 16). Massive street marches took place, with over 150,000 people demonstrating in Berlin in October 2015 (Delcker and Kroet 2015). By 2016, in Germany alone "a total of 310 cities, municipalities, counties, districts and regions [had] registered themselves with the Munich Environmental Institute as TTIP-free zones" (Deckstein, Salden, and Schießl 2016).

One of the most important European-level reactions involved a European Citizens' Initiative organized by Stop TTIP, a network of 483 organizations across Europe,[19] asking that TTIP and CETA negotiations come to an end. Supported by 148 civil society groups from 18 member states (Gheyle 2016, 6; Hübner, Deman, and Balik 2017), it collected over three million signatures. The European Commission rejected it in 2014.[20] However, that move was annulled by the Court of Justice of the EU in 2017. By then, CETA negotiations had ended, but those on the TTIP were still ongoing (European Commission 2017). As we shall see shortly, the EU Commission responded by undertaking an extensive public campaign to address the criticisms.

Civil groups mobilized against CETA early on too (Biuković 2012, 101). This was an unprecedented reaction. As Hübner, Deman, and Balik (2017) wrote, "the campaigns […] represent the largest cohesion amongst civil society in the EU's history" (853). They included Stop TTIP itself, which saw CETA as a potential precedent-setter for TTIP. The biggest opposition perhaps came from a European (and Canadian) network of 455 civil society groups which called for CETA's rejection in 2016. These included Greenpeace Europe, the European Federation of Public Service Unions, six national chapters of Friends of the Earth, Slow Food Italy, and other prominent organizations (see Seattle to Brussels Network 2016). Opposition came from local networks too. In early 2017, for instance, a coalition of Irish farmers, environmentalists, trade unionists, and small business associations asked their Members of the EP to stop CETA (see *Green News* 2017).

Once signed in 2016, CETA's ratification became highly contentious. "The battle for CETA," tweeted European Council President Donald Tusk, "was highly emotional" (*RT* 2016). It became, according to Paul Magnette, then minister-president of Belgium's Wallonia, a "soap opera" as the Wallonian government refused to approve it. "A four-letter word, CETA," Magnette wrote in *The Guardian*, "resonated on factory floors and offices, in homes, schools and cafes the length and breadth of Wallonia." Wallonia eventually relented but only after the Commission took the unprecedented step of negotiating with a member state's region. "That such an obscure topic as an economic and trade agreement should be the subject of such popular debate and controversy," continued Magnette, "is a phenomenon in itself" (Magnette 2016).

What can explain such difficulties? From the earliest stages, the key opponents adopted the language of European values, first in relation to TTIP and then to CETA, as the latter seemed increasingly likely to set the blueprint for the former. It is important to note that the EU itself also employed the language of values in explaining why it had decided to heed the protesters and not depart from the existing regulatory frameworks. We will consider the protesters' concerns first and then the EU's response.

Stop TTIP was perhaps the most vocal opponent. It used letters, videos, and demonstrations to depict multinational corporate interests as undermining what Europeans held dear and had secured in legislation over time. It described how the US industry was allowed "to use […] chlorine to disinfect chickens, to treat cattle with hormones, and to process genetically modified raw materials into foodstuffs." Letting those products into the EU would "be a huge gain for US agricultural conglomerates." As the Stop TTIP website explained,

> This is the reason that they are urging for European standards to be lowered. However, our standards were introduced for the protection of consumers, the environment, or animals, and they must not be forced out by a trade agreement! On the contrary: the public is discussing the raising of standards against factory farming, the use of chemicals, and in energy policies.[21]

The position was supported by major consumer-rights organizations such as foodwatch, with a presence in Germany, the Netherlands, and France. The organization's chief executive officer, Thilo Bode, described the transatlantic differences: "In Europe, nothing is allowed that is suspected of being hazardous to people's health" (as quoted in Deckstein, Salden, and Schießl 2016). In contrast, "in the US, there has to be a corpse, then things are regulated by litigation" (Deckstein, Salden, and Schießl 2016). Stop TTIP accordingly asked the EP in July 2015 to oppose TTIP and CETA because of their "lowering of standards" when it comes to the environment, social rights, consumers, and, with those, culture and democracy.[22]

Thus, TTIP generated an almost existential reaction. "The stakes," as War on Want, the UK-based anti-poverty charity stated, "could not be higher" (IER 2015). The regulatory "barriers" that the TTIP sought to remove "are in reality some of our most prized social standards and environmental regulations, such as labour rights, food safety rules (including restrictions on GMOs, regulations on the use of toxic chemicals)," and more.[23] Hence, when the EP trade committee agreed in May 2015 to have a resolution for a common position on TTIP be subject to a full parliamentary vote, John Hilary, War on Want's executive director, denounced the decision as treason:

> Millions of people across Europe have said no to TTIP, in the strongest trade campaign we have ever seen. Yet MEPs have turned their backs on their own

constituents, choosing instead to side with the business lobbyists of Brussels. This is an outright betrayal of the European people, and we shall not forget it.

IER 2015

CETA, too, was depicted with similar language, especially as it became clear it could potentially set a blueprint for the TTIP (Deckstein, Salden, and Schießl 2016). As with the TTIP, fears centered on GMOs and hormone beef. A 2016 open letter signed by 455 European and Canadian civil society groups calling for the rejection of CETA—and the most prominent initiative against ratification—offers an example (Seattle to Brussels Network 2016). It stated that "On both sides of the Atlantic, farmers, trade unions, public health, consumer, environmental […] groups, other NGOs [non-governmental organizations], as well as small and medium-sized enterprises (SMEs) have rejected the agreement." It then listed a number of "fundamental concerns," which included corporate greed, harm to consumers and product standards, harm to public health, and the ease with which the EU's precautionary principle could be challenged.

The alliance urged the EP (as well Canada's national and provincial legislatures) to broaden its dialogue to all concerned parties and develop the "foundations of a new, fair and sustainable trade agenda." Describing CETA as "an intrusive version of the old free trade agenda designed by and for the world's largest multinationals," it called for a "paradigm shift toward [… an] inclusive trade policy founded on the needs of our people and our planet."

The alliance worked in tandem with local groups. Events in Ireland, as already noted, provide an example. There, a coalition of over 80 civil society groups (unions, farmers, business owners, etc.) wrote a letter to the Irish members of the EP's Committee on Environment, Public Health and Food Safety, which gave its approval to CETA in 2017 ahead of the full parliamentary vote. One signatory (a Friends of the Earth manager) called the committee's vote "shocking." Another viewed it as "deeply disappointing given their remit for public health," and Canada's "lower standards." Yet another warned of the deal's "negative effect on public interest policies."[24]

The EU Commission could not ignore such unprecedented mobilization. It accordingly launched a counter-campaign addressing the concerns: The EU, it stressed, was resolute in its commitment to precisely the same values. We can consider TTP first. EU Trade Commissioner Cecilia Malmström logically became the leading voice for Europe. As she put it in 2016, debates on the TTIP have "focused very much on how to reconcile preserving identity and our individuality" (C-SPAN 2016). "Identity," she stressed, "hasn't always been part of trade negotiations, but [is] very much today" (see C-SPAN 2016). In a speech in Berlin in 2015, she made clear that "TTIP is just as much about responsibility [as it is about business]." That, she added, means ensuring that "European values [are] more protected not less so." In practical terms, Malmström reassured stakeholders that "TTIP will not change our laws on hormone beef and it will not change our laws on genetically modified food" (Malmström 2015). "I try to listen to the TTIP opponents," she stated, acknowledging that "sometimes they are worried that they will have to give up their European way of life" (see *Spiegel* 2015).

Karel De Gucht, European Commissioner for Trade from 2010 to 2014, had promised the same. In a January 2014 press release, he insisted that TTIP would be ratified only if it is "the right deal," something Europeans "consider worth supporting. A deal which pursues our interests and preserves our values" (European Commission 2014a). He then emphasized that "If – as a result of the negotiations – the EU was going to lower standards of protection for citizens regarding food or the environment […] if we were going to abandon our policy on genetically modified food or on beef hormones […] That would indeed be unacceptable" (European Commission 2014a). De Gucht stated that he knew that the EP "will not in the end approve a trade deal that undermines our European values or the social standards we have built over so many years" (European Commission 2014a). After meeting with US Trade Representative Michael Froman that same year, he promised that the TTIP would not become a "dumping agreement" and reaffirmed that "our standards on consumer protection, on the environment […] and on food are not up for negotiation" (European Commission 2014b; Harvey 2014).

In parallel, in 2016, the Commission published a factsheet, *Food Safety and Animal and Plant Health in TTIP*. It claimed the EU would adhere to "strict standards" with respect to GMOs, and "this will not change through TTIP." Moreover, "TTIP will not affect EU animal welfare laws." The EU will work with the US "to promote the highest standards of animal welfare possible."[25] No hormones would be allowed. "Tough EU laws designed to protect human life and health, animal health and welfare, or the environment and consumers," the sheet stressed, will not be changed "because of TTIP." The Commission also launched a TTIP-dedicated website with a Q&A section on the negotiations.[26]

Thus, the Commission also sought public input. Commissioner Malmström repeatedly affirmed that the EU negotiators were working with advisory groups comprising health, environmental, and other concerns. She noted that "people are interested in this deal [TTIP], more than any other deal in the past" (Malmström 2015). With this in mind, Commissioners reminded the public of their major 2013 Public Consultation effort on food involving roughly 43,000 EU citizens (Directorate-General for Agriculture and Rural Development 2013).

The Commission took similar steps with CETA. A key initiative was to ask Canada to commit to the Strategic Partnership Agreement—a document about fundamental values.[27] In 2015, it also made public the EU-Canada Trade Negotiating Mandate of 2009 and the accompanying negotiating directives, showing support for public, animal, and plant health (see Council of the European Union 2009, 2015). These were major public disclosures without precedent in EU history.

It was at this point that TTIP seemed finally doomed. The US had lost interest in what it excluded and the EU demanded, the incoming Trump administration practically abandoned it, and the EU formally walked away from the negotiating table. With CETA, as Canada seemed poised to accept the proposed requirements and those in the EU worried about food and other standards seemed somewhat reassured, concern grew over a second issue: The right of investors to sue local governments in case they felt discriminated against. The agreed-upon CETA text included a standard investor-state dispute settlement (ISDS) mechanism—common to many bilateral agreements—that made it easy for investors to take such actions. ISDS mechanisms historically have relied on ad-hoc panels, no appeals process, and no requirement to check for consistency with domestic laws after decisions are reached. As such, they can undermine regulations in areas like the environment, social rights, health, and food. Numerous civil society groups expressed their opposition. Some EU countries—including Germany, Austria, and France—announced they would reject CETA if any such mechanism was present (Hübner, Deman, and Balik 2017, 852–54).

When CETA was complete, it included an ISDS mechanism anyway. The reaction was fierce. The aforementioned dramatic events in Wallonia in 2016 were partly driven by this (Magnette 2016). CETA had, however, been finalized and could not be reopened for negotiations. Commissioner Malmström thus resorted to a legal "scrubbing" of the text that led to major changes. Among these were increased protection of national and EU laws, a permanent tribunal of independent judges, and an appeal system that allowed for legal correctness (European Commission 2016a).

As the final phases approached, the Commission praised its own accomplishments. "CETA ensures," it stated, that "economic gains do not come at the expense of consumer health and safety." "CETA," it continued, "will not affect food-related or environmental regulations in the EU […] Both the EU and Canada will keep the right to regulate freely in areas of public interest such as environment, health and safety" (European Commission 2016b). And the EU, according to EU Council President Tusk during the 16th EU-Canada Summit in 2016, stayed close to the people. "The battle for CETA," he said, showed how "important impressions and emotions are in the modern world […] The controversy around CETA has demonstrated that our first priority is to give people honest and convincing information about the real effects of free trade" (European Council 2016). The result, of course, was a diminished CETA in terms of regulatory reach and market penetration.

Conclusion: The Road Ahead

Vogel (1997) observed with considerable clairvoyance well ahead of TTIP and CETA that "Ironically, it is precisely because the EU and the US have so much in common and are so economically interdependent that they have clashed so frequently over each other's regulatory policies" (1). Thus, while the US and the EU have "an essential partnership," as Anthony Gardner (2020), President Barack Obama's ambassador to the EU, recently put it, their trade relationship remains vulnerable. The suffered fate of TTIP around regulatory alignment showed this. The Trump presidency, with its escalations of tariffs, did not help improve matters. TTIP is, of course, no longer in the cards. As we think about the future of transatlantic trade, and with CETA probably ratified at some point by all the member states, the spotlight turns to the Biden administration and its approach to the EU. We can close here by reflecting further on the three factors mentioned in the introduction that will likely shape the course of events.

First, and most obviously, the Biden administration has already signaled interest in closer economic ties with the EU. For real progress to be made, negotiations over one comprehensive trade agreement or the pursuit of more targeted ones will be necessary. In all cases, the lessons from TTIP and CETA will have to be kept squarely in mind. Since any future agreement will involve regulatory convergence in some areas at least, and given sensitivities in the EU especially around consumer protection, labor standards, environmental standards, and related issue areas, the Biden administration will face two very serious challenges. On the one hand, it will feel significant pressures from the EU to compromise on certain fronts: Civil society actors and other stakeholders will not allow for something different. On the other hand, any major agreement will require ratification in the US Congress. Here, Republicans but possibly some Democrats might have little appetite for significant regulatory adjustments or partial agreements that leave important economic sectors out of the equation. Thus, much will depend on how much political capital President Biden will be willing to spend on securing bipartisan support and, with that, how Republicans—many of whom remain committed to Trump's worldview—might react to his efforts.

Second, any future agreement will need to include provisions on the digital economy. Indeed, in June 2021, during Biden's first trip to Europe, the US and EU announced plans for a new Technology and Trade Council charged with devising new standards for emerging technologies and promoting democratic values (Wilkie 2021). More will come. However, the dynamics are bound to be very complex. The digital economy is rapidly increasing in size and constantly evolving. It is dominated by major US companies such as Facebook and Netflix. It is also a highly decentralized, non-tangible marketplace, with unclear boundaries, and numerous and varied supply and distribution channels. In addition, the EU has already launched its own concerted and multifaceted strategy (with the Digital Single Market Strategy, the Digital Markets Act, and Digital Services Act as centerpieces) for support and regulation. With all this in mind, the key regulatory issues will range from content to taxation, consumer rights, cultural preservation, anti-trust, and data control and use.

During President Biden's first trip to Europe in June 2021, various initiatives for collaboration and exchanges of ideas were explored. However, how, exactly, progress on the digital economy can be made remains a major question. Inevitably, we will see, once again, tensions rise between the need for convergence and the existence of divergent values and cultural understandings across the Atlantic. At the most basic level, it is practically certain that US big-tech companies will have to be regulated more than they are currently in the US—although in the US itself further regulation is likely coming, given bipartisan interest in it. Uncertainties on this front thus abound.

Third, we should recognize that powerful incentives for common ground may come not necessarily from within the transatlantic relationship but from the outside. This is in the form of competition in two regards. First, trade initiatives in other parts of the world are also deepening ties among countries. This will likely make the transatlantic partners more eager to find common ground. As it turns out, some of these partnerships involve one or more of the transatlantic partners themselves. The US's "pivot to Asia" under the Obama administration, for instance, and its participation in the Trans-Pacific Partnership negotiations (in which Canada also participated) in the late 2000s and through most of the 2010s is an important example. It undoubtedly encouraged the EU to seek closer integration with the US. The EU's dynamic pursuit of other trade agreements has had the same effect on the US (Griffith, Steinberg, and Zysman 2017, 579–80). The impact of these developments on transatlantic cooperation cannot be underestimated.

Second, and more importantly, China's rise as a political and economic superpower presents the EU, the US, and Canada with a serious strategic dilemma. If one or more of the partners wish to contain, challenge, or even confront China, deepening economic integration across the Atlantic is likely part of what must be done. The Trump administration's tough stances toward the EU and China may suggest otherwise: The US appeared inclined to assert itself unilaterally. However, history teaches that such positions are dangerous and not tenable long term. Indeed, President Biden indicated in his foreign policy speech in February 2021 that he intends to revitalize the US's ties to Europe (*Nikkei* 2021). In his June 2021 European trip, he followed that with explicit mentions of competition with China as a major reason for the US's renewed interest in collaborating with the EU. To this, we can add that, as India and other economies (many of them in Asia) grow, the need for further investment in the transatlantic partnership will make itself ever more obvious (Polyakova and Haddad 2019).

The necessity for a deepening of trade relations is thus quite clear. If and how this can be accomplished will depend on a number of complex challenges and developments.

Notes

1 https://ec.europa.eu/eurostat/statistics-explained/index.php/USA-EU_-_internationa l_trade_in_goods_statistics#:~:text=The%20trade%20surplus%20remained%20through out,2009%20(EUR%20169%20billion).
2 https://ustr.gov/countries-regions/europe-middle-east/europe/european-union#:~:text=U.S.%20goods%20and%20services%20trade,was%20%24109%20bill ion%20in%202018.
3 https://ustr.gov/countries-regions/americas/canada#:~:text=U.S.%20exports%20to%20 Canada%20account,and%20plastics%20(%2414%20billion.
4 https://ustr.gov/countries-regions/europe-middle-east/europe/european-union#:~:text=U.S.%20goods%20and%20services%20trade,was%20%24109%20bill ion%20in%202018.

5 https://ec.europa.eu/trade/policy/countries-and-regions/countries/united-states/#:~:text=Trade%20picture&text=EU%20investment%20in%20the%20US,both%20sides%20of%20the%20Atlantic.
6 https://ec.europa.eu/eurostat/statistics-explained/index.php?title=File:Imports,_exports_and_balance_for_trade_in_goods_between_the_EU-28_and_the_United_States,_2008-2018.png&oldid=428756.
7 https://ustr.gov/countries-regions/europe-middle-east/europe/european-union#:~:text=The%20United%20States%20had%20a,goods%20imports%20totaled%20%24488%20billion.&text=Services%20exports%20were%20%24256%20billion%3B%20Services%20imports%20were%20%24196%20billion.
8 https://ec.europa.eu/trade/policy/countries-and-regions/countries/united-states/.
9 www.transparency.org/en/cpi#.
10 www.wto.org/english/tratop_e/dispu_e/dispu_by_country_e.htm.
11 https://data.worldbank.org/indicator/TM.TAX.MRCH.WM.AR.ZS.
12 http://rtais.wto.org/UI/PublicMaintainRTAHome.aspx.
13 https://ec.europa.eu/trade/policy/countries-and-regions/negotiations-and-agreements/.
14 For the key priorities, see the Commission's 2002 European General Food Law, the earlier white paper on feed (Commission of the European Communities 2000), and Article 100a EEC of the Single European Act (Coggi and Deboyser 2016).
15 Estrogen, progesterone, testosterone, zeranol, melengestrol acetate, and trenbolone acetate.
16 For a summary of the US approach, see Lau (2015).
17 See http://trade.ec.europa.eu/doclib/press/index.cfm?id=685 and http://trade.ec.europa.eu/doclib/press/index.cfm?id=126.
18 This section draws from Duina (2019) and Duina and Smith (2019) for data and insights.
19 See https://stop-ttip.org/about-stop-ttip/.
20 http://ec.europa.eu/citizens-initiative/public/initiatives/non-registered/details/204.
21 See https://stop-ttip.org/what-is-the-problem-ttip-ceta/faqs/.
22 https://stop-ttip.org/wp-content/uploads/2015/07/Letter-to-MEPs-general-UK2.pdf.
23 https://waronwant.org/ttip.
24 http://environmentalpillar.ie/wp/wp-content/uploads/2017/01/ENVI-letter-final-Irish-version.pdf?utm_source=Press+release+CETA+group+letter+&utm_campaign=PR+CETA+GROUP+LETTER&utm_medium=email.
25 See http://trade.ec.europa.eu/doclib/docs/2015/january/tradoc_153004.3%20Food%20safety,%20a+p%20health%20(SPS).pdf.
26 See http://ec.europa.eu/trade/policy/in-focus/ttip/about-ttip/questions-and-answers/index_en.htm.
27 See https://eeas.europa.eu/headquarters/headquarters-homepage_en/13529/EU-Canada%20Strategic%20Partnership%20Agreement.

References

Acuti, Elena. 2009. "EU Safety Policy and Public Debate." In *The Search for a European Identity: Values, Policies and Legitimacy of the European Union*, edited by F. Cerutti and S. Lucarelli, 93–107. London: Routledge.

Barkham, Patrick. 1999. "The Banana Wars Explained." *The Guardian*, 5 March 1999. www.theguardian.com/world/1999/mar/05/eu.wto3.

BBC News. 2012. "Banana War Ends After 20 Years." 8 November 2012. www.bbc.com/news/business-20263308.

———. 2020. EU Imposes Tariffs on $4bn of US Goods in Boeing Row." 9 November 2020. www.bbc.com/news/business-54877337.

Beardsworth, Alan, and Alan Bryman. 1999. "Late Modernity and the Dynamics of Quasification: The Case of the Themed Restaurant." *The Sociological Review* 47 (2): 228–57.

Bernauer, Thomas. 2003. *Genes, Trade, and Regulation: The Seeds of Conflict in Food Biotechnology*. Princeton, NJ: Princeton University Press.

Biuković, Ljiljana. 2012. "Transparency Norms, the World Trade System and Free Trade Agreements: The Case of CETA." *Legal Issues of Economic Integration* 39 (1): 93–107.

Blenkinsop, Philip. 2020. "Analysis: EU Sees No Abrupt End to Trump Tariffs When Biden Takes Charge." *Reuters*, 8 December 2020. www.reuters.com/article/eu-usa-trade-analysis/analysis-eu-sees-no-abrupt-end-to-trump-tariffs-when-biden-takes-charge-idUSKBN28I20C.

Bown, Chad P. 2017. "Mega-Regional Trade Agreements and the Future of the WTO." *Global Policy* 8: 107–12.

Bossuyt, Fabienne. 2009. "The Social Dimension of the New Generation of EU FTAs With Asia and Latin America: Ambitious Continuation for the Sake of Policy Coherence." *European Foreign Affairs Review* 14 (5): 703–22.

Brown, Keith R. 2011. "Interaction Ritual Chains and the Mobilization of Conscientious Consumers." *Qualitative Sociology* 34 (1): 121–41.

Coggi, Paola T., and Patrick Deboyser. 2016. "The European Food Safety Authority: A View From the European Commission." In *Foundations of EU Food Law and Policy: Ten Years of the European Food Safety Authority*, edited by A. Alemanno and S. Gabbi, 195–205. Farnham: Routledge.

Commission of the European Communities. 2000. *White Paper on Food Safety*. https://eur-lex.europa.eu/legal-content/EN/TXT/?uri=LEGISSUM%3Al32041.

Council of the European Union. 2009. 2009 Negotiating Directives for an Economic Integration Agreement with Canada. http://data.consilium.europa.eu/doc/document/ST-9036-2009-EXT-2/en/pdf.

———. 2015. "EU-Canada Trade Negotiating Mandate Made Public." 15 December. www.consilium.europa.eu/en/press/press-releases/2015/12/15/eu-canada-trade-negotiating-mandate-made-public/.

C-SPAN. 2016. "Cecelia Malmstrom Says TPP Negotiations Will Move Forward After 'Brexit' Vote.' Video, 3:40. 30 June. www.c-span.org/video/?c4608594/cecilia-malmstrom-tpp-negotiations-move-forward-brexit-vote&start=561.

CNBC. 2021. "U.S. and EU Resolve 17-Year-Old Boeing-Airbus Trade Dispute." 15 June. www.cnbc.com/2021/06/15/us-and-eu-truce-boeing-airbus-dispute.html.

De Ville, Ferdi, and Gabriel Siles-Brügge. 2017. "Why TTIP Is a Game-Changer and Its Critics Have a Point." *Journal of European Public Policy* 24 (10): 1491–1505.

———. 2018. "The Role of Ideas in Legitimating EU Trade Policy: From the Single Market Programme to the Transatlantic Trade and Investment Partnership." In *Handbook on the EU and International Trade*, 243–62, edited by Sangeeta Khorana and María García. Cheltenham: Edward Elgar.

Deckstein, Dinah, Simone Salden, and Michaela Schießl. 2016. "The TTIPing Point: Protests Threaten Trans-Atlantic Trade Deal." *Spiegel ONLINE*, 6 May 2016. www.spiegel.de/international/world/protest-movement-threatens-ttip-transatlantic-trade-deal-a-1091088.html.

Delcker, Janosch, and Cynthia Kroet. 2015. "More Than 150,000 Protest Against EU-US Trade Deal." *Politico*, 9 October 2015. www.politico.eu/article/germany-mobilizes-against-eu-u-s-trade-deal-merkel-ttip-ceta/.

Directorate-General for Agriculture and Rural Development. 2013. *Report on the Results of the Public Consultation on the Review of the EU Policy on Organic Agriculture*. https://ec.eur opa.eu/agriculture/sites/agriculture/files/consultations/organic/final-report-full-text_en.pdf.

Dudek, Carolyn. 2015. "GMO Food Regulatory Frameworks in the US and the EU." In *The New and Changing Transatlanticism: Politics and Policy Perspectives*, edited by L. Buonanno, N. Cuglesan, and K. Henderson, 214–32. New York: Routledge.

Duina, Francesco. 2011. *Institutions and the Economy*. Cambridge: Polity Press.

———. 2019. "Why the Excitement? Values, Identities, and the Politicization of EU Trade Policy with North America." *Journal of European Public Policy* 26 (12): 1866–82.

Duina, Francesco, and Ezekiel Smith. 2019. "Affirming Europe with Trade: Deal Negotiations and the Making of a Political Identity." *Comparative European Politics* 17 (4): 491–511.

European Commission. 2006. New Strategy Puts EU Trade Policy at Service of European Competitiveness and Economic Reform. 4 October. https://ec.europa.eu/commission/presscorner/detail/en/IP_06_1303.

———. 2014a. "Stepping Up a Gear." http://europa.eu/rapid/press-release_STATEMENT-14-12_en.htm.

———. 2014b. "The Transatlantic Trade and Investment Partnership: Where Do We Stand on the Hottest Topics in the Current Debate?" http://europa.eu/rapid/press-release_SPEECH-14-52_en.htm.

———. 2016a. "CETA: EU and Canada Agree on New Approach on Investment in Trade Agreement." 29 February. https://ec.europa.eu/commission/presscorner/detail/lt/IP_16_399.

———. 2016b. *Comprehensive Economic and Trade Agreement (CETA)*. http://ec.europa.eu/trade/policy/in-focus/ceta/index_en.htm.

———. 2017. "European Citizens' Initiative: Commission Registers 'Stop TTIP' Initiative." http://europa.eu/rapid/press-release_IP-17-1872_en.htm.

———. 2020. Joint Statement of the United States and the European Union on a Tariff Agreement. 21 August. https://ec.europa.eu/commission/presscorner/detail/en/statement_20_1512.

European Council. 2016. "Remarks by President Donald Tusk at the 16th EU-Canada Summit." 30 October. www.consilium.europa.eu/en/press/press-releases/2016/10/30/tusk-remarks-eu-canada-summit/

Feinberg, Richard E. 2003. "The Political Economy of United States' Free Trade Arrangements." *World Economy* 26 (7): 1019–40.

Fourcade, Marion, and Kieran Healy. 2007. "Moral Views of Market Society." *Annual Review of Sociology* 33: 285–311.

Gardner, Anthony Luzzatto. 2020. *The Essential Partnership between the European Union and the United States*. Cham: Palgrave.

Gheyle, Niels. 2016. "Trade policy With the Lights On: Linking Trade and Politicization." Paper presented at EU Trade Policy at the Crossroads: Vienna Conference on EU Trade Policy. Vienna, 4–6 February 2016. https://biblio.ugent.be/publication/7104966/file/7104968.pdf.

Gheyle, Niels, and Ferdi DeVille. 2017. "How Much Is Enough? Explaining the Continuous Transparency Conflict in TTIP." *Politics and Governance* 5 (3): 16–28.

Grande, Edgar, and Swen Hutter. 2016. "Beyond Authority Transfer: Explaining the Politicisation of Europe." *West European Politics* 39 (1): 23–43.

Granovetter, Mark. 1985. "Economic Action and Social Structure: The Problem of Embeddedness." *American Journal of Sociology* 91 (3): 481–510.

The Green News. 2017. "Over 80 Irish Civil Society Groups, Including Unions, Farmers and Business Owners, Are Calling on MEPs to Reject the EU Canada Trade Deal." 13 January 2017. https://greennews.ie/over-80-irish-civil-society-groups-including-unions-farmers-and-business-owners-are-calling-on-meps-to-reject-the-eu-canada-trade-deal/.

Griffith, Melissa K., Richard H. Steinberg, and John Zysman. 2017. "From Great Power Politics to a Strategic Vacuum: Origins and Consequences of the TPP and TTIP." *Business and Politics* 19 (4), 573–92. https://doi.org/10.1017/bap.2017.16.

Gstöhl, Sieglinde. 2013. "The European Union's Trade Policy." *Ritsumeikan International Affairs* 11: 1–22.

Harrison, James, Mirela Barbu, Liam Campling, Ben Richardson, and Adrian Smith. 2019. "Governing Labour Standards Through Free Trade Agreements: Limits of the European Union's Trade and Sustainable Development Chapters." *Journal of Common Market Studies* 57: 260–77.

Harvey, Fiona. 2014. "EU Under Pressure to Allow GM food Imports From US and Canada." *The Guardian*, 5 September 2014. www.theguardian.com/environment/2014/sep/05/eu-gm-food-imports-us-canada.

Hübner, K., Anne-Sophie Deman, and Tugce Balik. 2017. "EU and Trade Policymaking: The Contentious Case of CETA." *Journal of European Integration* 39 (7): 843–57.

Huidrom, Raju, Nemanja Jovanovic, Carlos Mulas-Granados, Laura Papi, Faezeh Raei, Emil Stavrev, and Philippe Wingender. 2019. *Trade Tensions, Global Value Chains, and Spillovers: Insights for Europe*. International Monetary Fund Departmental Paper Series No. 19/10.

Institute of Employment Rights (IER). 2015. "TTIP Update: MEP Trade Committee Backs TTIP." 29 May. www.ier.org.uk/news/ttip-update-mep-trade-committee-backs-ttip/.

Jolly, Jasper. 2020. "UK Drops EU Tariffs on Boeing as It Seeks Post-Brexit Trade Deal With US." *The Guardian*, 9 December 2020. www.theguardian.com/business/2020/dec/09/uk-drops-eu-tariffs-on-boeing-as-it-seeks-post-brexit-trade-deal-with-us-joe-biden?CMP=Share_AndroidApp_Other.

Lau, Jessica. 2015. "Same Science, Different Policies: Regulating Genetically Modified Foods in the U.S. and Europea" (blog). *Science in the News* (Harvard University). 9 August. https://sitn.hms.harvard.edu/flash/2015/same-science-different-policies/.

Laursen, Finn, and Christilla Roederer-Rynning. 2017. "Introduction: The New EU FTAs as Contentious Market Regulation." *Journal of European Integration* 39 (7): 763–79.

Malmström, Cecelia. 2015. *TTIP: Freedom and Responsibility*. http://europa.eu/rapid/press-release_SPEECH-15-4473_en.htm.

Magnette, Paul. 2016. "Wallonia Blocked a Harmful EU Trade Deal – But We Don't Share Trump's Dreams." *The Guardian*, 14 November 2016. www.theguardian.com/commentisfree/2016/nov/14/wallonia-ceta-ttip-eu-trade-belgium.

Meunier, Sophie, and Rozalie Czesana. 2019. "From Back Rooms to the Street? A Research Agenda for Explaining Variation in the Public Salience of Trade Policy-Making in Europe." *Journal of European Public Policy* 26 (12): 1847–65.

Meunier, Sophie, and Kalypso Nicolaïdis. 2006. "The European Union as a Conflicted Trade Power." *Journal of European Public Policy* 13 (6): 906–25.

Nikkei. 2021. "Transcript: President Joe Biden Delivers Foreign Policy Speech." 5 February 2021. https://asia.nikkei.com/Politics/Transcript-President-Joe-Biden-delivers-foreign-policy-speech.

Organisation for Economic Co-operation and Development (OECD). n.d. "Global Value Chains and Trade." www.oecd.org/trade/topics/global-value-chains-and-trade/.

Polyakova, Alina, and Benjamin Haddad. 2019. "Europe Alone: What Comes After the Transatlantic Alliance." *Foreign Affairs* 98 (July): 109–12, 114–20.

Richardson, Laura. 2012. "The Post-Lisbon Role of the European Parliament in the EU's Common Commercial Policy: Implications for Bilateral Trade Negotiations." EU Diplomacy Paper No. 5. College of Europe, Department of EU international Relations and Diplomacy Studies.

RT. 2016. "Controversial CETA Deal Signed as Protesters Storm European Council in Brussels." 30 October 2016. www.rt.com/news/364743-ceta-canada-eu-signed-protest/.

Sardana, Saloni. 2020. "US Weighing New Tariffs on $3.1 Billion of European Goods, With Products Like Olives, Beer, Gin, and Planes on the List." *Business Insider*, 24 June 2020. https://markets.businessinsider.com/news/stocks/trade-war-us-tariffs-europe-3-billion-new-notice-2020-6-1029337397.

Scholderer, Joachim. 2005. "The GM Foods Debate in Europe: History, Regulatory Solutions, and Consumer Response Research." *Journal of Public Affairs* 5 (4): 263–74.

Seattle to Brussels Network. 2016. "European and Canadian Civil Society Groups Call for Rejection of CETA." 28 November. http://s2bnetwork.org/european-canadian-civil-society-groups-call-rejection-ceta/.

Shalal, Andrea, and David Shepardson. 2020. "U.S. Leaves Tariffs on Airbus Aircraft Unchanged at 15%." *Reuters*, 12 August 2020. www.reuters.com/article/us-usa-trade-eu/u-s-leaves-tariffs-on-airbus-aircraft-unchanged-at-15-idUSKCN2582WO.

Spiegel. 2015. "How a Trans-Atlantic Trade Deal Can Still Be Fixed." 6 August 2015. www.spiegel.de/international/world/how-ttip-and-an-eu-us-free-trade-deal-can-be-fixed-a-1036831.html.

US Library of Congress. 2015a. "Restrictions on Genetically Modified Organisms." www.loc.gov/law/help/restrictions-on-gmos/eu.php.

———. 2015b. Congressional Research Service. *The U.S.-EU Beef Hormone Dispute*, by Renée Johnson. R40449. 14 January. https://fas.org/sgp/crs/row/R40449.pdf.

Viju, Crina, May T. Yeung, and William A. Kerr. 2012. "The Trade Implications of the Post-Moratorium European Union Approval System for Genetically Modified Organisms." *Journal of World Trade* 46 (5): 1207–37.

Vogel, David. 1997. *Barriers or Benefits?: Regulation in Transatlantic Trade*. Washington, DC: Brookings Institution Press.

Washington Post. 2019. "How Trump Is Sabotaging Trades Ultimate Tribunal: QuickTake." 6 December 2019. www.washingtonpost.com/business/how-trump-is-sabotaging-trades-ultimate-tribunal-quicktake/2019/12/06/2a501aa2-1806-11ea-80d6-d0ca7007273f_story.html.

Wilkie, Christina. 2021. "America and Europe Will Create a Joint Tech Council to Craft New Rules on Trade." *CNBC*, 15 June 2021. www.cnbc.com/2021/06/15/america-and-eu-will-join-forces-to-craft-new-rules-on-trade-and-tech.html.

World Trade Organization (WTO). 2015. *Trade and Tariffs: Trade Grows as Tariffs Decline*. www.wto.org/english/thewto_e/20y_e/wto_20_brochure_e.pdf.

Wouters, Jan, Axel Marx, Dylan Geraets, and Bregt Natens. 2015. *Global Governance Through Trade*. Leuven Global Governance Series. Cheltenham: Edward Elgar.

Young, Alisdair R. 2016. "Not Your Parents' Trade Politics: The Transatlantic Trade and Investment Partnership Negotiations." *Review of International Political Economy* (23) 3: 345–78.

———. 2017. "The Politics of Deep Integration." *Cambridge Review of International Affairs* 30 (5–6): 453–63.

6
HUMAN RIGHTS IN US AND EU FOREIGN POLICIES

Joe Renouard

Introduction

By conventional wisdom, the transatlantic community is bound by robust economic ties, a long-standing collective security framework, and profound historical and cultural connections. However, beyond shared interests, is it also (and perhaps first) a community of shared democratic values? Do these states take seriously the call to promote human rights and democracy globally? In short, what does the transatlantic community stand for?

This chapter addresses human rights in United States (US) and European Union (EU) foreign policy. It describes US and European approaches to the promotion of human rights and democracy, scholarly perspectives on their policies and self-perceptions, and the significance of values and norms in their respective political systems and foreign policies. Three claims stand out in this narrative. First, contrary to those who insist on divergence in values and a widening transatlantic cultural gap, polling data and other sources suggest that Americans and Europeans do, in fact, share a set of fundamental beliefs and expectations about democracy, human rights, and the rule of law. Second, the US and EU do quite a lot—certainly much more than just about any other governments on Earth—to promote human rights and democracy. In a world where neither law nor custom requires governments to take this enterprise seriously, the US and EU are among the few that do. Third, differences in the approaches of the US and EU to human rights and democracy have less to do with values and more to do with the transatlantic power imbalance, US military primacy, occasional economic competition, the US's preference for unilateralism and hard-power solutions, and the agendas and personal styles of leaders (especially those who are more conservative or nationalistic). Because the US has taken on more security obligations than the EU, it is more likely to be accused of human rights violations in the pursuit of US interests, and it is somewhat

DOI:10.4324/9781003147565-9

more reluctant to take up human rights causes, especially in multilateral settings. Both face difficulties in claiming to lead on international human rights. The US's domestic problems and its inconsistent record of rights promotion have created a legitimacy problem for Washington, while the EU faces many obstacles in overcoming member states' parochial national interests and in building a strong, unified European foreign policy.

US and EU Approaches to International Human Rights

Human rights have a deep and complex history in Europe and the US, but it was only relatively recently that Western nations made international rights promotion part of their foreign policies. As a world power with a strong liberal tradition, the US has often taken a leading role in international human rights matters. This activism took shape in the post-war years of the 1940s before dissipating amid the Cold War tensions of the 1950s and 1960s. The real watershed was the 1970s and 1980s, when non-governmental organizations (NGOs) expanded in number and influence, and Congress began to challenge presidential foreign policy by setting human rights conditions for the nation's bilateral relationships. Beginning with President Jimmy Carter (1977–81), the executive branch then employed diplomacy, sanctions, and public criticisms to promote human rights in other states. The US government took on a wide array of causes in this era, including torture and political imprisonment in South America, persecution of Jews in the Soviet Union, civil wars in Central America, apartheid in South Africa, and state violence in China (Bradley 2016; Moyn 2010; Renouard 2016; Snyder 2018). Since that time, human rights requirements and bureaucratic institutions have been part of US foreign policy.

However, Americans also have a long history of zealously guarding their sovereignty and harboring a deep suspicion of multilateralism. The US's status as an economic and military superpower means that there may be little to gain and much to lose—including the possibility of politicized cases against Americans in international courts—by supporting some human rights causes and conventions. Unlike the EU, the US possesses a formidable military with global power projection capabilities, and between the Cold War era and the War on Terror, activists have accused US soldiers and covert operatives of human rights violations. Therefore, although Americans generally support the rule of law domestically and internationally, the US government routinely rejects the jurisdiction of international courts. Moreover, whereas EU member states' human rights approaches are strongly influenced and limited by the EU, the Council of Europe, and the Organization for Security and Cooperation in Europe, the US is not subject to the rules of a supranational organization or a regional human rights court (Forsythe 2000a, 2).

Much of the scholarship on this subject suggests that the US's approach to human rights is ambivalent, inconsistent, and even hypocritical, and that US policy does not live up to the nation's high ideals or to its deep domestic appreciation for individual liberties and the rule of law. Scholars point to the "paradoxical legacy" of US policy pursuits and the tendency toward "bait and switch" and "mixed signals" (Apodaca 2006; Forsythe 2000b, 145–48; Mertus 2004; Sikkink 2004). From the left, one hears much about US support of autocrats in the pursuit of economic and security interests (Chomsky 2004, 112–13). From the right, one hears that US leaders should eschew liberal universalism and instead separate values from interests and treat friends better than adversaries (Tillerson 2017). From realists and other skeptics, one hears that human rights claims are window dressing for naked national ambition, that the US's external orientation is highly militaristic ("perpetual war for perpetual peace"), and that the US acts much like other states in the pursuit of its interests (Bacevich 2010; Haas 2008, 268; Walt 2011). Murphy (2009) described three antinomies, or contradictory principles, which help explain US ambivalence in international human rights. The first is the conflict between institutionalism and realism in the pursuit of the nation's interests. The second is the conflict between the US as "responsible global actor," which engages with states based on sovereign equality and uniform rules, and the US as "exceptional nation," which shuns the limits of international law and institutions. And third is the conflict between a universalist willingness to embed US national law into international law and the exceptionalist defense of the autonomy of the US legal system (Murphy 2009, 49).

Criticism of US human rights efforts parallels suspicion of American exceptionalism (Hodgson 2009, 124–27, 153–54). Forsythe and McMahon (2017) noted that the US is willing to ignore human rights violations when other interests prevail. US foreign policy, they argued, is best described as "liberalized realism"—a kind of liberal internationalism that is implemented "when convenient" based on the context, the interests involved, and the ability to get results (Forsythe and McMahon 2017, ix, 5, 7). Donnelly and Whelan (2020) documented the Trump administration's deflating of exceptionalist myths and concluded that "it would only be a slight exaggeration to say that today the United States has no international human rights policy" (174). In addition, as Bradley (2018) noted, one could chart the "ever-diminishing place of the United States in the making of a global human rights order" long before Donald J. Trump's appearance on the political scene (331).

Others are willing to credit the US with doing at least *something* on behalf of human rights in—as the structural realists insist—an anarchic world with only limited global governance and in which states are compelled to prioritize security and economics in the pursuit of power. Far from ignoring human rights and humanitarian norms, the US has taken them seriously enough to legally require their consideration in bilateral relations, sometimes even to the point of conflict with other interests (Renouard 2016; Snyder 2018; Walldorf 2008). Whereas a relatively clear set of treaty clauses defines the EU's democracy and human rights promotion obligations, the legal and institutional basis of US human rights policy grows from congressional legislation and presidential initiatives. Since the 1970s, Congress has attached human rights conditions to a wide array of bilateral arrangements, including aid allocation, trade agreements, and export decisions (the Foreign

Assistance Act, the International Security Assistance and Arms Export Control Act), although there are loopholes for strategic and other reasons. Congress has denied most-favored-nation trade status to countries (e.g., the 1974 Jackson-Vanik Amendment), issued trade sanctions (e.g., the Comprehensive Anti-Apartheid Act of 1986), and required the president to promote religious freedom (International Religious Freedom Act of 1998), address human trafficking, and punish purveyors of "blood diamonds," among many other directives (Haas 2008, 258–66). The US's legal system has provided a forum for victims from other countries to take their abusers to court based on the principle of universal jurisdiction (Haas, 236–51). US courts have allowed limited use of the Alien Tort Statute for cases involving egregious violations outside the US, although in recent years the Supreme Court has limited the applicability of the statute (*Kiobel* 2013).

Congress and the executive branch have also created a human rights bureaucracy. The State Department's Bureau of Democracy, Human Rights, and Labor oversees human rights and democracy promotion activities and produces annual human rights reports on every country and region. The department also produces detailed annual reports on human trafficking and religious freedom. The National Security Council includes an office of human rights and democracy promotion that falls under the president's purview. Other agencies that carry out democracy promotion work include the United States Agency for International Development (USAID), the US-Middle East Partnership Initiative, and the government-funded private granting institution, the National Endowment for Democracy.

The US uses a wide array of tools to promote human rights, ranging from the persuasive to the coercive. On the discursive side of the ledger are private diplomacy ("constructive engagement"), public diplomacy (public statements of support or criticism), joint statements with other governments, calls for international investigations, and participation in international investigations. On the coercive side are cancelation of official visits, limits to cultural contacts, recall of diplomats, expulsion of diplomats, freezing assets, banning arms sales, reducing foreign aid and trade, economic sanctions, cutting diplomatic relations, and military action (Donnelly 2013b, 201). In the last half century, the US has reduced or terminated trade and aid to many strategic partners for human rights reasons, including South Africa, Turkey, Chile, Argentina, and Nicaragua. Moreover, given the inclusiveness of the US political system, activists and NGOs have had some success in highlighting illiberal behavior and pressuring legislators to act (Walldorf 2008, 1–7). Although the US has sanctioned selected rights-violating governments since the 1970s, in more recent years, Washington has used the "targeted sanctions" capabilities of the global Magnitsky Act to punish highly placed abusers while maintaining development assistance and humanitarian aid to needy populations. The US military has occasionally played a role in enforcing US or multilateral human rights directives, as in the 1999 North Atlantic Treaty Organization (NATO) bombing of Yugoslavia in response to Serbia's actions against Kosovar Albanians. At other times, the US military has supported international peacekeeping or enforced no fly zones. In the March 2011 intervention in Libya (ostensibly undertaken to stave off a massacre of civilians), the US took on a supportive role in NATO behind France and the United Kingdom (UK).

The EU's human rights evolution has involved far more constitutional steps and intra-European compromises. Europeans were at the forefront of human rights standard-setting after World War II via the 1950 European Convention on Human Rights (ECHR or the European Convention), the 1959 European Court of Human Rights (or the Strasbourg Court), and the 1961 European Social Charter. Although the European Economic Community (EEC) and the Organisation for Economic Co-operation and Development (OECD), established in 1957 and 1961, respectively, were largely concerned with economic development and integration, the EEC began incorporating human rights and democracy into its international activities in a modest way in the 1970s in concert with member states (Lorenzini, Tulli, and Zamburlini 2021). The 1986 Single European Act was the first EU document to mention human rights, stating that signatories were "determined to work together to promote democracy on the basis of fundamental rights [...] notably freedom, equality, and social justice." By the time of the 1992 Maastricht Treaty, which formally created the EU, Europeans had experienced the fall of the Berlin Wall, democratization in Central Europe, German unification, and dissolution of the Soviet Union. Unsurprisingly, then, the treaty included prescriptive human rights language drawn from the post-war conventions and charters. Article F declared that the EU "shall respect fundamental human rights, as guaranteed by the [ECHR]" and as enshrined in member states' constitutional traditions, and Article J.1 affirmed that developing and consolidating democracy, rule of law, and human rights was one objective of a future EU foreign policy.

Today, the legal and institutional basis of human rights in the EU lies in the Treaties of the European Union (TEU), of which the 2007 Lisbon Treaty (or the Treaty on European Union) is the most recent. Human rights became a formal part of the EU's body of common rights and obligations (or the Acquis communautaire) when the Treaty of Amsterdam came into force in 1999 (Jurado 2006, 121–22). Article 2 of the Lisbon Treaty declares that the union "is founded on the values of respect for human dignity, freedom, democracy, equality, the rule of law and respect for human rights." Via Article 6, the union accedes to the ECHR and recognizes the rights and principles laid out in the 2000 Charter of Fundamental Rights of the European Union.

Meanwhile, the concept of a common EU foreign policy grew from the 1970 Davignon Report and the proposal for European Political Cooperation, which eventually developed into the Common Foreign and Security Policy. The Lisbon Treaty clarifies that the promotion and protection of human rights is a central goal of all EU foreign policy fields. Article 21 of the TEU declares that the EU and its member states should "(seek) to advance" democracy and human rights "in the wider world," and Article 3 declares that the union shall contribute to the "eradication of poverty and the protection of human rights." In toto, the EU treaties, laws, and obligations define human rights and democracy as founding values and—depending on political and legal interpretation—either guiding foreign policy principles or aspirational objectives. Some legal scholars see them as binding upon EU officials, although they disagree as to whether they require strict compliance or a more flexible approach. Others interpret this language as offering only guidance rather than binding requirements (Kube 2019, 13–14; Larik 2016, 157–58; Oeter 2013, 840–42).

Like the US, the EU has adopted political and financial instruments with which it can encourage or pressure other governments to liberalize trade, respect human rights, and improve democratic governance. These begin with the Union's membership conditions (the 1993 Copenhagen criteria and Article 49 of the TEU), which require prospective states to have a functioning democracy, a market economy, minority protections, and respect for human rights and the rule of law. These obligations have led to internal reforms in applicant states during each enlargement negotiation, as when the states of the former Yugoslavia surrendered accused war criminals and Turkey implemented women's rights reforms (Haas 2010, 283).

All EU trade agreements with non-EU countries contain human rights clauses with provisions for monitoring and for withdrawal of trade terms if necessary. In 2020, for example, the Union partially withdrew Cambodia's trade preferences in response to serious human rights violations. Through the revamped Generalised Scheme of Preferences, the Union also offers tariff-free trade preferences to any developing nation willing to ratify and comply with key United Nations (UN) and International Labour Organization (ILO) conventions. Foreign aid conditionality—aka "positive conditionality," in which aid is conditioned on respect for human rights, increased as a reward for reforms, and reduced in response to violations—is among the most common EU methods of encouraging improvements in recipient countries. In this way, EU development aid is aimed not only at poverty reduction but also at democracy promotion and institution-building. European generosity gives the EU some leverage in this area: Although EU member states constitute just under ten percent of the world population, they and the EU provide 57 percent of development aid from OECD-Development Assistance Committee countries (European Commission 2019). Formal development agreements also include human rights provisions (e.g., the 2000 Cotonou Agreement, which was aimed at economic development and poverty reduction in the African, Caribbean, and Pacific Group of States). The 2021 renegotiation includes an even stronger role for democracy, human rights, and governance.

The so-called like-minded countries (smaller Western states led by Norway and the Netherlands and including Sweden, Canada, and Switzerland) have used development assistance as the chief instrument of their human rights policies. In contrast to the US and EU, which can afford a global approach to aid allocation, the like-minded have formed long-term development relationships with a smaller number of countries and have insisted that recipient governments respect a broad list of human rights. Other national interests may override these states' human rights concerns, but they have proved more willing than the US of holding recipient states accountable and even cutting ties with violators (Donnelly 2013a, 128–30).

Sanctions are another common EU human rights promotion instrument. As of 2021, country-specific human rights sanctions are in place against multiple states, including Belarus, Russia, Eritrea, North Korea, South Sudan, and Venezuela. The EU also maintains arms embargoes against China, Myanmar, and the Democratic Republic of Congo ostensibly for human rights reasons, and it embargoes transfers of equipment that can be used for internal repression, as in its 2011 ban on such sales to Iran. While the Union and its member states traditionally sanctioned individual countries, the December 2020 EU Global Human Rights Sanctions Regime (European Magnitsky Act) allows the European Council to sanction individuals, entities, and state and non-state actors for human rights violations anywhere in the world. Like its namesake in the US, this approach is intended to punish individual violators with asset freezes and travel bans while sparing innocent citizens. Following the February 2021 coup and subsequent repression in Myanmar, the EU led by bringing a special resolution to the UN Human Rights Council (UNHRC) and levying multiple sets of sanctions targeting high-ranking individuals and military-controlled companies. Meanwhile, the EU continued humanitarian aid to those affected by the Myanmar conflict.

In those rare cases when the EU has opted to use force to protect civilians, NATO has occasionally acted as the de facto military arm for EU (and US) decisions, as during the 1999 Kosovo War. In other cases, member states may take the lead, as when France led the Mali intervention of 2013–14 to head off an Islamist advance. Although as the Mali case suggests, while such interventions may stave off a humanitarian disaster in the short term, they do not necessarily establish the foundation for long-term strategic or humanitarian success (Cold-Ravnkilde and Nissen 2020). In the most egregious cases, such as the genocide in Darfur, the EU may refer the investigation and punishment to the International Criminal Court (ICC).

While the EU is not a leader in universal jurisdiction, some European states have invoked it to prosecute war crimes, crimes against humanity, genocide, and torture. Beginning with the groundbreaking 1998 indictment of Chilean dictator Augusto Pinochet, Spain and Belgium led in this area through prosecution of crimes committed in Latin America and Africa. But in response to pressure from powerful states and the charge that too many plaintiffs were pursuing politically motivated cases, these two nations restricted universal jurisdiction (Kaleck and Kroker 2018, 171–72; Langer 2015, 246; O'Sullivan 2017). Nevertheless, several European governments brought cases against US government officials and Central Intelligence Agency (CIA) agents for human rights violations or war crimes during the War on Terror (Haas 2008, 271–72). More recently, Germany has applied universal jurisdiction to prosecute those accused of torture in Syria (Kaleck and Kroker 2018).

The question of effectiveness is too substantial to be addressed here, but one can make a strong case that EU human rights promotion is not simply the product of European self-interest. One study of 50 EU economic and military interventions in 31 countries concluded that these actions correlated strongly with the other nations' human rights violations (Kreutz 2015). The effectiveness of development aid is another perennial question for donor nations. Conditioning aid can make a difference in human rights protection, although evidence suggests that increased aid funds can also allow ruling elites to maintain their legitimacy by sustaining their patronage networks. Yet, even if a government drags its feet on reforms, heightened domestic expectations may create pressure for legitimate changes (Carnegie and Marinov 2017, 672–73).

A Community of Shared Values?

Although most would agree that common interests are integral to the transatlantic relationship, the extent of common values is a matter of some debate. Some observers suggest that a structural divergence in values and cultural ties is causing significant damage to the US-Europe relationship (Sloan 2016a–b; Wickett 2018). This perspective was especially ubiquitous during the Trump presidency. Trump's aggressive nationalism, brusque style, and mercurial nature alienated European leaders and foreign policy elites, some of whom saw Trumpism as the death knell of both the liberal world order and the unified West that had nurtured it (Kimmage 2020; Tcherneva 2018). Trump dragged his feet on affirming Article 5 of the NATO treaty, upbraided member states for not paying their fair share and sparked transatlantic trade conflicts. In his failure to elucidate a vision for the transatlantic region, he encouraged US partners to hedge and perhaps even shift away from US alignment—to "take our fate into our own hands," in Angela Merkel's words.

These divides are substantial, and they may continue to hamper the relationship for years to come. Yet opinion polls and scholarly research provide ample evidence that the transatlantic region is, in fact, a community of shared values and common expectations about democratic politics and individual liberties. Irrespective of the many points of transatlantic disagreement, European and US promotion of human rights and democracy reflects, at some level, the expectations of elites and ordinary citizens alike.

There is broad transatlantic agreement on a common set of political and civil rights—namely, liberal individual protections, parliamentary political systems, a market economy, private property, and a basic (or even substantial) socioeconomic safety net. When asked to list the "main assets" of the EU, Europeans' top answer is "the EU's respect for democracy, human rights, and the rule of law"—the three core political values as defined in the Lisbon Treaty (European Union 2021a). Americans and Europeans express similar visions of what constitutes a "good democracy," including strong electoral institutions, social welfare, a robust economy, and civilian control of the military. Poll respondents in Europe and the US also support such democracy promotion efforts as election monitoring, civil society initiatives, and, when necessary, economic and political sanctions (Puzarina, Pötzschke, and Rattinger 2014). When asked about "areas of desired transatlantic cooperation," respondents rate "protection of human rights" as a high priority (GMFUS 2021, 13–14, 51–54).

Several scholars have demonstrated increasing transatlantic convergence on human rights and democracy promotion, although most concede that policy coordination and implementation have been difficult (Pérez de las Heras 2015). Heins, Badami, and Markovits (2010) disagreed with the common discourse of a "divided West" and saw instead relatively minor differences in shared understandings between the US, Germany, and Canada on international human rights. The rhetoric of transatlantic division, they concluded, even deflects from the increasing assertiveness of non-Western governments (Heins, Badami, and Markovits 2010). Babayan and Risse (2014) highlighted enhanced convergence in democracy promotion policies and a common interest in democratic domestic stability in target countries, although they also noted that the US and Europe do not represent a genuine partnership. "Common interests and collective identities," they pointed out, "have not led to institutional frameworks for sustained cooperation" in target countries (Babayan and Risse 2014, 3). Isernia and Basile (2014) showed that a majority of transatlantic elites (62 percent in the EU and 51 percent in the US) favored democracy promotion efforts, although in the neo-isolationist zeitgeist of 2014, the US public was somewhat lukewarm (46–53). The EU and US also differ slightly in their preferred instruments and in the kinds of domestic or international developments that spur them to respond (Babayan 2013; Babayan and Viviani 2013).

Researchers have consulted a wide array of sources to demonstrate a values convergence. Baldwin (2009) concluded that the US and Europe are far more alike than they are different and that transatlantic differences are no greater than the differences within Europe. Europe and the US, he argued, are "parts of a common, big-tent grouping—call it the West, the Atlantic Community, the developed world, or what you will" (Baldwin 2009, 10). McKean and Szewczyk (2021) have echoed this point more recently, adding that the very idea of "the West" is interchangeable with the liberal values that define it (3). Harrelson-Stephens (2013) similarly identified shared values as "the core of the transatlantic relationship" and the factor that most clearly distinguishes the region from the rest of the world. Shared values, she argued, are what have made the transatlantic relationship "enduring and necessary" and will continue to underpin regional economic and military cooperation. (Harrelson-Stephens 2013, 167–68). Larsen (2019) acknowledged that NATO's "unique institutional attributes" give the organization's democracy support efforts "a true value" despite challenges from illiberal states and countervailing forces in Eastern Europe. There is also strong evidence for a transatlantic values consensus in the UNHRC (Renouard 2020). And as the editors of this volume have pointed out, the distance between the US and European states in the World Values Survey and the Inglehart-Welzel cultural maps has shrunk over four decades and any actual transatlantic "values gap" has not increased since the 1990s. Given these data points, they argue, convergence is a more reasonable conclusion than divergence (see this volume's introduction).

Of course, there are some differences in values both within and between Europe and North America, and these may influence human rights pursuits and the transatlantic relationship. Some of these differences are unambiguous, such as the transatlantic divide over capital punishment and gun rights, as well as Americans' firmer adherence to religious values. Other differences are more nuanced. Europeans are generally more favorable to social welfare programs and a strong, centralized state, while Americans generally favor a weaker state and less regulation of the free market (Isernia and Basile 2013). Americans enjoy stronger constitutional protection of free expression than do Canadians and Europeans, and Americans are more likely than Europeans to prefer unilateral action in foreign policy. Americans are more willing to trust their own government over the UN on human rights matters, while Europeans and Canadians are more favorable to the UN and ICC (GMFUS 2021, 47–48; Puzarina, Pötzschke, and Rattinger 2014).

Suspicion of multilateralism is a long-standing US tradition. The US famously eschewed "entangling alliances" for a century and a half before forming NATO in 1949. And although the US took a leading role in developing the institutions of the post-war world order, it sidestepped a host of multilateral bodies and agreements in the ensuing decades, such as the Kyoto Protocol, the UN Convention on the Law of the Sea, and the Mine Ban Treaty. The US has also proved far less willing than European states to ratify international human rights covenants. It took the US nearly 40 years to ratify the Genocide Convention, and as of 2021, it has ratified only three of the nine core UN human rights conventions and only two of the nine optional UN human rights convention protocols. It has signed but not ratified many others, including the International Covenant on Economic, Social, and Cultural Rights, the ILO Forced Labour Convention, and the optional torture protocol. As of 2021, the US is the only nation in the world that has not ratified the Convention on the Rights of the Child and only one of seven not to have ratified the Convention on the Elimination of All Forms of Discrimination Against Women. Moreover, the US has ratified only two of the 8 fundamental ILO conventions and only 14 of the 189 ILO conventions overall. In many cases, the US has inserted reservations, understandings, and declarations or has declared articles or paragraphs "non-self-executing," which means they are not binding on the US without domestic legislation (Schabas 2000). Democrats and Republicans generally support the US's alliances, but the latter are particularly wary of UN "interference" in the US (Friedhoff 2021).

Nor has the US simply accepted the jurisdiction of international courts. The US has participated in the International Court of Justice (World Court) but has rejected some decisions unfavorable to US interests and has not acknowledged the court's plenary authority over the US (Murphy 2009, 46–47). President Bill Clinton reluctantly signed the Rome Statute of the ICC in 2000, but the Senate did not ratify it due to questions about the court's jurisdiction and the fear of Americans being prosecuted for unilateral military actions. President George W. Bush withdrew the US signature in 2002 (Mowle 2004, 88–98). As of 2021, the US is not a member and does not recognize that it applies to Americans. By contrast, all EU member states are ICC signatories, and the EU is the court's largest financial supporter. Each EU member state plus the UK has also ratified all eight of the fundamental ILO conventions and nearly all core UN human rights conventions and optional protocols.

Procedural difficulties play a part in American reluctance—it is difficult to win two-thirds support for a treaty in the Senate—but other factors are more significant. Fearing threats to their sovereignty, Americans are far less tolerant of multilateral arrangements, less willing to accept the jurisdiction of international courts and UN committees, and less willing to accept agreements that may conflict with the US Constitution, domestic laws, or cultural traditions. Forsythe (2018) pointed to "a certain intellectual isolationism" among American politicians and voters, who believe that the society does not need international standards or international review of human rights practices because the US Constitution is widely respected, and the nation has a strong, independent judicial system (14). The nation's size and superpower status also play a part, as the US faces more choices and more constraints on the use of power. As Donnelly (2013a) notes, whereas small states rarely need to choose between human rights and other goals, large states' varied interests and responsibilities preclude a strong, consistent human rights policy (130). In rejecting ICC oversight, for example, the US joins other non-signatories with powerful militaries or high per capita military spending, including China, Russia, India, Saudi Arabia, and Israel. Yet this US guardedness toward rights conventions does not equate with widespread domestic rights violations. As Mowle (2004) pointed out, the US has resisted international agreements in cases where its own domestic record was far superior to that of other signatories, and it has even withheld support for conventions that outlaw acts already prohibited by the US Constitution (110).

In contrast to US apprehension, the EU's human rights approach has long been entwined with multilateral perspectives, the European integration process, and the self-perception that Europe is a different kind of power. As Forsythe (2012) has suggested, a nation's self-image can strongly influence its approach to human rights, and many states' human rights policies "reflect the conviction that the state has some virtuous point to teach others" (205). Concurrent with the pro-globalization optimism of the 1990s and early 2000s, there was much discussion of Europe's post-Cold War identity and international role. If US foreign policy prioritized unilateralism and hard-power tools, as many argued, then perhaps the EU could forge a counter-identity in much the same way that smaller states like the Netherlands and Canada self-identified as liberal states that promote peace, human rights, international development, and international law (Forsythe 2000a, 2–3). In the tradition of François Duchêne's 1972 reference to Europe as a "civilian power," scholars at the turn of the 2000s portrayed the EU as a new kind of world actor—a "normative power" which used persuasion and attraction rather than force to promote democracy, human rights, and multilateralism (Duchêne 1972). The European project, wrote Rosecrance (1998), "is normative rather than empirical [… Europe] is now coming to set world standards in normative terms" (22).

Especially during the George W. Bush presidency (2001–9), much was made of Europeans' and Americans' supposedly conflicting values and foreign policies (e.g., Kagan's (2003) formulation that Europeans were from "Venus" and Americans from "Mars"). The US was the lone superpower, declared Kagan

(2003), and willing to exercise its power for the sake of democratic enlargement. *Contra* Kagan, Manners (2002) portrayed the EU as a unique international actor which could influence others' behavior through both its policies and its high moral standing. Menon, Nicolaidis, and Walsh (2004) praised Europe's "Kantian" approach to international affairs (as against Kagan's "Hobbesian" view) and called the EU "a pioneer in long term interstate peace building" and ultimately "one of the most formidable machines for managing differences peacefully ever invented" (11). Leonard (2005a–b) called Europe a "transformative power" based on the EU's track record of coaxing reforms in states seeking economic agreements or entry into the union.

Others spoke of Europe as a "responsible" power or an "ethical" power capable of combining civilian and military power (Mayer 2008). Aggestam (2008) argued that "ethical power Europe" represented a conceptual shift in the EU's global role from the mere "power of attraction" to "proactively working to change the world in the direction of its vision of the 'global common good'" (1). Toje (2008) described the EU as a "small" power, which, while it could certainly promote liberal democracy, human rights, and a market economy, could not build the foreign policy of a Great Power. Not only was a common strategic identity nearly impossible among so many member states and alongside a US security guarantee, but individual nations also desired to manage their own foreign and military policies (Toje 2008, 207, 210). These perceptions continued into the Barack Obama presidency (2009–17). Ferreira-Pereira (2012) noted the emergence of a "model-power Europe" which embraced civilian, military, and economic power. Simoni (2013) argued that the EU had developed an identity as a mature power that favors diplomacy in pursuit of humanitarianism, while the Americans had developed an identity as the provider of international security—a divergence that was clear in American and EU approaches to the Arab Spring. Taken together, these approaches signaled the appeal of normative theory in the study of European foreign policy (Sjursen 2015).

However, others have found claims of European "normative power" unrealistic. Scholars and activists have raised questions about European self-interest, migration and refugee/asylum policies, actions during the War on Terror and the fight against ISIL/ISIS, the rise of populism, and domestic challenges to the rule of law. In addition, although the EU and its member states face fewer accusations of human rights violations than does the US, Europeans also have fewer security obligations. Nicolaidis and Howse (2002) cautioned against representing the EU as an idealized "EUtopia," while Youngs (2004) argued that observers had oversold the claim of a values-based EU foreign policy and had largely ignored the strategic considerations in EU human rights policies. Sjursen (2006) similarly found all the talk of "normative" and "civilian" power to be overly generalized. How, she asked, would we know a "normative" or "civilizing" power when we see it, and would those features really set the EU apart (Sjursen 2006)? A skeptical Hyde-Price (2006), Jurado (2006), and Smith (2008, 129, 138) demonstrated that the EU did business with states with poor human rights records and that economic and strategic interests limited EU criticism of China and Russia. Mayer (2008) concluded that the EU's human rights conditions were too limited to get results and too inconsistent because of material interests, and he showed that Europe's power relative to the nation in question mattered far more than human rights concerns (70). Erickson (2013) found that European states' arms exports correlated more strongly to recipient nations' wealth than to non-material concerns (218). Balducci (2010) concluded that "normative Europe" certainly did not apply to China. On the contrary, member states delegated China's human rights issues to the EU and only held China dialogues for optics before dropping them altogether (49, 51). Kinzelbach (2015) similarly found very little European influence on China's human rights record.

Meanwhile, intra-European normative divides further weaken the argument for a transatlantic values divergence. Indeed, the entire European project has been hindered by nationalism, populism, and regional differences in values. Whereas the 2009 Financial Crisis highlighted north-south frictions in the EU (with southern states facing a balance-of-payments dilemma), the 2015–16 Migration Crisis illuminated east-west frictions (with eastern states refusing to open their borders). Populism has been steadily rising in Europe for more than two decades, and in recent years, populist energies have constituted a challenge to large-scale immigration, liberal refugee and asylum policies, regionalism, and the power and bureaucratic elitism of the EU, the US, and NATO. Populist parties won notable public support in most European countries' parliamentary elections in the 2010s; those on the right have had some success in Hungary, Poland, and Italy, while those on the left have been successful in Greece and Spain (Taggart 2017; Timbro n.d.; Verbeek and Zaslove 2017).

Poland and Hungary have emerged as the most vocal challengers to EU expectations. Poland's Law and Justice party and Hungary's Fidesz party grew in stature by embracing patriotic symbols and traditional values and opposing both large-scale immigration and domination by Brussels and Berlin. Beginning in 2017–18, the European Commission and European Parliament invoked Article 7 proceedings against Poland for its erosion of judicial independence and Hungary for civil society limits. Other regional states' tacit approval of some Polish and Hungarian policies reflects both a shared regional history and popular criticism of Brussels. Moreover, battles over LGBTQIA rights in East-Central Europe suggest that Europeans are enmeshed in "culture wars" not unlike those in the US. Polling data suggests high levels of public support for LGBTQIA equality and social acceptance in Scandinavia and Western Europe and low levels in Poland, Hungary, Russia, and the Balkans (ILGA Europe 2021; Pacewicz 2017; Pew Research Center 2020; Statista 2021). Religiosity on the continent varies widely from highly secular Sweden and Denmark to highly religious Poland and Romania (Pew Research Center 2018).

Populism and nationalism are animating factors in "Euroskepticism," as demonstrated in the 2016 Brexit vote and the growth of nationalistic political movements (Magone 2015). Between 2005 and 2015, 22 out of 28 countries saw a drop in trust in the EU and its institutions (Karv 2016). Those who claimed to be "optimistic" about the EU's future dropped from 69 percent in 2007 to

50 percent at the end of 2016 (European Union 2021a). More recent numbers suggest a rise in confidence, with 63 percent now calling their country's membership in the EU a good thing (the highest since 2007). But a near-majority still see "things going in the wrong direction" in the EU, with migration and refugee policy by far the greatest source of disagreement between national governments and the EU (European Parliament 2021, 26, 73–74, 83; European Union 2021a, b). However, populism has its limits. Populist figures in Central and Eastern Europe have challenged the ideological mainstream, but they have had limited influence over national parliaments, the European Parliament, and EU foreign policy (Stanley 2017; van Berlo and Natorski 2020).

Problems of Leadership and Legitimacy

Whereas EU ambitions to promote human rights run up against the national interests of member states, populist challenges to European unity, and the ever-present temptation of apathy, the US faces a human rights and democracy legitimacy problem due to its past foreign policy actions and its recent domestic divisions (Goldgeier and Jentleson 2020). US claims to moral leadership slipped during the War on Terror, as the effort to root out terror networks and protect American interests required significant trade-offs. In order to secure military bases, flyover rights, shared intelligence, and the support of partner governments, the US incarcerated enemy combatants at Guantánamo Bay, sent detainees to secret CIA "black sites" via "extraordinary rendition," cultivated ties of convenience with abusive regimes, occasionally killed civilians in targeted airstrikes, and watched helplessly while Iraq degenerated into civil war (Donnelly and Whelan 2020, 322–38; Forsythe and McMahon 2017, 94–104). The US human rights bureaucracy continued to publicize partner states' violations, but the US's political leaders were willing to overlook violations within states cooperating in the war (Foot 2004). Astute observers located these moral compromises in the Bush administration's neoconservative exceptionalism and its messianic belief that the US can and should shape other nations (Judis 2005; Micklethwait and Wooldridge 2005). In short, this was a vision of the US as (in a former secretary of state's words) the "indispensable nation" (Albright 1998). Critics believed that Bush's neoconservative vision represented a fundamental transatlantic divide, or even presaged the dissolution of the West (Anderson, Ikenberry, and Risse 2008; Kopstein and Steinmo 2007; Kupchan 2002). At the very least, it was clear that Bush's aggressive unilateralism contributed to anti-American feeling (Katzenstein and Keohane 2007; Kohut and Stokes 2006; O'Connor and Griffiths 2006).

The US's democratic reputation recovered somewhat during the Obama presidency, although many aspects of the Bush approach remained in place. The fight against al-Qaeda continued, Guantánamo remained open, and operations against ISIL/ISIS spurred military interventions in Libya, Yemen, the Horn of Africa, and Northern Mali. Obama presided over nearly 2,000 drone strikes, prompting much disagreement over civilian casualty figures.

Donald Trump oversaw even more drone strikes per annum and reduced transparency over civilian casualties, but it was not the excesses of counterterrorism that hurt the nation's democratic reputation in the Trump years. It was, instead, Trump's adoption of populist and nationalist symbols, his undiplomatic demeanor, his denunciation of globalization and the liberal world order, and his rejection of values in foreign policy. Even before Trump's victory, prominent scholars had recognized the waning Western enthusiasm for liberal political orders (Ikenberry 2013; Walt 2016). But Trump went much further in rejecting Wilsonian liberalism, interventionism, and multilateralism. Unlike conventional Western politicians, he scolded allies and partners, expressed admiration for dictators, and rarely paid lip service to liberal ideals. The momentous shift in tone was exemplified by his staunch defense of US sovereignty and borders; his withdrawal of the US from the Trans-Pacific Partnership, the Paris Climate Agreement, the New York Declaration for Refugees and Migrants, the UN Educational, Scientific and Cultural Organization, the World Health Organization, and the UNHRC; and his funding cuts to USAID, the State Department, and the UN.

Trump did little to promote human rights, instead embracing a selective and strategic Nixonian realist approach that differentiated between the nation's values and its foreign policies (Tillerson 2017). "One useful guideline," read a leaked internal memo, "is that allies should be treated differently—and better—than adversaries [...] We look to pressure, compete with, and outmaneuver [the US's adversaries]" and "should consider human rights as an important issue in regard to US relations with China, Russia, North Korea, and Iran" (*Politico* 2017). In stark contrast to the Bush administration, the US under Trump would not presume the universality of US values. "We lead by example," declared the December 2017 National Security Strategy (2017). "We are not going to impose our values on others." Speaking in Saudi Arabia, Trump assured the audience that "we are not here to lecture. We are not here to tell other people how to live, what to do, who to be, or how to worship" (Trump 2017a). He echoed these sentiments in his first UN speech: "We do not expect diverse countries to share the same cultures, traditions, or even systems of government" (Trump 2017b).

In Trump's first year alone, he did not publicly upbraid partners Egypt, the Philippines, Turkey, or Vietnam for clear rights violations. In those rare instances when the administration mentioned human rights, it was to challenge adversaries North Korea, Iran, and Venezuela. As a sign of Trump's attitude toward the State Department, he did not fill the top human rights position in the department until June 2018. The US even punished the ICC for investigating US actions in Afghanistan and Israeli actions in Palestine. In 2019–20, the US announced visa bans for ICC officials involved in such investigations and then took the unprecedented step of sanctioning two senior ICC officials for these investigations.

Trump's defenders pointed out the upsides of his approach. He rejected Bush's unilateral moralism and religiosity, and he did not embark on any major wars. He maintained the US alliance structure, and the post-war multilateral institutions remained in place. His defenders could also argue that his challenge to multilateralism was firmly within the American tradition and that his piercing of the myths of globalization offered a necessary corrective. And although Trump's rejection of the liberal order prompted countless establishment paeans to that order, some asked why the foreign policy elites were so willing to overlook the weaknesses of the status quo and of earlier US diplomacy (Bacevich 2017; Porter 2018). Finally, while the US and EU had their differences during the Trump presidency, their human rights bureaucrats found avenues of effective collaboration (Gilmore 2021).

The Biden administration certainly represents a change in tone, as President Joseph R. Biden, Jr., has expressed far more appreciation for alliances, the transatlantic relationship, and multilateralism. He has sanctioned the coup leaders in Myanmar and government officials in China and Cuba, and he has proposed a "united front" of democratic nations to address Beijing's violations. On the multilateral front, although the US continues to insist that the ICC has no jurisdiction over Americans, the administration lifted sanctions against the court. Biden has promised a US commitment to international criminal justice, and the US is now re-engaging with the UNHRC after an absence of nearly three years.

Conclusion: The Road Ahead

Yet, despite Biden's willingness to re-engage with the world and to take up human rights causes, however selectively, few Europeans believe that the US is as powerful as it once was. This attitude contrasts sharply with the early 2000s when even Europeans who strongly opposed the Bush administration also generally believed that America could shape the world (Krastev and Leonard 2021). The transformative vision of US exceptionalism has far fewer advocates today in light of its slipping global economic position, the rise of China, fallout from the "forever wars" in Iraq and Afghanistan, and the global authoritarian trend. The US's political and social ills have prompted questions about the nation's vitality, political stability, adherence to democratic values, ability to lead, and value to Europe. Whether the US system is truly under duress is perhaps less important than that the nation's reputation has been marred. Majorities in several EU nations not only believe that the US political system is broken, but they are also more positive about their own systems and see Berlin as a more important partner than Washington (Krastev and Leonard 2021).

The ambition to promote human rights faces other challenges. Despite Biden's internationalist credentials, US and European interests will occasionally collide in the Middle East, Africa, and Asia. The US will almost certainly press its European partners to get tougher on Beijing, including lobbying for Western unity on tougher human rights statements and policies. However, while there is much sympathy in Europe for such a position, Sino-European economic ties are formidable. European governments seeking to maximize their freedom of action and European companies seeking a presence in the US and Chinese markets will naturally work to skirt the US-China rivalry (Krastev and Leonard 2021). This may amount to an update of the Bush-era transatlantic conflicts, with Europeans seeing the US's aggressive approach to China as insufficiently nuanced and Americans seeing Europe as weak-willed and unwilling to subjugate economic interests to higher principles.

It remains to be seen whether the US can restore its credibility as a reliable actor that respects the transatlantic values of democracy, human rights, and the rule of law. It also remains to be seen whether the transatlantic community can reverse the global trend of advancing authoritarianism and show the world that liberal democracy is a more appealing system. The US is likely to remain more internally focused in the short term. American leaders will not only seek to rebuild domestic institutions, but they will also maintain some of the protectionist and populist elements of Trump's approach (Barkin and Kratz 2020). Given the ongoing political divide in the US, Europeans are likely to distance themselves from the US somewhat and take more responsibility for their own affairs. Moreover, owing to intra-European economic and cultural divides, some aspects of retrenchment and deglobalization will continue in Europe (Bomassi and Haenle 2021). Despite these challenges, human rights advocates can find comfort in the established laws, agencies, and bureaus of Washington, Ottawa, and the capitals of Europe. Transatlantic governments will naturally continue to prioritize national interests, but there is substantial space for elected leaders, bureaucrats, and their non-state partners to develop creative, bold approaches in the area of international human rights.

References

Aggestam, Lisbeth. 2008. "Introduction: Ethical Power Europe?" *International Affairs* 84 (1): 1–11.

Albright, Madeleine K. 1998. Interview, *Today Show*. 19 February. Department of State Archive. https://1997-2001.state.gov/statements/1998/980219a.html.

Anderson, Jeffrey J., G. John Ikenberry, and Thomas Risse, eds. 2008. *The End of the West: Crisis and Change in the Atlantic Order*. Ithaca: Cornell University Press.

Apodaca, Clair. 2006. *Understanding U.S. Human Rights Policy: A Paradoxical Legacy*. New York: Routledge.

Bacevich, Andrew J. 2010. *Washington Rules: America's Path to Permanent War*. New York: Metropolitan Books.

———. 2017. "The 'Global Order' Myth." *The American Conservative*. 15 June. www.theamericanconservative.com/articles/the-global-order-myth/.

Babayan, Nelli. 2013. "Home-Made Adjustments? US Human Rights and Democracy Promotion." Transworld Working Paper No. 20. www.iai.it/en/pubblicazioni/home-made-adjustments.

Babayan, Nelli, and Alessandra Viviani. 2013. "'Shocking' Adjustments? EU Human Rights and Democracy Promotion." Transworld Working Paper No. 18. www.iai.it/sites/default/files/TW_WP_18.pdf.

Babayan, Nelli, and Thomas Risse. 2014. "So Close, But Yet So Far: European and American Democracy Promotion." Transworld Working Paper No. 37. www.iai.it/sites/default/files/tw_wp_37.pdf.

Balducci, Giuseppe. 2010. "The Limits of Normative Power Europe in Asia: The Case of Human Rights in China." *East Asia* 27: 35–55.

Baldwin, Peter. 2009. *The Narcissism of Minor Differences: How America and Europe Are Alike*. New York: Oxford University Press.

Barkin, Noah, and Agatha Kratz. 2020. "Five Keys to a Transatlantic Agenda on China." Rhodium Group. 19 October. https://rhg.com/research/transatlantic-agenda/.

Bomassi, Lizza, and Paul Haenle. 2021. "Realigning the Transatlantic Relationship on China." In *Working with the Biden Administration: Opportunities for the EU*, edited by Rosa Balfour. Carnegie Europe. https://carnegieeurope.eu/2021/01/26/realigning-transatlantic-relationship-on-china-pub-83564.

Bradley, Mark Philip. 2016. *The World Reimagined: Americans and Human Rights in the Twentieth Century*. New York: Cambridge University Press.

———. 2018. "The United States and the Global Human Rights Order." In *Chaos in the Liberal Order: The Trump Presidency and International Politics in the Twenty-First Century*, edited by Robert Jervis, Francis J. Gavin, Joshua Royner, and Diane Labrosse, 331–36. New York: Columbia University Press.

Carnegie, Allison, and Nikolay Marinov. 2017. "Foreign Aid, Human Rights, and Democracy Promotion: Evidence from a Natural Experiment." *American Journal of Political Science* 61 (3): 671–83.

Chomsky, Noam. 2004. *Hegemony or Survival: America's Quest for Global Dominance*. New York: Owl Books.

Cold-Ravnkilde, Signe Marie, and Christine Nissen. 2020. "Schizophrenic Agendas in the EU's External Actions in Mali." *International Affairs* 96 (4): 935–53.

Donnelly, Jack. 2013a. *International Human Rights*. 4th ed. Boulder: Westview Press.

———. 2013b. *Universal Human Rights in Theory and Practice*. 3rd ed. Ithaca: Cornell University Press.

Donnelly, Jack, and Daniel J. Whelan. 2020. *International Human Rights*. 6th ed. New York: Routledge.

Duchêne, François. 1972. "Europe's Role in World Peace." In *Europe Tomorrow: Sixteen Europeans Look Ahead*, edited by Richard Mayne, 32–47. London: Fontana.

Erickson, Jennifer L. 2013. "Market Imperative Meets Normative Power: Human Rights and European Arms Transfer Policy." *European Journal of International Relations* 19 (2): 209–34.

European Commission. 2019. "Europe Remains the World's Biggest Development Donor." Press Release. https://ec.europa.eu/commission/presscorner/detail/en/IP_19_2075.

European Parliament. 2021. *Parlemeter 2020: A Glimpse of Certainty in Uncertain Times*. www.europarl.europa.eu/at-your-service/files/be-heard/eurobarometer/2020/parlemeter-2020/en-report.pdf.

European Union. 2021a. Future of Europe: Special Eurobarometer 500 – Annex. https://europa.eu/eurobarometer/surveys/detail/2256.

———. 2021b. "Standard Eurobarometer 94." https://europa.eu/eurobarometer/surveys/detail/2355.

Ferreira-Pereira, Laura C. 2012. "The European Union as a Model Power." In *The Foreign Policy of the European Union*, edited by Federiga Bindi and Irina Angelescu, 293–304. 2nd ed. Washington: Brookings.

Foot, Rosemary. 2004. *Human Rights and Counter-Terrorism in America's Asia Policy*. London: International Institute for Strategic Studies.

Forsythe, David P., ed. 2000a. *Human Rights and Comparative Foreign Policy*. New York: United Nations University Press.

———. 2000b. *Human Rights in International Relations*. Cambridge: Cambridge University Press.

———. 2012. *Human Rights in International Relations*. 3rd ed. New York: Cambridge University Press.

———. 2018. *Human Rights in International Relations*. 4th ed. New York: Cambridge University Press.

Forsythe, David P., and Patrice C. McMahon. 2017. *American Exceptionalism Reconsidered: US Foreign Policy, Human Rights, and World Order*. New York: Routledge.

Friedhoff, Karl. 2021. "Democrats, Republicans Support Alliances, Disagree on International Organizations." Chicago Council on Global Affairs. www.thechicagocouncil.org/research/public-opinion-survey/democrats-republicans-support-alliances-disagree-international.

German Marshall Fund of the United States (GMFUS). 2021. *Transatlantic Trends: Transatlantic Opinion on Global Challenges*. www.gmfus.org/sites/default/files/publications/pdf/TT2021_Web_Version.pdf.

Gilmore, Eamon. 2021. "Human Rights in the European Union's Foreign Policy." www.youtube.com/watch?v=aVVMThRbeoM.

Goldgeier, James, and Bruce W. Jentleson. "The United States Is Not Entitled to Lead the World." *Foreign Affairs*, 25 September. www.foreignaffairs.com/articles/world/2020-09-25/united-states-not-entitled-lead-world.

Haas, Michael. 2008. *International Human Rights: A Comprehensive Introduction*. New York: Routledge.

Harrelson-Stephens, Julie. 2013. "Cultural and Political Ties Within the Transatlantic Alliance in the New Century." In *Transatlantic Relations and Modern Diplomacy: An Interdisciplinary Examination*, edited by Sudeshna Roy, Dana Cooper, and Brian Murphy, 344–57. New York: Routledge.

Heins, Volker, Aditya Badami, and Andrei S. Markovits. 2010. "The West Divided? A Snapshot of Human Rights and Transatlantic Relations at the United Nations." *Human Rights Review* 11 (1): 1–16.

Hodgson, Godfrey. 2009. *The Myth of American Exceptionalism*. New Haven: Yale University Press.

Hyde-Price, Adrian. 2006. "'Normative' Power Europe: A Realist Critique." *Journal of European Public Policy* 13(2): 217–34.

Ikenberry, G. John. 2013. "The Liberal International Order and Its Discontents." In *After Liberalism?: The Future of Liberalism in International Relations*, edited by Rebekka Friedman, Kevork Oskanian, and Ramon Pachedo Pardo, 91–102. Houndmills: Palgrave Macmillan.

ILGA Europe. 2021. "Annual Review 2021." www.ilga-europe.org/annualreview/2021.

Isernia, Pierangelo, and Linda Basile. 2014. "To Agree or Disagree? Elite Opinion and Future Prospects of the Transatlantic Partnership." Transworld Working Paper No. 34. www.iai.it/sites/default/files/tw_wp_34.pdf, 46–53.

Judis, John. 2005. *The Chosen Nation: The Influence of Religion on U.S. Foreign Policy*. Carnegie Endowment for International Peace. March. https://carnegieendowment.org/files/PB37.judis.FINAL.pdf.

Jurado, Elena. 2006. "Assigning Duties in the Global System of Human Rights: The Role of the European Union." In *A Responsible Europe? Ethical Foundations of EU External Affairs*, edited by Hartmut Mayer and Henri Vogt, 119–39. New York: Palgrave MacMillan.

Kagan, Robert. 2003. *Of Paradise and Power: America and Europe in the New World Order*. New York: Alfred A. Knopf.

Kaleck, Wolfgang, and Patrick Kroker. 2018. "Syrian Torture Investigations in Germany and Beyond: Breathing New Life into Universal Jurisdiction in Europe?" *Journal of International Criminal Justice* 16 (1): 165–91.

Karv, Thomas. 2016. "Trust in the EU – Short-Term Fluctuations or a More Long-Term Trend?" Tampere Blogs. https://projects.tuni.fi/contre/blog/trust-in-the-eu-short-term-fluctuations-or-a-more-long-term-trend/.

Katzenstein, Peter J., and Robert O. Keohane, eds. 2007. *Anti-Americanisms in World Politics*. Ithaca: Cornell University Press.

Kimmage, Michael. 2020. *The Abandonment of the West: The History of an Idea in American Foreign Policy*. New York: Basic Books.

Kinzelbach, Katrin. 2015. *The EU's Human Rights Dialogue With China: Quiet Diplomacy and Its Limits*. New York: Routledge.

Kiobel v. Royal Dutch Petroleum Co. 569 U.S. 108 (2013).

Kohut, Andrew, and Bruce Stokes. 2006. *America Against the World: How We Are Different and Why We Are Disliked*. New York: Times Books.

Kopstein, Jeffrey, and Sven Steinmo, eds. 2007. *Growing Apart?: America and Europe in the Twenty-First Century*. New York: Cambridge University Press.

Krastev, Ivan, and Mark Leonard. 2021. "The Crisis of American Power: How Europeans See Biden's America." European Council on Foreign Relations Policy Brief. https://ecfr.eu/publication/the-crisis-of-american-power-how-europeans-see-bidens-america/.

Kreutz, Joakim. 2015. "Human Rights, Geostrategy, and EU Foreign Policy, 1989–2008." *International Organization* 69 (1): 195–217.

Kube, Vivian. 2019. *EU Human Rights, International Investment Law and Participation: Operationalizing the EU Foreign Policy Objective to Global Human Rights Protection*. Cham: Springer International.

Kupchan, Charles. 2002. "The End of the West?" *The Atlantic*. November.

Langer, Máximo. 2015. "Universal Jurisdiction Is Not Disappearing: The Shift From 'Global Enforcer' to 'No Safe Haven' Universal Jurisdiction." *Journal of International Criminal Justice* 13 (2): 245–56.

Larik, Joris. 2016. *Foreign Policy Objectives in European Constitutional Law*. New York: Oxford University Press.

Larsen, Henrik B. L. 2019. *NATO's Democratic Retrenchment: Hegemony after the Return of History*. New York: Routledge.

Leonard, Mark. 2005a. "Europe's Transformative Power." *Center for European Reform Bulletin* No. 40. www.cer.eu/publications/archive/bulletin-article/2005/europes-transformative-power.

———. 2005b. *Why Europe Will Run the 21st Century*. New York: Public Affairs Books.

Lorenzini, Sara, Umberto Tulli, and Ilaria Zamburlini, eds. 2021. *The Human Rights Breakthrough of the 1970s: The European Community and International Relations*. New York: Bloomsbury Academic.

Magone, José M. 2015. "Divided Europe? Euroscepticism in Central, Eastern and Southern Europe." In *The European Union in Crisis: Explorations in Representation and Democratic Legitimacy*, edited by Kyriakos N. Demetriou, 33–56. New York: Springer.

Manners, Ian. 2002. "Normative Power Europe: A Contradiction in Terms?" *Journal of Common Market Studies* 40 (2): 235–58.

Mayer, Hartmut. 2008. "Is It Still Called 'Chinese Whispers?' The EU's Rhetoric and Action as a Responsible Global Institution." *International Affairs* 84 (1): 61–79.

McKean, David, and Bart M. Szewczyk. 2021. *Partners of First Resort: America, Europe, and the Future of the West*. Washington: Brookings.

Menon, Anand, Kalypso Nicolaidis, and Jennifer Welsh. 2004. "In Defence of Europe. A Response to Kagan." *Journal of European Affairs* 2 (3): 5–14.

Mertus, Julie. 2004. *Bait and Switch: Human Rights and U.S. Foreign Policy*. New York: Routledge.

Micklethwait, John, and Adrian Wooldridge. 2005. *The Right Nation: Conservative Power in America*. New York: Penguin.

Mowle, Thomas S. 2004. *Allies at Odds?: The United States and the European Union*. New York: Palgrave MacMillan.

Moyn, Samuel. 2010. *The Last Utopia: Human Rights in History*. Cambridge: Harvard University Press.

Murphy, Sean D. 2009. "The United States and the International Court of Justice: Coping With Antinomies." In *The United States and International Courts and Tribunals*, edited by Cesare P. R. Romano, 46–111. New York: Cambridge University Press.

National Security Strategy of the United States. December 2017. www.acq.osd.mil/ncbdp/docs/NSS-Final-12-18-2017-0905.pdf.

Nicolaidis, Kalypso, and Robert Howse. 2002. "'This Is My EUtopia …': Narrative as Power." *Journal of Common Market Studies* 40 (4): 767–92.

O'Connor, Brendan, and Martin Griffiths, eds. 2006. *The Rise of Anti-Americanism*. New York: Routledge.

Oeter, Stefan. 2013. "Article 21." In *The Treaty on European Union: A Commentary*, edited by Hermann-Josef Blanke and Stelio Mangiameli, 833–74. Berlin: Springer.

O'Sullivan, Aisling. 2017. *Universal Jurisdiction in International Criminal Law: The Debate and the Battle for Hegemony*. New York: Routledge.

Pacewicz, Piotr. 2017. "Po raz pierwszy w Polsce zwolennicy jednopłciowych związków partnerskich są w większości" ["For the First Time in Poland, the Majority Support Same-Sex Partnerships"]. Oko Press. https://oko.press/pierwszy-polsce-zwolennicy-homoseksualnych-zwiazkow-partnerskich-sa-wiekszosci-moze-juz-czas/.

Pérez de las Heras, Beatriz. 2015. "EU and US External Policies on Human Rights and Democracy Promotion: Assessing Political Conditionality in Transatlantic Partnership." *Romanian Journal of European Affairs* 15 (2): 80–96.

Pew Research Center. 2018. "Eastern and Western Europeans Differ on Importance of Religion." www.pewforum.org/2018/10/29/eastern-and-western-europeans-differ-on-importance-of-religion-views-of-minorities-and-key-social-issues/.

———. 2020. "The Global Divide on Homosexuality Persists." www.pewresearch.org/global/2020/06/25/global-divide-on-homosexuality-persists/.

Politico. 2017. Memo. www.politico.com/f/?id=00000160-6c37-da3c-a371-ec3f13380001.

Porter, Patrick. 2018. "A World Imagined: Nostalgia and Liberal Order." Cato Institute Policy Analysis No. 843. www.cato.org/policy-analysis/world-imagined-nostalgia-liberal-order.

Puzarina, Kristina, Jana Pötzschke, and Hans Rattinger. 2014. "Attitudes Towards Human Rights and Democracy: Empirical Evidence in Europe and the United States." Transworld Working Paper No. 30. www.iai.it/sites/default/files/tw_wp_30.pdf.

Renouard, Joe. 2016. *Human Rights in American Foreign Policy: From the 1960s to the Soviet Collapse*. Philadelphia: University of Pennsylvania Press.

———. 2020. "Sino-Western Relations, Political Values, and the Human Rights Council." *Journal of Transatlantic Studies* 18: 80–102.

Rosecrance, Richard. 1998. "The European Union: A New Type of International Actor." In *Paradoxes of European Foreign Policy*, edited by Jan Zielonka, 15–23. The Hague: Kluwer Law International.

Schabas, William A. 2000. "Spare the RUD or Spoil the Treaty: The United States Challenges the Human Rights Committee on Reservations." In *The United States and Human Rights: Looking Inward and Outward*, edited by David P. Forsythe, 110–25. Lincoln: University of Nebraska Press.

Sikkink, Kathryn. 2004. *Mixed Signals: U.S. Human Rights Policy in Latin America*. Ithaca, NY: Cornell University Press.

Simoni, Serena. 2013. *Understanding Transatlantic Relations: Whither the West?* New York: Routledge.

Sjursen, Helene. 2006. "The EU as a 'Normative' Power: How Can This Be?" *Journal of European Public Policy* 13 (2): 235–51.

———. 2015. "Normative Theory: An Untapped Resource in the Study of European Foreign Policy." In *The Sage Handbook of European Foreign Policy*, edited by Knud Erik

Jørgensen, Aasne Kallan Aarstad, Edith Drieskens, Katie Laatinkainen, and Ben Tonra, 197–214. Thousand Oaks, CA: Sage.

Sloan, Stanley R. 2016a. *Defense of the West: NATO, the European Union, and the Transatlantic Bargain*. Manchester: Manchester University Press.

———. 2016b. "NATO's Hollowing Values Agenda." Atlantic Council Issue Brief. www.atlanticcouncil.org/in-depth-research-reports/issue-brief/natos-hollowing-values-agenda/.

Smith, Karen E. 2008. *European Union Foreign Policy in a Changing World*. 2nd ed. Malden, MA: Polity.

Snyder, Sarah B. 2018. *From Selma to Moscow: How Human Rights Activists Transformed U.S. Foreign Policy*. New York: Columbia University Press.

Stanley, Ben. 2017. "Populism in Central and Eastern Europe." In *The Oxford Handbook of Populism*, edited by Cristóbal Rovira Kaltwasser, Paul Taggart, Paulina Ochoa Espejo, and Pierre Ostiguy, 140–59. New York: Oxford University Press.

Statista. 2021. "Attitude Toward." 24 June. www.statista.com/statistics/1030193/russia-attitudes-toward-lgbt-persons/.

Taggart, Paul. "Populism in Western Europe." In *The Oxford Handbook of Populism*, edited by Cristóbal Rovira Kaltwasser, Paul Taggart, Paulina Ochoa Espejo, and Pierre Ostiguy, 248–65. New York: Oxford University Press.

Tcherneva, Vessela. 2018. *The End of the Concept of the West?* Brussels: Heinrich Boll Foundation.

Tillerson, Rex. 2017. Remarks to US Department of State Employees. https://2017-2021.state.gov/remarks-to-u-s-department-of-state-employees/index.html.

Timbro Authoritarian Populism Index. n.d. https://populismindex.com/.

Toje, Asle. 2008. "The European Union as a Small Power, or Conceptualizing Europe's Strategic Actorness." *Journal of European Integration* 30 (2): 199–215.

Trump, Donald J. 2017a. Remarks at the Arab Islamic American Summit. 21 May. Public Papers of the Presidents. www.presidency.ucsb.edu/ws/index.php?pid=124969.

———. 2017b. Remarks to the United Nations General Assembly. 19 September. Public Papers of the Presidents. www.presidency.ucsb.edu/node/331184.

van Berlo, Milan, and Michal Natorski. 2020. "When Contestation Is the Norm: The Position of Populist Parties in the European Parliament Towards Conflicts in Europe's Neighbourhood." In *European Union Contested: Foreign Policy in a New Global Context*, edited by Elisabeth Johansson-Nogués, Martijn C. Vlaskamp, and Esther Barbé, 191–211. Cham: Springer Nature.

Verbeek, Bertjan, and Andrej Zaslove. 2017. "Populism and Foreign Policy." In *The Oxford Handbook of Populism*, edited by Cristóbal Rovira Kaltwasser, Paul Taggart, Paulina Ochoa Espejo, and Pierre Ostiguy, 384–404. New York: Oxford University Press.

Walldorf, C. William. 2008. *Just Politics: Human Rights and the Foreign Policy of Great Powers*. Ithaca: Cornell University Press.

Walt, Stephen M. 2011. "The Myth of American Exceptionalism." *Foreign Policy* 189 (11 October): 72–75.

———. 2016. "The Collapse of the Liberal World Order." *Foreign Policy*. 26 June 2016. https://foreignpolicy.com/2016/06/26/the-collapse-of-the-liberal-world-order-european-union-brexit-donald-trump/.

Wickett, Xenia. 2018. *Transatlantic Relations: Converging or Diverging?* London: Chatham House.

Youngs, Richard. 2004. "Normative Dynamics and Strategic Interests in the EU's External Identity." *Journal of Common Market Studies* 42 (2): 415–35.

PART III
Broader Determinants of Transatlantic Relations

7
CANADA–EU–US RELATIONS

Emmanuel Brunet-Jailly

Introduction

Over the last 50 years, the European Union (EU), alongside its member states, has become a major international actor in matters of trade and foreign affairs. This transformation is as remarkable as it is noticeably recent—and understudied. Yet, it is having a distinct impact on all the international activities of EU member states. This chapter is a review of those changes and a critical assessment of the EU's transatlantic relations with Canada and the United States (US).

In the current international system, which emerged in 1648 with the signature of the Treaties of Westphalia, sovereignty is understood as the merger of four core functions of members of the international community: foreign policy, diplomacy, security, and defense. Today, in the case of the EU, such functions are split between the member states and the Union, with the EU now primarily controlling foreign policy and diplomacy, while its member states still control security and defense (Mérand and Rayroux 2018, 176). In other words, in International Relations studies, Canada, the US, and the EU do not share the same nature: Canada and the US are fully fledged federal systems and members of the international community with seats at the United Nations (UN), while the EU, despite some scholarly arguments to the contrary (Sidjanski 2001), is not a federation and is not a fullfledged member of the international community. Indeed, since May 2011, thanks to UN resolution 65/276, the EU is considered to be a regional organization. It has permanent observer status with enhanced participation rights, a unique set of rights including representation and presentation of proposals and amendments (European Council 2020) but not membership. This position of the EU in the UN, however, is only the tip of the iceberg. Indeed, reviewing and critically assessing such a relationship must consider differences that continue to affect its nature, its future, and its trajectory in the partnership.

DOI:10.4324/9781003147565-11

After a brief introduction, this chapter first focuses on the EU and its global strategy. Second, it presents the EU's own views on its transatlantic relationships and then on the past-and-present relationships with Canada and the US. The nature of the EU, the split nature of its international and foreign policy functions, and the values enshrined in its founding Treaty of Lisbon, guide our review and assessment of transatlantic relations to argue that, despite possible divergences in interests and policy with Canada and the US, the EU has become an inescapable and important partner. Because of both exogenous and endogenous reasons on both sides of the Atlantic, the transatlantic relationships remain very important, are resilient, and primarily cooperative.

Context: What Is the European Union?

Many legal scholars argue that, even before the signature of Lisbon, the "European Community" had "federalizing features" built in the common market treaty system (Hay 1966), and since Lisbon, it has continued to progressively implement similar structures across new supranational and intergovernmental domains where the federalizing leadership of the European institutions have made their mark. In his key work, *Federalism and Supranational Organizations*, Hay explained that

> One of the important reasons for the success of European integration is the organizational form which it adopted for the three "European Communities." Described as "supranational" [...] these organizations possess both independence from and power over their constituent states to a degree suggesting the emergence of a federal hierarchy.
>
> *Hay 1966, 4 cited in Martinico 2016, 35*

Nevertheless, as noted by Martinico (2016), the EU is not a federation. Instead, it is what legal scholars call *sui generis*—the EU is comparable to a federal system but is, at the same time, a unique and particular type of organization that is truly one of a kind. So, when looking at its international relations and foreign policy, we need to keep in mind the Union's sui generis nature as well as Mérand and Rayroux (2018) subtle suggestion that transfers in sovereignty include most of foreign policy and diplomacy, while its member states continue to hold back on much of security and defense policy.

Given the role of values in driving international relations (Harle 1990; Huntington 1993; Katzenstein 1996; Katzenstein, Keohane, and Krasner 1998; Pethiyagoda 2020), this chapter centers on European values as enshrined in the Union's founding treaty (Article 1a), which states that the Union

> *is founded on the values of respect of human dignity, freedom, democracy, equality, the rule of law and respect of human rights, including the rights of persons belonging to minorities. These values are common to Member States in a society in which pluralism,*

non-discrimination, tolerance, justice, solidarity and equality between women and men prevail [emphasis added].

Lisbon—EU 2007, 11

The EU has used a very particular method, known as the "Community Method" to implement observance of Community and then EU laws among its member states. In this chapter, I suggest that EU values enshrined in law play an important part in some of its blatant successes and failures (De Baere and Gutman 2012, 131). In the same vein, it is important to underscore here that the EU geopolitical approaches to politics and trade are framed by the pre-existing decision-making power the EU's Commission distinctly has in each area: With regards to market policy, diplomacy, and foreign affairs, the European Council has given the Commission and the European External Action Service (EEAS) a mandate only limited by qualified majority voting in Council. Whereas in matters of security and defense, national politics and intergovernmental relations continue to dominate, integration progress only results from unanimous decisions in Council. Hence, the well-documented and mediatic sense that European Council decisions take forever and take place within a theater of dissent.

This fundamental distinction between trade and political matters remains central to our understanding of the EU's strategy and trajectory. For instance, the EU's approach to recent notable internal tensions with Hungary and Poland have followed this framework: The EU always distinguishes, as a matter of principle, between market and political integration issues. When dealing with Hungary and Poland, it has become clear that political and value-dominated issues cannot spill over onto the areas of market integration. In the recent past, this line was not always so clear, as illustrated by the difficult decision-making process regarding the Multiannual Financial Framework and the Next Generation EU instrument of July 2019 (Brunet-Jailly and Hallgrimsdottir 2020). However, most recently, the European Commission has been reviewing, and has not yet approved, this same post-COVID-19 recovery funds for both Hungary and Poland because of tensions over fundamental values, such as the independence of the judiciary in Poland and LGBTQIA politics in Hungary.

Similarly, in the same line of thought in foreign policy, the EU has developed the concept of "systematic rivalry" to differentiate profoundly between political and economic matters when tensions arise. According to Blockmans and Hu (2019), when the European Commission reviewed the Road and Belt partnership investments in Hungary over Chinese state-owned initiative BorsodChem's investment, it found that "the investment in BorsodChem were not economically sound, [but] help job creation, regional development and the attainment of environmental objectives" (3). Likewise, according to Maçães (2021), recent tensions between the EU and China illustrate again how politics and market issues could have been entangled but confirm that the Union's strategy in its relationship with China is consistent and works. Indeed, the EU did join the United Kingdom (UK) and the US in implementing sanctions over human rights violations regarding Uighur Muslims in the Xinjiang Province. Indeed, while negotiating with China for the EU–China Comprehensive Agreement on Investment (CAI), the EU also implemented new regulations to prevent the Chinese state from interfering with more economic integration. And, in the end, the CAI is not a political agreement. It is a trade and market agreement only, and it has been designed to suit a European trading strategy. Hence, Maçães's (2021) conclusion: "They [Europeans] will keep insisting that to do business in their territory, China will have to do it on European terms" (19).

It is clear then that EU assertiveness is a progressive, structurally ambitious, and geopolitically complicated process, starting in 1999 with the previous three European Commissions, first under the leadership of president of the European Commission Romano Prodi (1999–2004) and then José Manuel Barroso (2004–14), Jean-Claude Juncker (2014–19), and Ursula von der Leyen (since July 2019). Prodi was the first president to work with a high representative of the EU for Foreign Affairs and Security Policy in the person of Javier Solana (1999–2009). He was succeeded by Catherine Ashton (2009–14), who was also first vice president of the Commission, and then Federica Mogherini (2014–19). The high representative today is Josep Borrell (since December 2019). Interestingly, it was only in December 2010 that the creation of the position of high representative came along together with the creation of the EEAS, that is, a very recent transformation of the European Commission. Indeed, for this purpose, the Commission merged two pre-existing services to implement this new service: the External Relations departments of both the Commission and the Council. Thus, a merger of EU diplomats along with national diplomats previously seconded to the EU. Today, this diplomatic corps is one of the largest in the world. It is independent from both the Commission and the Council and is currently headed by Borrell. The EEAS and the European Defence Agency work together and within the Permanent Structured Cooperation (PESCO), which is organizing the structured integration of 25 of the 27 national armed forces of the EU. Such integration has only taken place very progressively since 2017. PESCO was Mogherini's main policy breakthrough, signed in November 2017 and activated in December that same year.

In sum, for the EU to effectively engage internationally, it had to first address many important internal issues: issues of policy on trade developed as EU prerogatives progressively (agriculture, commerce, or trade), but as the very recent signature of the PESCO indicates, defense and security took many more years to become clearer intergovernmental issues. In other words, the fundamental question regarding this rather laggard evolution is to understand *why* regarding security and defense, the EU was not able to articulate a pan-Union strategy until very recently.

Context: What Is the European Union Strategy?

Concurrent to those institutional developments, for the EU, these changing contexts also include the *recent* process on the "Future of Europe" that started with the 2001 Laeken Declaration on the Future of the European Union (European

Commission 2001) and the subsequent 2009 Treaty of Lisbon. Both texts made important contributions to the formal expansion of the EU's foreign policy, defense, and security, and its diplomatic presence across the world.

Simultaneous negotiations of international agreements, the Strategic Partnerships, on common political, economic, and security issues were one important aspect of those developments. Today, the EU has Strategic Partnership engagements with ten countries: Brazil, Canada, China, India, Japan, Mexico, South Africa, South Korea, Russia, and the US. Canada, Japan, Russia, and the US are considered as established partners but originally had no such arrangements. On the contrary, Brazil (2007), China (2003), India (2004), Mexico (2008), and South Africa (2007) were formally approved by the EU Council first. Finally, South Korea did not follow a formal process but became a Strategic Partner in 2010.

From 2003 onward, and particularly after the 2008 *Report on the Implementation of the European Security Strategy*, the European Commission started implementing its security strategy under the leadership of Herman Van Rompuy and High Representative of the European Union for Foreign Affairs and Security Catherine Ashton. Since then, both the world and the EU have faced a turbulent global context. For instance, China asserted itself with renewed vigor in the South China Sea (2010 and 2016). In 2013, it launched infrastructure programs in about 60 partner countries worldwide (the Belt and Road Initiative); in 2014, Russia annexed Crimea. In 2014–15 as well, 1.2 million refugees crossed the Mediterranean Sea and peripheral countries to enter the EU during summer and fall 2014, winter 2015, and spring 2016.

Early observers and critiques such as Renard (2011) argued that those partnership agreements made it clear that specific partners were strategic while others were not and suggested that this approach influenced the relationship of EU with third countries because the partnerships implied a specific diplomatic game of inclusion and exclusion. Ultimately, Renard was skeptical and asked in his early report: "why" ten countries, "why" those specific ten countries, and for "what" strategic purpose? In a way, in an attempt to answer those questions for the EU, Ferreira-Pereira and Guedes Vieira (2016) argued that the Strategic Partnerships were multidimensional and multipurpose foreign policy instruments that pointed to the global regulatory ambition of the EU. But for Renard (2011), there was a lack of clarity behind the negotiations, and the rationale for the association of some of the partner countries was questionable, suggesting that "some countries (e.g., the US) are considered to be natural partners of the EU, whereas others (e.g., China and Russia) are considered simply to be too big to ignore" (iii).

Arguably, this tumultuous global environment has contributed to more European integration. Indeed, for the European Commission, one very important aspect of these partnerships is the acknowledgment of shared goals and values but also of the relative influence of each partners on global issues that matter to the EU such as human rights, security and defense, trade and investments, culture and education, and the environment. In 2016, High Representative Mogherini talked about "Our Union is under threat" and the EU needing "deepening partnership" so the EU can play its "collective role in the world" (EEAS 2016, 7, 13). In addition, beyond the advancement of Strategic Partnerships, Mogherini's leadership marked a turning point regarding discussion of the EU's Global Strategy (EU 2019). Mogherini wrote and said publicly that "a Global Strategy has been our collective compass in these difficult times."

However, more recently, Renard (2021) has remained unconvinced, arguing that there may be over 200 such partnerships in the world, with China leading the way in "Partnership Diplomacy" with about 50 established partnerships and the US with 31. Renard suggested, citing Cox, that "we no longer live in a world composed of clearly specified friends and well-defined enemies, but rather in one where partnership has become a necessity" (Cox 2012, 8; Renard 2021, 317). Furthermore, suggesting with Grevi (2012) that there were "partnerships of choices" and "partnerships of necessity." Also, since 2013, EU strategic autonomy has remained limited to the defense industry, which the European Council has managed to broker and reconfirm since then as "a more integrated, sustainable innovative and competitive defence technological and industrial base can contribute to enhance the EU's strategic autonomy and its ability to act with partners" (European Council 2019). This awareness led to two tools being developed, PESCO and the European Defence Fund (EDF), and since 2019, the realization that a common vision and an industrial policy were necessary for the development of such autonomy. For instance, the European Parliament recently noted the need to develop "strategic value chains that are key to EU industrial competitiveness and strategic autonomy" (European Parliament 2021, 4). Such awareness was further confirmed extremely clearly in April 2020 when President Charles Michel expressed the "utmost importance to increase the strategic autonomy of the Union and produce essential goods in Europe" (European Council 2021).

The Strategic Partnerships are part of an EU policy focusing on three groups of states: future European member states, neighboring states that are targeted by neighborhood policies, and Strategic Partnership states. These are three circles of friends that share values and/or some geopolitical proximity. Understanding Strategic Partnerships should be of great importance to our understanding of transatlantic relations, but the very recent institutional and strategic history of the European trajectory cannot be understated.

The EU View on Transatlantic Relations With Canada and the United States

On 24 March 2021, at the Berlaymont briefing session with US Secretary of State Antony J. Blinken, EU Commission President von der Leyen said, "The United States is an important and valued partner for the European Union, and we want to forge a new EU–US global agenda to meet the challenges, but also to seize the opportunity of our time" (European Commission 2021) and then carried on listing an agenda for discussions that included post-COVID vaccine supply chains; the suspension of tariffs regarding the Airbus/Boeing squabble; the need for discussion on the "multilateral trading system"; climate change and the return of the US administration to the Paris Agreement; and the North Atlantic Treaty Organization (NATO) and other foreign and security policies, including China, Russia, Turkey, and the Western Balkans.

What is important in such a declaration is that, for the EU, it is the core values, shared with Canada and the US, that are at the center of the relationship. These are the values of liberal democracies: democracy, human rights, the rule of law, economic and political freedom, and shared foreign policy and security interests. All are understood as contributing positively to more cooperation and strategic relations between the EU, Canada, and the US. Liberal internationalist and democratic values possibly form the bedrock of the transatlantic relationship. However, there are other issues important to the EU. They include cooperation in multilateral forums, climate and trade concerns, increased technological and digital competition, the relationship with Russia, and the rise of China.

Furthermore, shared history, values, and "strong people to people ties" (EU 2021, 4) and increased coordination on environmental issues, but also energy security and regional stability, and within the G7 and G20 contexts, are important to understand the EU side of the relationship.

Canada and the EU work together in EU common security and defense policy missions (e.g., Iraq, Mali, Ukraine, and Palestinian Territories) and in election observation missions. EU and Canadian parliamentarians have been meeting for 40 years to discuss common affairs, and since the 38th Interparliamentary Meeting, they have signed an agreement to maintain an uninterrupted dialogue that would complement other institutions set through their Strategic Partnership Agreement (SPA) (Council of the European Union 2016b). In addition, trade, economic, and investment relations with Canada have been transformed by ten years of negotiation and the signature of the Comprehensive Economic and Trade Agreement (CETA) (Council of the European Union 2016a). Particularly controversial, the CETA contains a special Investment Court System, whose application will have to wait for unilateral approval across all EU member states and regional parliaments. The SPA protects the rights of governments who are party to the Agreement to regulate public health, safety, the environment, and public morals, and provides social and consumer safeguards. The CETA signature led to a 7 percent increase in exports from the EU to Canada. With €38 billion in EU goods exported to Canada, the EU was and remains Canada's third-largest trading partner. Canada is the EU's 12th-largest trading partner with €20 billion worth of goods. EU services exported to Canada stood at €19 billion in 2018, while Canadian services imported by the EU remained at €13.5 billion. Investments stood at par with about €390 billion crossing the Atlantic from Canada and from the EU as foreign direct investments (FDIs).

Interestingly, the US Congress and the European Parliament also share a long-lasting relationship dating back to 1972, which was formalized as the Transatlantic Legislators' Dialogue with biannual interparliamentary meetings. In 2020, they issued a joint statement formalizing four main areas of shared concern across the

Atlantic: the health crisis, economic recession, the need for transatlantic leadership internationally, and collaboration with China and Russia. However, the European Parliament voted *against* the reopening of Transatlantic Trade and Investment Partnership (TTIP) negotiations in March 2019. In addition, in April 2019, the EU Council agreed to negotiate the elimination of industrial tariffs and conformity assessment. The EU and the US economies together represent nearly 50 percent of the world's gross domestic product (GDP) and about 30 percent of world trade. The US purchases about 18 percent of all EU exported goods and is its top partner. The EU, in return, imported about 12 percent of US exports and is its second top trading partner after China. The EU is the US's top purchaser of services with €196 billion to the EU versus €179 billion from the EU but with a strong steady increase of EU services sold in the US. Finally, they are each other's largest investors with a balanced amount of FDIs of about €375 billion year-to-year. However, beyond the failure of the TTIP negotiations, steel, aluminium, and cars as well as the aircraft industry have been issues of contention since 2018, with US tariffs being imposed on the EU and the EU filing a trade complaint to the World Trade Organization (WTO) in 2018. Also, the aircraft industry has seen the WTO authorize retaliation against the EU industry in the amount of €7.5 billion and against the US industry in the amount of €3.5 billion in 2020.

Past and Present Relationships of the EU With Canada

Canada and the EU only discovered each other as partners relatively recently. Until the turn of the last century, both Canada and the EU assumed that the structure of their alliances were set within NATO's parameters (i.e., through a narrow but very important security portfolio (Verdun 2021, 123)). Accompanying this was an assumption that their relationship was primarily dependent on their direct relationship with the US.

Internal politics played an important obstructing role in the resulting underdevelopment of a direct relationship between the EU and Canada. Québec separatist, nationalist, and sovereigntist ambitions were an ongoing frustration, and failures to reform either the Constitution or the federal system of equalization-preoccupied decision-makers (e.g., the 1992 Charlottetown Accord). Sovereigntists' ambitions culminated in a failed secessionist referendum in 1995. Furthermore, trade dependency on the US remained a core focus, but the signature of the North American Free Trade Agreement (NAFTA) crowned Canadian anxieties regarding its relationship with the US. NAFTA sealed and secured free trade between both countries.

In addition, there was reluctance to engage in furthering a relationship both on the Canadian and EU sides because, for Canada, in line with its historical relationship with the UK, diplomacy was primarily with each European member state directly, while, in return, the EU did not fully appreciate the nearly confederal structure of Canada in matters of trade. The complexity of both polities contributed to misunderstandings. Verdun (2021) underscored that EU officials did not understand the Canadian federal structure, which gives jurisdiction to provinces. For instance, Verdun argued with de Mestral and Fox-Decent: "The Canadian Constitution stipulates that the federal government has competence to negotiate trade agreements but cannot force provinces to implement them" (de Mestral and Fox-Decent 2008, 644; Verdun 2021, 132)—a federal peculiarity which Canadian scholar Grace Skogstad has deemed to be "shared jurisdiction" (Skogstad as quoted in Verdun 2021, 132). The resulting history of relations is a long list of specialized and sectoral agreements that are extremely well-documented in the literature but which prevent the formation of a broader "treaty" every time.

The idea of a comprehensive treaty came under the leadership of Nicolas Sarkozy, then president of the European Council, and then Canadian Prime Minister Stephen Harper. Negotiations had started in early 2008 and became public when famed Canadian journalist Doug Sanders wrote an article in Canada's national newspaper, *The Globe and Mail*, in early September 2008. At the time, it was interesting to hear diplomats disclose to journalists that Canada needed to get its act together and that provincial–federal relationships on issues of trade could derail agreement negotiations.

On the EU side, negotiators were also courting other important trade partners, such as Japan, which at the time was considered an easier negotiation than Canada. Interestingly, it was in September 2008 that the public ascent of Québec and Ontario's premiers gave a second wind to negotiations, and the realization that interprovincial trade barriers had disappeared but overlapping regulations, multiple licensing, and local preferences in government contracts remained as obstacles to doing business in the country (Sanders 2008). The negotiations took years to settle and the treaties—the SPA and CETA were both signed on 30 October 2016.

The SPA sets the stage regarding security and defense matters (Mérand and Rayoux 2018, 189–194) and thus is dependent on the EU's Common Security and Defence Policy (CSDP) and the Common Foreign and Security Policy (CFSP). CETA focuses exclusively on trade relations and was a model for the Brexit agreement that is now organizing the relationship between the UK and the EU today. Both the SPA and CETA are important agreements that remain popular in Canada even at a time when most political discussion focus on the post-pandemic recovery.

Finally, and most importantly, at a time when such treaties are not as popular as they may have been in 2008 when negotiations started, these treaties have yet to be ratified in the EU by both lower-level regional government and the national parliaments of EU member states. Indeed, as time goes by, EU citizen and sectoral non-profit organizations have criticized the often obscure negotiation and resulting agreements seemingly empower larger trade organizations and businesses, particularly with regard to dispute processes.

In the last five years, it is clear that multilateral cooperation in the G7 and the G20 formats have been contested, yet Canada presided over the 2018 G7 Summit and proposed a notably progressive agenda focusing on five topics: investing in growth that works for all, preparing jobs for the future, advancing gender equality and female empowerment, and working on climate change. Observers noted that such an agenda contravened NATO disputes with the US and the Trump administration's withdrawal from the multilateral Paris Climate Agreement (Trudeau 2017). However, these five topics are particularly interesting here because they signal that, in 2018, Canada and the EU shared strong views on international security, trade, and climate change.

Should the EU and Canada's close relationship be a surprise today? I argue that it should, in large part because for a long time that relationship was mitigated by the US as the dominant partner in matters of trade and security. The Trump presidency changed this situation. Partial disagreements and the White House's preference for bilateral relationships serving "America First" affected both Canada and the EU. In addition, the British exit from the EU (Brexit) also fundamentally and unanimously altered the views inside the Union of third states. What is particularly interesting is that during a rather unsettling Trump presidency, Brussels and Ottawa have signed and provisionally implemented the CETA and have concurrently started to concentrate on furthering their relationship. Hence, the notably enlightening remark by EEAS Secretary General Pedro Serrano "the EU Canada relationship—like brandy—has gotten better with age" which has been noted (Bendiek et al. 2018). Concomitantly, in the area of security, during the 4 December 2017 meeting of the EU–Canada Ministerial Committee (a first since the EU 2016 SPA) focused on deeper security and defense cooperation and the enhancement of EU–Canada cooperation around the world (Government of Canada 2017).

What is particularly significant is that both partners were interested in furthering multilateralism, while their traditionally most important partner (the US) was not and that they were working on issues of trade and security together and in front of both the WTO and NATO, reaffirming that EU–NATO cooperation provided a "solid basis for stepping up EU–Canada security and defence cooperation" (Government of Canada 2017, 7.i). This strengthening of the EU–Canada relationship and of shared views was also reaffirmed by Canada's minister of Foreign Affairs at the time, Chrystia Freeland, when she called "Canada's partnership with its European Allies [...] more essential than ever" (Freeland 2018).

This recent context of the close relationship between the EU and Canada points to the exceptionally unique relationship that Canada and the US have developed since the War of 1812 centered on a partnership resulting from shared geography; values; common interests; personal connections; and multilayered economic, social, and political ties. In 2021, Canada and the US still present the strongest trade relationship in the world, with more than CA$2 billion in goods crossing their common border each day. Their commitment to cooperation continues and was laid out again on 23 February 2021, in the *Roadmap for a Renewed U.S. Canada Partnership*, a document that establishes a renewed partnership in the fight against the COVID-19 pandemic and "mutual economic prosperity" (Trudeau 2021). However, trade with the US has been stable since the 2008 economic crisis. In this light, the past and present relationships of the EU and Canada demonstrates the recent alignment and strengthening of shared values and common economic interests, and the establishment of strong international agreements that confirm a trajectory of resilience and future commitment to cooperation. It is particularly notable that Canada and the EU signed two separate agreements, one on issues of trade and one regarding the broader value-laden political agreement. Since the CETA agreement went into force, the Port of Montréal has seen a 20 percent increase in goods going to Europe, and German motor vehicles have seen an increase of 168 percent. In sum, CETA works.

Past and Present Relationship of the EU With the US

The relationship of EU with the US is marked by eras of competition, as well as political, economic, and security cooperation and convergence. Competition takes place in the areas of economics, trade, and global economic policy. Recently, convergence has resulted from other difficult relationships with Iran and also, for instance, Russia and China, but tensions remain important with regard to the securitization of policy domains such as energy, the environment, or human rights, where the EU has promoted its soft normative power.

The Trump presidency was a period of serious challenges. It seems that the Biden presidency will be an era of further partnerships (Biden 2020; Cimoszewicz 2021). Indeed, on 24 March 2021, Secretary of State Blinken, a Francophile and supporter of Europe and the EU, said during the Berlaymont briefing session at the European Commission's headquarters (before the meeting with EU Commission President von der Leyen),

> I have to say, Madame President, as we consider our partnership with the European Union, we see the European Union as a partner of first resort on virtually everything you've already put on the agenda, and a number of other things that we'll discuss.
>
> US State Department 2021a

Undeniably, the EU–US partnership is steeped in a long tradition of outstanding cooperation, alignments, and crises. In the post-World War II period, the relationship existed alongside the creation and development of the European Communities (Janes 2021). This history, the Cold War, and the recent global transformation of the world from a juxtaposition of national-industrial powers to a world of global information and communication economies, the fragmentation of the Soviet Union and the emergence of Russia, and the more recent rise of Asian economies in the 1970s and 1980s, and of China (particularly since the post-Deng Xiaoping period, ending in 1989), all contributed major geopolitical shifts that affected the relationship. The development and affirmation of the EU as an international political actor furthered the partnership, but the euro, and trade and commercial policies brought along tensions as well.

At the core of this original relationship is a historically strong association that does not have a formal all-encompassing treaty. There are agreements in many different areas, from declarations on common interests to action plans. For instance, there is the post-World War II and post-Cold War Transatlantic Declaration (1990) and the 1995 New Transatlantic Agenda and New Transatlantic Agenda and Action Plan (which includes 150 security and trade potential initiatives) or again, the more recent Economic Partnership Agreement of 2008. None provided the architecture of a formal treaty.

Possibly more important are the people-to-people relationships that form the bedrock of these agreements, best illustrated by the 1995 TransAtlantic Business Dialogue (TABD) that has brought together business and government networks to discuss EU–US issues across networks covering numerous areas including legislative alignments, employment, and trade among many others. The TABD became a program of the Trans-Atlantic Business Council in 2013; meeting twice yearly, they make numerous policy recommendations aimed at the establishment of a barrier-free transatlantic market.

These organizations rest on the security foundations set by NATO, which brings together 30 European states and Turkey (i.e., not just the EU and/or member states). During the Trump presidency, it was the EU member states' own contributions to NATO that were raised as a core problem, hence fears of fissures in the foundations of the relationship.

However, the background remains that global economic forces are continually evolving. Together, the EU and the US contribute to about half of the world GDP and global trade in goods and services. For instance, more than 164,000 EU businesses are exporting to the US; 93,000 of those are small and medium enterprises. In terms of investments, US investments in the EU are three times larger than the whole of Asia's, and EU investments in the US are eight times greater than EU investments in India and China. Indeed, despite China becoming the EU's prime source of imports in 2021, the US and the EU have the world's largest trade and investment relationship, which also contributes to their uniquely integrated economic relations. Interestingly, despite such a unique economic relationship, the EU and US negotiations on the TTIP ended in 2016 after three years of failed negotiations.

In other words, there is tremendous evidence that the historical foundation of the relationship remains extremely strong across and beyond governments as a nearly 70-year-old networked partnership of non-governmental, non-profit, and private sector organizations persists—these are the interactions that may be at the core of what is referred to as a "strategic partnership" by the EU. Due to these foundations and networks, there is a particular resilience to transatlantic relations. With no overarching treaty providing a keystone to the edifice, such multitudes of linkages across various sectors and networks, institutions, and agreements make it difficult to actually characterize it as an institutionalized relationship. For instance, Smith (2021) argued that a difficulty resides with the EU itself, particularly with its incapacity to decide on a strategy and a role in relation to the US. Indeed, because of its sui generis nature and the complexities of internal coherence and external autonomy, the EU remains dependent on its relationship with its member states, thus internal cohesion and fragmentation continue to explain both its strength and fragility.

Many divergences emerged on the front of differing views on the nature of the relationship, the progressive but slow transformation of EU positions and shifting US policies. At the core is the worldwide transformation of security issues that are challenging the very foundation and management of transatlantic security. The soft "normative" position of the EU and the hard interventionist and nationalistic diplomatic messages of the US during the Trump presidency shed light on a relationship set in the shadow of the post-World War II era that was also affected by the slow-rising manifestation of EU foreign policy views on trade and security.

The unsuccessful negotiation of the TTIP is witness of the power of the European Commission vis-à-vis member states, yet regarding the Iran Nuclear Treaty, which the US left in 2018, the contribution of the EU through its member states (Britain, Germany, and France) is also recognized. Certainly, the transformation of the EU, which since the Lisbon Treaty has seen its role expanded with both diplomatic normative and economic powers, is unquestionable: a bureaucracy; the EEAS headed by a high representative who also serves as vice president of the European Commission; and a network of embassies present in 140 countries; and possibly less visible, but all the more important, legislative provisions such as the CFSP and CSDP, the recent Global Strategy, and even more recently, PESCO. All these internal changes have affected the relationship and shifted the institutional foundations of the relationship on numerous issues from member states to the EU.

On 1 December 2020, Karel Lannoo (2020), the chief executive officer of the Center for Policy Studies, one of the world's top-ten independent think tanks, published a call for European policymakers arguing that the Biden presidency is a rare opportunity to revive the transatlantic relationship but that conditions apply, namely "tangible progress in areas of defence, trade and global policy stances." For Lannoo, the Trump years' personal and open policy criticisms, and open support of European far-right movements, political parties, and governments, as well as threats on both security and trade portfolios clearly had strained the relationship.

However, for Lannoo, even if the style and language have changed, these strains remain unshaken by a new Biden presidency that is both under much pressure in the US but also cannot ignore the many unresolved issues that predated the Trump presidency.

In matters of security, for instance, the EU member states that are in NATO do not contribute to their own security, and their defense budgets do not meet the pre-agreed 2 percent GDP defense spending. Relying on the US military umbrella with underfunded national or European defense budgets means that relaying US strategical efforts across the EU is undermined because operational capacity and air transport of troops are limited. Also, Russian non-military threats (in particular, in Ukraine and Syria) and China's growing global influence and presence in and around the EU, together, form real hybrid threats (Gottemoeller 2019; Advisory Council on International Affairs 2020). For Lannoo, these are threats the EU is unable to deal with autonomously today, particularly in the post-Brexit era. The Dutch Advisory Council for International Affairs makes ten policy recommendations including, for instance, EU discussions on the operationalization of article 42(7) of the Lisbon Treaty, the creation of a European Interparliamentary network on defense, and a binding collective European defense plan to strengthen the current PESCO with regard to the procurement of defense material and sufficient funds for the EDF (Advisory Council 2020, 6) to self-reliance and operational capacity.

On the trade front, lagging issues are also in question: The EU–US trade imbalance in favor of the EU amounts to about €150 billion yearly, yet EU tariffs remain much higher. Using vehicle trade as an example, US tariffs stand at 2.5 percent, while EU tariffs remain at 10 percent.

In sum, there are important and complex issues that have not been addressed, and possibly the most disconcerting of all is the absence of a permanent structure of cooperation, Lannoo argued. In effect, because the EU and US's relative economic powers are slowly declining, it seems of great importance to assert their significant relationships and those with other international liberal democracies, above and beyond specific past, present, or future tensions.

EU–US Relations During the Trump Presidency (2016–20)

In November 2016, transatlantic relations for the US became much more challenging with the election of Donald J. Trump as the US's 45th president. One of the very first issues was that Europe would have to cooperate more on defense. Foreign ministers met in Brussels as early as 13 November 2016, to discuss European security. On that day, Boris Johnson, the UK's foreign secretary at the time, did not attend as a signal of his disapproval of the meeting (generally perceived as a muted criticism of President Trump). Manfred Weber, a close ally of German Chancellor Angela Merkel, and then-chair of the European Parliament's Conservative group, said "Trump will strengthen the need to establish a European defence community" (Mitchell 2016). Jean-Claude Juncker, then European Commission president, also said that Trump's election raised "the risk of upsetting intercontinental relations in their foundation and in their structure" (Mitchell 2016). For Europe and EU leaders, this was not a discovery but a realization that transatlantic relations were not guided by post-World War II principles but by the new contours set by contemporary global governance in an increasingly global economy where both the market shares of EU member states, Canada, and the US were proportionally smaller, yet still accounted for 43.5 percent of global GDP and trade in goods and services. In sum, during the Trump presidency, in the EU, the transatlantic relationship was in question. This time was qualified as "years of mistrust, recrimination and division" (Belfer Center 2020, 2).

Lessons from that time period remain, especially with regard to the importance of what European officials call the "Strategic Autonomy" of the EU. While the concept did not make unity in the Union originally (Mogherini 2016, 3–5), it is gaining ground in the face of recent challenges, and in particular, in its relationship with important trade partners such as China, security issues with Russia, and transatlantic partners such as Canada and the US. With the election of Joseph R. Biden, Jr., to the US presidency, many Europeans have become more hopeful. But one of the core goals set by Commission President von der Leyen in the State of the Union, was the Strategic Agenda and, in particular, the EU's ability to "act autonomously": Acting autonomously is a means-to-an-end bringing together much more support for broad political consensus on strategic autonomy and thus the EU's ability to implement its decisions (European Commission 2019).

The EU has become aware of the relative limits of its soft powers, such as economic sanctions and trade and climate diplomacy. The Union's member states are increasingly aware of their need to develop the tools of hard power. Although consensus remains an ongoing requirement, there are policy domains that are increasingly crystalizing attention, including the development of defense instruments.

The European Parliamentary Research Services published *On the Path to a 'Strategic Autonomy'* in fall 2020 to underscore two major venues that the EU could use to affirm its strategic autonomy: One, is to further "integration" across "horizontal—cross-policy basis [...] to strengthen EU multilateral action, reduce dependence on external actors, and made the EU less vulnerable in areas such as energy, disinformation and digital technology" (Anghel et al. 2020). A second possible option is to expand external relations and common defense programs by activating the Lisbon Treaty's "unused or underused [...] potential" (European Parliament 2021, 1).

It seems no one should assume that having signed such Strategic Partnership with the EU means that Canada and the US have *as close or clear a relationship as they have had from World War II*. In other words, it is very important to look into each partnership to understand the nature of these relations.

For many observers (Brattberg 2021), the Biden presidency means that a renewed transatlantic relationship is possible, and, in the words of Secretary Blinken, a "Europe whole, free, prosperous, and at peace" (US State Department (2021b) also cited in Brattberg 2021) could be the US's ultimate goal. Such changes in tone and style are a steep makeover of the relationship President Trump left behind (Bennhold 2020). However, European governments, the EU, and certainly, the people of Europe may have to be convinced that a new US president means that a new, and possibly a reinvented, relationship is possible. But in the EU, European views on the US have also changed: A recent European Council on Foreign Relations (ECFR) poll suggests that Europeans do not trust that Americans will not vote for another Trump presidency in four years (32 percent) (Krastev and Leonard 2021, 5–6). Sixty-one percent of the ECFR respondents believe that the US political system is either totally or partially broken. Poland and Hungary are the two exceptions to this view. There, 56 percent and 54 percent of respondents respectively, think otherwise. To underscore this important point of departure of the relationship: 66 percent of French, 67 percent of Spaniards, 68 percent of the Netherlands, 71 percent of Danes, 72 percent of Germans, and 77 percent of Swedes believe the US political system is broken (Krastev and Leonard 2021, 7). Also, in contrast, 59 percent of

Europeans believe that, in 2030, China will be a stronger power than the US; notably, nearly 80 percent of Spaniards, Italians, and Portuguese believe that China will be a stronger power in 2030.

Thus, what is important to our study of transatlantic relationships is that a majority of Europeans have doubts about the US and concurrently believe more in themselves and in the EU's own self-reliance. Furthermore, Europeans do not believe that their future is within a bipolar world (US/Russia or China). In the case of a major disagreement between China or Russia and the US, Europeans would like their country to remain neutral. On average 59–60 percent would like their country to take neither the China or Russian side (Krastev and Leonard 2021, 11–12, 16–19).

In sum, what we learn from the ECFR survey about European attitudes is that post-Trump transatlantic geopolitics now includes an important self-awareness and desire to see European countries assert themselves economically and remain neutral on China, Russian, or US relations. This is an important new context for the Biden administration because it suggests that European governments do not have the same liberty to act according to traditional transatlantic expectations as was the case in the 1950s and the 1990s when European government had some flexibility to take decisions that did not align with the views of their electorates (Krastev and Leonard 2021, 21–24). Indeed, both the US and the EU may have to reinvent their relationship along a trajectory that cannot be isolationist but possibly along a broader alliance going beyond past transatlantic relations and including the EU as a full-fledged economic power defending the interests of its member states and citizens, and as an emerging security actor, which alongside the US and Canada, can play a fuller role above and beyond its member states (i.e., playing member states against each other will have much less leverage than ever before). International and geopolitical issues nevertheless continue to frame the relationship.

Conclusion

Despite continual historical and recent vacillations, pauses, and delays, as suggested above, the trajectory of transatlantic relations as set by the EU remains strong and resilient, notwithstanding both endogenous and exogenous reasons. The foundations of such EU policies are found not only in both the recent institutional transformation of its decision-making, bureaucratic, and financial capacities but also the profound legislative advancements set by the Laeken Declaration and the Lisbon Treaty. Over the last 30 years, despite the remaining intergovernmental nature of European Union Security and Defence policies, those texts make all recent (CFSP, CSDP, and PESCO) and future legislative evolution possible and have profoundly transformed the EU into a potentially strong security partner.

At the same time, the EU emerges as a partner with an understanding of its own values, as enshrined in the Lisbon Treaty. Despite known disagreements, Canada, the EU, and the US share many liberal-international values and norms. These deep-seated values have continually fashioned their relationships since before World War

II, as well as during the Cold War, and, since the 1990s, deep transformation of the world in Asia, particularly because of the economic and military affirmation of China.

The three partners also have areas of divergence and disagreements that have emerged in the world of international politics over markets and security issues. Most clearly result from self-serving motivations. In a world where each one of their relative world-market share and collective world-economic domination decreases, their relationships continually result from a tug-of-war between adjusting trade partnerships; and concurrently, in the multifaceted world of security and defense, where very complex and enduring tensions force each partner into continual adaptations, the US especially remains a leading global power. However, continually challenged by China, Russia, and their allies, the US, Canada, and the EU have each striven to find common ground. Historically, those exogenous tensions have always brought them into converging trajectories. One recent notable exception took place under the Trump presidency, which notably brought Canada and the EU closer.

Over the last 30 years, EU member states have persistently relinquished more power and sovereignty to their European institutions. These member state decisions have fundamentally changed their own understanding of their global collective role with regard to security and defense. Such a transformation is very slow but continual. Hence, as illustrated above, intergovernmental decisions have been giving way to majority decisions progressively, and more areas of security and defense have become the responsibility of the Union, including the procurement of defense equipment, enhanced capacity, and funding. The EU's primary approach is grounded in a separation between trade and market issues, and fundamental values and takes two prominent treaty forms: international trade agreements and strategic partnerships. Although many observers have continually pointed at the multiple weaknesses of the unanimous political-determination requirement of member states, today, it is undeniable that the EU's security and defense mechanisms are much stronger than they were even only five years ago. As demonstrated very recently over human rights issues, this dual approach served the EU's relationship with China well. Indeed, the EU surprised the world when it did not hesitate to sanction Chinese officials over mass internments and human rights issues regarding the treatment of the Uighur Muslim minority in Xinjiang.

In sum, the EU's ability to negotiate international trade agreements is unquestionable, and on security and defense issues, the EU's interests and policy have not been limited but strengthened by endogenous factors. For the EU, the transatlantic relationships with Canada and the US is resilient and primarily cooperative.

References

Advisory Council on International Affairs. 2020. "Advisory Report 112: European Security: Time for New Steps." www.advisorycouncilinternationalaffairs.nl/documents/publications/2020/06/19/european_security.

Anghel, Suzana, Beatrix Immenkamp, Elena Lazarou, Jerôme Leon Saulnier, and Alex Benjamin Wilson. 2020. *On the Path to 'Strategic Autonomy': The EU in an Evolving Geopolitical Environment*. European Parliamentary Research Service. September. www.europarl.europa.eu/RegData/etudes/STUD/2020/652096/EPRS_STU(2020)652096_EN.pdf.

Belfer Center. 2020. *Stronger Together. A Strategy to Revitalize Transatlantic Power*. www.belfercenter.org/publication/stronger-together-strategy-revitalize-transatlantic-power.

Bendiek, Annegret, Milena Geogios, Philip Nock, Felix Schenuit, and Laura von Daniels. 2018. "EU-Canada Relationship on the Rise: Mutual Interests in Security, Trade and Climate Change." SWP (German Institute for International and Security Affairs) Working Paper No. 3. October. www.swp-berlin.org/publications/products/arbeitspapiere/1_WP_Bendiek_etal_EU-Canada_relations_final_01.pdf.

Bennhold, Katrin. 2020. "Has 'America First' Become 'Trump First'? Germans Wonder." *New York Times*, 6 June 2020. www.nytimes.com/2020/06/06/world/europe/germany-troop-withdrawal-america.html.

Biden, Joseph. 2020. "Why America Must Lead Again. Rescuing U.S. Foreign Policy After Trump." *Foreign Affairs*, 23 January. www.foreignaffairs.com/articles/united-states/2020-01-23/why-america-must-lead-again.

Blockmans, Steven, and Weinian Hu. 2019. "Systemic Rivalry and Balancing Interests: Chinese Investment Meets EU Law on the Belt and Road." *CEPS [Centre for European Policy Studies] Policy Insights* No. 2019-04. www.ceps.eu/wp-content/uploads/2019/03/PI_2019_04_SB-WH_EU-China_0.pdf.

Brattberg, Erik. 2021. "Transatlantic Relations After Biden's First 100 Days." Carnegie Endowment for International Peace. https://carnegieendowment.org/2021/05/06/transatlantic-relations-after-biden-s-first-100-days-pub-84472.

Brunet-Jailly, Emmanuel, and Helga Kristin Hallgrimsdottir. 2020. "Covid-19 & the MFF 2021-27: Accountability and Transparency for All Europeans." *European Community Studies Association Canada*. 6 August. www.ecsa-c.ca/post/the-future-of-the-european-union-in-2020.

Cimoszewicz, Włodzimierz. 2021. "The Russian Factor in EU Security Policy and Transatlantic Relations." *European View* 20 (1): 34–39. https://doi.org/10.1177%2F1781685821999846.

Council of the European Union. 2016a. Comprehensive Economic and Trade Agreement (CETA). https://data.consilium.europa.eu/doc/document/ST-10973-2016-INIT/en/pdf.

———. 2016b. Strategic Partnership Agreement (EU and Canada). https://data.consilium.europa.eu/doc/document/ST-5368-2016-REV-2/en/pdf.

Cox, Michael. 2012. "Power Shifts, Economic Change and the Decline of the West?" *International Relations* 26 (4): 369–88.

De Baere, Geert, and Kathleen Gutman. 2012. "Federalism and International Relations in the European Union and the United States: A Comparative Outlook." In *Federalism in the European Union*, edited by Elke Cloots, Geert De Baere, and Stefan Sottiaux, 131–66. Portland, OR: Hart Publishing.

de Mestral, Armand, and Evan Fox-Decent. 2008. "Rethinking the Relationship Between International and Domestic Law." *McGill Law Journal* 53: 573–648. http://165.22.229.17/wp-content/uploads/pdf/1233672-De_Mestral_and_FoxDecent.pdf.

European Commission. 2001. Presidency Conclusions European Council Meeting in Laeken, 14 and 15 December 2001. https://ec.europa.eu/commission/presscorner/detail/en/DOC_01_18.

———. 2019. Opening Statement in the European Parliament Plenary Session by Ursula von der Leyen, Candidate for President of the European Commission. https://ec.europa.eu/commission/presscorner/detail/en/SPEECH_19_4230.

———. 2021. Press Statement by President von der Leyen and U.S. Secretary of State Antony Blinken. https://ec.europa.eu/commission/presscorner/detail/en/STATEMENT_21_1362.

European Council. 2019. A New Strategic Agenda, 2019–2024. Press Releases. www.consilium.europa.eu/en/press/press-releases/2019/06/20/a-new-strategic-agenda-2019-2024/.

———. 2020. EU at the UN General Assembly. European Council Policies. www.consilium.europa.eu/en/policies/unga/.

———. 2021. Conclusions of the President of the European Council Following the Video Conference of the Members of the European Council, 23 April 2020. www.consilium.europa.eu/en/press/press-releases/2020/04/23/conclusions-by-president-charles-michel-following-the-video-conference-with-members-of-the-european-council-on-23-april-2020/.

European External Action Service (EEAS). 2016. European External Action Service. Shared Vision, Common Action: A Stronger Europe – A Global Strategy for the European Union's Foreign and Security Policy. https://eeas.europa.eu/archives/docs/top_stories/pdf/eugs_review_web.pdf.

European Parliament. 2021. *Transatlantic Relations: The USA and Canada*. www.europarl.europa.eu/ftu/pdf/en/FTU_5.6.1.pdf.

European Union (EU). 2019. *The European Union's Global Strategy: Three Years on, Looking Forward*. https://eeas.europa.eu/sites/default/files/eu_global_strategy_2019.pdf.

Ferreira-Pereira, Laura C., and Alena Vystoskaya Guedes Vieira. 2016. "Introduction: The European Union's Strategic Partnerships: Conceptual Approaches, Debates and Experiences." *Cambridge Review of International Affairs* 29 (1): 3–17. https://doi.org/10.1080/09557571.2015.1130341.

Freeland, Chrystia. 2018. "Let's Not Underestimate Our Collective Power." Atlantik-Brücke Eric M. Warburg-Award for Transatlantic Commitment Speech. www.atlantik-bruecke.org/en/chrystia-freeland-lets-not-underestimate-our-collective-power-2/.

Gottemoeller, Rose. 2019. "NATO Is Not Brain Dead: The Alliance Is Transforming Faster Than Most People Think." *Foreign Affairs*, 19 December. www.foreignaffairs.com/articles/united-states/2019-12-19/nato-not-brain-dead.

Government of Canada. 2017. Joint Statement – EU and Canada: A Progressive and Dynamic Strategic Partnership. 4 December. www.international.gc.ca/world-monde/international_relations-relations_internationales/europe/2017-12-04-spa-aps.aspx?lang=eng.

Grevi, Giovanni. 2012. "Why EU Strategic Partnerships Matter." European Strategic Partnerships Observatory (ESPO) Working Paper No. 1. Brussels: ESPO.

Harle, Vilho, ed. 1990. *European Values in International Relations*. London: Bloomsbury Academic.

Hay, Peter. 1966. *Federalism and Supranational Organizations. Patterns for New Legal Structures*. Urbana, IL: University of Illinois Press.

Huntington, Samuel P. 1993. "The Clash of Civilizations." *Foreign Affairs* 72 (32): 22–169.

Janes, Jackson. 2021. "Transatlantic Relations Under US President Joe Biden." *Zeitschrift für Außen- und Sicherheitspolitik* [Foreign Affairs and Security Policy] 14: 57–73. https://doi.org/10.1007/s12399-021-00841-0.

Katzenstein, Peter Joachim, ed. 1996. *The Culture of National Security: Norms and Identity in World Politics*. New York: Columbia University Press.

Katzenstein, Peter J., Robert O. Keohane, and Stephen J. Krasner. 1998. "International Organization and the Study of World Politics." *International Organization* 52 (4): 645–85.

Krastev, Ivan, and Mark Leonard. 2021. *The Crisis of American Power: How Europeans See Biden's America.* European Council on Foreign Relations Policy Brief No. 363. https://ecfr.eu/wp-content/uploads/The-crisis-of-American-power-How-Europeans-see-Bidens-America.pdf.

Lannoo, Karel. 2020. "The Biden Presidency Is a Last Call for Europe." Centre for European Policy Studies. 1 December. www.ceps.eu/the-biden-presidency-is-a-last-call-for-europe/.

Lisbon – European Union. 2007. Treaty of Lisbon amending the Treaty on European Union and the Treaty establishing the European Community, signed at Lisbon, 13 December 2007. Official Journal of the European Union. C306. 2007/C306/01. https://eur-lex.europa.eu/LexUriServ/LexUriServ.do?uri=OJ:C:2007:306:FULL:EN:PDF.

Maçães, Bruno. 2021. "Surprise! The EU Knows How to Handle China." *Politico*, 21 June. www.politico.eu/article/eu-china-strategy-geopolitics/

Martinico, Guiseppe. 2016. "The Federal Language and the European Integration Process: The European Communities Viewed From the US." *Politique Européenne* 3 (53): 38–59. www.cairn.info/revue-politique-europeenne-2016-3-page-38.htm#s1n3.

Mérand, Frédéric, and Antoine Rayroux. 2018. "Foreign, Security, and Defence Policies." In *European Union Governance and Policy Making: A Canadian Perspective*, edited by Emmanuel Brunet-Jailly, Achim Hurrelman, and Amy Verdun, 176–95. Toronto: University of Toronto Press.

Mitchell, David. 2016. "EU Ministers Meet to Discuss Trump Presidency." *The Guardian*, 13 November 2016. www.theguardian.com/us-news/2016/nov/13/eu-leaders-to-meet-with-aim-of-forging-common-response-to-trump-boris-johnson.

Mogherini, Frederica. 2016. *Shared Vision, Common Action: A Stronger Europe – A Global Strategy for the European Union's Foreign and Security Policy.* June. https://eeas.europa.eu/archives/docs/top_stories/pdf/eugs_review_web.pdf.

Pethiyagoda, Kadira. 2020. "Chapter 1: Culture in International Relations." In *Indian Foreign Policy and Cultural Values*, 3–11. London: Palgrave Macmillan. https://doi.org/10.1007/978-3-030-54696-0_1.

Renard, Thomas. 2011. *The Treachery of Strategies: A Call for True EU Strategic Partnerships.* Egmont Paper 45. Brussels: Egmont Institute. http://aei.pitt.edu/32321/1/ep45.pdf.

———. 2021. "Conclusions: The Rise and Fall of an Idea." In *The European Union's Strategic Partnerships: Global Diplomacy in a Contested World*, edited by Laura C. Ferreira-Pereira and Michael Smith, 311–23. London: Palgrave MacMillan.

Sanders, Doug. 2008. "Europe to Canada: Get Your Act Together." *The Globe and Mail*, 4 October 2008. www.theglobeandmail.com/news/world/europe-to-canada-get-your-act-together/article20388332/.

Sidjanski, Dusan. 2001. *The Federal Approach of the European Union or The Quest for an Unprecedented European Federalism.* Notre Europe Research and Policy Paper No. 14. July. https://institutdelors.eu/wp-content/uploads/2020/08/etud14-en-1.pdf.

Smith, Michael. 2021. "The European Union and the United States: Competition, Convergence, and Crisis in a Strategic Partnership." In *The European Union's Strategic Partnerships: Global Diplomacy in a Contested World*, edited by Laura C. Ferreira Pereira and Michael Smith, 97–120. London: Palgrave Macmillan.

Trudeau, Justin. 2017. Prime Minister Unveils Themes for Canada's 2018 G7 Presidency. 14 December. https://pm.gc.ca/en/news/news-releases/2017/12/14/prime-minister-unveils-themes-canadas-2018-g7-presidency.

———. 2021. Roadmap for a Renewed U.S. – Canada Partnership. https://pm.gc.ca/en/news/statements/2021/02/23/roadmap-renewed-us-canada-partnership.

US Department of State. 2021a. Secretary Antony J. Blinken and European Commission President Ursula von der Leyen Before Their Meeting. Remarks to the Press. 24 March. www.state.gov/secretary-antony-j-blinken-and-european-commission-president-ursula-von-der-leyen-before-their-meeting/.

———. 2021b. "Secretary Blinken Remarks on the Three Seas Initiative." YouTube video, 2:37. 17 February. www.youtube.com/watch?v=0eLEHM-fAoU.

Verdun, Amy. 2021. "The EU-Canada Strategic Partnership: Challenges and Opportunities." In *The European Union's Strategic Partnerships: Global Diplomacy in a Contested World*, edited by Laura C. Ferreira Pereira and Michael Smith, 121–48. London: Palgrave Macmillan.

8
THE RISE OF CHINA AND TRANSATLANTIC STRATEGY

Emiliano Alessandri[1]

Introduction

Although it was not a prominent transatlantic topic until relatively recently, China has rapidly climbed the ladder of transatlantic priorities to the point that competition between the West and China is now presented as the defining geopolitical contest of the twenty-first century. Whereas Washington, in a rare instance of bipartisanship, has veered toward a decidedly adversarial stance, Europe is keeping a more open mind. But its own assessment has become more cautious, with internal factors playing as much of a role as American influence toward a partial transatlantic alignment. The suspension, in May 2021, of the long-sought European Union (EU)-China Comprehensive Agreement on Investment, in a tit for tat following Beijing's retaliation against EU sanctions on Xinjiang, and the shift of Germany's political elites toward a more vigilant approach are notable manifestations of the new attitude.

While this growing awareness about the multifaceted challenge posed by an increasingly assertive China is long overdue, a rushed shift from engagement to containment may not be the best course. Much needed initiatives aimed at rolling back China's influence in key domains—from new technologies to critical infrastructure—should be anchored to a joint strategic assessment, the main goal of which would be to articulate a new engagement policy no longer based on the flawed expectation of an eventual convergence between China and the West. A thorough review of transatlantic priorities vis-à-vis China—one that would include a frank exchange about respective interests, assets, and approaches—would help mitigate the risk of transatlantic tensions, such as those that suddenly erupted around the ill-communicated and ill-received decision by the United States (US) in September 2021 to proceed with a trilateral security pact with Australia and the United Kingdom (UK) for the Indo-Pacific to the exclusion of France (with Paris losing a lucrative submarine deal with Canberra in the process).

To turn the emerging but still far from fine-tuned transatlantic alignment on China into something resembling a coordinated strategy, ongoing exchanges between the EU and the US should focus on defining success and failure in Western policy toward Beijing over the next ten-to-twenty years. While addressing urgent matters in their specific domains, existing transatlantic dialogue formats—starting with the working groups of the recently launched Trade and Technology Council—should articulate key elements of a transatlantic strategy fit for different political cycles and capable of bridging the differences that are to persist in China policy at the EU-US and intra-European levels. Initiatives now pursued on parallel or disjointed tracks should be streamlined into a transatlantic bargain that rejects the notion that only a pivot to Asia will allow the US to concentrate on the China challenge—or that Washington might suddenly veer for an "America First" approach to China if Europe showed hesitancy along the way (a fairly likely scenario). Then again, the idea—still popular in some European circles—that the EU can remain neutral in the looming US-China standoff should also be questioned. Rather, the focus of transatlantic partners should be on preserving core elements of the Western-designed liberal international order which Beijing's policies now threaten, yet which China itself much benefited from to its present current strength.

In this respect, the Biden administration's focus at the 2021 G7, North Atlantic Treaty Organization (NATO), and EU-US summits—which culminated in the Summit for Democracy in December of the same year—on "rallying the world's democracies" has charted a path forward (Biden 2021). After four years of transatlantic turbulence accompanied by erratic US policy, an allied-centered approach is being laid out, one that rejects the inevitability of a "cold war" with China but seeks the renewal of the liberal order to tackle a challenge that will test democratic societies for generations and whose outcome is far from certain. In the hard task of moving from blueprint to action, talk of US leadership and Europe's "strategic autonomy" should be tempered by the full acceptance of the inextricable strategic interdependence binding the US and Europe in the twenty-first century. While reaching consensus will remain a complicated process—with Brussels (and Washington) already nervous about the possible impact of electoral dynamics in Germany and France on future China policy—what should ultimately drive transatlantic strategy is the lucid recognition that no single country is in the position to meet the China challenge alone. Although specific interests and perspectives will continue to differ across national contexts, it should be clear that Europe and the US are bound to succeed or fail together in the high-stakes contest that is before them.

Strategic Neglect?

Until recently, transatlantic debates rarely addressed China as a strategic priority, let alone as a security challenge.[2] Now, China has become an inescapable transatlantic topic, entering not only trade discussions within the World Trade Organization (WTO) but also strategic discussions held on the occasion of the

G7 and NATO summits (see, among others, Besch, Bond, and Schuette 2020). Transatlantic cooperation on China is the subject of a growing range of policy initiatives, from digital infrastructure to economic connectivity, as well as the focus of unprecedented media and think tank attention.[3] Public opinion on both sides of the Atlantic is increasingly aware of the risks posed by a powerful China, although Europeans generally hold more nuanced views and are not eager to be drawn into a new cold war of sorts.[4]

To his credit, President Donald J. Trump directly contributed to elevating China in the global and transatlantic agendas. He was among the first Western leaders to sound the alarm about the wide-ranging strategic implications of a rising China, adopting an openly adversarial posture after successive US administrations had renewed faith in the West's ability to manage—even shape—China's international trajectory.[5] Certain analysts would point to a mix of Western naiveté and China's dissimulation as the possible explanation for the alleged "strategic neglect" (Schadlow 2020).[6]

According to a certain narrative bordering on conspiracy theory, Beijing was able to disguise its growing ambition for decades, in a long "marathon" for primacy that would rectify a "century of humiliation."[7] Transatlantic partners, so the argument goes, proved to be extremely short-sighted in their approach to China by actively supporting their future strategic rival both bilaterally and through Western-led financial institutions as if China's rise was mainly an international development rather than geopolitical issue. In the post-Cold War era, the same narrative continues, Washington focused on anything else, from the global threat posed by terrorist networks to a resurgent Russia. Meanwhile, China forged ahead largely unhindered and unchecked, expanding its influence from its immediate neighborhood to Oceania, Africa, and Latin America. All this while Western attention and resources—including military ones—were largely employed elsewhere. In 2049, on the occasion of the 100th anniversary of the People's Republic, Beijing would crown its seemingly successful strategy by unseating the US as the new international leader. Many fear the reckoning may now come much earlier.[8]

While not without some appeal, the view that Beijing "outsmarted" the West is based on a highly selective and fundamentally flawed interpretation of history. Among other problems, it tends to eliminate the nuances and trivialize the decision-making processes that need, on the contrary, to be comprehended if the goal is course correction with China. A more plausible explanation of why it "took so long" for the US and Europe to recognize the looming challenge posed by a rising China rests with the partial but nonetheless significant results that the Western-led policy of engagement achieved. While certainly not uniformly effective, the policy of engagement did accompany the transformation of the People's Republic from a militant state supporting revolutionary movements around the world in the 1960s to a notably restrained international actor—and an economy deeply integrated in global trading networks—just a few decades later.

Rather than engagement itself, a certain dogmatic belief in the transformative power of globalization is to be blamed for misplaced expectations about the results a policy of engagement could yield over the long term. For decades, the paradigm guiding US and European policy toward China was broadly based on the tenet that economic integration would also lead to a more democratic China. This view was embraced by President Bill Clinton in the late 1990s, at a time when globalization and US hegemony were widely seen as two sides of the same coin but had underpinned US policy for much longer.[9]

Both in the Cold War and post-Cold War eras, the US—often followed by Europe—took highly consequential decisions vis-à-vis China driven by sheer interest as much as by ideological confidence in the superiority of the Western model. President Richard Nixon's much celebrated China opening helped drive already existing wedges between Beijing and Moscow, leading to a split in the communist camp. This policy, together with détente toward the Soviet Union, paved the way for the demise of the bipolar era and the emergence of the US as the uncontested international leader. By the 1990s, Washington could take credit for a series of strategic initiatives which had allowed the "free world" to prevail, expanding the appeal of Western liberalism among countries that had pursued alternative models of socioeconomic development in the aftermath of World War II. China's entry into the WTO in 2001—a process whose groundwork was laid down before the Clinton years—marked a major turning point in Beijing's relations with the world, not just the West. Beyond the idea that economic globalization would, in due time, bridge the significant gap that still separated China from the West, the calculus was that it would be harder for Beijing to challenge the international system from within than from without.

This certainly optimistic approach—one that continued to look at US-China relations as a positive sum game and at China's rise in terms of the benefits for the world economy—was not outright naïve.[10] For one, it went through different phases combining cycles of cooperation with phases of confrontation, one being the cooling of relations that ensued after Beijing's repression of popular movements in 1989. Although Tiananmen was quickly metabolized, the fallout led to policies that are in place until today, including an arms embargo that the West has enacted together for the past 30 years. More importantly, Western engagement—even the "comprehensive" type pursued by the Clinton administration—was always coupled with clear elements of containment. After the Cold War, the US preserved, and at various turns expanded, its strategic assets in the Pacific (whereas it significantly reduced its footprint on the European continent). Successive US administrations invested in a vast system of military bases in East Asia—something Beijing has, unsurprisingly, resented as encirclement.

Even the engagement-oriented Obama administration pursued, in parallel, a policy of containment: The "Asia pivot" comprising different initiatives aimed at taming Chinese influence, from strengthened military power projection in the Pacific to an expanded network of relations with traditional and new Asian partners. It is often overlooked that President Barack Obama, whom detractors describe as being too soft on the US's rivals, designed an international strategy aimed at containing China between two new trade blocs, the Trans-Pacific and

Transatlantic Trade and Investment Partnerships (TPP and TTIP, respectively). The TTIP intended to deepen the already unparalleled interdependence between the US and European economies with the double objective of further integrating the transatlantic market and reaffirming the role of the West as the world's standard-setter in trade and investment matters. Protectionist tendencies on both sides of the Atlantic, not pressure from China, derailed the initiative toward the end of the second Obama presidency. For its part, the TPP was aimed at countering China's influence in its own region by rallying Asian partners around an economic project of strategic relevance which notably excluded China. The successful accomplishment was jeopardized by Trump's decision (made shortly after his inauguration) to withdraw the US from it in an act of disdain toward multilateralism.

While the US tailored the mix of engagement and containment to different circumstances and cycles, Europe followed a similar path, combining growing economic engagement with Beijing with a vigilant approach that did not overlook normative aspects. In 2003, the EU entered a "comprehensive strategic partnership" with China, a decision that was driven by economic calculus as well as by growing political and cultural interest in each other models.[11] While some EU member states were willing to put the human rights issue on the backburner to prioritize their growing trade and investment relationships with China, the European Parliament and other EU institutions continued to closely scrutinize China's domestic record, from human rights to media freedom. While warming up to Beijing, the EU has repeatedly refused to grant China "market economy status," a decision based on economic parameters but laden with political implications.

Aware of the strategic dimension of China's rise, Europeans initially welcomed Obama's trade initiatives before a wary public and organized corporate interests forced a rethinking. Fearing the emergence of a "G2" of sorts, European capitals looked at the TTIP as a counterweight to the US's Asia pivot. After the US withdrew from the TPP, Europeans continued deepening ties with Asian partners, diversifying EU's trade relations and supporting regional initiatives, starting with the Association of Southeast Asian Nations, providing potential alternatives to a China-centric Asian order.

The Crisis of the Engagement Paradigm

If containment was integral to Western policy throughout, what then explains the recent shift toward a more confrontational approach? At a close look, the "death of engagement" has less to do with the fact that "it did not work"—or that China "cheated"—than with domestic factors and changing power balances (Schell 2020).

Washington had no hesitations about engaging China, even directly supporting it financially and scientifically, when US preeminence was not in question and until the American public was broadly supportive of an internationalist US foreign policy trading short-term gains with long-term dividends deriving from commitments. US policy toward China has started to shift when the base of this internationalist consensus has begun eroding. Due to mounting international fatigue and growing concerns about globalization's impact on the US's own domestic economy, a situation which China's rise certainly aggravated but was not chiefly responsible for, Washington has come to the conclusion that a policy of open-ended engagement no longer served US interests.

Undoubtedly, China's deviation from the reform path it had taken in the 1990s also played a role in changing US views. From 2013, China has regressed on a series of democracy and human rights indicators, pursued an increasingly aggressive economic policy, and expanded its military capabilities to buttress a Chinese sphere of influence in East Asia and beyond.

The combination of the above-described dynamics is now correctly seen as directly undermining the US standing with regard to China, making a course correction imperative. After all, US policy toward China has been closely aligned with the evolving US international strategy from the outset. In the late nineteenth century, with its "Open Door policy," Washington put a check on European colonial powers and protected the growing interests of US business. The policy was well-suited for a rising commercial power that intended to expand its influence without necessarily joining the imperialist camp.

In the 1970s, President Nixon's opening reflected a challenging time in which Washington felt that the Cold War had to be altered in order to preserve US leadership. The policy gave the US significant new leverage over the Soviet Union while creating a basis for the resolution of the inconclusive and increasingly ruinous Vietnam War. In the post-Cold War period, the US's unrivaled military might was seen as a guarantee that China's fast economic rise would not meaningfully challenge US primacy.

However, the US-China bargain, wherein Beijing would buy shares of the US debt and import technological commodities and know-how, while flooding the US market with cheap goods, became increasingly untenable in the 2000s. This was due to a series of reasons, including China manipulating its currency to sustain exports, unfulfilled commitments about a level playing field for foreign companies operating in the Chinese market, as well as proliferating cases of intellectual property theft and forced technological transfer. Perhaps more crucially, Chinese products started climbing up global value chains to cover intermediate and high-end goods once mainly manufactured in advanced economies. Beijing also increasingly focused on expanding the domestic market while building unequal relationships with smaller trading partners around the world.

By the time President Trump was elected in 2016, it had become abundantly clear to US policymakers across the aisle that the US-China relationship would be defined by competition as much as by cooperation. The change from the Obama administration—based on ideological factors *and* indicators pointing to a further loss of US competitiveness—was the assessment that competition increasingly worked to the US's disadvantage. Hence, the need to use all available means of statecraft to preserve a remaining but receding hedge.

The Trump administration used strong rhetoric against China and presented US-China competition in a Manichean way that clearly drew on Cold War terminology and symbolism. The rivalry between the US and the Chinese Communist Party was presented as one between two alternative systems, not just two international actors pursuing separate interests. Whereas members of the Trump administration described the competition in "civilizational" terms, a major difference with the Cold War script was that the focus was almost exclusively on US rather than Western interests.[12] Vice President Michael Pence's much-quoted 2018 Cold War–like speech on China tellingly did not give Europe any mention (Pence 2018).

During the Trump years, ever present security-related concerns were given higher status in the US-China relationship, from the future of Taiwan to China's claims in the South China Sea. Gradually but steadily, Washington became increasingly uncomfortable with a more assertive Chinese foreign policy that openly questioned the US's military dominance in East Asia and freedom of navigation in the Pacific. China's activities in the digital and cyber domain also came under close scrutiny, and the notion of "techno" or "digital" autocracy gained currency in policy circles.[13] Looking at trade balance sheets through the prism of national security, President Trump initiated a trade war aimed at rebalancing the relationship as well as progressively "decoupling" the highly interconnected Chinese and US economies. The Department of the Treasury took the step in 2019 to label China a "currency manipulator" (a designation later withdrawn).

While President Joseph R. Biden, Jr., has chosen a more balanced approach that avoids the excesses of the Trump administration—above all the notion that containment can be pushed so far as to "decoupling" the highly interconnected US and Chinese economies while pressuring partners around the world to fully align or face consequences—the tenets of US policy have not been fundamentally altered (*Financial Times* 2021a; Leary and Davis 2021). Across the aisle, Washington now looks at China as the US's top strategic rival, and a whole-of-government approach is being leveraged to tame Chinese power. On both the left and the right, China's rise is blamed for many of the domestic difficulties the US faces.[14]

A key difference from the Trump years is that—at least in these early phases of the Biden presidency—the US administration sees allies and partners around the world as key assets in the containment of China. For the Biden administration, a revival of US internationalism offers a powerful antidote to US decline. The revitalization of US alliances, especially with democratic nations in Europe and Asia, is seen as instrumental to the restoration of US leadership.

The EU-China Cooling Off

A policy of engagement with China has been a central aspect of European foreign policy for decades. EU member states have established varyingly close relationships with China with trade policy being decided at the EU level. Over the years, China has become an increasingly important trading partner. In 2020, it overtook the US to become the EU's largest trading partner (the transatlantic economy remains much more integrated when it comes to investment). Like the US, the EU has also been running a sizable trade deficit with China (hovering at or above US$100 billion for many years). But Brussels has been far more hesitant than Washington in drawing security implications from this. In fact, the EU does not generally look at the relationship with China in terms of direct strategic competition. Unlike the US, the EU has no hegemonic position to preserve. Because of its limited power projection and vastly inferior military assets, the EU has mainly concentrated on soft security aspects. Although some European countries—notably France and the UK—have significant historical legacies and remain actively engaged in East Asia, Europe as such is not a major player when it comes to Asian security.

The strategic partnership the EU entered with China in 2003 mainly looked at the opportunities opened up by growing economic exchanges. Yet, witness the difficulties in its post-Cold War relationship with the US. The EU had started early on flirting with the idea that China could be also a political partner in navigating an increasingly multi-polar world. For its part, Beijing initially showed considerable interest in the European integration process and expressed a certain admiration for the "European model"—even as it continued to leverage a series of often unequal bilateral relationships with select EU and non-EU countries (Tocci 2008).

Building on a track record of increasingly warm relations, China seized opportunities along the way during the 2010s. During the Euro crisis, it offered to help struggling European economies at a time of Brussels-mandated austerity (Small 2012). Although China's concrete support was overestimated, Beijing made new partners in those years, especially in Eastern and Southern Europe. The so-called 17+1 (a platform allowing China to engage EU as well as non-EU members bypassing EU-wide structures) was launched in 2012–13 against the backdrop of the Euro crisis and the roll out of the Belt and Road Initiative (BRI).[15] During the Trump years, Beijing skilfully drew a contrast with the US by presenting itself as a supporter of globalization and an advocate of multilateralism at a time when the "America First" agenda belittled the value of alliances and international institutions (State Council Information Office 2017).

With its relationship framed in mainly economic terms, Europe's recent change of heart about China is only partially motivated by political dynamics in Beijing or military-security developments in Asia. Certainly, Brussels and European capitals have taken note of President Xi Jinping's leadership style and Beijing's increasingly repressive and anti-democratic policies. The European Parliament has been proactive in exposing violations of human and minority rights in China. But what really triggered Europe's rethink was the evolving assessment of key segments of the European business community, particularly Germany with its very direct experience of China's unfair practices. These European interests sounded the alarm in 2019 by choosing to refer to China both as a partner and a "systemic competitor" (see BDI 2019). European institutions followed suit, with the European Commission naming China a "systemic rival" in March 2019 (European Commission 2019).

Whereas the EU position is the product of a difficult synthesis and is nothing but consolidated, a trend is discernible (Small 2020). While engagement remains the cornerstone of EU policy, based on the 2016 Strategy on China, the EU is increasingly resorting to elements of containment. Among other measures, the EU has adopted new schemes for vetting and, in some cases, restricting the operations of Chinese companies in the European market (although the last word still largely rests with individual EU member states). Like the US, the EU has taken action on human rights, adopting sanctions in 2021 against entities and individuals implicated in China's highly controversial policies toward the Uighurs.

More broadly, there is a new awareness about the risks posed by China's assertive international strategy and a new determination about presenting Beijing with a united front in crucial files affecting the bilateral relationship. Especially on the competition between "techno-autocracies" and the world's democracies, the US government under both the Trump and Biden administrations has played a direct role in influencing the views of European elites. Meanwhile, think tanks and the media have contributed to changing perspectives among the larger public (Cohen and Fontaine 2020; Shahbaz 2018).

A Looming Cold War?

The Biden administration's emphasis on uniting the world's democracies, coupled as it is with a sharp focus on China as the defining strategic, inevitably leads to the question about whether we are entering a new Cold War-like era of geopolitical and ideological competition—and what the transatlantic dimension of this contest may be. While the media and a growing number of pundits find it irresistible to draw parallels, the differences between the Cold War and the US-China standoff are incomparably more significant than the possible similarities (Fontaine and Ratner 2020).

The Cold War analogy is not entirely misplaced because, as during the Cold War era, the rivalry that is shaping up between the West and China pits alternative systems against each other (see, among others, Westad 2019). Competing values and world views—not only economic and security interests—are part of the contest, and the confrontation promises to be a long, generational one. Although the distribution of international power is becoming more diffused overall, China is the only country that can realistically compete with the US for superpower status and is, in fact, already described as a near-peer competitor in US official documents (see, among others, ODNI 2021). Although multi-polar, the international system will be largely defined by the US-China rivalry in key areas, including the military field.

There are, however, notable differences with the Cold War. These are mainly to be found in the hard-to-change reality of economic interdependence. The Soviet Union was never integrated into the global free-market economy. Even in a post-COVID era, trade and financial links will, on the contrary, continue to bind the US and China, and China and the rest of the world, in very significant ways.

A second difference with the Cold War is that while ideological differences between the West and China are getting sharper, Beijing seems content, for now at least, with embodying rather than actively exporting an alternative model. As a result, there is also no "Chinese bloc," with Beijing having formalized alliances and security partnerships with less than a handful of nations. This might change in the future, of course. Beijing increasingly seeks close ties with countries whose assets can be leveraged in the competition with the US. It is noteworthy that Chinese companies are now exporting not only commodities but also technology, including the type that can be used to establish or strengthen forms of digital authoritarianism.

One further difference with the Cold War is Europe's position. Europe was at the center of the bipolar era not because of its strength but because of its weakness following two world wars. The Iron Curtain cut across the continent, manifesting the division between East and West and the decline of Europe as a center of power. The current rivalry between the US and China is global—not only in a geographical sense but also because it plays out against a backdrop of global markets and global value chains. Key areas of the unfolding confrontation are inherently transnational, such as cyberspace. Against this backdrop, Europe is not as central to the US-China standoff as it was during the US-Soviet one. However, the European continent is already a major theater of the unfolding competition, a fact that is yet to be fully appreciated on either side of the Atlantic. China's drive for technological leadership and its BRI have made advanced European economies a key target. Europe is also a central factor in the US-China confrontation because a divided Western camp would give Beijing a decisive advantage.

For the time being, the risk is as much that China drives wedges between the EU and the US as it undermines European unity within. Initiatives such as the 17+1 have attempted precisely at creating a circle of China's European friends, leveraging bilateral relationships with smaller and more vulnerable European countries. China's charm offensive is playing out visibly in the Balkans and in Eastern Europe among prospective EU members or disenchanted ones. China has also targeted sluggish Southern European economies that have deeply resented post-global recession austerity policies imposed by the German-led European core.

Beijing's outreach strategy has somewhat lost traction in recent years because large EU members, such as Germany and France, have actively encouraged EU-wide approaches.[16] Balkan and Central Eastern European countries have had their share of disillusionment with China, either because some of their deals with China have failed to deliver or because local elites had experienced firsthand the risks of entering unequal relationships with Beijing. Against the backdrop of the pandemic, however, China has remained a crucial source of diversification, including when it comes to the supply of vaccines. Countries as disparate as Hungary, Serbia, and Turkey have strengthened their engagement with China even as their Western partners cautioned them against doing so.

A reason why Europe is an important piece of the new competition is precisely because China's rise has reverberations on the "neighborhoods" the EU intended to "Europeanize" until not long ago. China is already an important economic actor in the Middle East and North Africa region and seems eager to play a more political role there too, in places like post-war Syria, for instance. China controls the Port of Piraeus and other assets in the Mediterranean basin, and the Chinese navy has participated in joint maneuvers with Russia in the area (Ekman 2018; Müller-Markus 2016). With the BRI, China is strengthening or opening new venues of influence from Central Asia to the Adriatic.

While Moscow is all too aware of China's expanding sphere of influence in the former Soviet Bloc, it has pragmatically built a close relationship with China. Even though it does not amount to an alliance and may never transform into one, it is cemented by interest and by shared antagonism toward the West. As Western-Russian tensions over Ukraine and other issues have become even more acute in recent years, any suggestion that transatlantic allies may engineer a Cold War-like split between Moscow and Beijing, this time luring Russia into a Western orbit, is close to fanciful at this stage.

Transatlantic Aspects of China Policy

The fact that until recently China was not seen as a pressing transatlantic subject does not mean that a track record of US-EU dialogue on China is missing. Quite the contrary, the US and Europe have taken momentous decisions about China both in the Cold War and post-Cold War periods, often coordinating their respective policies and initiatives. These have reflected a broad transatlantic alignment behind the vision of integrating China into the world economy and co-opting it into Western-designed global governance structures.

Among the reasons why China rarely made it to the top of the transatlantic agenda is that China policy has not caused any major transatlantic disagreement, at least not to the level of significance of the 2003 Iraq War, to mention a relatively recent case.

The US opening to China in the early 1970s took place against the backdrop of a larger shift in US international strategy, from the demise of the Bretton Woods system to détente, which forced Europe to face a different type of US leadership, one which often bypassed European partners. US strategy created some uneasiness but Europe reaped benefits from de-escalation and revamped international dialogue. After the Cold War, transatlantic tensions on China policy surfaced around discussions in Europe about lifting the arms embargo, an initiative by Germany and France in 2004–5, later withdrawn in light of Washington's opposition. A decade later, China's Asian Infrastructure Investment Bank (AIIB), which became operational in 2015, also exposed transatlantic differences. The UK, France, Germany, Italy, and other European countries decided to join the new multilateral development entity—to Washington's irritation—even if the initiative reflected was clearly aimed at challenging Western leadership.

These and other tensions notwithstanding, the transatlantic dialogue on China has been constructive overall. Before President Trump's focus on the China challenge, Beijing's controversial policies had already prompted intensified transatlantic exchanges, initiated by Europe as much as by the US. During the second George W. Bush administration, German Chancellor Angela Merkel traveled to Washington in 2007 to propose a new US-EU free trade agreement with a focus on pressuring China (Chase 2020). Washington did not show particular interest in the German initiative at the time. Nonetheless, ensuing discussions led to the establishment of the Transatlantic Economic Council, an institution that has offered an early forum for comparing notes on economic policy toward China.

During the Obama years, the Asia pivot predictably irritated the Europeans, who feared being sidelined. Only during Obama's second term, and especially after the outbreak of the Ukraine crisis, Europe regained priority status in US strategy. Yet, channels that had been established around the arms embargo controversy in 2004–5 were expanded and reinforced. Assistant Secretary of State for East Asian and Pacific Affairs Kurt Campbell spearheaded a major initiative aimed at engaging Europe on China. The latter led to the key 2012 joint US-EU declaration on common objectives in the Asia-Pacific region (US Department of State 2012).

Following the AIIB disagreement, no major transatlantic tensions took place on issues relating to China. To the contrary, the US worked profitably with the EU and Japan on rare earths and China within the WTO. Washington lobbied for and was pleased by Brussels's decision not to grant China market economy status in 2016 (Small 2019).

The Trump years were marked by transatlantic turbulence. On China, the Trump administration adopted a seemingly contradictory approach that risked antagonizing Europe precisely at a time when the US demanded allies to align on an openly confrontational China policy. Washington approached the EU and European capitals bilaterally, calling for a rollback of Chinese influence, especially when it comes to the development of 5G networks. The Trump administration offered to share its track record of vetting Chinese investments and acquisitions in strategic sectors and pushed Europeans in the direction of adopting instruments similar to the Foreign Investment Risk Review Modernization Act and the Committee on Foreign Investment in the US.

Although these pressures certainly added a sense of urgency to a review of Europe's China policy, which was already underway, US lobbying led to mixed results. This is because, at the very same time, Washington was targeting the EU with tariffs and questioning the value of the European integration project overall. Faced with the US's mercantilist turn, Europeans were made, if anything, even more aware of the need for differentiation. Often disparaging the EU and its leaders, President Trump showed virtually no interest in coordinating US policy on China with his European counterparts. He passed on a proposal made by French President Emmanuel Macron in 2018 to launch a transatlantic dialogue at the highest level. In fact, the Trump administration put unprecedented pressure on Europe on issues concerning China while remaining highly ambivalent about the US's traditional commitment to European and transatlantic security.

Washington alerted transatlantic allies about China acquiring sensitive information through Huawei-operated 5G networks and warned them about US-European intelligence cooperation being jeopardized as a result. Several European countries did not find these arguments as compelling as they would have under different circumstances. While the US lobbied against European contracts with Huawei (which in some cases had already been signed), much less attention was paid to how to create viable alternatives to Chinese technology. Although some proposals were floated about better leveraging European tech leaders such as Ericsson and Nokia, the impression was that the US was much more interested in targeting Chinese operators rather than promoting new transatlantic champions.

The problem with the Trump administration's transatlantic engagement rested with its "America First" approach. President Trump adopted a dismissive approach at best toward the US's traditional alliances and showed disdain toward the EU and European integration. Although the US Congress reaffirmed the US commitment to NATO, transatlantic relations became very transactional during the Trump years, leaving Europe in the uneasy spot of either aligning with a unilateralist US or hedging its bets on issues of growing strategic consequence, including its relationship with China. Europeans also feared that for all the China-bashing, President Trump could cut a bilateral deal with Beijing that would bypass Europe. This indeed happened with the Phase One trade deal, signed by Trump and Chinese officials in January 2020. The truce in US-China trade relations was welcomed in Europe, but the good news was tempered by concerns that US trade policy would target the EU next.

The US's unpredictability during the Trump years reinforced trends in Europe toward greater "strategic autonomy," a notion that had already been introduced in the EU Global Strategy in 2016, before Trump's election. When it came to relations with China, this led several leaders to advocate a "European way," with EU High Representative Josep Borrell semi-facetiously referring to it as Europe's "Sinatra Doctrine" (Borrell 2020).

The Future of US-EU Cooperation on China

With President Biden—a self-declared Atlanticist whose first presidential overseas trip was to Europe—transatlantic cooperation is again at the center of the US international agenda. While the "US is back," the old transatlantic relationship in which Europeans could comfortably rely on US leadership may never be resurrected. Always a difficult endeavor, transatlantic alignment will remain the prize of hard diplomatic work in a rapidly changing international environment in which the West will not call all the shots and in which the US may be tempted at several turns to lean on ad hoc coalitions rather than structured US-EU coordination.

While the current approach aims to remedy the problematic aspects of recent US policy, many questions remain on the table including how far the current administration really is ready to go to coordinate the design—not just the implementation—of China policy with the EU. The Biden administration is also yet to convincingly address the key question—left notably unaddressed in recent years and of great interest to the Europeans who are adamant about avoiding unnecessary polarization—of what a realistic and satisfactory endgame with China may look like. Both the US and the EU are rightly opposed to the consolidation of a Chinese sphere of influence from Asia to Africa and Europe itself. Yet, the US and

Europe are yet to come up with a set of clear redlines that may contribute to setting boundaries to China's ambitions.

When such lines are drawn, such as around the independence of Taiwan, their enforcement leads to conundrums for which transatlantic allies are not necessarily prepared. The Biden administration is rightly insisting on holding Beijing accountable for deviations or attacks on the rules-based international order. The focus on the preservation of international principles and standards marks a change from the previous administration and is a smart one. One key advantage is that it frames the US-China rivalry not so much in terms of an ideological clash but one between custodians and challengers of rules that have served the world (not just the West) well for decades. It also makes it easier to recruit Europe to the task as the EU's external action is geared toward the preservation of international law and the multilateral system.

The weakness of the current approach is that it tends to discount the extent to which China has already been able to bend the rules of the system from within, by virtue of its sheer power and size as well as by offering an alternative model—political as well as normative—to Western liberalism. At a minimum, Beijing is only selectively engaging Western-designed regimes while increasingly using its clout to create parallel structures and networks. As the Chinese approach unfolds, Biden's "rallying the world's democracies" goal must be accompanied by the articulation of a new type of engagement policy with China that is no longer based on the expectation of an eventual convergence with the West. The question on the table, therefore, is as much about how to contain China as how to work out an acceptable modus vivendi that avoids a ruinous escalation.

In fact, a meaningful transatlantic dialogue on China needs to combine specific subjects with a broad vision of success and failure in China policy over the next two decades. The latter will have to be as detailed as possible as to which elements of the international order shall be preserved at all costs and which regional and global regimes may have to adapt or be renegotiated entirely as power balances change. This necessary transatlantic exchange should aim at nothing less than a joint strategic assessment placing China at the center of a larger reflection on the future of the West. The ongoing EU-US dialogue on China should therefore work on technical issues as much as on strategic ones, outlining a first of its kind "transatlantic strategy." The latter should provide a long-term plan for dealing with China—one that shall survive political cycles on both sides of the Atlantic and bridge, wherever possible, the differences that will continue to characterize transatlantic as well as intra-European approaches.

Among its other goals, this exercise should highlight the strategic interdependence that links the US and Europe as they develop their respective relationships with China. This interdependence is perhaps even deeper than the one that brought transatlantic allies together during the Cold War. For one, the West-China competition takes place against the backdrop of a global economy that is incomparably more interconnected and integrated than during the bipolar era. Moreover, it is widely recognized that China poses a more formidable challenge to Western dominance. Already the leading world economy in purchasing power terms, China can count on a vast population and a successful industrialization process fueled by capitalistic development. Perhaps more crucially, China's rise builds on a long history of statehood and strong national traditions. While the current political regime in China is not as stable as it is generally believed, it would be incautious at best to bet on its demise—at least in the short-to-medium term.

While certainly more declaratory than operational, a transatlantic strategy could nonetheless articulate cooperation on China in very concrete ways. Ideas that have been floated in recent years and months could be fleshed out with a view to their operationalization. For example, as NATO adopts its new strategic concept recognizing the new security dynamics triggered by China's rise, serious thought could be given to establishing a NATO-China Council patterned after the NATO-Russia one. To strengthen transatlantic engagement in the Indo-Pacific, an area beyond the Atlantic Alliance's security perimeter, NATO could accelerate the process of updating and expanding its partnerships in Asia with a clearer China focus. This would provide a way for Europeans to meaningfully contribute to Asian security policy without necessarily deploying new assets in the Pacific. As strategic coordination transcends strictly defined regional boundaries, current cooperation within the Quadrilateral Security Dialogue (comprising the US, India, Japan, and Australia) could be expanded to include the UK and select EU countries.

As the US continues to focus on military deterrence in the Indo-Pacific, Europe can also complement the economic side of the Asian security equation, from coordinating future trade deals with the US to leveraging scientific and technological cooperation with established and rising Asian players, from Japan to India. Encouragingly, EU's "connectivity" partnerships in the Indo-Pacific are being revisited with a much clearer geostrategic focus—and a larger budget—than initially envisaged.

When it comes to the transatlantic economy, it may be difficult to resurrect projects on the scale of the TTIP as post-pandemic recovery might be accompanied by free-trade skepticism on both sides of the Atlantic. Recent developments, such as the launching of a Trade and Technology Council, however, should focus on aligning transatlantic approaches on China as well as on further integrating the transatlantic market while preserving the West's role as a global standards-setter.

Synergies should be found between the functional and geographic levels, with strategic clarity underpinning any proposed new initiative. The US should signal that Europe remains central to its international strategy even as attention focuses on the competition with China. As noted, Europe will be a key "battleground" going forward. At the same time, Europe can actively contribute to key functional aspects of the emerging transatlantic agenda, from leveraging its role in regulatory sphere to leading efforts on sustainable development and the energy transition, including in the context of the G7-backed "Clean Green Initiative."

The challenges facing the latter initiative are many, from at least partly matching the scale of the BRI to assigning specific roles to the countries involved. In this context, the EU could probably focus its action on the transitional region between Europe and the Indo-Pacific. Although the EU is not the leading actor, a number of countries there look at the European market with great interest. This is a region that stretches from Central Asia all the way to Eastern and Southeastern Europe, one where the EU maintains leverage through its neighborhood and enlargement policies.

While it is natural for the US and Europe to tailor their engagement in key regions to different capabilities and levels of influence, transatlantic allies should aim at a co-participation rather than a division of responsibilities. China will continue to pose not fully symmetrical challenges to the US and Europe. But only transatlantic unity will give the US and the EU the hedge that is needed in a long-term contest whose outcome is far from decided.

Notes

1 Views expressed in this chapter are strictly personal and do not reflect any of the author's affiliations.
2 At the Track II and 1.5 levels, transatlantic dialogue formats on China were already developed in the early 2000s. However, 9/11, the global War on Terror, and the ensuing transatlantic tensions redirected attention away from China to other pressing challenges.
3 Among the earliest transatlantic think tank initiatives on China is the German Marshall Fund of the United States' Stockholm China Forum and Asia Program, launched in the 2000s, bringing together analysts and practitioners from Europe, the US, and Asia.
4 See, among others, the findings of opinion surveys by the German Marshall Fund of the United States (2021).
5 On some of the novelties of Trump's approach, from a critical perspective, see Medeiros (2021).
6 For a balanced assessment of faults and failures in US China policy, see Campbell and Ratner (2018).
7 Pillsbury (2016) offers an influential example of this line of thinking.
8 See, among others, Jacques (2009) on China's coming hegemony.
9 In fact, even during the Clinton years, different approaches co-existed. For an assessment, see Kamath (1998).
10 Steinberg (2020) presents a practitioner's account of US China policy across post-Cold War administrations.
11 For an interpretation of the recent evolutions in EU-China relations, see among others, Godement (2020).
12 Policy Planning Staff Director Kiron Skinner was much criticized for her civilizational—even racial—cauterization of the US competition with China. For a critique, see Harris (2019).
13 For an enumeration of China's challenges to US primacy and security, see White House (2017).
14 The consensus conceals a plurality of perspectives dividing progressive and conservative views of the US's China policy. See Sanders (2021) for a critique from the left.
15 The initiative has lost some of its steam recently due to increased scrutiny from larger EU member states. Smaller EU countries have also faced an expectations gap and questioned the usefulness of this format. Lithuania was the first country to official withdraw from the forum in 2021.
16 Barkin (2021) discussed the evolution of German policy on China.

References

Barkin, Noah. 2021. "Rethinking German Policy Towards China: Prospects for Change in the Post-Merkel Era." Chatham House Briefing Paper, US and the Americas Programme, Europe Programme. May. www.chathamhouse.org/sites/default/files/2021-05/2021-05-26-german-policy-towards-china-barkin.pdf.

Besch, Sophia, Ian Bond, and Leonard Schuette. 2020. *Europe, the US and China: A Love-Hate Triangle?* Centre for European Reform. September. www.cer.eu/sites/default/files/pbrief_us_china_eu_SB_IB_LS.pdf.

Biden, Joe. 2021. "My Trip to Europe Is About America Rallying the World's Democracies." *Washington Post*, 5 June 2021.

Borrell, Josep. 2020. "The Sinatra Doctrine: How the EU Should Deal With the US-China Competition." *IAI (Istituto Affari Internazionali) Papers* 20 (24). www.iai.it/sites/default/files/iaip2024.pdf.

Bundesverband der Deutschen Industrie (BDI). 2019. *Partner and Systemic Competitor – How Do We Deal With China's State-Controlled Economy?* BDI Policy Paper. January.

Campbell, Kurt, and Ely Ratner. 2018. "The Chia Reckoning." *Foreign Affairs* (March–April). www.foreignaffairs.com/articles/china/2018-02-13/china-reckoning.

Chase, Peter. 2020. "The Missing Partnership: The United States, Europe, and China's Economic Challenge." German Marshall Fund of the United States Policy Paper No. 14. September. www.gmfus.org/sites/default/files/publications/pdf/Chinas%20Economic%20Challenge%20-%2011%20September.pdf.

Cohen, Jared, and Richard Fontaine. 2020. "Uniting the Techno-Democracies: How to Build Digital Cooperation." *Foreign Affairs* (November–December). www.foreignaffairs.com/articles/united-states/2020-10-13/uniting-techno-democracies.

Ekman, Alice. 2018. "China in the Mediterranean: An Emerging Presence." *Notes d L'Ifri*. February. www.ifri.org/sites/default/files/atoms/files/ekman_china_mediterranean_2018_v2.pdf.

European Commission. 2019. *EU-China – A Strategic Outlook*. Joint Communication to the European Parliament, the European Council and the Council. 12 March. https://ec.eur opa.eu/info/sites/default/files/communication-eu-china-a-strategic-outlook.pdf.

Financial Times. 2021. "Blinken Rejects Claims of 'Cold War' Between US and China." *Financial Times*, 4 May 2021. www.ft.com/content/f77604cd-cb6b-45df-a9ec-4f4b63959ad5.

Fontaine, Richard, and Ely Ratner. 2020. "The U.S.-China Confrontation Is Not Another Cold War. It's Something New." *Washington Post*, 2 July 2020. www.washingtonpost.com/opinions/2020/07/02/us-china-confrontation-is-not-another-cold-war-its-something-new/.

German Marshall Fund of the United States. 2021. "Relations With China." 7 June. www.gmfus.org/publications/relations-china-2021.

Godement, François. 2020. "China's Relations With Europe." In *China and the World*, edited by David Shambaugh, 251–69. Oxford: Oxford University Press.

Harris, Peter. 2019. "Conflict With China Is Not About a Clash of Civilizations." *The National Interest*, 3 June 2019. https://nationalinterest.org/feature/conflict-china-not-about-clash-civilizations-60877.

Jacques, Martin. 2009. *When China Rules the World: The End of the Western World and the Birth of a New Global Order*. London: Penguin Books.

Kamath, P. M. 1998. "US-China Relations Under the Clinton Administration: Comprehensive Engagement or the Cold War Again?" *Strategic Analysis* 22 (5): 691–709.

Leary, Alex, and Bob Davis. 2021. "Biden's Policy Is Emerging—and It Looks a Lot Like Trump's." *Wall Street Journal*, 10 June 2021. www.wsj.com/articles/bidens-china-policy-is-emergingand-it-looks-a-lot-like-trumps-11623330000.

Medeiros, Evan. 2021. "How to Craft a Durable China Strategy." *Foreign Affairs*, 17 March. www.foreignaffairs.com/articles/united-states/2021-03-17/how-craft-durable-china-strategy.

Müller-Markus, Christina. 2016. "China Moors in the Mediterranean: A Sea of Opportunities for Europe?" *Notes Internacionals* CIDOB [Barcelona Centre for International Affairs] No. 156 (September).

Office of the Director of National Intelligence (ODNI). 2021. *Annual Threat Assessment of the US Intelligence Community*. 9 April. www.dni.gov/files/ODNI/documents/assessments/ATA-2021-Unclassified-Report.pdf.

Pence, Michael. 2018. Remarks by Vice President Pence on the Administration's Policy Toward China. 4 October. https://china.usembassy-china.org.cn/remarks-by-vice-president-pence-on-the-administrations-policy-toward-china/.

Pillsbury, Michael. 2016. *The Hundred-Year Marathon: China's Secret Strategy to Replace America as the Global Superpower*. London: St. Martin's Press.

Sanders, Bernie. 2021. "Washington's Dangerous New Consensus on China: Don't Start Another Cold War." *Foreign Affairs*, 17 June. www.foreignaffairs.com/articles/china/2021-06-17/washingtons-dangerous-new-consensus-china.

Schadlow, Nadia. 2020. "Consider the Possibility That Trump Is Right About China." *The Atlantic*, 5 April. www.theatlantic.com/ideas/archive/2020/04/consider-possibility-trump-right-china/609493/.

Schell, Orville. 2020. "The Death of Engagement." *The Wire China*, 7 June 2020. www.thewirechina.com/2020/06/07/the-birth-life-and-death-of-engagement/.

Shahbaz, Adrian. 2018. "Freedom on the Net 2018: The Rise of Digital Authoritarianism." Freedom House. https://freedomhouse.org/report/freedom-net/2018/rise-digital-authoritarianism.

Shapiro, Jeremy. 2021. "Biden Talks a Big Game on Europe. But His Actions Tell a Different Story." *Politico*, 4 June. www.politico.com/news/magazine/2021/06/04/biden-administration-europe-focus-491857.

Small, Andrew. 2012. China-Europe Relationship and Transatlantic Implications. Testimony before the US-China Economic and Security Review Commission. 19 April. www.uscc.gov/hearings/hearing-china-europe-relationship-and-transatlantic-implications.

———. 2019. "Transatlantic Cooperation on Asia and the Trump Administration." German Marshall Fund of the United States Policy Paper No. 25. October. www.gmfus.org/sites/default/files/publications/pdf/Small%20-%20Transatlantic%20Cooperation%20Asia%20-%2029%20Oct.pdf.

———. 2020. "The Meaning of Systemic Rivalry: Europe and China Beyond the Pandemic." European Council on Foreign Relations Policy Brief. 13 May. https://ecfr.eu/publication/the_meaning_of_systemic_rivalry_europe_and_china_beyond_the_pandemic/.

Steinberg, James B. 2020. "What Went Wrong? U.S.-China Relations From Tiananmen to Trump." *Texas National Security Review* 3 (1): 119–33.

State Council Information Office. 2017. Full Text: Xi Jinping's Keynote Speech at the World Economic Forum. People's Republic of China. 6 April. www.china.org.cn/node_7247529/content_40569136.htm.

Tocci, Nathalie, ed. 2008. *Who Is a Normative Foreign Policy Actor?: The European Union and Its Global Partners*. Brussels: Centre for European Policy Studies.

US Department of State. 2012. U.S.-EU Statement on the Asia-Pacific Region. 12 July. https://2009-2017.state.gov/r/pa/prs/ps/2012/07/194896.htm.

Westad, Odd Arne. 2019. "The Sources of Chinese Conduct: Are Washington and Beijing Fighting a New Cold War?" *Foreign Affairs* (September–October). www.foreignaffairs.com/articles/china/2019-08-12/sources-chinese-conduct.

White House. 2017. *National Security Strategy of the United States of America*. December. https://trumpwhitehouse.archives.gov/wp-content/uploads/2017/12/NSS-Final-12-18-2017-0905.pdf.

9
PUBLIC AND ELITE OPINION RELATING TO THE EU–US RELATIONSHIP

Stephen Brooks

Introduction

"Are the United States and Europe heading for divorce?" This was the title of a 2001 article written by Ivo Daalder at a time when the transatlantic relationship was widely seen as entering an unprecedentedly rocky phase (Daalder 2001). Just how rocky would soon be apparent. On 15 February 2003, some of the largest demonstrations in history took place in Europe's capitals, protesting the imminent United States-led invasion of Iraq. In Rome, an estimated 3 million people demonstrated against the invasion, earning this protest a Guinness World Record as the world's single largest anti-war protest.

Daalder's (2001) reflections on the future of the transatlantic alliance were, in fact, prompted by the transition from the Bill Clinton administration to that of George W. Bush and not by the storm clouds of war. In terms of both his rhetoric and actions, newly elected President Bush appeared to favor a unilateralist approach that placed the United States (US) at odds with its European partners on a range of issues. As it happened, of course, the transatlantic differences that caused many to fret about the foreign policies and style of the Bush administration during its first several months were, comparatively speaking, mere bumps in the road. The decision to invade Iraq and specific American policies associated with the War on Terror, including claims of Geneva Convention violations and the use of force to extract information from prisoners, saw the US and many of its most important European allies on opposing sides of these issues. Although many Americans shared the criticisms of their government's actions that were so widely held by Europeans, it was also true that many did not (Asmus 2004). Public opinion on the two sides of the Atlantic was quite different and was argued by many to be an important driver of a widening transatlantic gap (Kohut and Stokes 2006).

DOI: 10.4324/9781003147565-13

On the face of it, the argument that public opinion influences foreign policy and the relations between countries has often seemed rather compelling. Those North Atlantic Treaty Organization (NATO) allies that declined to join in the Anglo-American mission to bring down the regime of Saddam Hussein were also countries where, for the most part, public opinion was overwhelmingly opposed to this decision. The significant losses experienced by the Republican Party in the 2006 congressional elections were surely due, in no small measure, to widespread dissatisfaction among Americans with the Iraq War and aspects of the Bush administration's War on Terror. German Chancellor Gerhard Schröder's re-election in 2002, after a campaign in which strong criticism of the US government's apparent resolve to use force to bring about regime change in Iraq became the most prominent part of his message to voters, both tapped into and mobilized anti-American sentiment in that country's electorate (*Deutsche Welle* 2007; Finn 2002). More recently, the 2016 election of Donald J. Trump, whose "America First" slogan clearly resonated with millions of voters, and the pro-Brexit forces victory in the United Kingdom's (UK) 2016 referendum, attested to the importance of public opinion on matters beyond the water's edge.

No US election since 1940 has been decided by or, arguably, significantly affected by the US's relationship with Europe (Moe 2013). In the other direction, relations with the US have been, from time to time, a prominent factor during elections in some European countries, as was true in Greece in 1984, Germany in 2002, and Spain in 2004.[1] Elections aside, this is a street where the traffic runs mainly in one direction, the views of European populations toward the US having a greater impact on their respective politics and government actions than American views of Europe have had on US politics and policies. This does not mean that American public opinion, as it concerns that country's relations with Europe, has no influence on American elections and the actions of government. But that influence is, I will argue, diffuse and indirect.

On both sides of the Atlantic, public opinion may and indeed has evolved in ways that have affected the transatlantic relationship. The rise of nationalist populism in recent years in the US and across much of Europe, while not about transatlantic relations in any specific sense, has influenced these relations in a couple of ways. At the most general level, it has done so through the challenge it poses to certain aspects of globalization and to the architecture of liberal internationalism that seeks to impose limits on state sovereignty. This rather general influence has assumed a more specific form in the case of Brexit and in trade skirmishes between the European Union (EU) and the US. In the Brexit case, dissatisfaction over the UK's membership in the EU and what many Britons perceived to be their country's inability to determine certain matters free from the hand of Brussels, ultimately led to that country's exit from the EU. Already, before the 2016 Brexit referendum, the claim that Britain would be able to negotiate better terms of trade with international partners was a prominent message in the pro-Brexit campaign. This belief was, of course, encouraged by

President Trump who rather famously promised in the 2016 presidential campaign and after his election that a US-UK trade deal would be imminent and welcome after Brexit (Frum 2018). In the case of trade disputes between the EU and the US, these have been part of transatlantic family squabbles for many years. For the most part, however, and certainly before Trump assumed the presidency, these disputes were mainly unknown to the general public, engaging special interests and state elites but seldom mobilizing public opinion to any serious degree. (The mobilization of European public opinion, especially but not only in France, against American agricultural imports involving genetically modified organisms or growth-hastening chemicals in the case of meat, is an exception to this generalization.) This changed when candidate and then President Trump regularly complained about what he argued were unfair terms of trade with Europe and other regions of the world. The transatlantic trade relationship became part of the larger "America First" narrative that resonated powerfully with many Americans (Mead 2019). Nationalist populism aside, public opinion has, according to some, contributed to a widening gap between the EU and the US and to a decline in the ability of their respective governments to work together. Stokes (n.d.) wrote, "The partisan divide in U.S. public opinion around issues of importance to Europeans is a far more serious challenge to the future of transatlantic relations than the presidency of Donald Trump. Whether he is re-elected or not, Europeans need to prepare for a world in which the United States still behaves in many Trump-like ways for the foreseeable future" (see also, Pew 2020a).

On such issues as climate change, human rights, military spending, and trust in science, the views of Americans and Europeans appear to have become increasingly divergent. Reactions to the COVID-19 pandemic on the two sides of the Atlantic, some observers argue, have exacerbated this divergence (Butler 2020; Dennison and Zerka 2020). The US that many Europeans see is one that they and their leaders find to be less comprehensible and less admirable. This, it is argued, has contributed to the US's diminished standing in Europe, not to mention in the rest of the world. Particularly during the Trump presidency, but also during the presidency of George W. Bush, the US's European allies have been less willing to look to and accept American leadership.

This chapter examines the impact that public opinion has on relations between the US and its European partners. I begin from the premise that public opinion can indeed matter when it comes to transatlantic relations. In what circumstances, how, and to what degree public opinion affects foreign policy are, of course, questions that have long been debated and on which there exists no consensus (Kertzer 2020). For purposes of the present analysis, I think it unnecessary to revisit these important issues. Instead, I start from the premise that the impact of public opinion on matters related to foreign policy and, in particular, on transatlantic relations, is often indirect and less significant than other factors affecting government policies and actions. Moreover, when it comes to transatlantic relations, as is also true of other aspects of foreign policy, it is entirely reasonable to expect that some differences in public opinion will be more impactful than others.

To better understand the role that public opinion plays, I organize the analysis under the following three headings:

- friendship and an affinity of values,
- the desirability of US leadership, and
- similarities and differences on the issues.

What emerges is a very mixed picture of public opinion's impact on transatlantic relations. It certainly is not one that poses an existential threat to the Atlantic partnership, although there have been, including recently, some worrisome trends. Foremost among these is the existence in the US population of a significant minority that is skeptical and even hostile toward the idea and institutions of multilateralism. This, perhaps more than any other aspect of public opinion, represents a destabilizing element in the transatlantic partnership.

Friendship and an Affinity of Values

For as long as survey data have been collected on what Americans and Europeans think of each other, the assessment has been mainly positive, most of the time (Buchanan and Cantril 1953). They have tended to see each other as friends and allies, rather than rivals and enemies. Even during periods of unusual tension in transatlantic relations, sharp downturns in measures of friendliness have been mainly directed at particular leaders and policies and not so much at the US and Americans or, from the American side, at Europeans or a particular European society. Moreover, these downturns have been quite transient, usually not outlasting a particular conflict or presidency.

Two of the most cited measures of what I am calling friendliness include the following response items: "Do you have a favorable view of the United States?," asked of non-American populations by the Pew Research Center's Global Attitudes project since 2003 (Pew n.d.), and "Please say whether you consider [country name] an ally of the United States, friendly, but not an ally, or an enemy of the United States," asked of Americans by Gallup since the late 1980s (Gallup n.d.). Other measures that tap this sentiment toward the other include a question about whether European respondents perceive the US in a favorable light, reported from time to time since 2002 in the German Marshall Fund of the United States' (GMFUS) annual *Transatlantic Trends* and various more specific questions asked of Europeans about the US and Americans for the Eurobarometer surveys, going back to the 1970s.

The Pew measure of how favorable national populations are toward the US shows significant variation over the period between 2003 and 2021. They range between a high of 75 and a low of 37 percent in France, 64 to 30 percent in Germany, and 75 to 50 percent in the UK. These variations track closely with changes in confidence in the president to do the right thing in world affairs, where the range is from a high of 91 to a low of 9 percent in France, 93 to 10 percent in Germany, and 86 to 16 percent in the UK. It is clear that views of the US president have an impact on favorable ratings toward the US, a relationship observed in all of the European countries included in the Pew survey. It is also clear that a reservoir of goodwill toward the US exists that, although tested by a particular presidency, can rebound very quickly.

This variability in opinion toward the US has long existed. Survey questions asking Europeans whether they have a favorable view of the US, of Americans, and of the US president have been asked by Gallup, Eurobarometer, and other surveys since the 1970s. These evaluations were low at various points in the 1970s and then for most of the Reagan presidency, rebounded during the presidency of George H.W. Bush, fell rather sharply during the first Clinton administration before improving during his second term, after which they fell dramatically during the George W. Bush presidency.[2] There is no evidence of a long-term decline in favorability toward the US among Europeans. Most striking is how closely this measure of American standing is related to the views that Europeans hold of particular presidents and their policies (Brooks 2016, 23–28).

No such variability is found in Americans' sentiments toward Europe. Since 1991, Gallup has asked US respondents about their opinion of countries throughout the world. Canada usually has occupied the first spot, followed closely by the UK, and then three or four other European countries among the top ten, including France and Germany. Only in 2003, when France, Germany, and many other European allies opposed the US-led invasion of Iraq, did these favorability levels drop. Most of the time, they have been and continue to be very high, with 80–90 percent of respondents expressing a very or most favorable view of the US's European G7 partners, as well as Canada and Australia (Gallup n.d.).

Given the generally high levels of favorability that Americans express toward major European countries, it is not surprising that these countries also tend to be viewed as allies. Gallup occasionally asks whether Americans view about two dozen countries as allies, friends but not allies, unfriendly, or enemies. France, Germany, and the UK were among the European countries included in the list presented to American respondents in 2018, the last time this question was asked. Overwhelming majorities said that these European countries were either allies (most Americans view the UK as an ally, about twice as many who say that it is a friend) or friends (Americans are somewhat more likely to view France and Germany as allies than as friends) (Gallup 2018). A February 2019 survey carried out for the Chicago Council on Global Affairs, at a moment when relations between the US and some of Europe's major leaders were as frosty as they had been at any time since President Trump's election, found that 77 percent of Americans considered the EU to be mostly a partner and only 19 percent expressed the view that the EU was mainly a rival. To provide a bit of perspective, this compared to 32 percent who saw China as mainly a partner and 63 percent as a rival (Chicago Council 2019b). Finally, since 2014, the Pew Research Global Attitudes Project has asked respondents in countries across the world, including the US, whether they have a favorable or unfavorable opinion of the EU. The percentage of Americans expressing a favorable view of the EU has remained steady at between 51 and 58 percent during these years (Pew n.d., indicator 28).

The numbers reported in the preceding paragraphs do not disclose what is surely an important difference between the *intensity* of sentiments of Europeans toward the US and those of Americans toward its European partners: The US and its actions matter more to Europeans than those of European nations and the EU do for Americans. When pollsters ask European respondents to express an overall view of the US, these respondents may well have in mind the current US president and the actions and policies of their government, as these are perceived abroad. Americans, on the other hand, are much less likely to know or have opinions about particular circumstances or leaders in Europe. It was a rare European who could not, unprompted, identify George W. Bush, Barack Obama, or Donald Trump as the US president. Americans were far less likely to know who was the president of France, German chancellor, UK prime minister, or, least of all, the president of the European Commission.

The high levels of goodwill that Americans feel toward their major European partners were not affected by President Trump's unprecedented incivility toward Europe and European leaders on issues of trade and defense spending. Indeed, as will be shown later in this chapter, there is good evidence that Americans did not share Trump's position on these matters. It could be, as was also true of Canada, which was also and often in the crosshairs of President Trump's highly critical tweets and other public pronouncements, that Americans realize that these countries do not pose any serious threat to the well-being of their country and that compared to many other regions of the world, the populations and governments of these countries share important affinities with the US.

From the other side of the Atlantic, the elasticity in Europeans' opinion of the US, and the fact that it is closely tied to their assessment of the person who occupies the White House, suggests that there is a reservoir of goodwill toward the US that becomes most apparent when the US president appears to share values and take positions that accord with those widely held across western Europe. These include multilateralism in the management of global affairs, a preference for diplomacy over military solutions to international conflicts, serious attention to and action on climate change, and human rights as a primary value in foreign policy. When these values appear to be embodied in the American government, the French speak of "*l'Amérique qu'on aime*," which, of course, implies the existence of another America that is disliked and disparaged. This is an ambivalence toward the US that has long characterized most European populations (Brooks 2016, ch. 3).

The Desirability of American Leadership

The Pew Research Center's question asking whether respondents have confidence that the US president will do the right thing in world affairs already provides a

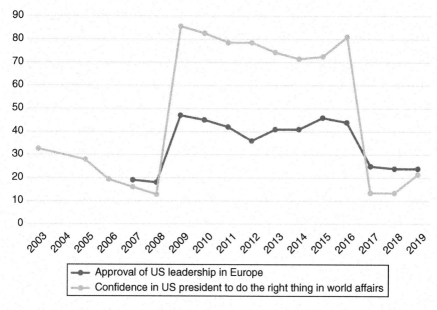

FIGURE 9.1 Confidence in the US president and desirability of US leadership

Source: Adapted from Gallup data (Ray 2020) on approval of US leadership in the world and Pew Center (n.d.) data on confidence in US president to do the right thing in world affairs.

good indication of what Europeans think when it comes to the desirability of US leadership at a particular moment in time. However, it does not tell the whole story. As Figure 9.1 shows, even during periods when Europeans' approval of the US president's performance in world affairs is very high, as it was during most of the Obama presidency, the percentage of Europeans agreeing that strong US leadership in the world is important is much lower. Indeed, according to Gallup surveys, it has never been agreed by a majority of Europeans since 2007, when this question was first asked. Among the larger European countries, the main outlier is the UK, where strong majorities supported US leadership in the world between 2009 and 2016 (Ray 2020).

A somewhat different picture emerges, however, from surveys conducted by the GMFUS and published in its annual report, *Transatlantic Trends*, between 2002 and 2013. These surveys found that, just before the US-led invasion of Iraq, two-thirds of Europeans expressed the view that strong US leadership in world affairs was desirable. This fell to about half in 2003 and slightly more than one-third of Europeans throughout the remainder of the George W. Bush presidency. It then rebounded, however, to a majority after the 2008 election of Barack Obama, ranging from 52 to 56 percent during the years from 2009 to 2013, the last year this question was asked for the annual *Transatlantic Trends* report (GMFUS 2014, chart 1, 15). During these same years, approval among Europeans of President Obama's handling of international affairs, which was very high at the beginning of his presidency, dropped quite significantly. This suggests that Europeans' view of the desirability of American leadership in the world, although tending to track in the same direction as their assessment of his performance in world affairs, is not a mere reflection of this assessment (GMFUS 2014, chart 3, 18).

However, perhaps the most interesting finding of the GMFUS surveys and others on the desirability of US world leadership involved what was, for a time, a rather large gap between mass and elite opinion in Europe. The European public appeared to be much more skeptical than Members of the European Parliament and EU officials about US leadership during the years 2006–10 (GMFUS 2011, chart 3, 4). This gap between elite and mass opinion disappeared by 2013, by which point European elites appear to have become disillusioned with US leadership and were no more likely that European citizens as a whole to be very or somewhat supportive of strong US world leadership, slightly more than half agreeing (Isernia and Basile 2014, figure 2, 15). Unfortunately, systematic polling of mass and elite groups on this and other transatlantic issues that took place has not continued since 2013. Based on non-survey evidence, however, including the pronouncements in recent years of such European leaders as Angela Merkel and Emmanuel Macron and support by EU officials for the concept of "European strategic autonomy" (Franke and Varma 2019), there is little reason to think that European elites have returned to the short-lived love affair with the idea of US global leadership that existed during the first Obama administration.

The fact that Europeans' support for strong US leadership in the world declined during the George W. Bush presidency, then during Obama's second term in office, and most recently and dramatically under President Trump is not unprecedented. Based on non-identical questions asked since 1960 by the United States Information Agency, Eurobarometer, the GMFUS, and the Pew Research Global Attitudes Project, dramatic swings in public opinion on this matter are not recent. Opposition to a strong US leadership role in the world had already weakened during the Vietnam War, and then increased sharply by the beginning of the 1980s. "A tide of anti-Americanism and neutralism was spreading," wrote Ziegler, "as evidenced by large peace marches, protests, and the growing nuclear freeze movement" (Ziegler 1998, 21).

Europeans' desire for strong leadership in the world has always tracked closely, although not perfectly, as was seen during the Obama presidency, with the US president's perceived handling of international affairs. This suggests that, at least in the past, it has not been so much a question of whether the US *should* lead, but of *how* and *where* the US leads. European populations have not been of a single mind on these matters. As mentioned earlier, British support for strong US leadership regularly tracked about 10 percentage points higher than that for Europe as a whole during the period from 2002 to 2013, when this question was asked annually by the *Transatlantic Trends* survey. This was the case notwithstanding that British respondents' approval of the US president's handling of international affairs was about the same as that of Europeans as a whole during these years. Poland and some of the other eastern European members of the EU, as well as Albania and Kosovo, also have shown higher levels of support—much higher than in western Europe—for US leadership in the world and also in their approval of President Trump's handling of international affairs (Pew n.d.).

Since the turn of the century, years that have seen the EU grow from 15 to 27 member states and the emergence of the idea that the EU could and should be more influential and independent in global affairs, various surveys have asked Europeans whether they believe the EU should play a leadership role in global affairs. Over the past several years, this has been joined by Gallup questions asking respondents whether they approve of the performance and leadership of Germany, China, and Russia. All of this reflects the more multipolar image of geopolitics that has succeeded the unipolar moment that lasted from the fall of the Soviet Union in 1991 to the invasion of Iraq in 2003. Initial confidence that the EU could and should carve out a larger role in global affairs, independent of US leadership, was probably in significant part a reaction to what was seen as the George W. Bush administration's unilateralism and policies in the Middle East that were widely rejected by European publics. The more recent decline in European support for US leadership in the world is more likely a combination of reaction against the style and substance of the Trump administration's actions on the world stage and the belief that geopolitical realities have changed in ways that make leadership from other countries more feasible and desirable.

The fact that the wording of questions about the importance of strong US leadership in the world is quite different and that the *Transatlantic Trends* question was dropped after the GMFUS's 2013 survey complicates the assessment of European public opinion on this matter.[3] Moreover, evolving geopolitical realities, in particular the rising influence of China, makes it difficult to draw conclusions about the underlying meaning of changes in Europeans' views of whether and in what circumstances US leadership is desirable. What can be concluded from the somewhat fragmentary survey record is that as recently as the Clinton presidency, the first two years of the George W. Bush presidency, and most of the Obama presidency, those who supported such a role for the US outnumbered those opposed by a significant margin.

Since then, this has not been the case. In recent years the percentage of Europeans who look elsewhere, and particularly to the EU, for global leadership has increased significantly. Nevertheless, international leadership is not a zero-sum game, and so the fact that a majority of Europeans now believe that the EU should play a strong leadership role on the world stage, or that they give Germany higher marks for its performance in global affairs than the US, does not signify opposition to US leadership. It is more reasonably understood as support for shared leadership between the US and the EU. It also happens to be a vision of transatlantic leadership that appears to have considerable support in the US among both foreign policy elites and the general public (Monten et al. 2020).

The Trump years reinforced what was already a growing tendency for European publics to have less confidence in the older model of a Western world in which

US leadership was widely thought to be a necessary and effective guarantee of their security and the liberal world order. An 11-country survey carried out by the European Council on Foreign Relations (ECFR) in December 2020 suggests that this tendency to rely less on the US security guarantee has three components (Krastev and Leonard 2021). They include declining US power globally (and China's ascendance), the unreliability of the US as a partner, and a widespread preference for neutrality between the great powers.

On the matter of US decline, the ECFR survey found that six-in-ten Europeans believe that in ten years' time China will be a stronger power than the US. Only one in five said that this would probably or definitely not be the case. A Pew survey carried out a few months earlier found that in none of the ten European countries surveyed, or in Canada, did a majority express the view that the US was the world's leading economic power. The national percentages mentioning the US ranged from 37 percent in Sweden to only 17 percent in Germany. Mentions of China outnumbered those of the US in every European country, as well as in Canada, in most cases by a very significant margin (Pew 2020b, Q14).

The second factor contributing to the decline in Europeans' faith in the idea of the US security guarantee involves unreliability. There is little doubt that much of this decline can be laid at the doorstep of what has been called the "Trump Effect," expressed in Merkel's May 2017 statement: "The times in which we could completely depend on others are, to a certain extent, over [...] We Europeans truly have to take our fate into our own hands" (Henley 2017). The 2020 election of Joseph R. Biden, Jr., and the flurry of steps taken during the early days of his administration to demonstrate that, in his words, "America is back," appear not to have dispelled fears that the domestic forces that produced Trump's election could see the presidency or Congress, or both, return to the control of a Republican Party still under the influence of the ideas and policies that characterized the Trump presidency. The 2020 ECFR survey reports that about one-third of Europeans agree that Americans cannot be trusted after voting for Trump in 2016, about one-quarter disagreeing, and six in ten say that the US political system is completely or somewhat broken. Two-thirds of Europeans, including large majorities in every country surveyed, agreed with the statement, "Europe can't always rely on the US; we need to look after our own defence capabilities." Only one in ten expressed the view that the US will always protect Europe. At the same time, however, a clear majority of Europeans, including majorities in every one of the 11 countries surveyed, with the exception of Germany, agreed that their country needs the US security guarantee to be safe from military invasion (Dennison and Zerka 2020).

It is perhaps surprising, therefore, that Europeans express a strong preference for neutrality in their relations with the US, China, and Russia, and that only in the UK is there still a majority believing in the primacy of their country's relationship to the US. Asked whether in a disagreement between the US and either China or Russia, they would prefer that their country take a side or remain neutral, majorities in almost all of the European countries surveyed opted for neutrality. The only exceptions involved disagreement between the US and Russia, where a plurality of

Danes and Poles favored neutrality but by comparatively small margins over siding with the US (Krastev and Leonard 2021).

A preference for neutrality, even a rather strong preference among most European populations, could be interpreted in various ways. Whatever else it may signify, it seems to indicate that there remain only vestiges of a sort of any deferral to Washington reflex in great power conflicts that were once more common in Europe. This may be seen when responses to these questions on disagreements between the US, on the one hand, and China and Russia on the other, are disaggregated by age. Older Europeans are significantly more likely to side with the US and less likely to opt for neutrality in such a conflict, compared to their younger compatriots. While it could be that this is an age cycle effect, it seems more reasonable to interpret this difference as generational. It is also reflected in generational views of NATO, older Europeans being more likely than younger age cohorts to have a favorable view of the alliance (GMFUS 2021, 23). Those who remember the Cold War are more likely to have greater trust in or an affective attachment to the US in matters of geopolitics.

In regard to public opinion on the relationship of the US to one's country, Europeans do not display an indifference between the US and its great power rivals. As shown in Figure 9.2, the number of respondents mentioning the US as the most important country with which their own country should have good relations far surpasses the numbers for Russia and China combined among most member-state populations. But only in the UK, where 55 percent of respondents mentioned the US as being their country's most important bilateral partner, does a majority express this sort of special relationship. In most of the surveyed member states, Germany is at least as likely as the US to be mentioned as the first country with which it is important to have a good relationship. This reflects an important economic reality, Germany being the single largest trading partner for all the countries in this survey with the exception of Great Britain (US), Spain (France), and Portugal (Spain). Country-to-country relationships are, however, based on more than economics. Security concerns were clearly more important in the minds of Poles when they answered this question than was the case among many of the other European populations surveyed. But as the Cold War recedes ever further in European memories, and as the contours of geopolitics evolve in ways that appear to most Europeans to signify a declining stature for the US, it is not surprising that perhaps only the British are left with the idea of having a "special relationship" with the US.

Similarities and Differences on the Issues

Values and beliefs are the foundation on which opinions and sentiments rest. Over the past few decades, the argument has often been made that a significant gap separates the values and beliefs of Americans and Europeans and that this gap is an important driver of transatlantic disharmony (Kagan 2003; Wallace 2001). Differences on issues that are reasonably seen as crucial to transatlantic unity are

214 Stephen Brooks

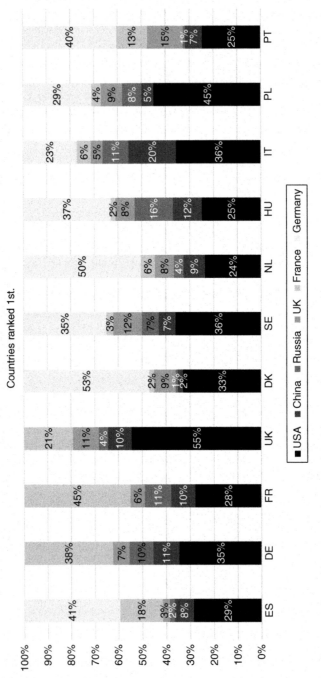

FIGURE 9.2 Ranked importance of relationships with other countries

Source: Figure provided by Pawel Zerka, ECFR.

reflections of this deeper rift at the level of values and beliefs (Pew 2016; Stokes 2019). And, indeed, there certainly have been and continue to exist many issues on which the opinions of Americans and at least some European populations, including those of the leading countries of the EU, diverge. The 2003 decision to invade Iraq was, of course, the most dramatic case of an impactful difference in policy and public opinion.

The claim that a values gap is one of the root causes of disharmony in transatlantic relations is not agreed upon by all, and, in fact, the evidence in support of this claim is not particularly strong. In the introduction to this volume, it is argued that the values gap between the US and European populations on a number of survey questions that are widely accepted as valid measures of attitudes and beliefs relating to important aspects of equality, personal freedom, and the role of democratic government has not widened over the past three decades. Indeed, on most measures, differences appear to have narrowed. Moreover, the gap between the US population and those of the leading member states of the EU and the UK is no greater than exists between some member states of the EU. Even on attitudinal measures associated with Kagan's well-known thesis that "America's power and its willingness to exercise that power—unilaterally if necessary—constitute a threat to Europe's new sense of mission" (Kagan 2003, 61), a values difference that he argued is rooted in history and the asymmetry of power between the US and Europe, the transatlantic values gap is not particularly significant. When it comes to willingness to use force to maintain order in the world (Pew 2020c, Q50h), willingness to fight for one's country (WVS 2017, Q151), and national pride (WVS 2017, Q254), recent surveys show little or variable difference between Americans and the populations of such countries as the UK, France, Sweden, the Netherlands, Spain, and Italy.

Moreover, not all public opinion differences on policy issues have destabilizing consequences for the transatlantic relationship, and it is rare that any become nearly as consequential as the Iraq War. Nonetheless, sustained and large differences in public opinion on issues that have to do with key goals and institutions of the transatlantic partnership may have the potential to create serious tension. Among these are the public's views on trade, defense and security, climate change, and multilateralism.

Trade

The Trump presidency will be remembered, among other things, for the "America First" slogan and policy. Much of this policy had to do with trade and President Trump's frequently repeated claims that the US had been taken advantage of by all of its major trading partners, including the EU (which he rather famously characterized as a "foe" on the eve of a 2018 meeting with Vladimir Putin), through deals negotiated under previous presidents. The fact that the US had a large and persistent trade deficit with the EU was adduced by Trump as proof of this claim. It was an argument that clearly resonated with a significant part of his base and that also tapped a current of anti-globalism that, as in many other Western democracies, is not insignificant in the US. Although expressed in a very different manner and alongside a foreign policy that embraces internationalism, the Biden administration's "Buy American" policy retains some of the Trump presidency skepticism about how the liberal world trade order treats American business and workers (Frum 2021; Hughes 2021).

It is not at all clear, however, that Americans are or have been more protectionist when it comes to matters of trade than their European or Canadian counterparts. Survey data reported by the Chicago Council on Global Affairs finds that in annual surveys since 2004 a majority of Americans have agreed that international trade benefits the US economy and US consumers. There has been more skepticism about whether it benefits American workers, although during the Trump presidency a strong majority of Americans concluded that it did (Chicago Council 2020, figure 3). The Pew Global Attitudes Project's 2014 and 2018 surveys found that support for the statement, "Trade with other countries is good," was very high in both the ten EU countries surveyed and in the US (EU: 79 percent, 2014 and 85 percent, 2018; US: 68 percent, 2014 and 74 percent, 2018). And like Americans, they were much more dubious about its employment benefits (Pew 2018).

On transatlantic trade, more specifically, support for the proposed Transatlantic Trade and Investment Partnership (TTIP) had fallen sharply on both sides of the Atlantic even before President Trump canceled it just days after his 2017 inauguration. What had been generally high if uneven levels of support across the EU fell during 2016 when the negotiations were stalled, and European interest groups and some political parties opposed to the TTIP became more vocal (Pew 2015). In the US, the TTIP was in the crosshairs of both Republican presidential aspirant Donald Trump and Democratic hopeful Bernie Sanders, whose opposition to TTIP and the proposed Trans-Pacific Partnership elevated the importance of trade as an issue and was surely key to the mobilization of public opposition to such deals (Elliott 2016). What had been solid public support for the TTIP in principle (Pew 2014), melted during the year leading up to the 2016 presidential election.

It is well established that elite cueing can have a significant and rapid influence on public opinion regarding matters of foreign policy (Dür 2019). In an analysis that draws on a wide range of survey data, Lincicome (2018) refuted the widely accepted claim that public support for trade protectionism was rising among Americans during the Trump years. Instead, he argued,

> [T]o the extent there is a protectionist problem in the United States, it originates in our political class, not the American electorate. Most Americans generally support freer trade, globalization, and even oft-maligned trade agreements, but the understandable disinterest of many voters means that isolated polls on specific trade policy issues [...] more likely reflect partisan cues or broader macroeconomic conditions than actual support for or opposition to the trade measure at issue.
>
> *Lincicome 2018, 9*

Elite cueing also appears to have been an important factor when it comes to the collapse of support in the EU—more dramatic in some countries than in others—for the TTIP (Bluth 2019; Dür and Schlipphak 2021). In addition, however, some studies indicate that individual attitudes toward the US also affected perceptions of the TTIP, negative attitudes making it more likely that one would be open to arguments opposed to the agreement (Sojka, Díaz-Lanchas, and Steinberg 2019).

On both sides of the Atlantic (and acknowledging the existence of minorities in national populations that are more disposed to oppose international trade), the majority opinion is supportive of international trade while also wary of some of its specific impacts, particularly on employment. There is not a difference between US and European public opinion on such matters that, in itself, should make the negotiation of a transatlantic trade agreement unachievable or contribute more generally to a climate hostility in matters of transatlantic trade. However, elite cueing by interest groups and political parties appears to have a significant impact on public opinion in regard to particular trade proposals, as appears to have been the case in the TTIP negotiations.

Defense and Security

The Trump administration's policy of "America First" was also associated with an expressed reluctance to engage militarily in parts of the world and in circumstances where the vital interests of the US were not at stake. The understanding of "vital interests" was narrower than at any point in time since before World War I and certainly more restrictive than President Obama's policy regarding the protection of America's "core interests" and the necessity of US leadership in the world. Obama's statement that "Strong and sustained American leadership is essential to a rules-based international order that promotes global security and prosperity as well as the dignity and human rights of all peoples," found no echo during the Trump administration (White House 2015, President Obama's introduction). With respect to Europe, the Trump years were ones of considerable stress when it came to matters of security. President Trump's public questioning of NATO's continuing relevance, his refusal to affirm US support for Article 5 of the NATO treaty, and a policy toward Russia that, on the whole, was perceived to embolden the Putin regime in its conflict with Ukraine were among the major stress points. Although widely criticized by the US foreign policy establishment and even some members of the Republican Party on all these counts, and more generally for his indifference toward matters of European security, Trump's refusal to treat European leaders as allies and his obvious disdain for transatlantic cooperation on security matters appeared to be supported by much of his base.

As was also true on issues of trade, there was a rather wide gap between US public opinion on matters of defense and security, the US's leadership role in the world, and the transatlantic security relationship, and the policies and tweets of President Trump. There simply is no support for the argument that most Americans, before, during, or after the Trump administration, wished or wish to see a significant retrenchment in the US's commitment to global security or, more particularly, the NATO alliance. At the very time that President Trump was questioning the relevance of NATO, a 2019 survey showed that Americans with a favorable view of NATO outnumbered those with an unfavorable view by a two-to-one ratio (52 percent to 26 percent; see Pew 2020c). This level of favorability was the same as the median across NATO member states and remained largely unchanged between 2009 and 2019. The Chicago Council's question regarding NATO is more sharply worded, asking respondents whether they believe NATO is still "essential to our country's security." A solid majority of Americans have answered yes since this question was first asked in 2002, and the percentage actually increased over the course of the Trump presidency, reaching 73 percent agreement in 2019 (Chicago Council 2019a, figure 6, 18). Only about one-in-five respondents believe that America's security alliance with Europe mainly benefits the latter, six of ten saying that it benefits both parties (Chicago Council 2020, figure 2, 11).

Americans are not alone in their belief in the importance of NATO to their country's security. A 2020 GMFUS survey found that 53 percent of the French, 74 percent of Germans, and 70 percent of Americans expressed the view that NATO is very or somewhat important to the security of their country (Institut Montaigne 2020). Although agreement is somewhat lower in France, it is still the case that those viewing NATO as important to national security outnumber those who do not by a two-to-one ratio. A separate survey of UK residents in 2019 by the British Foreign Policy Research Group found that two-thirds agreed that NATO was critically or somewhat important to the UK's future national security (British Foreign Policy Group 2019).

It appears, therefore, that public opinion does not pose a threat to transatlantic unity on security matters, at least with respect to the NATO alliance. If there is a transatlantic gap in public opinion, it may be with respect to the challenge that China poses to the security and values of the West. We have already seen that Europeans are inclined, by large margins in most countries, to indicate their preference for neutrality in the event of a conflict between the US and China. Concretely, this has played out in differences between the EU and the US over the adoption of the Chinese 5G data infrastructure, although it is not at all clear that publics on either side of the Atlantic understand arguments that the Trump and now the Biden administration have made about the security implications of this issue (Gorman 2020).

Even before the worldwide spread of the COVID virus, public opinion toward China was trending downward on both sides of the Atlantic. Since then, negative sentiments have spiked in all but a handful of Western democracies (Pew 2021). A combination of factors explains this, including, *inter alia*, China's lack of transparency and cooperation in determining the origins and spread of COVID-19, Beijing's crackdown on dissent in Hong Kong, the treatment of the Uighur Muslim minority in China, and evidence of a more aggressive foreign policy in China's near neighborhood. This increased public negativity toward China might have the potential to strengthen the transatlantic security alliance through the shared perception of a threat to Western values. While this is difficult to predict, more certain is that public opinion on the two sides of the Atlantic is seldom the main driver in transatlantic relations on matters of security, occasional rifts such as that over the Iraq War notwithstanding.

Climate Change and Energy

Within hours of his inauguration, President Biden signed an executive order to rejoin the Paris Agreement, reversing a decision taken by his predecessor. Differences between Europe and the US on matters of climate change go back to the Bush administration's formal rejection of the Kyoto Protocol on greenhouse gas emissions in 2001. Since then, policy on climate change has been a major point of disagreement in transatlantic relations and between the Republican and Democratic parties.

It is probably fair to say that the issue of climate change has been a significant factor contributing to the perception among Europeans and their governments that the US cannot be counted on to provide the sort of global leadership that was expected in the past and that this abdication of a leadership role on climate matters was most egregious during the Trump presidency (CRS 2021, 6–8). The Biden administration took immediate steps to redress this perception, but the legacy of past disengagement is a wariness about US commitments and the capacity to follow through on them in the event of a change in government.

Public opinion explains some of this rift between the US and Europe on climate and energy issues, but not in a simple manner of Americans being less concerned than Europeans about the reality and consequences of climate change. There is a transatlantic gap on these issues, but it is not as wide as often believed. A major international survey conducted in late 2019 asked respondents whether they believed that climate change posed a serious threat to the people of their country over the next 20 years. In the seven largest Western European countries, an unweighted average of 60 percent said that climate change posed a very serious threat. This compared to 49 percent in the US and 56 percent in Canada. In two of the Western European countries, Sweden (40 percent) and the Netherlands (41 percent), there was less concern that climate change would pose a very serious threat than among Americans (Lloyd's Register Foundation 2020). The Pew Global Attitudes Survey, conducted in the summer of 2020, found that the percentage of Americans agreeing that global climate change is a major threat to their country was not strikingly lower, at 62 percent, than in the UK (71 percent), Germany (69 percent), or Sweden (63 percent) (Pew 2020d).

Underneath these numbers for national populations are two rather important differences. First, Americans are much less likely than Western Europeans to consider climate change the major threat to their country or even one of the leading threats. The 2020 Pew survey mentioned above found that, among Americans, global climate change received the fifth highest number of mentions as a threat to the country. In seven-of-nine European countries, it ranked first and second in the other two countries. In Canada, it ranked first (Pew 2020e).

Second, there is much greater polarization in the American population on the issue of climate change. This polarization, which overlaps with ideology and partisanship, has increased over time. Data reported by the Program on Climate Communication at Yale University show that the gap between liberal Democrats and conservative Republicans on whether global warming should be a "high" or "very high" priority for the president and Congress increased from 50 to 74 percentage points between 2009 and 2020. The gap between moderate Democrats and moderate Republicans was only 18 percentage points in 2009 but grew to 34 percentage points by 2020 (Yale 2020, 7). This wide partisan gap is confirmed by a 2021 Pew survey. It found that whereas 70 percent of Democratic Party supporters agreed that dealing with climate change should be a top priority as a long-range foreign policy goal, only 14 percent of Republican supporters agreed. This was the widest margin of disagreement by far between supporters of the two parties with respect to their views on foreign policy priorities (Pew 2021).

Ideological/partisan polarization on climate and energy issues in the US is reinforced politically by the two-party system and the primary system of choosing party candidates. At this conjuncture (2022), it is simply unthinkable that a Republican candidate for president, or Republican candidates for Congress in the vast majority of districts and states, could win their primary election (or elections and caucuses, in the case of presidential aspirants) by embracing climate change as a foremost issue. This is because of not only the opinions held by the party's base, which plays a key role in the selection of candidates, but also because the part of the electorate that leans toward the Republican Party is much less convinced about the need to scale back or even abandon traditional modes of generating energy and carbon-generating lifestyles. Skepticism about climate change and the threat that it poses is not unknown in Europe, particularly among supporters of right-wing populist parties (Kulin, Sevä, and Dunlap 2021). But it is neither a defining feature of the right to the degree that it is in the US nor is the influence of these parties in most European countries comparable to that of the Republican Party in the US, at both the state and national levels. Proportional representation and the multi-party systems of Europe have the effect of blunting to some degree the influence of climate change skepticism and opposition to alternative energy policies.

Multilateralism

After the attacks of 9/11, and as the Bush administration's War on Terror unfolded, one increasingly heard accusations of US unilateralism emanating from the capitals of Europe. In fact, worries and charges of this sort were already heard in the Clinton years, during that rather brief unipolar moment when France's minister of Foreign Affairs, Hubert Védrine (1999), lamented that the US had become a "hyper-power" and that Europe needed to push back in order to ensure a healthier balance of power in the world. In the awarding of the 2009 Nobel Peace Prize to Obama, just weeks into his first term of office, the Nobel committee explicitly acknowledged its expectation that the US would turn toward multilateralism on the global stage, an expectation that was widely shared across Europe. The pendulum swung away from multilateralism during the Trump years, only to see a return to the more engaged rhetoric and diplomatic style of the Obama years—and many of the same foreign policy advisers—under President Biden (Crowley 2020).

The multilateralism/unilateralism continuum is, of course, not so much an issue as about institutions and processes for the management of issues. Nevertheless, it has often been seen as a major point of difference between the US and its European allies, as well as Canada, and one that has roots in the different foreign policy preferences of Americans and the publics of these other countries (Ignatieff 2005). Public support for such institutions of international governance and shared sovereignty as the United Nations (UN) and its agencies, the International Criminal Court, the International Joint Commission, the Paris Agreement, and other treaties that impose requirements on signatories and that involve collective decision-making and that limit individual state sovereignty is sometimes thought to be significantly less in the US than in Europe, and particularly in Western Europe. In fact, whatever the truth of this belief might have been at various points in the past, there is very little evidence that it has been true in recent decades (Kull 2005).

Surveys by the Chicago Council on Global Affairs have regularly shown high levels of support among Americans for international engagement, a shared as opposed to a dominant leadership role, and a belief that participating in international organizations makes the US safer (Chicago Council 2019a, 2020). The Pew Global Attitudes Project corroborates this clear preference for multilateralism among a majority of Americans and shows, moreover, that this preference is not lower on most measures than in Western Europe or Canada. Surveys between 2004 and 2020 reveal that US support for the UN has been about as high as in most of these other countries. In a 2020 survey, respondents were asked whether, "When dealing with major international issues, our country should take into account the interests of other countries even if it means making compromises with them" or "our country should follow its own interests even when other countries strongly disagree." Six-of-ten Americans agreed that their country should take into account the interests of other countries. And on the related question, "Do you think countries around the world, including ours should act as part of a global community that works together to solve problems" or "[countries should act as] independent nations that compete with other countries and pursue their own interests?," three-quarters of Americans supported the cooperative approach. In the case of both questions, Americans' level of support for the multilateral option was about the same as the average for the seven largest Western European countries and Canada (Pew 2020f).

Not only do foreign audiences commonly underestimate Americans' support for multilateralism, so too do Americans and many of their leaders. In an article published at the time of the Iraq War, when the idea of American unilateralism was riding high, Todorov and Mandisodza (2004) provided survey data showing that although Americans tended to support multilateral policies, they overestimated, by a wide margin, public support for unilateral ones. This was quite probably the case during the Trump years too, when majority opinion remained solidly in support of multilateralism, but the rhetoric of the president and his supporters in the media conveyed a very different impression. Kull and Destler (1999) showed that this tendency to get it wrong when it comes to public opinion on multilateralism is not limited to the general public. Based on elite interviews, they found that members of the foreign policy community, including members of Congress, tended to misread the preferences of the public (Kull and Destler 1999).

There is, however, a significant minority of the US population that is opposed to multilateralism and to anything that appears to reduce the capacity of the US to act based on its own sovereign interests, as defined by Americans. About three-in-ten Americans believe that their country should follow its own national interests, even when its allies strongly disagree (Pew 2019). Conservative Republicans are those most likely to support hold this view (55 percent). The experience with COVID-19 certainly has not attenuated the differences within the US population on whether multilateralism is the best way to pursue the country's foreign policy aims. A Chicago Council survey carried out in the summer of 2020 found that fewer than one-in-five Republican supporters agreed that the US should rely more on participation in international organizations, compared to six-in-ten Democratic Party supporters. Asked whether "The coronavirus outbreak has made it clear that it is more important for the United States to be self-sufficient as a nation so we don't need to depend on others," 58 percent of Republicans agreed, compared to 18 percent of Democrats and 36 percent of Independents (Chicago Council 2020).

Ideologically conservative Republican supporters are those most likely to be skeptical about multilateralism. They are, of course, the citizens most likely to be active in Republican Party politics and to vote in the party's primary elections. As in the case of climate and energy issues, discussed in the previous section, the US's two-party system and the method of selecting party candidates amplify the policy influence of this segment of the population.

Conclusion

Public opinion has often been thought of as a destabilizing force in transatlantic relations, and on occasion, it has certainly contributed to a short-term rift between the US and its European partners. It is not at all clear, however, that it has been a major driver of transatlantic quarrels. Part of the reason for this is that the differences in public opinion on the two sides of the ocean are, on many issues of trade and security, not particularly wide, and certainly not so wide as to pose an unbridgeable gap.

In one important respect, however, public opinion may have acquired the potential to render the relationship less predictable and make the management of differences more challenging. This involves the fact of a significant minority of Americans who are wary of their country's engagement in the world, skeptical if not downright hostile toward multilateralism and structures of international governance, and who embraced the message of "America First" that was a hallmark of the Trump presidency. Many Europeans worry that the return of such an orientation in US foreign policy could be only a presidential election away and that for this reason the US needs to be thought of as a less reliable partner than in the past.

Two decades ago, Ivo Daalder asked rhetorically, "Are the United States and Europe heading for divorce?" His answer was "no," and the reasons that he gave are as valid today as at that earlier moment of stress in transatlantic relations. "More issues unite than divide the two," Daalder argued:

> Both sides of the Atlantic share a commitment to market democracy and to the underlying values that have given rise to it over centuries. Both hold key economic and strategic interests in common (even if they often differ on how best to protect or advance them). And cooperation between the two is necessary (and in many cases sufficient) to address many of the most important global issues.
>
> *Daalder 2000*

On balance, and as is true of the economic, strategic interests that are shared, public opinion contributes more to the resilience of transatlantic relations that to their destabilization.

Notes

1 Historically, relations with the US have often been a major issue in the elections of Mexico and some other Latin American countries. This is also the case in Canada, where the country's relationship with the US was the overriding issue of the 1911 and 1988 elections.
2 See figure 2 in Katzenstein and Legro (2009), 3.
3 Pew, "[T]ell me how much confidence you have in each leader to do the right thing regarding world affairs"; Gallup, "Do you approve or disapprove of the job performance of the leadership of the United States?"; GMFUS, "How desirable is it that the United States exert strong leadership in world affairs?"

References

Asmus, Ronald D. 2004. "Power, War, and Public Opinion." *Policy Review* (February and March). www.hoover.org/research/power-war-and-public-opinion.
Bluth, Christian. 2019. "Lessons From TTIP Toxicity for EU-US Trade Talks." In Perspectives on the Soft Power of EU Trade Policy, edited by San Bilal and Bernard Hoekmano, 173–82. London: CEPR Press.
British Foreign Policy Group. 2019. "Public Opinion on Global Threats and the Future of NATO." 3 December. https://bfpg.co.uk/2019/12/public-opinion-on-global-threats-future-of-nato/.
Brooks, Stephen. 2016. *Anti-Americanism and the Limits of Public Diplomacy*. New York: Routledge.

Buchanan, William, and Hadley Cantril. 1953. *How Nations See Each Other: A Study in Public Opinion*. Urbana, Ill.: University of Illinois Press.

Butler, Katherine. 2020. "Europeans' Trust in US as World Leader Collapses During Pandemic." *The Guardian*, 29 June 2020. www.theguardian.com/world/2020/jun/29/europeans-trust-in-us-as-world-leader-collapses-during-pandemic.

Chicago Council on Global Affairs. 2019a. "Rejecting Retreat: Americans Support US Engagement in Global Affairs." www.thechicagocouncil.org/sites/default/files/2020-11/report_ccs19_rejecting-retreat_20190909.pdf.

———. 2019b. "Russians Say Their Country Is a Rising Military Power; And a Growing Percentage of Americans View Russia as a Threat." 21 March. www.thechicagocouncil.org/publication/lcc/russians-say-their-country-is-rising-military-power.

———. 2020. "Divided We Stand: Democrats and Republicans Diverge on US Foreign Policy." 17 September. www.thechicagocouncil.org/research/public-opinion-survey/2020-chicago-council-survey.

Congressional Research Service (CRS). 2021. "U.S. Role in the World: Background and Issues for Congress." 19 January. https://fas.org/sgp/crs/row/R44891.pdf.

Crowley, Michael. 2020. "An Obama Restoration on Foreign Policy? Familiar Faces Could Fill Biden's Team." *New York Times*, 9 November 2020. www.nytimes.com/2020/11/09/us/politics/biden-cabinet.html.

Daalder, Ivo H. 2000. "Europe: Rebalancing the U.S.-European Relationship." Brookings Institution. 1 September. www.brookings.edu/articles/europe-rebalancing-the-u-s-european-relationship/.

———. 2001. "Changing Patterns of European Security and Defence." *International Affairs* 77 (3): 553–67.

Dennison, Susi, and Pawel Zerka. 2020. "Together in Trauma: Europeans and the World After COVID-19." *European Council on Foreign Relations Policy Brief*. 29 June. https://ecfr.eu/publication/together_in_trauma_europeans_and_the_world_after_covid_19/.

Deutsche Welle. 2007. "Expert: Iraq Not the Only Reason for German Anti-Americanism." 8 August 2007. www.dw.com/en/expert-iraq-not-the-only-reason-for-german-anti-americanism/a-2728847.

Dür, Andreas. 2019. "How Interest Groups Influence Public Opinion: Arguments Matter More Than the Sources." *European Journal of Political Research* 58 (2): 514–35. https://doi.org/10.1111/1475-6765.12298.

Dür, Andreas, and Bernd Schlipphak. 2021. "Elite Cueing and Attitudes Towards Trade Agreements: The Case of TTIP." *European Political Science Review* 13 (1): 41–57. doi:10.1017/S175577392000034X.

Elliott, Larry. 2016. "Trade Policy Is No Longer Just for Political Nerds: It Matters in the UK and US." *The Guardian*, 27 March 2016. www.theguardian.com/business/2016/mar/27/trade-policy-uk-eu-referendum-us-bernie-sanders-donald-trump-ttip-globalisation.

Finn, Peter. 2002. "U.S.-Style Campaign With Anti-U.S. Theme." *Washington Post*, 19 September 2002. www.washingtonpost.com/archive/politics/2002/09/19/us-style-campaign-with-anti-us-theme/c9d368ab-b3f9-43f8-936a-fd9109fae5cb/.

Franke, Ulrike, and Tara Varma. 2019. "Independence Play: Europe's Pursuit of Strategic Autonomy." European Council on Foreign Relations Flash Scorecard. 18 July. https://ecfr.eu/special/independence_play_europes_pursuit_of_strategic_autonomy/.

Frum, David. 2018. "Trump's Betrayal of Britain: During His Campaign, the President Encouraged Brexit. Now, as Britain Struggles With Its Transition From the EU, He's Turned His Back." *The Atlantic*, 12 July 2018. www.theatlantic.com/ideas/archive/2018/07/post-brexit-britain-needs-americas-help/565043/.

———. 2021. "The Trump Policy That Biden Is Extending." *The Atlantic*, 28 April 2021. www.theatlantic.com/ideas/archive/2021/04/bidens-speech/618745/.
Gallup. n.d. Country Ratings. news.gallup.com/poll/1624/perceptions-foreign-countries.aspx.
———. 2018. "Fewer Americans Say Mexico Is a U.S. Friend or Ally." 19 July. https://news.gallup.com/poll/237443/fewer-americans-say-mexico-friend-ally.aspx.
German Marshall Fund of the United States (GMFUS). 2011. *Transatlantic Trends: Leaders 2011.* 15 March. www.gmfus.org/publications/transatlantic-trends-leaders-2011.
———. 2014. *Transatlantic Trends 2014.* 10 September. www.gmfus.org/publications/transatlantic-trends-2014.
———. 2021. *Transatlantic Trends 2021.* 7 June. www.gmfus.org/publications/transatlantic-trends-2021.
Gorman, Lindsay. 2020. "5G Is Where China and the West Finally Diverge." *The Atlantic*, 5 January 2020. www.theatlantic.com/ideas/archive/2020/01/5g-where-china-and-west-finally-diverge/604309/.
Henley, Jon. 2017. "Angela Merkel: EU Cannot Completely Rely on US and Britain Any More." *The Guardian*, 28 May 2017. www.theguardian.com/world/2017/may/28/merkel-says-eu-cannot-completely-rely-on-us-and-britain-any-more-g7-talks.
Hughes, Justin. 2021. "How Biden's 'Buy American' Plan Is Different From Trump's." *The Hill*, 17 February 2021. https://thehill.com/opinion/finance/539283-how-bidens-buy-american-plan-is-different-from-trumps.
Ignatieff, Michael, ed. 2005. *American Exceptionalism and Human Rights*. Princeton, NJ: Princeton University Press.
Institut Montaigne. 2020. *Transatlantic Trends 2020*. June. www.institutmontaigne.org/en/publications/transatlantic-trends-2020.
Isernia, Pierangelo, and Linda Basile. 2014. *To Agree or Disagree? Elite Opinion and Future Prospects of the Transatlantic Partnership*. Transworld Working Paper No. 34 (June). http://transworld.iai.it/wp-content/uploads/2014/06/TW_WP_34.pdf.
Kagan, Robert. 2003. *Of Paradise and Power: America and Europe in the New World Order*. New York: Knopf.
Katzenstein, Peter J., and Jeffrey W. Legro. 2009. *US Standing in the World: Causes, Consequences, and the Future*. Long Report of the Task Force on U.S. Standing in World Affairs. American Political Science Association. September. https://scholarship.richmond.edu/cgi/viewcontent.cgi?article=1230&context=polisci-faculty-publications.
Kertzer, Joshua D. 2020. "Public Opinion and Foreign Policy." *Oxford Bibliographies*. www.oxfordbibliographies.com/view/document/obo-9780199743292/obo-9780199743292-0244.xml.
Kohut, Andrew, and Bruce Stokes. 2006. *America Against the World: How We Are Different and Why We Are Disliked*. New York: Times Books.
Krastev, Ivan, and Mark Leonard. 2021. "The Crisis of American Power: How Europeans See Biden's America." European Council on Foreign Relations Policy Brief. 19 January. https://ecfr.eu/publication/the-crisis-of-american-power-how-europeans-see-bidens-america/.
Kulin, Joakim, Ingemar Johansson Sevä, and Riley E. Dunlap. 2021. "Nationalist Ideology, Rightwing Populism, and Public Views About Climate Change in Europe." *Environmental Politics*. https://doi.org/10.1080/09644016.2021.1898879.
Kull, Steven. 2005. "Public Attitudes toward Multiculturalism." In *Multilateralism and U.S. Foreign Policy: Ambivalent Engagement*, edited by Stewart Patrick and Shepard Forman, 99–120. Boulder, CO: Lynne Rienner Publishers.

Kull, Steven, and I. M. Destler. 1999. *Misreading the Public: The Myth of the New Isolationism.* Washington, DC: Brookings Institution Press.

Lincicome, Scott. 2018. "The 'Protectionist Moment' That Wasn't: American Views on Trade and Globalization." *Free Trade Bulletin* [Cato Institute] No. 72 (2 November). www.cato.org/sites/cato.org/files/pubs/pdf/ftb-72.pdf.

Lloyd's Register Foundation. 2020. World Risk Poll. https://wrp.lrfoundation.org.uk/.

Mead, Walter Russell. 2019. "Allies Worry Over U.S. Public Opinion: The Gap Between Voters and Foreign-Policy Elites Shows Little Sign of Closing." *Wall Street Journal*, 4 March 2019. www.wsj.com/articles/allies-worry-over-u-s-public-opinion-11551741006.

Moe, Richard. 2013. *Roosevelt's Second Act: The Election of 1940 and the Politics of War.* New York: Oxford University Press.

Monten, Jonathan, Joshua Busby, Joshua D. Kertzer, Dina Smeltz, and Jordan Tama. 2020. "Americans Want to Engage the World: The Beltway and the Public Are Closer Than You Think." *Foreign Affairs*, 3 November 2020. www.foreignaffairs.com/articles/united-states/2020-11-03/americans-want-engage-world.

Pew Research Center. n.d. Global Indicators Database. www.pewresearch.org/global/database/indicator/1/.

———. 2014. "Support in Principle for U.S.-EU Trade Pact." 9 April. www.pewresearch.org/global/2014/04/09/support-in-principle-for-u-s-eu-trade-pact/.

———. 2015. "Is Europe on Board for a New Trade Deal with the U.S.?" 29 January. www.pewresearch.org/fact-tank/2015/01/29/is-europe-on-board-for-a-new-trade-deal-with-the-u-s/.

———. 2016. "Where Americans and Europeans Agree, Disagree on Foreign Policy." 14 June. www.pewresearch.org/fact-tank/2016/06/14/where-americans-and-europeans-agree-disagree-on-foreign-policy/.

———. 2018. "1. Spotlight on Views of Trade in the U.S., EU and Japan." Americans, Like Many in Advanced Economies, Not Convinced of Trade's Benefits, Ch. 1. 26 September. www.pewresearch.org/global/2018/09/26/spotlight-on-views-of-trade-in-the-u-s-eu-and-japan/.

———. 2019. "6. In a Politically Polarized Era, Sharp Divides in Both Partisan Coalitions." Views of Foreign Policy, Ch. 6. 17 December. www.pewresearch.org/politics/2019/12/17/6-views-of-foreign-policy/.

———. 2020a. "Americans and Germans Differ in Their Views of Each Other and the World." 9 March. www.pewresearch.org/global/2020/03/09/americans-and-germans-differ-in-their-views-of-each-other-and-the-world/.

———. 2020b. "U.S. Image Plummets Internationally as Most Say Country Has Handled Coronavirus Badly." 15 September. www.pewresearch.org/global/2020/09/15/us-image-plummets-internationally-as-most-say-country-has-handled-coronavirus-badly/.

———. 2020c. "NATO Seen Favorably across Member States." 9 February. www.pewresearch.org/global/2020/02/09/nato-seen-favorably-across-member-states/.

———. 2020d. "Despite Pandemic, Many Europeans Still See Climate Change as Greatest Threat to Their Countries." 9 September. www.pewresearch.org/global/2020/09/09/despite-pandemic-many-europeans-still-see-climate-change-as-greatest-threat-to-their-countries/.

———. 2020e. "Unfavorable Views of China Reach Historic Highs in Many Countries." 6 October. www.pewresearch.org/global/2020/10/06/unfavorable-views-of-china-reach-historic-highs-in-many-countries/.

———. 2020f. "International Cooperation Welcomed Across 14 Advanced Economies." 21 September. www.pewresearch.org/global/2020/09/21/international-cooperation-welcomed-across-14-advanced-economies/.

———. 2021. "Majority of Americans Confident in Biden's Handling of Foreign Policy as Term Begins." 24 February. www.pewresearch.org/politics/2021/02/24/majority-of-americans-confident-in-bidens-handling-of-foreign-policy-as-term-begins/#economic-and-security-issues-are-publics-top-foreign-policy-priorities.

Ray, Julie. 2020. "U.S. Leadership Remains Unpopular Worldwide." Gallup. 27 July. https://news.gallup.com/poll/316133/leadership-remains-unpopular-worldwide.aspx.

Sojka, Aleksandra, Jorge Díaz-Lanchas, and Frederico Steinberg. 2019. "The Politicization of Transatlantic Trade in Europe: Explaining Inconsistent Preferences Regarding Free Trade and the TTIP." European Commission, Joint Research Centre Working Papers on Territorial Modelling and Analysis No. 9.

Stokes, Bruce. n.d. "For Europe, A Deeply Polarized U.S. Public Is a Bigger Challenge Than Trump." *Transatlantic Take*, German Marshall Fund of the United States.

———. 2019. "US Foreign Policy Will Continue to Divide Americans Beyond 2020." Chatham House. March. www.chathamhouse.org/2019/03/us-foreign-policy-will-continue-divide-americans-beyond-2020.

Todorov, Alexander, and Anesu Mandisodza. 2004. "Public Opinion on Foreign Policy: The Multilateral Public That Perceives Itself as Unilateral." *The Public Opinion Quarterly* 68(3): 323–48.

Védrine, Hubert. 1999. «Déclaration de M. Hubert Védrine, ministre des affaires étrangères, sur les relations internationales depuis l'effondrement de l'URSS, les équilibres géostratégiques et la sécurité internationale» [Statement of French Minister of Foreign Affairs, Hubert Védrine, on international relations, geo-strategic equilibrium and international security since the collaps of the USSR]. 3 November. www.vie-publique.fr/discours/131274-declaration-de-m-hubert-vedrine-ministre-des-affaires-etrangeres-sur.

Wallace, William. 2001. "Europe, the Necessary Partner." *Foreign Affairs* (May–June). www.foreignaffairs.com/articles/europe/2001-05-01/europe-necessary-partner.

White House. 2015. National Security Strategy. February. https://obamawhitehouse.archives.gov/sites/default/files/docs/2015_national_security_strategy_2.pdf.

World Values Survey (WVS). 2017. Seventh Round of the WVS. www.worldvaluessurvey.org/WVSOnline.jsp.

Yale University. 2020. *Politics and Global Warming*. Program on Climate Change Communication. December. https://climatecommunication.yale.edu/wp-content/uploads/2021/01/politics-global-warming-december-2020b.pdf.

Ziegler, Andrew. 1998. *European Public Perceptions of the Atlantic Alliance: Implications for Post-Cold War Security Policy*. NATO. www.nato.int/acad/fellow/96-98/ziegler.pdf.

10

THINK TANKS AND TRANSATLANTIC RELATIONS

An Overview

Donald E. Abelson and Christopher J. Rastrick

Introduction

As several contributors to this volume have observed, speculation about the resilience and, at times, fragility of transatlantic relations has preoccupied scholars, policymakers, and journalists—even casual observers of American-European affairs—for decades. In recent years, the impact of a shifting economic and political landscape in Europe and the United States (US) has also captured the attention and interest of many prominent public policy research institutes or think tanks. Concerned about how changes in leadership and a reorientation of political priorities in some countries could threaten the stability of transatlantic ties, many of these institutions have invested considerable time and resources tracking developments on both sides of the Atlantic. Indeed, high-profile think tanks inside and beyond the Washington Beltway, and in many European capitals, have and continue to weigh in on the future of this historically significant relationship.

While over 11,000 think tanks are scattered across the globe (McGann 2021), it is not surprising given their rich history, evolution, and growth (Abelson 2018; Rastrick 2018) that North America and Europe are home to almost half of the world's public policy institutes. With large concentrations of think tanks in Washington, DC, and in various European cities, including Paris, London, Bonn, and Brussels, there is no shortage of policy experts prognosticating about the multitude of transatlantic issues that find their way into various national legislatures and executive councils. From inside paneled boardrooms on Capitol Hill and in the White House, to the halls of the European Parliament, there are regular discussions among think tanks and policymakers about how to move this strategic partnership forward without compromising the integrity and durability of the alliance.

For scholars committed to explaining how policy ideas informing transatlantic relations are generated, transmitted, and in some cases, acted upon by those occupying positions of power, identifying and deciphering the role, function, and perceived impact or influence of think tanks can pay handsome dividends. As organizations committed to shaping how policymakers and other key stakeholders think about a wide range of issues, including Washington's attitudes toward burden-sharing in the North Atlantic Treaty Organization (NATO), a familiar talking point during Donald J. Trump's tumultuous presidency, it stands to reason why scholars have begun to pay closer attention to the tactics they employ to affect policy change. Recognizing that ideas matter and that those that are poorly conceived and recklessly executed may have dire consequences, it is understandable why think tanks, as incubators of ideas, have been subjected to more intense scrutiny. While those who study think tanks may not agree on how best to assess their policy influence, they generally concede that in many ways, these institutions are well positioned and equipped to make their presence felt on the public policy landscape.

As the academic literature on think tanks has matured in recent years, some scholars have broadened the scope of their research to highlight the efforts of think tanks in China and in other parts of Asia, Africa, and the Middle East to shape the political discourse around important policy issues (Abelson and Rastrick 2021; Abelson, Brooks, and Hua 2017). Despite the considerable progress made in exploring the role think tanks play in these and other regions, the political leverage they may or may not wield often remains cloaked in mystery. Indeed, securing access to the material required to test hypotheses about the influence of think tanks in many non-democratic countries continues to present formidable obstacles. However, the same cannot be said of experts who examine think tanks located in Washington, DC, in Brussels, or indeed in many other European capitals where their public interactions with policymakers often make the news.

How think tanks are perceived by policymakers, the media, and other important stakeholders who both support and often consume their research products, and the extent to which their involvement in policymaking is welcomed or discouraged at various levels of government, has and will undoubtedly continue to yield many interesting findings. However, our focus here is not to revisit normative discussions about the democratic or undemocratic nature of unelected experts, or whether think tanks are primarily concerned about advancing the public good and/or their private interests and those of their benefactors. Much of this work has already been undertaken and has led to fertile discussion among academics and journalists (Abelson 2018; Parmar 2012). Rather, our intent is to draw upon the experiences of a handful of think tanks in the US and in Europe to demonstrate how, in an increasingly competitive marketplace of ideas, they have been able to position themselves as vocal participants and commentators on the transatlantic relationship. We do this by explaining that despite a shared commitment to influencing public opinion and public policy, think tanks in the US and in much of Europe have at times embraced a very different approach to engaging stakeholders around key policy issues. Put simply, for many think tanks in the US, the most effective way to transmit their ideas is through various forms of advocacy. By contrast, for many of their European counterparts, facilitating discussions among important officials, rather than trying to impose their own policy agenda, is their preferred modus operandi.

To be clear, the purpose of this chapter is not to simply identify a select group of think tanks in the US and in Europe, which, as part of their mandate, have a commitment to study transatlantic relations. It is well known in the think tanks community that the New York-based Council on Foreign Relations (CFR) and London's Chatham House have, for many years, engaged in important research on the transatlantic relationship (Parmar 2004). To these organizations, we could add the RAND Corporation, the American Enterprise Institute (AEI), the Center for Strategic and International Studies (CSIS), the Hoover Institution on War, Revolution and Peace, the Brookings Institution and several think tanks located in France, Germany, Great Britain, Brussels, and the Netherlands. Still, as important as it is to acknowledge public policy institutes that possess the most expertise and notoriety in this policy field, keeping track of the scholars on their payroll, the number of conferences, workshops, and seminars they sponsor, and how frequently their staff testifies before legislative bodies, takes observers of think tanks only so far. Even if one adds to these metrics the volume of studies they generate, and how often their scholars appear in, or are quoted by, the print, broadcast, and electronic media, several questions about the impact or influence of these institutions invariably remain unanswered.

Rather, our goal in this chapter is more sweeping. It is to explore how think tanks on both sides of the Atlantic are able to take advantage of the political systems they occupy, and the unique position they enjoy on the public policy landscape, to affect policy change. First, we examine the role of think tanks within the context of the transatlantic relationship, with a particular focus on how some of the peculiarities and distinctions between the US and European think tank communities have informed different roles within this relationship. Second, we assess the nature and scope of collaboration between think tanks in the US and Europe, and how these interactions have helped shape the transatlantic relationship. Finally, we identify several contemporary features of the broader transatlantic relationship that may inspire and facilitate enhanced collaboration between these two think tank communities. The election of President Joseph R. Biden, Jr., the Brexit withdrawal, and the fragile defense relationship present unique opportunities for the US and the European Union (EU) think tanks to broker key solutions to these and other timely and important transatlantic issues.

Given the variety of think tank typologies and classifications that have been constructed and employed by various scholars (Abelson 2018; McGann 1992; Stone 1996; Weaver 1989), it is important for us to be clear about what we believe constitutes a "think tank." While there is persistent disagreement among scholars as to what criteria must be satisfied for an organization to be considered a think tank (Abelson 2006, 11; Abelson and Rastrick 2021; Kelstrup 2021; Mendizabal 2021), for the purposes of this chapter, think tanks will be defined as independent, non-governmental, non-partisan public policy research organizations that provide research and analysis to help shape public opinion and public policy. Furthermore, given the vast geographic reach of these organizations, and the multiple and diverse communities within them, we will limit our study to think tanks in Washington, DC, and supranational think tanks in Brussels. More specifically, in these geographic centers, we will focus primarily on think tanks that are widely respected for their expertise on transatlantic relations.

Think Tanks in the US and Europe

Although the origin of the first commonly understood think tank can arguably be traced to Europe (the Royal United Services Institute in London), the global development of think tanks since that point have of course spread well beyond the continent. While approximately 47 percent of think tanks are based in North America and Europe (McGann 2021), the development of think tanks within these jurisdictions has not necessarily been symmetrical.

In the EU, there have been two principal tracks of think tank development: within member states (with a domestic-level constituency and focus) and within Brussels (with an EU-wide orientation). While the development of think tanks within member states has been subject to a modest degree of scholarly attention (particularly those member states—past and present—with more established think tank histories, such as France, Germany, and the UK), think tanks with an EU-specific mandate (and most typically operating within Brussels, the *de facto* capital of the EU) have only recently started to be analyzed by scholars. In fact, the first distinct analysis of the EU think tanks originated from Philippa Sherrington (2000), who noted "the deepening of EU competences, the increased impact of EU policy-making on member states, and thus a heightened awareness of all things European" (173). As such, while the limited attention to these organizations may be attributable to limited attention to transnational think tanks within the literature, it is also significantly attributable to the relative nascence of "supranational think tanks" as veritable epistemic actors within the EU public policy space.

Perhaps it is not surprising, then, that the scale and ostensible role for supranational think tanks has correlated with an enhanced deepening of competence of the EU, which has augmented considerably since at least the mid-to-late 1980s. As the decision-making competence of the EU has evolved and enhanced, the think tank community within Brussels has augmented as well. With the new scope and increased complexity of policy decisions and discussions within the EU (not to mention a characteristic consultative instinct adopted by many EU institutions), the opportunity was ripe for the development of a robust think tank community. Accordingly, throughout the 1990s and into the early 2000s, the number of supranational think tanks increased significantly as some of the more visible think tanks came onto the scene (such as the European Policy Centre, Friends of Europe, and Bruegel). As these organizations have established themselves as long-term features of the Brussels public policy community, scholarly attention has turned toward, first, understandings of their definition and number and, second, their role and constituencies within the multiple policy processes of the EU. Still undetermined, in these authors' minds, is the role that these organizations have played in fostering relationships with their member state colleagues, which ostensibly takes on increasing relevance and opportunity in the wake of the UK withdrawal from the EU.

While many of the functions that observers and scholars would associate with the "core business" of think tanks are certainly present among supranational think tanks, there are ways to distinguish these organizations from many of their counterparts around the world. For example, while supranational think tanks can and do produce original research and analysis, their priority and indeed comparative advantage within the EU public policy space relates to their ability to provide a networking function. In other words, supranational think tanks have concentrated many of their activities on cultivating, maintaining, and nurturing policy networks, and by ensuring that the proper settings are established to accommodate policymakers, non-governmental actors, and any policy-adjacent individuals/organizations that could benefit by accessing these networks. To do so, "supranational think tanks can be seen to play a 'matching' role whereby individuals and organizations are exposed to each other under the auspices of a given think tank, so that policy actors (like-minded or ideologically disparate) are introduced and begin building the basis of a constructive policy-oriented relationship" (Rastrick 2018, 70). In providing a forum for these exchanges to take place, supranational think tanks "are able to promote consensus-building and discussion among actors/organizations with a vested interested in policy outcomes and public policy in general, regards of whether these actors' desired outcomes are initially mutually exclusive" (Rastrick 2018, 70).

Despite supranational think tanks possessing neither institutional nor official "power," we can now see how these organizations may exert various forms of "influence" and socialization with those actors who are capable and charged with exerting formal power. Some scholars have even suggested that formal policymakers do not need to be directly involved in a policy network for non-governmental network actors to exercise influence in policymaking. As Marin and Mayntz (1991) argued, "if 'policy' usually means public policy in policy network studies, this does not imply that state agents must be the focal or dominant participants," adding "in largely self-regulated sectors, on the other hand, public policy may well be formulated by private actors (to be initiated or subsequently endorsed by the proper political authorities)" (17).

The priority think tanks in the EU place on creating networking opportunities for key stakeholders at times stands in stark contrast to how several think tanks in the US seek to influence policy discussions. Although it is not uncommon for many high-profile US think tanks to invite policymakers, journalists, academics, and representatives from other non-governmental organizations (NGOs) and government agencies to their workshops, conferences, and seminars, more advocacy-oriented US think tanks place a higher premium on relying on their research profile and media contacts to drive discussions around key policy issues. Unlike many of their European counterparts who are intent on facilitating policy discussions, think tanks in the US are generally more committed to shaping the outcome of those decisions. Indeed, as the US think tanks have become more engaged in political advocacy since the early 1970s (Abelson 2006, 2018), they have developed even more sophisticated strategies to ensure their voices are heard. How the US think tanks came to be more advocacy-oriented and the implications of this shift are discussed in the following section. This overview will lead to a broader discussion about US-European think tank collaboration.

The American Think Tank Experience

When the US and European scholars observe the behavior of more advocacy-oriented think tanks such as The Heritage Foundation and the Center for American Progress, they often become nostalgic about early twentieth-century policy research institutions that took root in the UK, Germany, and in the US. Reflecting on think tanks of this period, social and cultural historian James A. Smith (1991a), political scientist David M. Ricci (1993), and several others conjured up images of experts working tirelessly at their desks to identify the underlying causes of economic, social, and political unrest. Given the avowedly ideological leanings of many of today's think tanks, it is understandable why these and other admirers of Britain's Fabian Society and Chatham House, home of the Royal Institute of International Affairs, and of the Brookings Institution during its formative years, are concerned about the direction think tanks have taken in recent decades. For those longing for the re-emergence of more traditional policy research institutes, it is both troubling and worrisome that think tanks such as The Heritage Foundation (Edwards 1997, 2013), the Adam Smith Institute (Pirie 2012), and countless others have, in effect, become lobbyists for various political causes. With the recent announcement that Donald Trump, who displayed nothing but contempt for think tanks during his four years in office (Abelson 2021), has launched the America First Policy Institute, admirers of the golden age of think tanks have more cause for concern. Rather than helping government think its way through complex policy problems—a goal articulated by institutions during the Progressive Era—critics of think tanks (Stefancic and Delgado 1996) contend that contemporary think tanks have embarked on a far less virtuous and more dangerous path. Have they?

In retracing the history of think tanks, it is tempting to portray Progressive Era think tanks as high-minded and virtuous, and advocacy think tanks as opportunistic and sinister. To label advocacy think tanks (which often promote progressive policies) as nefarious and self-serving would be inaccurate and misleading. At the turn of the twentieth century, think tanks such as the Russell Sage Foundation (1907) and the Carnegie Endowment for International Peace (1910) may very well have made a concerted effort to inject both social science and a social conscience into discussions around various public policy issues. Nonetheless, it would be naive to suggest that their goals were entirely altruistic. They did not ignore how their research could influence policy debates in ways that they deemed important both for their institution and for their country.

Exercising influence need not have negative repercussions. Heralded as the quintessential think tank because of its commitment to policy research, the Brookings Institution, for example, took great pride in advising members of Congress to draft the Budget and Accounting Act of 1921 (Critchlow 1985; Smith 1991b). This legislation resulted in the creation of institutions and practices that are still used to oversee and implement the federal budget. Similarly, in the same year, the New York-based CFR was established as an exclusive club for intellectuals and statesmen to discuss America's role in the world (Parmar 2004). Some of the earliest think tanks refrained from interfering directly in deliberations on Capitol Hill and in the White House. However, from the time these institutions took root in the US, they were well aware of how their ideas could shape and influence the politics of the day.

Think tanks created during the Progressive Era understood the power of ideas. After all, this is why Andrew Carnegie, Robert Brookings, Herbert Hoover, and other philanthropists invested in these institutions. They were established to help inform, educate, advocate, and, yes, at times, to indoctrinate. What allowed them to succeed was their ability to make their views known. Progressive Era think tanks might have assigned a far higher priority to generating rigorous policy research than do many advocacy think tanks of the late twentieth and early twenty-first centuries, but they should not be seen as altruistic guardians of the public interest. Institutions, regardless of whether they are classified as think tanks, interest groups, or lobbyists, are motivated by similar goals—to shape and influence public opinion and public policy in ways that satisfy their core interests. Where they differ is with respect to how they define their priorities, the resources they allocate to research and marketing, and the strategies they employ to achieve their desired objectives.

Early twentieth-century think tanks, as well as those created over the past 40 years, perform similar roles and functions. Yet regardless of when they were incorporated, what sustains them is their ability to engage in policy research and public advocacy. It is not the role of think tanks that has changed. What has changed is the higher premium think tanks place on advocacy and marketing over policy research, a trend that was popularized by The Heritage Foundation in the early 1970s. Indeed, no other think tank in the US or, for that matter, around the globe, has had a greater impact in changing the complexion and orientation of think tanks than Heritage (Edwards 2013). It was The Heritage Foundation that stressed the importance of providing policymakers with timely and policy-relevant research, and it was Heritage that influenced generations of think tanks to combine policy research with aggressive marketing. The rise of The Heritage Foundation and hundreds of other advocacy think tanks continues to generate concerns in scholarly circles, but the decision of think tanks to become more invested in advocacy than in research was predictable, particularly in a political system that values political expediency over the creation and dissemination of knowledge. In fact, think tanks such as The Heritage Foundation that can provide policymakers and other key stakeholders with the ammunition they need to achieve their political goals are handsomely rewarded. By satisfying the wishes of their core constituents, think tanks may, at the very least, become even more entrenched in the policymaking process.

Recognizing the importance of conveying their ideas to multiple target audiences, think tanks have become adept at making their presence felt. They rely on a range of governmental and non-governmental channels to make their views known. These range from taking part in interviews on political talk shows and network newscasts to testifying before congressional committees and serving as advisers on presidential campaigns and transition teams. As the marketplace of ideas has become increasingly congested, think tanks have devoted even more time and resources to extending their reach (Abelson 2006).

The Strategies of American Think Tanks

Determining what constitutes a think tank continues, as noted, to elude most scholars in the field, but identifying the various ways these kinds of organizations interact with decision-makers and other influential stakeholders is hardly a mystery. During the Progressive Era, think tanks communicated their findings primarily by producing and disseminating reports, and by holding conferences and meetings with policymakers, business leaders, academics, and journalists. In recent years, several studies have documented the extensive ties that were established between prominent think tanks such as Brookings, the CFR, and RAND Corporation (Abella 2008; Parmar 2004; Smith 1991b) and the leading political and business leaders with whom they discussed and debated a range of issues.

By the late 1960s and early 1970s, think tanks began to think more strategically about how to capture the attention of policymakers and the public. And as noted, no organization would prove to have more of an impact in shaping how think tanks would communicate in the future than the Washington, DC–based Heritage Foundation. Established in 1973 by former congressional aides Edwin Feulner and Paul Weyrich, The Heritage Foundation not only changed the complexion of the think tank community but also introduced new and revolutionary techniques for think tanks to enhance their visibility (Abelson, Brooks, and Hua 2017; Edwards 1997, 2013). For Feulner and Weyrich, think tanks could become far more relevant in the policymaking process if they better understood the needs of policymakers. Rather than replicating what the Brookings Institution and other more traditional think tanks had done for years, Heritage, as noted, introduced a model based on what they called "quick response policy research." Simply put, instead of only producing book-length studies that policymakers rarely had the time or inclination to read, Heritage researchers were instructed to write and disseminate briefs on timely and relevant policy issues. The briefs were typically four-to-six pages in length, offered recommendations on how the US could address specific domestic and foreign policy challenges, and, in the pre-internet age, were hand-delivered to every member of Congress. In addition, Heritage produced several other types of publications that catered to different target audiences.

By the time Ronald Reagan assumed the presidency in January 1981, Heritage had become one of the leading think tanks in the country, thanks in part to the publication of *Mandate for Leadership* (Heatherly 1981), a weighty tome that served as a blueprint for the incoming administration. Heritage's meteoric rise was also due in no small measure to its commitment to marketing ideas aggressively, the hallmark of advocacy think tanks. For Feulner, a graduate of the Wharton School of Business who held onto the presidency of Heritage for over three decades, ideas were no different from commodities being traded on the New York Stock Exchange. During his lengthy tenure, he often noted that ideas could only gain traction if they were properly marketed to and endorsed by large segments of the population. As important as it was to Feulner and Weyrich to strengthen their ties to key business, media, and political figures, they never lost sight of the importance of connecting with the American people. In its early years, a large percentage of Heritage's budget was derived from thousands of small donations.

Heritage's approach to marketing its ideas to multiple stakeholders has been adopted by hundreds of other think tanks both inside the Beltway and across the US. Not surprisingly, those institutions that have bought into the Heritage model rely on similar channels to enhance their visibility. Scholars from think tanks appear regularly as "talking heads" on television and radio programs; testify before legislative committees; organize seminars, workshops, and conferences for policymakers, journalists, congressional staffers, and academics; establish close ties to appointed officials throughout the bureaucracy; distribute publications electronically; maintain blogs on their web sites; use social media, including Twitter, Instagram, and Facebook to communicate to younger audiences; deliver lectures at various universities; and occasionally take a leave of absence to work on congressional and presidential campaigns.

The strategies employed by think tanks are carefully coordinated for maximum results. However, unlike for-profit organizations, their success or failure is not measured by quarterly losses or gains. It is determined by how much of an impact they have had in influencing public policy. Directors of think tanks employ several metrics such as media exposure and the frequency with which their scholars testify before congressional committees to gauge their standing in the policymaking community. Unfortunately, these and other indicators have proven to be unreliable measures of policy influence. While think tanks have a vested interest in convincing stakeholders that their organizations wield tremendous influence, the scholars who study them have yet to agree on how to evaluate their performance.

On the surface, think tanks in the US and those with a focus on the EU perceive their roles very differently. For the US think tanks, becoming more advocacy-oriented which, as noted, has manifested itself in different ways, is seen as the most effective way to ensure their voices are heard. With an eye to shaping the political climate for an extended period of time, think tanks inside the Beltway are not shy when it comes to their intentions. They are committed to influencing what policymakers and other stakeholders think about critical domestic and foreign policy issues and waste little time constructing a well-coordinated strategy to affect policy change. But in much of Europe, think tanks have adopted a different approach, one that relies more on facilitating discussions among key stakeholders rather than one that emphasizes advocacy at all costs. In some ways, these differences may help to explain why collaboration between and among the US and European think tanks on the transatlantic file tends to be more infrequent and episodic, a subject to which we now turn.

Obstacles to US-EU Think Tank Collaboration

While observers might expect there to be a strong and storied tradition of collaboration among think tanks in the US and EU—in accordance and in movement with the vagaries of the transatlantic relationship—the degree and pace of collaboration has in actual fact largely been modest, infrequent, and ephemeral. The extent of think tank collaboration in a transatlantic context is variant, although there are two principal modes of collaboration: European "branches" and project-specific collaboration.

In the case of European "branches," we are referring to the American think tanks that have established permanent operations within Europe. As one might infer, this operating model is largely endemic to among the more well-endowed and enduring US think tanks including, for example, the Carnegie Endowment for International Peace (which operates Carnegie Europe in Brussels) and the German Marshall Fund of the United States. While these organizations are able to leverage their considerable endowments and operating revenue to sustain international activities in Europe, the fact is most US think tanks are not in a financial position where such operational extension is feasible. While European "branches" are by no means the norm for the US think tanks, the far more regularized mode of engagement centers on project-specific collaboration, either organically or as a requisite for granting purposes. In this instance, think tanks from both continents can leverage the particular research expertise of scholars and staff in their respective organizations, while also tapping into the dissemination networks that each think tank uniquely serves. This approach is most opportune for think tanks working within specific areas of expertise or focus, where there are natural synergies that can be exploited from a smaller number of experts working within a limited audience. As will be discussed shortly, one might suggest that the ongoing discussions that will culminate in a US-UK trade agreement might be well-served by a collaborative dimension between trade-focused think tanks in the US and EU (and, of course, those in the UK).

As we know that the history of collaboration between US and European think tanks is neither as extensive nor enduring as one might expect, it would be helpful to turn our attention to the reasons that might underpin these characteristics. In particular, we identify two key reasons why the transatlantic think tank relationship has not necessarily corresponded to leaps within the broader transatlantic relationship: Different roles fulfilled by think tank communities and increasing competition within the "marketplace of ideas."

Between US and supranational think tanks, there are different goals and outcomes that they archetypically seek to fulfil and compete upon (Rastrick 2018, 22). For supranational think tanks, we know that they are generally disposed to facilitating a network-oriented role, whereby their comparative advantage is providing decision-makers and non-governmental actors the opportunities to engage, when such engagement may not have occurred expediently or at all. While research and public policy analysis serves as a component of supranational think tanks' activity, it is not, in our estimation, their core competency nor is it their comparative advantage within the Brussels public policy community. For the US think tanks, by contrast, their core competency is very much aligned with timely, substantive, and "briefing-friendly" research and analysis that serves to edify and influence policymakers and those around them. For the US think tanks, their metrics of success align with the volume of their output, the extent to which it is captured within the (typically) mainstream press and social media, and the opportunities availed to present these findings in front of decision-makers. For supranational think tanks, in comparison, their metrics of success certainly capture a component of the aforementioned indicators. However, their primary metrics serve their primary audience and goals: Namely, the number and breadth of opportunities for their networking function to be maximized and the depth and caliber of individuals and organizations they count as members or participants through their fora. In short, while the US and supranational think tanks pursue fundamentally different goals and metrics of success, this belies the reality that they serve fundamentally differently prioritized functions within their particular constituencies. While this collaboration may make sense under situations in which the goal is to leverage their respective counterparts' strength (impactful advocacy in the case of US think tanks and meaningful network-facilitating in the case of supranational think tanks), the differences in goals do not broadly entice deeper collaboration between these organizations.

The second reason we identify as inhibiting expectedly closer relations between the US and supranational think tanks lies in the sustained, but increasing, competition in the "marketplace of ideas" of which think tanks have until recently enjoyed perhaps an oligopolistic, or at least market-moving, status. However, in recent years especially, we have seen a proliferation in thought leadership activities and institutes among organizations that have traditionally operated outside the epistemic community, or at least had an irregular interaction in this space. For example, many multinational banking institutions, management-consulting firms, and other multinational corporations have created thought leadership institutes or departments as part of their operations. Whereas previously these corporations or organizations may have sought and retained the research and analytical expertise of a think tank within their jurisdiction, they are increasingly turning toward their own in-house capabilities to fulfil this part of their operations. Of course, there are several reasons for doing so, including not only the prestige that comes with sustaining an in-house thought leadership institute capable of attracting media and public policy attention based on research/analytical bona fides, but also the ability to create a "revolving door" of data, research, and insights that can serve clients in a more traditional profit-making aspect of these organizations. This phenomenon is an understudied development, but in light of the transatlantic and globalized nature of the organizations producing this type of in-house alternative to think tanks, it is entirely conceivable that this pole in the marketplace of ideas on transatlantic relations may in the future become increasingly important and relevant.

What this means for think tanks in the context of the transatlantic relationship is that the opportunities for uniquely cross-Atlantic research and analytics that may have previously been proprietary to think tanks and similarly oriented research organizations (for-profit or otherwise) have become challenged by the willfully expanded capacity of multinational organizations to bypass think tanks altogether and fulfil the research and dissemination activities themselves. As these organizations continue to expand and make their in-house thought leadership function permanent, think tanks on both sides of the Atlantic will continue to face increased competition in their funding and value proposition to funders.

While there are reasons for the transatlantic think tank relationship failing to bloom, this is not an evergreen condemnation. In times of significant policy and socioeconomic upheaval, think tanks often stand poised to exert disproportionately higher impact and influence, given their ability to provide quick, accessible, and relevant research and analysis. Furthermore, the previously modest transatlantic think tank connections ought not be a definitional trait of this relationship, especially given the public policy voids and opportunities that think tanks on both sides of the Atlantic seem uniquely positioned to support.

Opportunities for Collaboration

Notwithstanding a modest history of cross-Atlantic collaboration among think tank communities, it remains the case that there is an opportunity for deepening this relationship to mutual advantage and, indeed, to the advantage of the public policy discussion and debates surrounding the transatlantic relationship. For many years, the Chicago Council on Foreign Relations under the skilled leadership of Ivo Daalder, and the Woodrow Wilson Center's Global Europe Program, have made important contributions to scholarly discussions around transatlantic relations, and there is no doubt that far more research could be undertaken by these and other research institutes on both sides of the Atlantic. In particular, there are novel geopolitical challenges that could be well-served by a more integrated and productive relationship between scholars populating think tank communities. It is also worth noting that while a handful of US think tanks, including AEI, Brookings, and the Hoover Institution have and continue to devote serious attention to transatlantic relations, several European studies centers and institutes based at prominent American universities, including the Center for European Studies at Harvard, the Center for West European Studies at the University of Washington, and the Institute for European Studies at the University of California, Berkeley, deserve closer consideration. Through their many publications, conferences, workshops, visiting professorships, and fellowship programs, university-based research institutes have made their presence felt. Typically, university-based research centers do not possess the resources available at standalone think tanks, but this does not mean that they do not contribute to enhancing conversations about transatlantic relations. How has the changing political landscape in the US afforded these and other research institutes devoted to the study of European affairs with more opportunities to engage key stakeholders about transatlantic relations?

First, the election of Joe Biden to the US presidency on 3 November 2020—and the several months into his term at the time of writing—has marked an important rethinking of US foreign policy after four years of President Trump. While President Trump's foreign policy outlook was sustained by a protectionist, "American First" approach to trade (such as through the rollercoaster application and subsequent revocation of tariffs, even upon traditionally friendly trading partners), combined with a preference for bilateral relationships over established multilateral fora and organizations (such as the US role in NATO), it is clear that President Biden's instinct is toward a more stable, traditional approach to trade and foreign relations. While the insinuation (and likely the preference of many) would seem to suggest that transatlantic relations can "snap back" into place following four years of President Trump, that is not necessarily the case. While institutional bureaucracies can certainly be "sticky" and slowly responsive to changes in delivery and tactics, think tanks can offer their nimbleness and strategic advice to policymakers and their teams who are tasked with returning to a more traditional transatlantic relationship over at least the next four years.

In this sense, the US and supranational think tanks are well-positioned to assist this process of fostering diplomatic rehabilitation. For US think tanks, their predisposition to substantive and timely policy research and recommendations can allow policymakers to move quickly and in an evidence-based approach to restoring a more collegial relationship among the US and European counterparts, while supranational think tanks are similarly and uniquely positioned to afford policymakers and NGOs the space and deliberate discussion to establish (or re-establish) the transatlantic relations that fuel productive diplomatic and economic activity.

Second, the UK's 2016 decision to withdraw its membership within the EU has only recently concluded, and the UK is now in a position to (or rather, face the imperative to) enter into bilateral trade and diplomatic agreements with states around the world. The consequences of Brexit are, of course, of significant relevance not just for the UK but also for its historic trading and diplomatic partners (of which the US and the EU are among the largest and most enduring). What this means is that the US and EU will be undertaking the process of negotiating the formal terms of a trading relationship (which has already been accomplished in the case of the EU, effective 1 January 2021) while also reconstituting the nature of diplomatic relationships as well. This will be different for the EU and the US, and its think tank communities are interestingly well-positioned to offer their comparative advantage to the situation. For supranational think tanks, their networking function could prove especially helpful in introducing and forging key diplomatic relationships between officials operating within Brussels, in addition to the economic and trade relationships that can be enabled through supranational think tank fora (although, admittedly, the current COVID-19 pandemic is making the kind of in-person engagement intermittent).

For the US think tanks, providing well-reasoned and evidence-based analysis and recommendations to President Biden and his senior advisers would be welcomed, especially in the early days of his administration. Indeed, there is good reason for several US-based think tanks to be optimistic about re-establishing strong ties with both the White House and with several agencies in the Executive Office of the President. Unlike during Trump's term in office when all but a select few think tanks had the president's ear (Abelson 2021), Biden's style of governing and his respect and admiration for policy experts will bode well for the country's top policy institutes. For Biden, like Barack Obama (Abelson 2009), being a Washington insider (Abelson and Carberry 1998) should not prevent or dissuade a president from soliciting and embracing the policy recommendations from leading experts. On the contrary, it should be encouraged.

President Biden is acutely aware of how the think tank community in and around the nation's capital can help his administration face the many political, economic, and social challenges presented by COVID-19. During the 2020 US presidential primaries and general election that saw Biden and Kamala Harris defeat an embattled president, he held "regular briefings [...with] a small group of liberal economists," many of whom with close ties to leading public policy institutes (Think Tank Watch 2020). Included among this elite group were Jared Bernstein, a senior fellow at the Center on Budget and Policy Priorities; Lawrence Summers, who is affiliated with the Center for Global Development, the Brookings Institution, the Peterson Institute for International Economics, and the Center for American Progress; Byron Auguste, Council on Foreign Relations; Jack Lew, Council on Foreign Relations and the Brookings Institution; and Anthony Blinken, formerly a senior fellow at CSIS who was later appointed by Biden as US secretary of state. Had Neera Tanden, former head of the Center for American Progress, been confirmed as director of the Office of Management and Budget, think tank representation in Biden's cabinet would have been greatly enhanced. However, as a result of mounting opposition to Tanden, the Biden White House decided in early March 2021 to pull her nomination.

In addition to holding briefings with a small group of leading economists, Biden and his team had access to over 100 other advisers who were assembled to offer policy advice on a host of economic issues (Think Tank Watch 2020). Moreover, similar arrangements were made to ensure that Biden could rely on leading foreign policy experts, many with strong connections to prominent think tanks. For example, on his Department of Defense transition team, eight of 23 members were recruited from top military and strategic studies think tanks, including Kathleen Hicks, senior vice-president at CSIS; Ely Ratner and Susanna Blume, Center for a New American Security; and Christine Wormuth, Stacie Pettyjohn, and Terri Tanielian, RAND (Coleman and Barrickman 2020).

But Biden's connection to the think tank community runs even deeper. In 2017, Biden and his alma mater, the University of Delaware, announced "a partnership to form the Biden Institute, a research institute dedicated to policy discussion and advancement of several issues, including criminal justice, civil rights, women's rights, environmental reform, and more" (Higgins 2021). Biden served as founding chair of the Institute until he declared his candidacy for president in 2020. His sister, Valerie Biden-Owens, has played "a central role in the operation of the Biden Institute" (Higgins 2021).

Biden's close ties to several members of the think tank community remain strong. The question that remains is how much of an impact will those with think tank ties both inside and outside his administration have on his policy agenda. Of particular interest to those monitoring the US-European file, is how and to what extent will US-based think tanks affect the future of the transatlantic alliance. Although there are indications that the negotiation of a US-UK trade agreement is not an immediate foreign policy priority for President Biden (Mayes and Martin 2021), the complexity that US negotiators and decision-makers face would no doubt be assisted by the deep and nuanced foreign policy expertise of many of Washington's leading think tanks. While some think tanks have expressed initial agreement with suggestions that the negotiation of a US-UK free trade agreement may indeed be an extended affair (Barfield 2019; Hufbauer 2020), other think tanks have already offered specific and principle-based guidance for how the US should approach these negotiations (Conley, Renison, and Suominen 2019; Ikenson, Lester, and Hannan 2018). All this is to say, the deep expertise that the think tanks can offer policymakers in the midst of a highly complex and technical negotiation of trade terms for two of the world's largest economies is a clear opportunity for think tanks to exert significant impact. This is especially true for a new presidential administration.

Finally, in addition to the imperative of negotiating a new trade agreement between the US and the UK and assisting a new presidential administration in reorienting the transatlantic relationship in a more traditional direction, there is a not insignificant dimension to the transatlantic relationship that merits its own consideration: defense relations. Over the course of the Trump administration, there were multiple shifts, pivots, and walk-backs on some key defense and military matters that are fundamentally important and existential to the transatlantic relationship. Principally, the fascination and disdain that President Trump expressed for NATO in his administration were no doubt one of the most existentially compromising and concerning positions that were taken on defense matters through the course of his administration. While the material impact to President Trump's suspicion of NATO was reflected in proposed spending reductions, restoring the US integration with NATO will not take place immediately. Fortunately, for the US policymakers, think tanks inside "the Beltway" possess considerable military and defense expertise, with many think tanks dedicated specifically to security and defense matters. While few supranational think tanks offer the kind of specialization and depth in military matters that exists among the US think tank community, once again we can aver that supranational think tanks may offer their comparative advantage to policymakers, NGOs, and the defense community in resuscitating the fervor for multilateral defense cooperation.

Conclusion

Despite the failure of the Trump administration to take steps necessary to enhance the transatlantic "special relationship," there is renewed vivacity to the promise of this special relationship on both sides of the Atlantic. What shape and pace this ultimately takes will, of course, be subject to future analyses, but at the time of writing, a considerable rollback of many Trump-era foreign policy pronouncements and policies are occurring, thus creating a window for the transatlantic relationship to reset itself. As scholars and pundits alike turn to exploring how this new period of the transatlantic relationship, the goal of this chapter was to contemplate how think tanks on both sides of the Atlantic may, if properly incentivized, enhance collaboration among polities and societies. We have also sought to show that despite having different priorities think tanks in the US and throughout Europe can add significant value to conversations around key policy issues.

This chapter has also identified two key reasons why this type of collaboration has not historically blossomed. First, we argued that the fundamentally different roles, goals, and outcomes think tanks on opposite sides of the Atlantic pursue do not significantly incentivize robust interaction and integration of efforts. As noted, the US think tanks pursue an advocacy-oriented role, whereby they leverage their research and analytical capacity in an effort to affect policy change. In doing so, they rely heavily on various communication strategies such as fostering ties with media outlets across the globe and taking advantage of opportunities to provide testimony before congressional committees and sub-committees. Their efforts to sway public opinion and public policy can also take the form of off-the-record meetings and conversations with elected officials and their advisers. By contrast, for supranational think tanks, there is a greater tendency toward creating networking opportunities where they can encourage governmental and non-governmental actors to engage in much broader policy discussions. Given these fundamentally different roles and priorities, it is perhaps not surprising that a more significant overlap of operations and activities between US and European-based think tanks has not emerged.

We also suggest that the heightened competition in the "marketplace of ideas" has encouraged think tanks to be more singularly focused on their organizational advancement, as opposed to building relationships that might result in a modest increase in their public profile. Put simply, engaging in more collaboration with think tanks in other countries and policy domains may appeal to some donors, but it may also detract from the outputs and outcomes they are trying to achieve at home. Thus, while the number of civil society and public policy institutions have increased, so too has the necessity of distinguishing or differentiating themselves from their competitors. In turn, think tanks in the US and the EU have largely avoided competing with the more established and financially-secure think tanks that are able to bankroll a transatlantic profile and operation.

While the verdict on the past and present of the transatlantic think tank community is not entirely clear, there is little doubt that there are opportunities for enhanced collaboration that can emerge in response to shifting geopolitical and relational features of the broader transatlantic relationship. It is quite possible, then, that there are several contemporary variables that might provoke or otherwise encourage a healthier relationship between think tanks on both sides of the Atlantic. Principally, the change of leadership in Washington, the fallout from the Brexit negotiations, and the fragile defense relationship between the US and the EU are all reasons that think tanks may take on an enhanced spirit of collaboration (at least in the short term). There is a lengthy—although occasionally interrupted—tradition of think tanks playing a key briefing and staffing role in the event of presidential transitions, and President Biden has indicated a desire to return to a more traditionalist foreign policy orientation. With that, there is some rehabilitation that will need to occur, and think tanks can assist in this process. For instance, establishing joint cross-Atlantic working tables, hosting diplomatic representatives at their various fora, and co-authoring key public policy research and recommendations for kickstarting the reignition of the transatlantic special relationship are all ways this collaboration can be supportive and beneficial to a new administration.

Second, the withdrawal of the UK from the EU continues to present a major policy mess for trade analysts, foreign policy speculators, and geopolitical pundits alike. Many aspects of the path forward for a UK outside the EU (and an EU outside the UK, depending on perspective) will not be seamless or taken for granted, including the remaking of a UK-US relationship beyond the context of broader multilateral engagement in which the EU seems predisposed. With that in mind, Washington and multiple European capitals are well-stocked with think tank scholars and fellows with issue-specific expertise on trade matters and could be beneficial to supporting a post-Brexit trade relationship between the US and the EU. This trade negotiation is almost certain to be a multi-year, complex, and issue-by-issue negotiation, and the institutional knowledge, experience, and advocacy of think tanks in both jurisdictions would well serve this cumbersome process. Finally, the fragility of defense relations between the US and the EU after President Trump's shirking of traditional defense norms and processes certainly created challenges for the health and function of well-established defense systems and relations. As President Biden ostensibly seeks to revert to a more traditional and recognizable defense relationship between the US and the EU, there are a number of think tanks in both jurisdictions (but especially in the US) that can shepherd these conversations and transitions in a de-escalated, rational, and reasoned manner.

So what does this mean for the future of collaboration between US and EU think tanks? In many ways, the future of the transatlantic think tank relationship is one of the very limited expectations and therefore significant opportunity for growth. While there are few who would be under the illusion that a strengthened transatlantic think tank relationship would fundamentally heal or damage the broader relationship, we have argued that there is nonetheless an opportunity for incremental benefit to all actors involved. However, this may not be an organic process or one that is immediately obvious to officials, decision-makers, and perhaps even think tanks themselves. In fact, it may require a deliberate effort by those within the public policy community to spur these relationships and build the case for collaboration, with the goal that there would be sufficient momentum to sustain and build enhanced relationships between think tanks in both jurisdictions. However, again, that takes deliberate efforts and actions by those committed to spurring a transatlantic think tank community.

While this chapter focused on the extent of think tank relations between the US and the EU, it would be interesting for future analyses to consider whether the limited engagement is unique to think tanks or a reflection of limited mobility and relationships among other actors. For example, we know that there are very active lobbying communities within Washington, Brussels, and other political capitals, and the plethora of truly transnational special interests means that decision-makers are oftentimes dealing with the same arguments for and against certain policies. Whether lobbyists cross borders as seamlessly as policy imperatives would be an interesting avenue of further exploration. Furthermore, the much more established and ostensibly permanent features of epistemic communities—which is to say, universities—deserve analysis on their transatlantic relationships. As the competition for international students grows, universities must become more proactive, especially in a post-pandemic world. As such, a consideration of the congruence of transatlantic university relationships to the broader ebbs and flows of the transatlantic relationship would be an interesting question to consider.

This chapter set out to understand why the relationship and practice of collaboration between the US and the EU think tanks have historically been so limited, particularly when set against the backdrop of deep and enduring diplomatic, economic, and defense ties between the US and Europe. In the immediate aftermath of the Trump years, scholars and observers of transatlantic relations will consider whether the return to a more traditional and recognizable transatlantic relationship will lead to more collaborative activity between the US and the EU think tanks. Only in the fullness of time, however, will we be able to witness whether this relationship blossoms or remains relatively stagnant.

References

Abella, Alex. 2008. *Soldiers of Reason: The Rand Corporation and the Rise of the American Empire.* New York: Harcourt, Inc.

Abelson, Donald E. 2006. *A Capitol Idea: Think Tanks & US Foreign Policy.* Montreal: McGill-Queen's Press.

———. 2009. *Do Think Tanks Matter? Assessing the Impact of Public Policy Institutes.* Montreal: McGill-Queen's University Press.

———. 2018. *Do Think Tanks Matter? Assessing the Impact of Public Policy Institutes.* 3rd ed. Montreal: McGill-Queen's University Press.

———. 2021. "An Uphill Battle; Donald Trump, Think Tanks and the War of Ideas." In *Critical Perspectives on Think Tanks: Power, Politics and Knowledge*, edited by Julien Landry, 97–116. Cheltenham, UK: Edward Elgar.

Abelson, Donald E., and Christine Carberry. 1998. "Following Suit or Falling Behind? Analysis of Think Tanks in Canada and the United States." *Canadian Journal of Political Science* 31 (3): 525–55.

Abelson, Donald E., and Christopher J. Rastrick, eds. 2021. *Handbook on Think Tanks in Public Policy*. Cheltenham, UK: Edward Elgar.

Abelson, Donald E., Stephen Brooks, and Xin Hua, eds. 2017. *Think Tanks, Foreign Policy and Geo-Politics: Pathways to Influence*. London: Routledge.

Barfield, Claude. 2019. *The US-UK Free Trade Agreement: Not So Fast*. Washington: AEI. www.aei.org/economics/international-economics/the-us-uk-free-trade-agreement-not-so-fast/.

Coleman, Ray, and Nick Barrickman. 2020. "Biden Names Pro-War Think Tank and Former Pentagon Officials to Transition Team." *World Socialist Website*. www.wsws.org/en/articles/2020/11/17/bide-n17.html.

Conley, Heather A., Allie Renison, and Kati Suominen. 2019. *A Policy Roadmap for U.S.-UK Digital Trade*. Washington: Center for Strategic & International Studies.

Critchlow, Donald T. 1985. *The Brookings Institution, 1916–52: Expertise and the Public Interest in a Democratic Society*. Dekalb, IL: Northern Illinois University Press.

Edwards, Lee. 1997. *The Heritage Foundation at 25 Years*. Ottawa, Illinois: Jameson Books.

———. 2013. *Leading the Way: The Story of Ed Feulner and the Heritage Foundation*. New York: Crown Forum.

Heatherly, Charles L., ed. 1981. *Mandate for Leadership: Policy Management in a Conservative Administration*. Washington, DC: The Heritage Foundation.

Higgins, Drew. 2021. "The Biden Institute and the Biden Presidency." *The Review*, 3 April 2021. http://udreview.com/the-biden-institute-and-the-biden-presidency/.

Hufbauer, Gary Clyde. 2020. *Prospects for a US-UK Trade Accord Are Daunting*. Washington: Peterson Institute for International Economics.

Ikenson, Daniel, Simon Lester, and Daniel Hannan. 2018. *The Ideal U.S.-U.K. Free Trade Agreement: A Free Trader's Perspective*. Washington: Cato Institute.

Kelstrup, Jesper D. 2021. "Methodological challenges and advances in studying think tanks." In *Handbook on Think Tanks in Public Policy*, edited by Donald E. Abelson and Christopher J. Rastrick, 33–43. Cheltenham, UK: Edward Elgar.

Marin, Bernd, and Renate Mayntz. 1991. "Introduction: Studying Policy Networks." In *Policy Networks: Empirical Evidence and Theoretical Considerations*, edited by Bernd Marin and Renate Mayntz, 11–23. Boulder, CO: Westview Press.

Mayes, Joe, and Eric Martin. 2021. "U.K.-U.S. Trade Deal Is Likely Years Away as Biden Shifts Focus." *Bloomberg*, 26 March 2021. www.bloomberg.com/news/articles/2021-03-26/u-k-u-s-trade-deal-is-likely-years-away-as-biden-shifts-focus.

McGann, James G. 1992. "Academics to Ideologues: A Brief History of the Public Policy Research Industry." *PS: Political Science and Politics* 25 (4): 733–40.

———. 2021. *2020 Global Go To Think Tank Index Report*. Think Tanks and Civil Societies Program, University of Pennsylvania. https://repository.upenn.edu/cgi/viewcontent.cgi?article=1019&context=think_tanks.

Mendizabal, Enrique. 2021. "Describing and Comparing Think Tanks." In *Handbook on Think Tanks in Public Policy*, edited by Donald E. Abelson and Christopher J. Rastrick, 16–32. Cheltenham, UK: Edward Elgar.

Parmar, Inderjeet. 2004. *Think Tanks and Power in Foreign Policy: A Comparative Study of the Role and Influence of the Council on Foreign Relations and the Royal Institute of International Affairs, 1939–1945*. London, UK: Palgrave Macmillan.

———. 2012. *Foundations of the American Century: The Ford, Carnegie, and Rockefeller Foundations in the Rise of American Power*. New York, NY: Columbia University Press.

Pirie, Madsen. 2012. *Think Tank: The Story of the Adam Smith Institute*. London: Biteback.

Rastrick, Christopher J. 2018. *Think Tanks in the US and EU: The Role of Policy Institutes in Washington and Brussels*. New York: Routledge.

Ricci, David M. 1993. *The Transformation of American Politics: The New Washington and the Rise of Think Tanks*. New Haven: Yale University Press.

Sherrington, Philippa. 2000. "Shaping the Policy Agenda: Think Tank Activity in the European Union." *Global Society* 14: 173–89.

Smith, James A. 1991a. *Brookings at Seventy-Five*. Washington, DC: The Brookings Institution.

———. 1991b. *The Idea Brokers: Think Tanks and the Rise of the New Policy Elite*. New York: Free Press.

Stefancic, Jean, and Richard Delgado 1996. *No Mercy: How Conservative Think Tanks Changed America's Social Agenda*. Philadelphia: Temple University Press.

Stone, Diane. 1996. *Capturing the Political Imagination: Think Tanks and the Policy Process*. London: Frank Cass.

Think Tank Watch. 2020. "Think Tankers Advising Joe Biden on the Economy." 17 June.

Weaver, R. Kent. 1989. "The Changing World of Think Tanks." *PS: Political Science and Politics* 22 (2): 563–78.

11
THE RISE AND CHALLENGE OF POPULISM

Andrea Wagner, Eric Pietrasik, and Dorian Kroqi

Introduction

The aftermath of the 2020 United States (US) presidential election and the Capitol Hill insurrection have sent shockwaves throughout the world, prompting questions about the ideal of American exceptionalism and the resilience of the country's institutions. With his unanticipated ascendancy to the presidency in 2016, Donald J. Trump wrote a new chapter in campaign history to demonstrate how, at times, a course of action replete with pomposity, chicanery, and unpredictability pays off. Four years later, in 2020, the US faced the health and socioeconomic consequences of the deadly COVID-19 pandemic exacerbated by the choices of the Trump administration (Zamarripa 2020). This extraordinary event permeated the 2020 presidential election. Three months of polarizing debates and unwarranted attacks climaxed with the election of former Vice President Joseph R. Biden, Jr., as the US's 46th president (Fabian and Page 2020). In the wake of a projected Biden victory, President Trump contested the numbers by claiming voter fraud and election misconduct. He prematurely declared himself the winner of Pennsylvania and Georgia despite a significant number of mail-in ballots in these states still to be included in the tally (Kelly 2020). Pre-election concerns over the effectiveness of postal voting had been compounded by Trump's opposition to the process. In the immediate post-election days, the Republican president doubled down on this opposition when challenging the legality of mail-in voting, declaring it a fraudulent maneuver "to steal the election" (Rupar 2020).

The Trump campaign alleged that its observers had not been enabled access to observe the ballot counting. On 6 November 2020, Supreme Court Justice Samuel Alito issued an order requiring county boards officials in Pennsylvania to comply with a state directive and separate late ballots (Rizzo 2020). The next day, US public opinion influencers and legislators were divided. Major media outlets were

DOI:10.4324/9781003147565-15

speaking of Biden as president-elect; several prominent Republicans repudiated Trump's fraud tirade as fallacious and dangerous, while others endorsed his specious quest for transparency. Courts of different jurisdictions overwhelmingly rejected lawsuits initiated by Trump and his allies (Helderman and Viebeck 2020). The failure of the judicial route gave way to an offensive at the state and local levels pressuring Republican officials to find systemic loopholes that would serve Trump's goals (Kumar and Orr 2020).

Despite the indisputability of hard numbers, President Trump remained steadfast and dauntless in his pretensions of electoral fraud and refused to concede (Herb 2020). His narrative galvanized his most fanatic cheerleaders. On 8 December 2021, President Trump called on his supporters to attend a rally in preparation for Congress's 6 January 2021 Electoral College vote count (Bump 2021). On 6 January, the "March to Save America" (or the "March for Trump") set up a rally of Trump's supporters at the Ellipse, but it was the president's speech that fired them up against the Capitol (Tanfani, Berens, and Parker 2021). Alternative sources also suggest that the rioters had planned a disruption of the Congressional election session weeks before the Ellipse speech (Schwartz 2021). Later investigations uncovered a well-coordinated plot that had been first articulated in alternative-tech websites and platforms, such as those on TheDonald.win, Parler, and Telegram (Lytvynenko and Hensley-Clancy 2021). Confessions from "Stop the Steal" fringe group, an FBI report, and findings from the *New York Times* revealed that the final intent of the insurrectionists was that of resorting to armed violence (Goldman 2021). The storming of the US Capitol caused a stir in international public opinion. Prominent political figures, governments, and other institutions did not recoil from voicing their opinions on this moment in US history. Opponents and critics of Trump, such as former European Council President Donald Tusk, took the opportunity to warn of the dangers of a radicalized mob under the sway of charismatic leaders (Brzozokowsi, Moscovenko, and Grüll 2021).

This chapter seeks to investigate European right-wing populists' reaction to the 6 January 2021 insurrection at the US Capitol. Did these parties denounce the violence? Did they perceive Trump's role as an inciter or did they exonerate him? There was no question of the intense support for Trump among the European rightists, especially, in the wake of the 2020 election. What we were curious to learn is whether the support from a few of these actors wavered in the aftermath of the presidential election and 6 January? Since 2016, right-wing populists in Europe have revered Trump as an inspiring role model and leader. He spoke a nativist, xenophobic language and propped up the legitimacy of their aspirations. However, the outcome of the 2020 election and the Capitol unrest may test the electoral prowess of Trump's European cheerleaders. It may equally call into question the coexistence of the right-wing populist Zeitgeist with constitutional democracy.

Public perception of a crisis is susceptible to different types of framing proposed by either the media, various power-holders, or power-seekers. Framing entails the salience-focused selection of particular facets from an event or phenomenon with the intent of shaping and structuring the public perception of a problem's definition, its cause-and-effect interpretation, potential remedies, and ethical implications. Frames convey knowledge through an ensemble of select facts organized around peculiar interrelated concepts, colorful descriptive narratives, and image representations that ultimately define the pre-debate situation. The actors who engage in frame-creation may be politicians or media actors (Entman 1993; Gamson and Modigliani 1989; Tankard 2001). Semetko and Valkenburg's (2000) categorization best exemplifies how the nature of a frame reflects the intent of the framer. Whether it is to underscore the stakeholders' disagreements (conflict), bring human adversity to the fore (human interest), identify the root causes and culprits (attribution of responsibility), question the propriety of the actions (morality), or evaluate the pecuniary implications (economic consequences), frames seek to instil an understanding of the social world that suits a framing agenda (de Vreese 2004; de Vreese and Boomgaarden 2003).

Legitimation is another concept that overlaps with framing. Van Leeuwen and Wodak (1999) introduced four major interconnected categories through which legitimation is expressed. They are authorization, moral evaluation, rationalization, and mythopoesis. Authorization is legitimation with reference to authority, be this source a person, tradition, custom, or law. Moral evaluation abides by a value system. Rationalization relies on knowledge claims or arguments. Mythopoesis is legitimation through anecdotal or fragmentary narratives on the past or the future. Legitimation represents a discursive strategy that justifies an actual or potential course of action to the public. For instance, right-wing populist rhetoric employs moral evaluation and mythopoesis to legitimize "othering" and, hence, argue for the implementation of more restrictive immigration policies (Said 2017).

This chapter draws on Hawkins' (2012) discourse-centered and Mudde's (2013) ideology-centered approaches to populism. An understanding of populism as a discursive manifestation of a thin-centered ideology with a special emphasis on "the language that unwittingly expresses a set of basic assumptions about the world" allows us to examine the discursive strategies that underpin European right-wing populists' rhetoric (Hawkins 2012; Mudde 2013). Our analysis purports to measure legitimation in claims supporting Trump and exonerating him from all responsibility in the Capitol riots. It also seeks to identify the framing right-wing populist actors resorted to most frequently to evaluate or (de)legitimize the 2020 US election and the Capitol Hill riots. We completed a content analysis of 409 claims from eight European countries. We sought to explain the alternation and interplay of evaluative and (de)legitimizing claims in the discourse of right-wing populist politicians in Germany, France, the United Kingdom (UK), Spain, the Netherlands, Italy, Hungary, and Poland. While an empirical analysis of legitimacy debates may encompass a variety of political discourse arenas, this chapter's emphasis is on the framing and rhetoric from the populist right. Our research looks at how an aggregate of frames can offer new insights into varying degrees of legitimation and support in these actors' argumentation.

Methodology

Our inquiry pooled two methods: frame analysis and political claims analysis. We purport to see how discursive action generates negative or positive evaluations of the current events in US politics (Hurrelmann and Wagner 2020; Hurrelmann, Gora, and Wagner 2013; Koopmans and Statham 1999). We are particularly interested in claims from European right-wing populist leaders and parties. We have coded claims linked to the 2020 US election, the Capitol Hill insurrection, general perceptions of Trump, Biden, and the Republican and Democratic parties. In addition, we deal with legitimizing and delegitimizing claims on election fraud allegations and Trump's social media ban. We identified 409 claims and coded them with the help of the seven variables listed below (see Appendix 11A.1).

- *Claimant*—This variable indicates the author of the claim. Our codebook distinguishes between claims pronounced by right-wing populists in Germany (Alternative für Deutschland (Alternative for Germany), AfD), France (Marine Le Pen and National Front (FN)), UK (Nigel Farage and the Brexit Party), Spain (Santiago Abascal and Vox), the Netherlands (Geert Wilders and Partij voor de Vrijheid (Party for Freedom)), Italy (Matteo Salvini, Lega Nord (Northern League)) and Fratelli d'Italia (Brothers of Italy)), Hungary (Viktor Orbán and Fidesz (Hungarian Civic Alliance)), and Poland (Andrzej Duda and Prawo i Sprawiedliwość (Law and Justice), PiS).
- *Addressee*—This variable indicates the actor mentioned in the claim. Our codebook distinguishes between claims that touch upon Trump, Biden, the Republican Party, the Democratic Party, the US news media, social media outlets, as well as Capitol Hill rioters.
- *Object*—We differentiate between claims containing perceptions about Trump and his policies, Biden and his future presidency, the Republican and Democratic parties, the 2020 US presidential election, the Capitol Hill riots, and Trump's role in the unrest. We have also focused on claims about election fraud allegations, the integrity of US elections, and the media's role in the US presidential election.
- *Evaluation*—This variable captures whether we have a negative or positive evaluation of the claim's object.
- *Legitimation*—This variable indicates an attempt to legitimize or delegitimize the object of the claim.
- *Justification*—This variable has to do with the reasons supporting an evaluation and/or (de)legitimation.
- *Frame used*—We rely on the conflict-, responsibility-, human interest-, morality-, and economic consequences frames. In our case, the conflict frame embodies the various areas of contention in US politics and the way these are perceived by the European populist leaders. The human interest frame describes how a given issue or problem, such as a Trump or Biden administration decision affects the US citizens or the European countries in our study. The attribution

of responsibility-frame associates the root cause of events with individuals (e.g., Trump/Biden) and/or political parties (e.g., the Republicans/Democrats). The morality frame underscores the normative aspect of an event, the common denominator distinction between right and wrong when evaluating the behavior of the actors. The economic consequences frame concentrates on the implications of political events for the general economic welfare of the society.

To investigate the degree of Europe's right-wing populists' disassociation from Trump following the US Capitol insurrection, we carried out an in-depth quantitative and qualitative content analysis. We examined the discursive strategies of the German, French, British, Spanish, Dutch, Italian, Polish, and Hungarian populist leaders and their respective parties. In total, we have identified 409 claims. In this sample of claims, we discovered that 63.3 percent were evaluative claims (36.7 percent positive and 34.2 percent negative). What's more, 47.9 percent of the claims contained an attempt to legitimize the object, while 48.4 percent of the claims sought to de-legitimize (see Tables 11.1 and 11.2).

Claim Analysis

The AfD is a German nationalist ultra-conservative populist party, known for its opposition to the Eurozone and disapproval of the European Union's (EU) migration policy (Berning 2017). The party was formed in 2013. It narrowly missed the 5 percent threshold in that year's election. However, it secured, the following year, seven seats in the European Parliament (EP), and, in the 2017 federal election, it became the country's third-largest party and the official opposition. In its infancy, the AfD was merely fostering a critical view of EU politics among the more conservative constituencies, thus, challenging the mainstream parties. However, since 2013, AfD has embraced nationalism, anti-immigrant bigotry, and ethno-religious prejudice. Political commentators and analysts have described the party as a union of two factions, that is, a moderate national-conservative branch, represented by politicians such as Jörg Meuthen, and the identitarian Der Flügel subgroup (Klikauer 2019). At the European level, the AfD left the Europe of Freedom and Direct Democracy group (EFDD) in the EP to join the newly created Identity and Democracy, a family of populist inspiration. The party's leader in the EP, Meuthen, has been a prominent voice in championing border protection, democratization, and Euro-area reform.

Most of the claims from the AfD members contained positive evaluations of Trump (18.4 percent). They commended the president's indisposition to new wars, his success in Arab-Israeli reconciliation, and his assertive approach on China. We also came across an isolated instance of criticism by co-chair Alexander Gauland. He disapproved of Trump's decision to withdraw US troops from Germany, wishing it would apply to other North Atlantic Treaty Organization (NATO) countries. Unlike most of the European right-wing populists, AfD saw promise in a Biden presidency. In a sample of 49 coded claims, we found 10.2 percent of the claims containing a positive evaluation of Biden's victory. AfD member Armin-Paul Hampel welcomed "Biden's desire to work closely with Western allies" in reshaping transatlantic relations (*Sputnik News* 2021). Yet, criticism was not far from the surface. Germany's right-wing populists conjectured the imperilment of the country's affordable energy supply. It forecast new wars and censorship under a new Democratic presidency. In fact, Beatrix von Storch, AfD's deputy leader, deplored the crackdown on the freedom of expression by monopolistic internet giants such as Google, Facebook, Twitter, and Amazon. Numerous claims relied on a combination of the conflict and responsibility frames (30.6 percent) followed by a medley of the conflict, responsibility, and economics consequences frames (18.4 percent).

Marine Le Pen is a French right-wing populist politician and lawyer who has been president of the National Rally (RN) (formerly known as the Front National) since 2011. In 2010, Le Pen became leader of the FN by embodying the desire of the party's membership to move away from the jingoism and pariahism of her father and predecessor, Jean-Marie Le Pen. In 2018, the party rebranded itself as the Rassemblement National to mark a watershed with the past (Stockemer 2017). Still, her leadership campaign and tenure have not been free from controversy. Early in her candidacy, Le Pen drew unseemly parallels between the observance of Muslim religious practices and the Nazi occupation of France during World War II. This instance presaged the birth of a new communication strategy, a strategy that has effectively adjusted to new events and developments such as the 2015 migrant crisis and the terrorist attacks in France (Shields 2013). The emphasis was now on militant Islam and Islamization posing both cultural and security dilemmas for French society. The other archnemesis of the renewed FN is the EU, perceived as the incarnation of a destructive ultra-liberalism. Le Pen opposes the current levels of European integration and Turkey's membership in the EU and has pledged to hold a referendum on French EU and Eurozone membership. While the party has suffered a setback in the recent parliamentary elections, its success in the regional and EU elections has been impressive. Le Pen came second in the first round of the 2017 presidential election. Therefore, it should not come as a surprise that Le Pen will most likely face President Emmanuel Macron in the 2022 presidential election, as opinion polls show a closer second-round runoff than in 2017 (Benoit 2021).

In France, we found the highest percentage of claims (38.5 percent) that contained a positive evaluation of Trump. Marine Le Pen pronounced most of these claims as she looked forward to a second Trump presidency that, according to her, "is better for France" (*Sputnik News* 2020). For the RN leader, "Donald Trump means the return of nations; and the end of rampant globalization, the weakening regulations and the disappearing borders," which "harm nations" (*Sputnik News* 2020). In contrast to Germany, the prevalent media frame (15.4 percent) was morality followed by the conflict and responsibility frames. The morality frame, emphasizing the normative aspect of an event, recurred when claimants made a stand against the Capitol Hill riots.

Farage was a key participant in the Brexit movement and the 2016 campaign referendum. His support for Brexit was first associated with the 2015 migrant crisis

(Hughes 2019). Yet, the UK Independence Party (UKIP) leader did not just fear a Muslim takeover. He often intimated sentiments of Europhobia directed at British residents from Central and Eastern Europe (Evans and Mellon 2019). His opposition to further monetary integration, as exemplified by the bailout fund, proved to be another bone of contention. His role in the UK and EU earned UKIP 3.8 million votes in the 2015 general election making it the third largest party in Britain. In 2016, with the success of the referendum, he chose to leave public life only to make a comeback in 2019 with the Brexit Party. Farage was a prominent figure in the Euroskeptic EFDD parliamentary group. In the EP plenaries, he became notorious for his outbursts against European Commission Presidents José Manuel Barroso and Jean-Claude Juncker, as well as European Council President Herman Van Rompuy (Weber 2018). These fiery exchanges touched upon discordant visions of the EU integration process, corruption scandals, democratic credentials, and monetary sovereignty.

The highest percentage of claims in our sample comes from the UK (20.6 percent). Within this sample, we found a record high percentage of negative evaluations compared to other countries (18.2 percent). Nigel Farage is the author of the majority of these claims, and they consist primarily of negative evaluations of Joe Biden and the Democratic Party. For instance, he wrote in a tweet that the new US president was someone who "hates the UK" (Harris 2020). He did not mince his words even for the BBC when prating that "foe Biden is anti-Brexit, foe Biden is pro-the European Union, foe Biden is profile Irish nationalist cause" (Roy 2021). As in Germany, 34.1 percent of the claims relied on a combination of the conflict and responsibility frames followed by the conflict, responsibility, and economics consequences (8 percent) as well as morality frames (6.8 percent).

Spain was an exception in Europe insofar as it remained largely immune to the advancement of the populist right. The change came with the Andalusian regional elections of December 2018 when voters pushed the Vox outside the area of political insignificance (Marcos-Marne, Plaza-Colodro, and O'Flynn 2021). In the April 2019 election, the party won 10.26 percent of the vote, which translated into 24 seats in the Congreso de los Diputados. In the November 2019 elections, Vox more than doubled its share of seats becoming the third-largest party in the chamber. African migration and the country's constitutional turmoil inspired a host of nativist, centralist, and anti-immigrant attitudes. Like its counterparts across Europe such as the RN, AfD, and UKIP, Vox advocates a policy of tighter border controls. Promotional videos for VOX used symbolic content to invoke the glorious history of the *Reconquista* as an allusion to what they regard as an inner and outer Islamic invasion (Caparrós 2019). Others argue that support for Vox is an inevitable corollary of Catalonia's sovereignty crisis (Turnbull-Dugarte 2019). Nonetheless, Vox's eccentric unitarian conception of Spain and its emphasis on repression against the Catalan sovereignty movement turned out to be effective themes for an electoral feat.

In Spain, we found the second-highest percentage of negative evaluative claims (6.3 percent) against Biden. Yet, in comparison to the UK, the gravity of the accusations against the current president was bewildering. Spain's populists portrayed Biden as someone who was "a great unknown" because "no one knows what he really thinks" in spite of his lifelong career as a public servant (*CE Noticias Financieras* 2020b). Abascal echoed his disdain for Biden by considering him a liability and insinuating that the Democratic Party had kept him hidden during the campaign. Without forethought and analysis, he would release statements such as "Biden is El País'es favourite. Podemos's favourite. Otegui's favourite. Maduro's favourite. China's favourite. Iran's favourite. A paedophile's favourite" (Dunham 2020). Spain's populists recurred to the same frames as consentient German and British: 37.5 percent of the coded claims relied on the conflict and responsibility frames followed by the conflict, responsibility, and morality frames (6.3 percent).

Geert Wilders, a Dutch businessman and politician, is the founder and leader of PVV (Partij voor de Vrijheid [Party for Freedom]). A former member of the Volkspartij voor Vrijheid en Democratie (People's Party for Freedom and Democracy), he has been an outspoken critic of Islam and Turkey's EU accession. His proposals, declarations, and statements are some of the most contentious postulations in the European political scene. In an op-ed in *de Volkskrant*, he considered the Koran a "fascist book" likening it to Hitler's *Mein Kampf* and equating Mohammed to "the devil" (*de Volkskrant* 2007). In a speech before the Dutch parliament, Wilder warned of the mortal threat of Islamification and Arabization to the European and Dutch civilizations. From 2006 to 2010, the PVV's popularity soared due in large part to its ability to criticize the Dutch government and the EU for the Eurozone Crisis (van Kessel 2015). In the 2010 parliamentary elections, the PVV won 24 seats (15.5 percent of the vote), therefore becoming a significant power broker as the third-largest party in the country. The 2017 parliamentary election enshrined the PVV as the second-largest party in the States General with 20 seats. However, the other parliamentary parties blacklisted Wilders' party by refusing ex-ante a coalition government with the Vrijheidists. While the PVV and its leader have been ostracized at home, at the European level, Wilders has been a remarkable force behind the alliance of right-wing populists (Rivera and Davis 2019). Of all the countries studied, the lowest percentage of claims came from Dutch populists. A large percentage of the coded claims praised Trump (33.3 percent), conveyed disappointment over the Capitol Hill riots (8.9 percent), and used the conflict and responsibility frames (41.7 percent).

The creation of the Lega Nord in 1991 was the upshot of a resurgent populist movement that assayed to redress the deep-seated frustrations of Italians in the country's northern regions (Albertazzi, Giovanni, and Seddone 2018). In the 2010s, Lega Nord under Salvini spoke to those constituencies who saw themselves on the losing end of the European integration process. Since then, the party's traditional anti-immigration, pro-life, homophobic, and neoliberal positions have been carried to new extremes. Salvini secured the leadership of Lega Nord in 2013 after gaining visibility and popularity as a Euroskeptic in the EP. There, he distinguished himself as a feisty critic of the Eurozone policies, a fierce opponent of the EU-managed asylum system, and a friend of Vladimir Putin's Russia. Along with Le

Pen and Wilders, he fomented a rightist movement committed to Euroskepticism, cultural chauvinism, national sovereignty, jobs creation, law and order, controlled immigration, and Islamophobia. It eventually paved the way, in 2014, for the birth of the ID group in the EP (Rivera and Davis 2019). Salvini's Lega abandoned regionalism to discover the spirit of pan-Italian nationalism. It reinvented itself in 2018 by removing the "Nord" that made it identifiable with a particular section of the country. This nationalist turn marshalled a new paradigm: The primary enemy were no longer the southern Italians but the foreigners and immigrants who were blamed for the scourge of economic and social insecurity. Lega's 2018 parliamentary election campaign funneled this message through an effective communication strategy that won it the plurality of the votes (Albertazzi, Giovanni, and Seddone 2018). The two populist movements, on the right and on the left (Lega and the Movimento 5 Stelle (Five Star Movement)) obtained an absolute majority, allowing them to form a coalition government. Salvini became minister of the Interior and deputy prime minister. Once in government, he acted in line with his campaign oratory by shutting down the ports to prevent refugees from entering the country. Slogans such as "Stop Immigration!" and "Defend Italians from the invasion" became part of a discursive gambit aimed at re-energizing xenophobic sentiments against Islamic communities and irregular immigrants (Chiaramonte et al. 2018).

We have coded 46 claims by Italy's right-wing populists. We found the highest percentage of positive evaluations for Trump (47.8 percent) and the highest percentage of negative evaluations for the Capitol Hill riots (17.4 percent). Salvini also expressed his disapproval over Trump's social media ban. In his words,

> Twitter and Facebook are private companies, but I wonder where are we going? If someone decides that Salvini should be blocked, who decides that? There's a certain left that considers itself superior. I condemn violence, but censorship, I do not like it.
>
> *CE Noticias Financieras 2021a*

The prevalent media frame was conflict and responsibility (19.6 percent) followed by the morality frame (10.9 percent).

In Hungary, Orbán's career trajectory has been unusual, with his transition from an activist for a liberal democracy to the helmsman of an untamed ethnocentric Christian fundamentalist movement (Bogaards 2018; Rajcsányi 2018). Orbán's ethnocentrism combines the vision of a family-oriented society with a streak of nativism and xenophobia (Ilikova and Tushev 2020). He views African and Middle Eastern migration as a demographic threat seeking to minoritize Europe's autochthonous populations (Ilikova and Tushev 2020). His Christian fundamentalism rejects diversity, secularism, and European unity in favor of a crusading holy alliance of Central and Eastern European countries (Komuves 2020). The migrant crisis has set the background for an uncompromising ideological juxtaposition between the government of Hungary and the EU. In turn, anti-EU rhetoric has provided Orbán with the necessary domestic support for a new authoritarian turn. At the same time, while shunned by the EU, the Hungarian leader has set out to become a trendsetter for analogous movements across Europe and beyond.

In Hungary, we found the highest percentage of negative evaluations of President Biden and the Democratic Party (30.8 percent). Like Salvini in Italy, Hungary's justice minister, Judit Varga, rebuked Trump's permanent interdiction from Facebook and Twitter and reassured her co-citizens that Prime Minister Orbán would "not tolerate intrusions on free speech" (Hopkins, Shotter, and Espinoza 2021).

Andrzej Duda is a Polish politician and lawyer who has served as Poland's president since 2015. The PiS is a right-wing Euroskeptic political party. In 2005, its founders, twin brothers, Lech and Jarosław Kaczyński, secured a parliamentary victory that gave rise to a coalition government. Over the years, the party elite has grown increasingly Euroskeptic and has moved further to the right. In 2015, Duda rejected the EU's redistribution of asylum seekers by invoking the primacy of national interest over any other consideration. In the proximity of the 2020 presidential elections, he manifested his opposition to LGBTQIA marriage, adoption, and education (Kinowska-Mazaraki 2021). The Polish president characterized the movement as "a foreign ideology" comparable to Soviet Communism (Wirwicka 2020). Despite his open anti-LGBTQIA and xenophobic stances, in June 2020, Duda was re-elected for a second term defeating Warsaw's mayor, Rafał Trzaskowski, by a narrow margin.

A number of evaluative claims from Poland expressed support for Trump and his policies (27.9 percent). Duda reassured his constituents that cooperation with President Trump would bring concrete benefits to the country. In contrast with their Hungarian counterparts, Polish populists showed more restraint and leveled far less criticism (3.3 percent) at Biden and his party. In contrast to Hungary, where 36.6 percent of the claims relied on the conflict and responsibility frames, Poland's populists adopted a combination of conflict and responsibility (8.2 percent), conflict, responsibility, and morality (6.6 percent) as well as morality (6.6 percent) frames.

Election Outcome and the Capitol Hill Riots

Our claim analysis revealed that there was profuse support among populists for a second Trump presidency. Farage, a long-time Trump supporter, was extremely confident of the success of his 2020 bid. One day before the election, the former UKIP leader compared the now former US president to a "human dynamo" and "the single most resilient and brave person" he had ever met (Singh et al. 2020). Farage also expressed concern over the potential for fraud in the system of early mail-in voting. Once the election results were in, expectation left room for incredulity. Farage stepped up Trump's fraud allegations reiterating time and again that Democratic Party-run states delivered ballot harvesting on an "industrial scale" (*Daily Telegraph* 2020). Le Pen, who referred to Trump's 2016 win as "an additional stone in the building of a new world," also reckoned that the US presidential election was rigged (Tidman 2021). Of all the populist claims examined, we found

258 Andrea Wagner et al.

TABLE 11.1 Variations within right-wing populists' perception of the most important 2020–21 US events

CLAIMANT	Country	Total Evaluative Claims N=409 (100%)				Perceptions of Trump N=151 (36.9%)		Perceptions of Biden and the Democrats N=58 (14.2%)		Perceptions of the 2020 US Election Integrity/Trump Losing N=83 (20.2%)		Perception of the Capitol Hill Insurrection N=31 (7.6%)	
		TOTAL	negative	positive	no evaluation	negative	positive	negative	positive	negative	positive	negative	positive
	TOTAL	409 (100%)	140 (34.2%)	150 (36.7%)	119 (29.1%)	1 (0.7%)	138 (91.4%)	47 (81%)	5 (8.6%)	17 (20.5%)	0 (0%)	27 (87.1%)	0 (0%)
Meuthen/AfD	Germany	49 (12%)	17 (34.7%)	15 (30.6%)	17 (34.7%)	1 (2%)	9 (18.4%)	1 (2%)	5 (10.2%)	1 (2%)	0 (0%)	6 (12.2%)	0 (0%)
Le Pen/FN	France	39 (9.5%)	12 (30.8%)	15 (38.5%)	12 (30.8%)	0 (0%)	15 (38.5%)	0 (0%)	0 (0%)	2 (5.1%)	0 (0%)	6 (15.4%)	0 (0%)
Farage/UKIP	UK	88 (21.5%)	44 (50%)	29 (33%)	15 (17%)	0 (0%)	28 (31.8%)	16 (18.2%)	0 (0%)	7 (8%)	0 (0%)	4 (4.5%)	0 (0%)
Abascal/Vox	Spain	32 (7.8%)	9 (28.1%)	8 (25%)	15 (46.9%)	0 (0%)	8 (25%)	2 (6.3%)	0 (0%)	0 (0%)	0 (0%)	0 (0%)	0 (0%)
Wilders/PVV/VVD	The Netherlands	12 (2.9%)	5 (41.7%)	4 (33.3%)	3 (25%)	0 (0%)	4 (33.3%)	0 (0%)	0 (0%)	0 (0%)	0 (0%)	1 (8.9%)	0 (0%)
Salvini/Lega Nord/Fratelli d'Italia	Italy	46 (11.2%)	13 (28.3%)	23 (50%)	10 (21.7%)	0 (0%)	22 (47.8%)	0 (0%)	0 (0%)	3 (6.5%)	0 (0%)	8 (17.4%)	0 (0%)
Orbán/Fidesz	Hungary	82 (20%)	32 (39%)	39 (47.6%)	11 (13.4%)	0 (0%)	39 (47.6%)	26 (30.8%)	0 (0%)	1 (1.2%)	0 (0%)	1 (1.2%)	0 (0%)
Duda/PiS	Poland	61 (14.9%)	8 (13.1%)	17 (27.9%)	36 (59%)	0 (0%)	13 (21.3%)	2 (3.3%)	0 (0%)	1 (1.6%)	0 (0%)	1 (1.6%)	0 (0%)

The Rise and Challenge of Populism **259**

TABLE 11.2 Variations within right-wing populists' legitimation and de-legitimation attempts

CLAIMANT	Country	Total Claims	Claims addressing Trump N=175 (42.8%)		Claims addressing Biden and the Democrats N=126 (30.8%)		Claims addressing the Media N=21 (5.1%)		Claims addressing the Capitol Hill Rioters N=12 (2.9%)	
			de-legitimation	legitimation	de-legitimation	legitimation	de-legitimation	legitimation	de-legitimation	legitimation
TOTAL		409 (100%)	14 (8%)	149 (85.1%)	88 (69.8%)	37 (29.4%)	21 (100%)	0 (0%)	11 (91.7%)	1 (8.3%)
Meuthen/AfD	Germany	49 (12%)	1 (0.6%)	12 (6.9%)	4 (3.2%)	1 (0.8%)	3 (14.3%)	0 (0%)	2 (16.7%)	1 (8.3%)
Le Pen/FN	France	39 (9.5%)	3 (1.7%)	16 (9.1%)	3 (2.4%)	3 (2.4%)	3 (14.3%)	0 (0%)	0 (0%)	0 (0%)
Farage/UKIP	UK	88 (21.5%)	2 (1.1%)	32 (18.3%)	33 (26.2%)	3 (2.4%)	1 (4.8%)	0 (0%)	4 (33.3%)	0 (0%)
Abascal/Vox	Spain	32 (7.8%)	5 (2.9%)	10 (5.7%)	5 (4%)	0 (0%)	8 (38.1%)	0 (0%)	0 (0%)	0 (0%)
Wilders/PVV/FVD	The Netherlands	12 (2.9%)	0 (0%)	5 (2.9%)	0 (0%)	0 (0%)	0 (0%)	0 (0%)	0 (0%)	0 (0%)
Salvini/Lega Nord/ Fratelli d'Italia	Italy	46 (11.2%)	2 (1.1%)	17 (9.7%)	1 (0.8%)	0 (0%)	2 (9.5%)	0 (0%)	4 (33.3%)	0 (0%)
Orban/Fidesz	Hungary	82 (20%)	1 (0.6%)	40 (22.9%)	26 (20.6%)	6 (4.8%)	3 (14.3%)	0 (0%)	0 (0%)	0 (0%)
Duda/PiS	Poland	61 (14.9%)	0 (0%)	17 (9.7%)	16 (12.7%)	24 (19%)	1 (4.8%)	0 (0%)	1 (8.3%)	0 (0%)

that only Wilders refused to back Trump's victory narrative. He expressed support for US democracy and placed his trust in the country's institutions concluding that, while unfortunate, Trump had lost the election. Unlike Wilders, von Storch, the AfD's deputy party leader, moved in another direction. Few days after the election, on 7 November, she released a Twitter message alleging "massive evidence of election fraud" that only the "democratic constitutional state" could rectify (Labbe 2020). In Italy, Guglielmo Picchi, a member of parliament for Lega, accused the Democrats of an attempt "to steal the election" (Labbe 2020). Trump's Italian advocate, Salvini, was reluctant to acknowledge Joe Biden's win by either hinting at the absence of explicit headlines in the newspapers or regurgitating the "more votes than voters" conspiracy (Perrone 2020).

No wonder the populists who held power in Central European countries zealously endorsed Trump's re-election efforts. In an essay published in *Magyar Nemzet*, Orbán regarded the Democratic Party's foreign policy as "moral imperialism" akin to a sense of US superiority marked by a lecturing posture on democracy (Hjelmgaard 2020). Wishful thinking about Trump's victory also emanated from animosity inside Fidesz toward Hungarian-born American billionaire George Soros, a Biden supporter. Sycophantic pro-government media went so far as to liken Biden to a Marxist and a communist. In Poland, Duda praised the four years under Trump as essential for improving the country's cooperation with the US. Following Biden's victory, PiS member Krzysztof Szczerski regretted the end of an era during which Poland had a place of privilege in US politics at par with its Western European neighbors. With Trump's defeat, the PiS politicians echoed the Trump team's arguments. Szczerski declared that the outcome was far from definitive and that a second round of litigation in the courts would have determined the real winner. Polish President Andrzej Duda wrote an awkward tweet congratulating Biden for his "successful presidential campaign" without truly acknowledging his win (*bne IntelliNews* 2021b).

Unaware of the systemic subtleties in the US presidential election, Vox leader Abascal posited in no uncertain terms the victory of the man who, in his view, stood against everyone. He admonished the media, the pollsters, and the commentators for their biases and applauded Trump for exposing their lies. The Vox leader also congratulated Florida's Hispanic community for taking a position against socialism. Vox Member of European Parliament (MEP) and political spokesperson Jorge Buxadé aroused like-minded social media viewers with slogans like "Spanish Patriots with Trump" (*CE Noticias Financieras* 2020a). Right-wing populists in Spain focused less on the election fraud narrative and more on celebrating Trump as a winner. The Disenso Foundation, a Vox think tank, interpreted the 2020 election outcome as "the great failure of the Democratic Party's cultural project" to bridge the elite-people divide (*CE Noticias Financieras* 2020c). Their study argued that Trump's vote in 2020 had swelled by an additional 10 million because of a surge in support from Hispanics, Blacks, the LGTBQIA community, and women.

For some of the Trump's populist peers, the insurrection on Capitol Hill was an aberrance. After viewing the broadcast, Wilders could not hide his shock. In a tweet, he stated that "the outcome of democratic elections should always be respected, whether you win or lose" (*Soualiga Newsday* 2021). Others minimized the insurrection's severity. Farage spoke of "protesters," while Abascal considered Trump a victim of "media manipulation" (*CE Noticias Financieras* 2021b). The general secretary for Vox in the Congreso de los Diputados, Macarena Olona Choclán, called for a Nobel Peace Prize for Trump as the only president who, in the last three decades, had refrained from waging war. She whitewashed Trump of any responsibility for the events at the Capitol because, in her view, leaders can't "take responsibility for citizens' actions" (*CE Noticias Financieras* 2021b). Also, in support of Trump, Le Pen expressed dismay and shock over the outgoing president being described as a coup inciter in the aftermath of the 6 January events. She also suggested that the media had aggrandized the events well beyond their true reach. When speaking of the rioters, Le Pen even raised doubts about whether they were really Trump supporters.

In Italy, Salvini denounced and condemned the episodes of violence in Washington without openly criticizing Trump. Nicola Procaccini, a MEP from the populist Fratelli d'Italia, compared the rioters to a "series of fanatics who in some cases border on the ridiculous, starting with that one who seemed to have come out of the Village People" (Van Housen and Radaelli 2021). In Germany, the AfD's Meuthen described the events as "frightening, disturbing and completely out of the question," reaffirming his party's aversion to brutality and anarchy (Brzozowski, Moscovenko, and Grüll 2021). Meuthen's party colleague Gottfried Curio downplayed the insurrection as just a "demonstration that escalated" and expressed his concerns over the potential instrumentalization of the Washington events to undermine the legitimacy and credibility of AfD itself (Thurau 2021).

In a Facebook post, Fidesz MEP Tamás Deutsch ridiculed the situation by writing "First Black Lives Matter, now Nothing Matters. United States of Anarchy" (*bne IntelliNews* 2021a). Hungarian Family Minister Katalin Novák bemoaned the US's anti-democratic setback. Orbán instead focused on the lessons that such experience could teach. He invited Hungarians to refrain from passing judgment and expressed confidence in the US's ability to settle its own disputes. In the same vein with their Hungarian peers, Poland's right-wing populists did not ascribe blame to Trump for the diatribe against the electoral process and the subsequent attack on the US's seat of government. In agreement with Orbán, Andrzej Duda tweeted that the events in Washington were an "internal affair," adding that "Poland believes in the strength of the American democracy" (Polish Press Agency 2021). In a stupefying twist, former minister of Foreign Affairs Witold Waszczykowski accused former US president Barack Obama of the societal divisions that hastened the 6 January events.

Conclusion

Our claim analysis revealed that while right-wing populism seems to have lost its impetus following Trump's defeat, it is far from vanished. Our analysis discovered that the majority of European populist actors continued to endorse the former president in his post-election course. Concurrently, they covertly and openly delegitimized President-elect Biden and the Democratic Party through a rhetoric of disapproval, slander, and denial. However, the 6 January events thwarted—in unanticipated ways—their political ambitions.

The European right-wing populists found themselves in the uneasy position of either condoning an ideological ally or condemning the subversive acts at the Capitol. They got themselves out of this quandary by denouncing the violence against the institutions but leaving Trump out of it. Polish President Duda reprobated the riots but deemed the responsibility for them to be treated as a strictly US internal matter (Bodalska 2021). He and Brexit Party leader Farage had to walk the tightrope between understating the gravity of the situation and feigning an inability to ascertain the full facts (Al Jazeera 2021). While support for Trump was the norm in the rightist populist family, some of its members broke ranks. The RN leader Marine Le Pen not only denounced the rampage on Capitol Hill but also invited the then incumbent in the White House to recognize his defeat (Brzozowski, Moscovenko, and Grüll). Germany's AfD co-chairs and parliamentarians were firm in their rejection of violence and anarchy as they acknowledged the official US presidential election result.

The dilemma of the right-wing populists across Europe was that of attending to their political ambitions at home while maintaining a correct position on the insurrection in Washington without rejecting Trumpism. It is for this reason that the varying responses revealed a cost-benefit analysis on the part of each populist leader. For powerholders such as Poland's Duda and Hungary's Orbán, rejecting Trump was unnecessary, but for power-seekers such as Le Pen or Meuthen, the political cost of remaining silent could have been fatal.

We may hypothesize that keeping Trump at arm's length would be more of a pragmatic rather than ideological deliberation. The populist forces who want to be in government cannot condone or abet an insurrection. It would portray them as obstructers of the democratic process. This predicament is particularly constraining for those forces like France's RN who are promising atonement for decades of racism, xenophobia, and anti-Semitism. Our findings show that no claimant resorted to a "will of the people" argument to defend the Capitol Hill insurrection as an exertion of rights. Instead, the majority integrated the morality, conflict, and responsibility frames to oppugn the rightness of the insurrectionists' actions by perceiving the latter as a threat to democracy and its foundational institutions.

Appendix

TABLE 11A.1 Examples of right-wing populist statements and their coding

Claims	Coding
It's no surprise that Abascal also had this to say about the Democratic frontrunner: "Biden is El País's favourite. Podemos's favourite. Otegui's favourite. Maduro's favourite. China's favourite. Iran's favourite. A paedophile's favourite" (Dunham 2020).	**Claimant:** Abascal **Addressee:** Biden **Object:** Perception of Biden and his policies **Evaluation:** Negative **Legitimation:** De-legitimation **Justification:** N/A **Media Frame:** Conflict and responsibility
"Salvini echoed the president's attempt to discredit the results of the US election, saying that parts of the country had "more votes than voters" and that polling stations should stop counting" (Perrone 2020).	**Claimant:** Mateo Salvini **Addressee:** Not specified **Object:** US 2020 election **Evaluation:** Negative **Legitimation:** De-legitimation **Justification:** Evidence of voter fraud **Media Frame:** Morality
"'I think Donald Trump's re-election is better for France. Because Donald Trump means the return of nations; and the end of rampant globalization, the weakening regulation and the disappearing borders, which, I think, harm nations,' Le Pen said live on the CNews channel" (*Sputnik News* 2020).	**Claimant:** Le Pen **Addressee:** Trump **Object:** Perception of Trump **Evaluation:** Positive **Legitimation:** Attempt to legitimize **Justification:** In the best interest of France **Media Frame:** No frame
"What happened there is frightening, disturbing and completely out of the question," MEP Jörg Meuthen (ID) and co-chair of the AfD said. "The AfD rejects any form of violence and anarchy" (Brzozowski, Moscovenko, and Grüll 2021).	**Claimant:** Jörg Meuthen **Addressee:** No addressee **Object:** Capitol Hill riots **Evaluation:** Negative **Legitimation:** De-legitimation **Justification:** No violence **Media Frame:** Conflict and responsibility

References

Albertazzi, Daniele, Arianna Giovannini, and Antonella Seddone. 2018. "'No Regionalism Please, We are Leghisti!' The transformation of the Italian Lega Nord Under the Leadership of Matteo Salvini." *Regional & Federal Studies* 28 (5): 645–71. https://doi.org/10.1080/13597566.2018.1512977.

Al Jazeera. 2021. "How Europe's Far Right Responded to Pro-Trump Capitol Riots." *Al Jazeera*, 7 January. www.aljazeera.com/news/2021/1/7/far-right-capitol-riots.

Berning, Carl C. 2017. "Alternative für Deutschland (AfD) – Germany's New Radical Right-Wing Populist Party." *ifo DICE Report* 15 (4): 16–19.

Benoit, Angeline. 2021. "France's Le Pen Gains Ground for 2022 Elections, Poll Shows." *Bloomberg*, 11 April. www.bloomberg.com/news/articles/2021-04-11/france-s-le-pen-gains-ground-for-2022-elections-poll-shows.

bne *IntelliNews*. 2021a. "Hungarian Government Remains Silent After Capitol Riots." 8 January. https://intellinews.com/hungarian-government-remains-silent-after-capitol-riots-199839/?source=hungary.

———. 2021b. "VISEGRAD BLOG: Central Europe's Populists Need a New Strategy for Biden." 19 January. https://intellinews.com/visegrad-blog-central-europe-s-populists-need-a-new-strategy-for-biden-200683/.

Bodalska, Barbara. 2021. "Polska: Prezydent Duda krytykowany za reakcję na wydarzenia w Waszyngtonie" [Poland: President Duda Criticized for His Reaction to Events in Washington]. *EURACTIV.pl*, 8 January. www.euractiv.pl/section/polityka-zagraniczna-ue/news/polska-reakcje-usa-atak-kapitol-duda-rau-grodzki-tusk-miller-kierwinski-kowal-schnepf-szczerski-jablonski-sikorski-mosbacher/.

Bogaards, Matthijs. 2018. "De-Democratization in Hungary: Diffusely Defective Democracy." *Democratization* 25 (8): 1481–99. https://doi.org/10.1080/13510347.2018.1485015.

Brzozowski, Alexandra, Louise Rozès Moscovenko, and Philipp Grüll. 2021. "Europe's Right-Wing Populists Beat About the Bush After US Capitol Assault." *EURACTIV*, 11 January. www.euractiv.com/section/politics/news/europes-right-wing-populists-walk-a-tightrope-after-mob-storms-the-us-capitol/.

Bump, Philip. 2021. "When Did the Jan. 6 Rally Become a March to the Capitol." *The Washington Post*, 10 February 2021. www.washingtonpost.com/politics/2021/02/10/when-did-jan-6-rally-become-march-capitol/.

Caparrós, Martín. 2019. "Vox and the Rise of the Extreme Right in Spain." *The New York Times*, 13 November 2019. www.nytimes.com/2019/11/13/opinion/spain-election-vox.html.

CE *Noticias Financieras* English. 2020a. "Abascal Believes Trump Can Feel the Winner for Standing Against Everyone and Celebrates Democratic Defeat in Florida." 4 November 2020.

———. 2020b. "U.S.-Vox Believes It Is 'Not Yet Clear' the Outcome of the US Election and It Is 'Premature' to Give Biden the Winner." 9 December 2020.

———. 2020c. "Vox's Foundation Believes Trump's Agenda 'Has Come to Stay' and the 'Cultural Battle' Gives Votes." 12 November 2020.

———. 2021a. "Salvini Says He 'Doesn't Copy' Trump, Bolsonaro or Macron." 10 January 2021.

———. 2021b. "Vox Argues That Trump Be Awarded the Nobel Peace Prize." 20 January 2021.

Chiaramonte, Alessandro, Vincenzo Emanuele, Nicola Maggini, and Aldo Paparo. 2018. "Populist Success in a Hung Parliament: The 2018 General Election in Italy." *Southern European Atlas* 23 (2): 479–501. https://doi.org/10.1080/13608746.2018.1506513.

The Daily Telegraph. 2020. "Nigel Farage: No Doubt There Was 'Industrial Scale' Ballot Harvesting in US Election." 2 December 2020. www.dailytelegraph.com.au/news/national/nigel-farage-no-doubt-there-was-industrial-scale-ballot-harvesting-in-us-election/video/ba40dc8137eeb1b201fad1617649ee41.

de *Volkskrant*. 2007. "Wilders will den Koran verbieten" [Wilders Wants to Ban the Koran]. 8 August 2007. www.volkskrant.nl/nieuws-achtergrond/wilders-wil-koran-verbieden~b061f12d/.

de Vreese, Claes. 2004. "The Effects of Frames in Political Television News on Issue Interpretation and Frame Salience." *Journalism & Mass Communication Quarterly* 81 (1): 36–52. https://doi.org/10.1177/107769900408100104.

de Vreese, Claes, and Hajo G. Boomgaarden. 2003. "Valenced News Frames and Public Support for the EU." *Communications* 28 (4): 261–81. https://doi.org/10.1515/comm.2003.024.

Dunham, Alex. 2020. "Trump or Biden: Who Is Better for Spain-US relations?" *The Local*, 5 November 2020. www.thelocal.es/20201105/trump-or-biden-who-is-better-for-us-spain-relations/.

Entman, Robert M. 1993. "Framing: Toward Clarification of a Fractured Paradigm." *Journal of Communication* 43 (4): 51–58. https://doi.org/10.1111/j.1460-2466.1993.tb01304.

Evans, Geoffrey, and Jonathan Mellon. 2019. "Immigration, Euroscepticism, and the Rise and Fall of UKIP." *Party Politics* 25 (1): 76–87. https:doi.org/10.1177/1354068818816969.

Fabian, Jordan, and Tyler Page. 2020. "Biden Called U.S. Election Winner After Bitter Contest With Trump." *Bloomberg News*, 7 November 2020. www.bloomberg.com/news/articles/2020-11-07/joe-biden-wins-u-s-presidency-after-bitter-contest-with-trump.

Gamson, William A., and Amadeo Modigliani. 1989. "Media Discourse and Public Opinion on Nuclear Power: A Constructionist Approach." *American Journal of Sociology* 95 (1): 1–37. https://doi.org/10.1086/229213.

Goldman, Adam. 2021. "F.B.I. Report Is said to Have Warned of Plans for Violence at the Capitol." *The New York Times*, 12 January 2021. www.nytimes.com/2021/01/12/us/fbi-report-capitol.html.

Harris, Katie. 2020. "Boris Fires Deal Warning to EU as He Issues Update on UK-US Trade Agreement." *The Express*, 11 November 2020. www.express.co.uk/news/politics/1357549/Brexit-latest-news-boris-johnson-michel-barnier-david-frost-EU-UK-trade-talks.

Hawkins, Benjamin. 2012. "Nation, Separation and Threat: An Analysis of British Media Discourses on the European Union Treaty Reform Process." *Journal of Common Market Studies* 50 (4): 561–77. https://doi.org/10.1111/j.1468-5965.2012.02248.x.

Helderman, Rosalind S., and Elise Viebeck. 2020. "'The Last Wall': Judges Across the Political Spectrum Rejected Trump's Efforts to Overturn the Election." *The Washington Post*, 12 December 2020. www.washingtonpost.com/politics/judges-trump-election-lawsuits/2020/12/12/e3a57224-3a72-11eb-98c4-25dc9f4987e8_story.html.

Herb, Jeremy. 2020. "As Trump Refuses to Concede, His Agencies Awkwardly Prepare What They Can for a Biden Transition." *CNN*, 14 November. www.cnn.com/2020/11/13/politics/transition-agencies-wait-biden/index.html.

Hjelmgaard, Kim. 2020. "'Our Time Is Far From Over': Without Donald Trump, What Happens to Global Populism?" *USA Today*, 12 November 2020. www.usatoday.com/story/news/world/2020/11/12/without-donald-trump-what-happens-populist-right-wing-leaders/6234085002/.

Hopkins, Valerie, James Shotter, and Javier Espinoza. 2021. "Hungary Follows Poland in Taking on Big Tech 'Censors.'" *Financial Times*, 3 February 2021. www.ft.com/content/6a315d26-c6fe-4906-886d-04cec27a6788.

Hughes, Ceri. 2019. "It's the EU Immigrants Stupid! UKIP's Core-Issue and Populist Rhetoric on the Road to Brexit." *European Journal of Communication* 34 (3): 248–66. https://doi.org/10.1177/0267323119830050.

Hurrelmann, Achim, and Andrea Wagner. 2020. "Did the Eurozone Crisis Undermine the European Union's Legitimacy? An Analysis of Newspaper Reporting, 2009–2014." *Comparative European Politics* 18 (1): 707–28.

Hurrelmann, Achim, Anna Gora, and Andrea Wagner. 2013. "The Politicization of European Integration: More than an Elite Affair?" *Political Studies* 63 (1): 43–59.

Ilikova, Lilia, and Andrey Tushev. 2020. "Right-Wing Populism in Central Europe: Hungarian Case (Fidesz, Jobbik)." *Utopía y Praxis Latinoamericana* [Latin America Utopia and Praxis] 25 (12): 325–31.

Kelly, Makena. 2020. "Trump Declares Premature Victories in Battleground States on Twitter." *The Verge*, 4 November 2020. www.theverge.com/2020/11/4/21550017/trump-pennsylvania-premature-victory-twitter-rules-tweets-biden-election-2020.

Kinowska-Mazaraki, Zofia. 2021. "The Polish Paradox: From a Fight for Democracy to the Political Radicalization and Social Exclusion." *Social Sciences* 10 (3): 112. https://doi.org/10.3390/socsci10030112.

Klikauer, Thomas. 2019. "Germany's AfD – Members, Leaders and Ideologies." *Asian Journal of German and European Studies* 4 (4). https://doi.org/10.1186/s40856-019-0041-5.

Komuves, Anita. 2020. "Hungary's Orban Calls for Central Europe to Unite Around Christian Roots." *Reuters*, 20 August 2020. www.reuters.com/article/us-hungary-monument-idUSKBN25G0XS.

Koopmans, Ruud, and Paul Statham. 1999. "Political Claims Analysis: Integrating Protest Event and Political Discourse Approaches." *Mobilization: An International Quarterly* 4 (2): 203–21. https://doi.org/10.17813/maiq.4.2.d7593370607l6756.

Kumar, Anita, and Gabby Orr. 2020. "Inside Trump's Pressure Campaign to Overturn the Election." *Politico*, 21 December 2020. www.politico.com/news/2020/12/21/trump-pressure-campaign-overturn-election-449486.

Labbe, Chine. 2020. "Election Misinformation Isn't an American phenomenon – It's Spreading Across Europe, Too." *Euronews*, 8 December 2020. www.euronews.com/2020/12/08/election-misinformation-isn-t-an-american-phenomenon-it-s-spreading-across-europe-too-view.

Lytvynenko, Jane, and Molly Hensley-Clancy. 2021. "The Rioters Who Took Over the Capitol Have Been Planning Online in the Open For Weeks." *Buzzfeed News*, 6 January 2021. www.buzzfeednews.com/article/janelytvynenko/trump-rioters-planned-online.

Marcos-Marne, Hugo, Carolina Plaza-Colodro, and Ciaran O'Flynn. 2021. "Populism and New Radical-Right Parties: The Case of VOX." *Politics* (June). https://doi.org/10.1177/02633957211019587.

Mudde, Cas. 2013. "Three Decades of Populist Radical Right Parties in Western Europe: So What?" *European Journal of Political Research* 52 (1): 1–19. https://doi.org/10.1111/j.1475-6765.2012.02065.x.

Polish Press Agency. 2021. "Poland Believes in Strength of US Democracy Says President." 7 January. www.pap.pl/en/news/news%2C788995%2Cpoland-believes-strength-us-democracy-says-president.html.

Perrone, Alessio. 2020. "Trump's Italian Cheerleader Spreads Baseless Conspiracy Theories Over Votes." *The Independent*, 6 November 2020. www.independent.co.uk/news/world/europe/salvini-trump-election-fraud-us-b1640668.html.

Rajcsányi, Gellért. 2018. "Viktor Orbán's Hungary: Orbanist Politics and Philosophy From a Historical Perspective." *Political Change*, 123–34. www.semanticscholar.org/paper/Viktor-Orbán's-Hungary%3A-Orbanist-Politics-and-fromRajcsányi/5e985d59cf396e5c01c38ef87ac8f4a9bee2c1c4.

Rivera, Ellen, and Marsha P. Davis. 2019. "Dissecting Identity & Democracy, the EU's New Far-Right Super Group." Institute for European, Russian and Eurasian Studies Occasional Papers, No. 3. Transnational History of the Far Right Series. https://ieres.elliott.gwu.edu/research-publications/occasional-papers/.

Rizzo, Salvador. 2020. "Trump Campaign Was Not Denied Access to Philadelphia's Ballot count." *The Washington Post*, 19 November 2020. www.washingtonpost.com/politics/2020/11/19/trump-campaign-was-not-denied-access-philadelphias-ballot-count/.

Roy, Amit. 2021. "College to Study Churchill's Views on Race and Empire." *Eastern Eye*, 5 February 2021. www.easterneye.biz/college-to-study-churchills-views-on-race-and-empire/.

Rupar, Aaron. 2020. "Trump Signals He's Counting on the Supreme Court to Help Him Steal the Election." *Vox*, 4 November. www.vox.com/2020/11/4/21545914/trump-tweet-biden-steal-the-election-poles-polls.
Said, Hala Mohammed. 2017. "Legitimation Strategies in Egyptian Political Discourse: The Case of Presidential Speeches." MA thesis, the American University in Cairo. https://fount.aucegypt.edu/etds/674/.
Schwartz, Brian. 2021. "Pro-Trump Dark Money Groups Organized the Rally That Led to Deadly Capitol Hill Riot." *CNBC*, 9 January. www.cnbc.com/2021/01/09/pro-trump-dark-money-groups-organized-the-rally-that-led-to-deadly-capitol-hill-riot.html.
Semetko, Holli, and Patti M. Valkenburg. 2000. "Framing European Politics: A Content Analysis of Press and Television News." *Journal of Communication* 50 (2): 93–109. https://doi.org/10.1111/j.1460-2466.2000.tb02843.x.
Singh, Maanvi, Lauren Aratani, Martin Belam, and Tom McCarthy. 2020. "Trump and Biden Make Final Pitches as Historic Election Arrives – As It Happened." *The Guardian*, 3 November 2020. www.theguardian.com/us-news/live/2020/nov/02/us-election-2020-live-updates-president-donald-trump-joe-biden-kamala-harris-latest-news-update.
Shields, James. 2013. "Marine Le Pen and the 'New' FN: A Change of Style or of Substance?" *Parliamentary Affairs* 66 (1): 179–96. https://doi.org/10.1093/pa/gss076.
Sputnik News. 2020. "Le Pen Says Trump 'Better for France' Than Biden." 4 November 2020.
———. 2021. "Germany's AfD Calls Biden's Diplomacy Address 'Signal of Hope,' Warns Against Contradictory Actions." 5 February 2021. https://sputniknews.com/europe/202102051081993578-germanys-afd-calls-bidens-diplomacy-address-signal-of-hope-warns-conflicting-action/.
Soualiga Newsday. 2021. "Dutch Politicians Say Storming of the Capitol Is a Warning and a Lesson." 7 January 2021. www.soualiganewsday.com/index.php?option=com_k2&view=item&id=35366:dutch-politicians-say-storming-of-the-capitol-is-a-warning-and-a-lesson&Itemid=535.
Stockemer, Daniel. 2017. *The Front National in France: Continuity and Change Under Jean-Marie Le Pen and Marine Le Pen*. Cham: Springer International Publishing AG.
Tanfani, Joseph, Michael Berens, and Ned Parker. 2021. "How Trump's Pied Pipers Rallied a Faithful Mob to the Capitol." *Reuters*, 11 January 2021. www.reuters.com/article/us-usa-trump-protest-organizers-insight-idUSKBN29G2UP.
Tankard, James. "The Empirical Approach to the Study of Media Framing." In *Framing Public Life: Perspectives on Media and Our Understanding of the Social World*, edited by Stephen D. Reese, Oscar H. Gandy, and August E. Grant, 95–106. Mahwah, NJ: Erlbaum.
Thurau, Jens. 2021. "Bundestag Discusses Support for Biden After Capitol Riots." *Deutsche Welle*, 14 January 2021. www.dw.com/en/bundestag-discusses-support-for-biden-after-capitol-riots/a-56229734.
Tidman, Zoe. 2021. "Le Pen Could Win Next Election, Minister Warns." *The Independent*, 14 February 2021. www.independent.co.uk/news/world/europe/marine-le-pen-2020-france-election-bruno-le-maire-b1801918.html.
Turnbull-Dugarte, Stuart J. 2019. "Explaining the End of Spanish Exceptionalism and Electoral Support for Vox." *Research and Politics* 6 (2). https://doi.org/10.1177/2053168019851680.
Van Housen, Jon, and Mariella Radaelli. 2021. "Europe'd Better Learn a Lesson From the Capitol Madness." *Khaleej Times*, 12 January 2021. www.khaleejtimes.com/editorials-columns/europed-better-learn-a-lesson-from-the-capitol-madness.

van Kessel, Stijn. 2015. "Dutch Populism During the Crisis." In *Populism in the Shadow of the Great Recession*, edited by Hanspeter Kriesi and Takis S. Pappas, 109–24. Colchester: ECPR Press.

van Leeuwen, Theodoor J., and Ruth Wodak. 1999. "Legitimizing Immigration Control: A Discourse-Historical Analysis." *Discourse Studies* 1 (1): 83–118. https://doi.org/10.1177/1461445699001001005.

Weber, Lorène. 2018. "Barroso at Goldman Sachs, or the Mistreatment of European Ethics." *The New Federalist*, 29 March. www.thenewfederalist.eu/barroso-at-goldman-sachs-or-the-mistreatment-of-european-ethics?lang=fr.

Wirwicka, Alicja. 2020. "Rodziny jednopłciowe to w Polsce fakt. 'Mój brat ostatnio przyszedł do mnie i zapytał, czy będzie musiał wrócić do domu dziecka.'" [Same-Sex Families Are a Fact in Poland. 'My Brother Recently Came to Me and Asked If He Would Have to Go Back to the Orphanage.']. *Onet.pl*, 8 July 2020. https://wiadomosci.onet.pl/kraj/duda-chce-zmienic-konstytucje-w-kwestii-adopcji-rodziny-jednoplciowe-to-w-polsce-fakt/3lwr1jf.

Zamarripa, Ryan. 2020. "5 Ways the Trump Administration's Policy Failures Compounded the Coronavirus-Induced Economic Crisis." *Center for American Progress*, 3 June. www.americanprogress.org/issues/economy/news/2020/06/03/485806/5-ways-trump-administrations-policy-failures-compounded-coronavirus-induced-economic-crisis/.

INDEX

Note: Pages in *italics* represent figures; **bold** represent tables.

Abascal, Santiago 251, 255, **258–59**, 260–61, **263**; *see also* populism; Vox
Acheson, Dean 33, 42, 44–45
AfD (Alternative für Deutschland) 251–52, 254; and Biden presidency 252–53; 6 January insurrection **258–59**, 261–62, **263**; and Donald J. Trump 252; *see also* 6 January insurrection; populism; public opinion; Trump, Donald J.; 2020 US presidential election
Afghanistan *see individual countries and US presidents*
Al-Qaeda *see* War on Terror
"America First" 3; America First Policy Institute 233; and China 185, 191; and defense and security 217; and trade 215; and transatlantic relations 196; and Trump administration 9, 172; and US public opinion 204–5, 223; *see also* isolationism; trade; Trump, Donald J.
anti-Americanism 105, 109, 152, 204, 210; *see also* public opinion; Trump, Donald J.
ASEAN *see* Southeast Asia
Ashton, Catherine 48, 166–67; *see also* EU; European Commission; trade
asylum system *see* migration
Atlantic Charter 41, 44, 110
Atlantic community 29, 32–36, 41, 47–48, 50, 147
Atlanticism 2; Atlanticists 33–34, 101, 196; New Atlanticism 39; *see also* transatlantic relations; World War II; *and individual countries, leaders, and officials*
Austin, Lloyd J., III 50; *see also* Biden, Joseph R., Jr.
Australia 9; and China 65–66; and EU 123; and "Five Eyes" 71; and Iraq War 48; Quadrilateral Security Dialogue 66, 198; and US 66, 184; US public opinion of 207; *see also individual countries and trade agreements*
authoritarianism 9, 59–60, 68, 111, 154, 257; *see also* China; populism; public opinion; Russia; Trump, Donald J.

Baker, James A. 39, 46–47; *see also* Bush, George H.W.
Biden, Joseph R., Jr. 67, 69, 103, 251–52; and Afghanistan 106–7; and China 59, 62, 64–65, 190, 192, 196–97, 218; and democracy 30, 192; election of 212, 230, 240, 248–49, 262; environmental policy 88, 94–96, 219; and EU 49–51, 132, 173, 177–78, 192, 244; foreign policy 29–30, 74, 105, 133, 185, 216, 221–22, 240–42, 244; and human rights 154–55; and Iran 50, 62–63; and NATO 50–51, 103, 185; and Paris Climate Agreement 50, 95, 219; Plan for a Clean Energy Revolution and Environmental Justice 80, 95; public opinion of 254–55, 257, **259**, 260, **263**; and think tanks 241–42; and trade 64, 120, 122, 216; and transatlantic relations

3, 30, 154, 175, 177, 196, 253; *see also* Obama, Barack; populism; transatlantic relations; Trump, Donald J.; 2020 US presidential election
bilateralism 39, 64, 92, 94, 122–25, 191–93, 196, 240; and environmental policy 90, 93; and transatlantic relations 89–90, 130–31, 172; *see also* multilateralism; *and individual countries and relationships*
Blinken, Antony J. 168, 173, 241; and NATO 18; and transatlantic relations 177; *see also* EU-US relations; foreign policy; NATO; transatlantic relations
Borrell, Josep 50, 166, 196; *see also* EU; European Commission
Brexit 102, 120, 151, 176, 204–5; Brexit Party 251, 253–54, 262; and EU-US relations 230, 240, 244; Donald J. Trump 204; and UK-EU relations 171–72, 204, 240, 244; *see also* Farage, Nigel; populism, think tanks; Trump, Donald J.; UK
BRI (Belt and Road Initiative) 59, 61, 67, 167, 191, 193–94, 198; *see also* China
Brookings Institution 2–3, 114n5, 230, 233–35, 241; *see also* think tanks
Bush, George H.W. 18, 46, 84, 207; environmental policy 97n2; and trade 39; *see also* Reagan, Ronald
Bush, George W. 148–49, 154, 194, 208–11; and Afghanistan 17, 47, 153–54; environmental policy 84, 89, 219; foreign policy 9, 203; and human rights 153, 186; and Iraq War 47, 152, 203–4; and neoconservative exceptionalism 9, 152–54; transatlantic relations 2–3, 8, 205; unilateralism 47, 203, 211; and US transatlantic leadership 205, 207, *209*, 210–11; and War on Terror 18, 46, 152, 203–4, 220; *see also* EU-US relations; multilateralism; public opinion

CAI (Comprehensive Agreement on Investment) 166, 184, 188; *see also* China; EU-China relations
Canada: Afghanistan 48; and China 133; and Cold War 34; and COVID-19 12, 51; defense policy 104, 109, 169; environmental policy 95; "Five Eyes" 71; foreign policy 34; and Iraq War 48; multilateralism 32; and NATO 18, 30, 36–37, 39–40, 51, 170; nuclear policy 46; population movement 9–10, 12–13, 17; and populism 9; and Suez Crisis 43; transatlantic relations 19, 31–32, 164, 177, 179; transatlantic values 8–9, 169, 178–79; US relations 9, 31, 39, 41, 80, 163, 170, 172, 177, 207–8, 223n1; UK relations 31–32; *see also* climate change; human rights; intelligence; transatlantic relations; WTO; *and individual relationships and trade agreements*
CETA (Comprehensive Economic and Trade Agreement) 16, 119–20, 131–32, 169, 171–73; opposition to 126–30; *see also* Canada; EU-Canada relations; GMOs
China 59–60, 197–98; and Africa 186, 193; cyber security 63; dependency on 60–61, 193; engagement with 14, 62, 73, 168, 188; economic development 60, 64–65, 67, 72, 179, 187; foreign policy 58; foreign students from 12; increasing influence of 66, 68, 112, 120, 133, 154, 167, 178, 194, 211; and Middle East 193; and NATO 198; Regional Comprehensive Economic Partnership 65; and Russia 169–70, 173, 194; technology 63, 67–68, 113, 169; and trade 59–60, 65, 67; and transatlantic relations 113, 179, 184–86, 194–99; and Uighur Muslims 179, 218; and Western debt 70; *see also* BRI; 5G technology; Huawei; human rights; trade; Xi Jingping; *and individual countries and relationships*
Churchill, Winston 7, 33; *see also* transatlantic relations; transatlantic values; UN; World War II
CIA (Central Intelligence Agency) *see* intelligence
climate change 169; and Canada 79–80, 95, 96–97n1, 219–20; challenges of 79–80; and civil society institutions 88; and China 67, 88, 90–93; emissions targets 85, 92, 95–96; EU policy 80, 82–85, 89; global warming 92, 220; international summits 85, 88, 91; public attitudes on 205, 208, 215, 217, 219–20; skepticism 220; transatlantic cooperation 87–96, 171–72, 177, 219; US policy 80, 82–85, 89, 95; *see also* Biden, Joseph R., Jr.; environment; Obama, Barack; Paris Climate Agreement; Trump, Donald J.
Clinton, Bill 47, 114n8, 148, 199n9, 207; and China 187; environmental policy 84; and US transatlantic leadership 203, 211, 220; *see also* transatlantic relations
Clinton, Hillary 48; *see also* Obama, Barack
Cold War 61, 140, 173–74, 179, 213; with China 185–87, 189–90, 192, 194, 197;

end of 110–11; and EU 191; and Europe 10, 19, 46, 149, 193; and NATO 17, 104, 108, 110–13; and trade 123; and US foreign policy 106, 187, 189; *see also* Kissinger, Henry; Nixon, Richard; Soviet Union; transatlantic relations
Conference on Security and Cooperation in Europe 39; *see also* EU
Council of Europe 140
COVID-19 16–17, 51, 79, 241; and Canada-US relations 172; and China 58, 66, 68, 102, 192, 218; and Donald J. Trump 69, 248; and EU 72, 101, 165, 168; and transatlantic relations 11–12, 35, 96, 101–2, 205; and US foreign policy 222; *see also* Canada; China; public opinion; US; World Health Organization

Duda, Andrzej 251, 257, **258–59**, 260–62; *see also* populism; Prawo i Sprawiedliwość

ECSC (European Coal and Steel Community) 14, 32, 38, 42
Eisenhower, Dwight 33, 38, 41, 43, 104; *see also* Cold War; NATO; World War II
11 September 2001 17–18, 47, 50, 59, 220; *see also* Bush, George W.; Iraq War; War on Terror
environment 86, 167, 169, 242; anti-environmentalism 95; cap-and-trade 85, 89–90; civil society groups 128, 130–31; environmental degradation 79–81, 83, 94–96; environmental movement 80, 82–83, 86; environmental politics 90–91, 93–94; EU policy 79, 80–85, 96, 121–25, 129–32; EU-US cooperation on 80, 87–91, 93–95, 173; pollution 4, 79, 82–83, 86, 90, 94–95; public attitudes on 8, 81; Transatlantic Environmental Dialogue 40, 88; and transatlantic relations 6, 80, 88–90, 96, 128; US policy 79–84, 96; *see also* climate change; EPA; GMOs; Paris Climate Agreement; *and individual countries and leaders*
Environmental Action Programmes 83; *see also* climate change; environment
environmentalism *see* environment
EPA (Environmental Protection Agency): history of 82–84, 86; and Barack Obama 85–86, 90; and Donald J. Trump 84; *see also* climate change; environment
EU (European Union) 1, 102, 163; and Asia 69, 198–99; defense and security policy 3, 167, 178; history of 32, 163–64; NATO 49, 172, 175; and population movement 2, 20n4, 252; strategic autonomy 166, 168, 176; and transatlantic relations 37, 71, 68, 163–64, 168–70, 178; and trade 124–25, 127, 144, 163, 165–67, 177, 179; values of 165; *see also* climate change; environment; foreign policy; trade; Treaties of the European Union; *and individual countries, organizations, relationships, and trade agreements*
EU-Canada relations 30, 96–97n1, 163–64, 172, 179; history of 38–41, 170–73; and security 169, 171, 178; Strategic Partnership Agreements 130, 167–69, 171–72, 177, 188; and trade 119, 121, 130, 169–72, 176; *see also* Canada; trade; transatlantic relations; *and individual trade agreements*
EU-China relations: cooling off 190–93; rapprochement 67–68, 178, 185; sanctions 179, 184, 192; and security 73, 145; Strategy on China 165–67, 188, 191–93, 196; and trade 121, 166, 174, 177, 184, 190–91; *see also* China; human rights; trade; *and individual trade agreements*
Europe 59, 71, 102, 177, 213; and China 58, 61–63, 67–68, 72, 113, 184–88, 191–99; defence community 11, 14, 10–8, 113, 175–76, 217; history of relations with North America 31–34, 40–41, 43–48, 104; power and 149–51; population movement 11–14; and trade 16–17, 127, 173, 205; and US 3–4, 7, 9–10, 29, 44, 102, 116, 146–47, 220–1, 223; *see also* EU; human rights; intelligence; trade; transatlantic relations; *and individual countries, relationships, and trade agreements*
European Commission 15, 49–50, 175–76, 208, 254, 167; and China 67, 191, 121, 165–66; and climate change 85; "Global Europe" initiative 122–23; and GMOs 82; and human rights 151, 165; and trade 129–30; *see also* trade; von der Leyen, Ursula; WTO; *and individual trade agreements*
European Community/Communities 32, 38–39, 44, 83, 173; as concept 35, 164; *see also* EU
European Council 165, 249, 254; and environment 83; and defense 168; and human rights 145; and trade 127, 171; *see also individual trade agreements*
European Council on Foreign Relations 177–78, 212

European Defence Fund 70, 168, 176
European External Action Service 165–66, 172, 175
European Green Deal 80, 88, 96; *see also* climate change; environment
European Parliament: and defense 177; environmental policy 88; and human rights 151, 188, 191; and populism 152, 252, 260; and trade 125, 168, 170; and US 15, 169, 210, 228; *see also* EU; Europe; European Commission; European Council; populism; trade; *and individual trade agreements*
European Union Economic Community 38, 143; *see also* EU; trade
European Union Emissions Trading System 85, 89–90; *see also* climate change; environment
Euroskepticism 151, 254, 256–57; *see also* populism; public opinion
EU-US relations 1–3, 30, 41, 49–50, 131, 163–64, 168, 178; history of 15–16, 37–41, 173–76; and China 185, 195–99; EU-US trade 16, 119–22, 132–33, 170, 174, 176, 215; foreign policy and security 40, 73; and human rights 139; summits 14, 40–41, 51, 185; and trade 16, 122, 131–32, 173–76, 194, 204; and Trump administration 3, 176; *see also* bilateralism; environment; NATO; public opinion; trade

Farage, Nigel 251, 253–54, 257, **258–59**, 261–62; *see also* Brexit: Brexit Party
Fidesz 251, **258–59**, 260–61; *see also* Orbán, Viktor; populism
Financial Crisis (2007–8) 35, 48, 60, 69, 151
"Five Eyes" *see* intelligence
5G technology 63, 68, 71, 195, 218; *see also* Huawei
foreign policy 163; and China 112, 188, 190, 218; EU 73, 139, 143, 150, 152, 164–69, 175, 244; European 10, 59, 190; US 10–11, 103, 106, 108, 140, 148–50, 260; and France 114n8; and public opinion 204–6, 208, 211, 216, 218, 220; and US 10–11, 34, 140–41, 217, 222; *see also* human rights; *and individual countries and US presidents*
France 72, 108; and Barack Obama 107, 208; and China 61, 191, 193–94; and climate change 91–92; and Donald J. Trump 51, 109, 208; and Iraq War 47, 207; French public opinion 207–8, *214*, 215, 218; and NATO 43, 101–2, 107,
143, 145; US public opinion of 207; and US relations 42, 44, 104–5, 109, 113, 114n8, 184–85, 194; *see also* EU; Macron, Emmanuel; transatlantic relations
Fratelli d'Italia 251, **258–59**, 261; *see also* populism
free trade *see* trade
Front National 251, 253, **258–59**; *see also* Le Pen, Marine; populism; Trump, Donald J.

General Agreement on Tariffs and Trade *see* WTO
geoeconomics: and China 62, 67–68, 72; *see also* trade
geopolitics 2, 73, 173, 178, 184, 192, 213, 244; and China 67, 173, 184, 186, 192, 211; and EU 165, 168, 178; and NATO 102; transatlantic relations 239, 244; and Trump administration 211; and US 9–10, 31; *see also* power
Germany: and China 59, 61, 63–64, 67–68, 109, 184–85, 191, 193–95; defense 46, 70, 72–73; environmental policy 83, 88, 127; and human rights 145, 147; and NATO 39, 43, 45–46, 69, 102, 108, 113, 218; public opinion 177, 206–7, 211–13, *214*, 219; and trade 128, 131, 173, 175; and transatlantic relations 34, 46; and Trump administration 49–50, 176, 194–5; and US 109, 204; US public opinion on 207–8; *see also* EU; intelligence; Merkel, Angela; populism; trade; transatlantic relations
"Global Europe" initiative *see* European Commission
globalization 60, 103, 189; anti-globalization 204, **263**; and China 64, 112, 187, 191; deglobalization 155; pro-globalization 149, 186–87; and Trump administration 153–54, 253; *see also* populism; trade; Trump, Donald J.
global warming *see* climate change
GMOs (genetically modified organisms) 87, 94, 128; and Canada 126, 129; and EU 82, 87, 125–26, 129–30, 205; hormone beef 125–26, 129; and US 81, 87, 126, 205; *see also* climate change; environment; *and individual trade agreements*
Gorbachev, Mikhail 45–47; *see also* Cold War; Reagan, Ronald; Russia; Soviet Union
Green New Deal 95; *see also* Biden, Joseph R., Jr.; climate change; environment
G7 (Group of 7) 19, 46, 169, 207; environmental policy 198; summits 4, 49,

51, 171, 185–86; *see also* NATO; trade; *and individual countries and relationships*
G20 (Group of 20) 169, 171; *see also* G7; NATO; trade; *and individual countries and relationships*

Heritage Foundation, The: as advocacy think tank 233–34; and policymaking 235–36; politicization of 233; *see also* Reagan, Ronald; think tanks
hormone beef *see* GMOs
Huawei 63, 68, 195–6; *see also* China; 5G technology
human rights 140; and Canada 144, 147, 149; and China 140, 145, 149–51, 153–54, 166, 179, 188–89, 191–92; and EU 124, 128, 139–40, 143–46, 148–54, 167, 173; international 140–41, 147–48, 155; LGBTQIA 151, 165, 257; public opinion on 205, 208; sanctions 140, 142, 145, 154, 166, 184, 192; and trade 141–42, 144; and transatlantic relations 122, 147, 155, 169; and US 18, 139–43, 146, 149–50, 152–54; *see also* authoritarianism; populism; public opinion; *and individual countries, events, leaders, organizations, relationships, and treaties*
Hungary: and Biden presidency 257; and China 165, 193; and Donald J. Trump 257, 261; and EU 151, 165, 256; and NATO 110–11; *see also* populism; Orbán, Viktor
Huntington, Sam: Huntingtonianism 107; and NATO 108–9

immigration 9, 151; anti-immigration 255; restriction of 250, 256; and right-wing populism 151; *see also* migration; populism
India 12, 16–17; and China 66, 90, 92; and EU 92, 121, 123, 167, 174; and human rights 149; Quadrilateral Security Dialogue 66, 198; and US 92, 133, 198; *see also* EU; US; *and individual trade agreements*
intelligence: CIA 46, 152; "Five Eyes" 71; sharing 63, 71, 152, 195, 198
International Criminal Court 145, 148, 154, 221; US rejection of 149, 153–54; *see also* human rights
Iran: Green movement 60; Joint Comprehensive Plan of Action 18, 48, 50, 175; and EU 63, 145, 173; and Trump administration 18, 49, 153; *see also* EU; *and individual US presidents*
Iraq War 1, 154, 203, 211; and Germany 47, 204; and France 47; history of 152; and NATO 18, 48; opposition to 47, 204, 207, 209, 215, 219; and transatlantic relations 19, 194; *see also* War on Terror; *and individual countries and US presidents*
ISIL/ISIS *see* War on Terror
isolationism 107, 149; and US 31, 147, 178; *see also* Trump, Donald J.

Japan 14; and China 64–66, 70; environmental policy 91, 95; and EU 123, 125, 167, 171; and US 65, 69–70, 195; *see also* Kyoto Protocol; trade; *and individual trade agreements*
Joint Comprehensive Plan of Action *see* Iran
Juncker, Jean-Claude 166, 176, 254; *see also* European Commission; trade

Kennedy, John F. 43–44, 106; *see also* Cold War; NATO
Kerry, John *see* Biden, Joseph R., Jr.: environmental policy
Kissinger, Henry 44–46; as Atlanticist 34; and China 61; *see also* Cold War; NATO; Nixon, Richard
Kyoto Protocol 84–85, 94, 148; negotiation 89, 91; ratification 88; US rejection of 219; *see also* climate change; environment; Japan

Lega Nord 251, 255, **258–59**; *see also* populism; Salvini, Mateo
Le Pen, Marine 251; and Donald J. Trump 257, 261–62; and 6 January insurrection 253, **258–59**; 261–62, **263**; *see also* Front National; populism; public opinion; Trump, Donald J.; 2020 US presidential election
LGBTQIA (lesbian, gay, bisexual, trans, queer, intersex, and asexual) rights *see* human rights
Liberal International Order 33, 103, 105–7, 113, 169, 178, 204; and China 185
liberalism 110, 126, 140–41, 147, 187, 197; liberal democracy 6–8, 59, 61–62, 106, 109–12, 150, 155, 169; and China 60; liberal world order 18, 146, 153–54, 212; and right-wing populism 256; Wilsonian 153; and World War II 6, 103, 187; *see also* authoritarianism; human rights; nationalism; populism

Lisbon Treaty 124–25, 143, 146, 167, 177–78; and EU 175–76, 178; signing of 164; *see also* EU; Europe; trade; Treaties of the European Union

Maastricht Treaty 40, 82–83, 143
Macdonald, John A. 31–33; *see also* Canada; transatlantic relations
Macron, Emmanuel 114n1, 253; as Atlanticist 101; and China 72, 102; and Biden administration 51, 68, 107; and NATO 102–3, 107; and transatlantic relations 101; and Trump administration 51, 102–3, 107, 109, 195; and US leadership 210; *see also* EU-US relations; France; Merkel, Angela; NATO; *and individual US presidents*
Malmström, Cecilia 129–31; *see also* European Commission; trade
Marshall Plan 37–38, 42; *see also* Cold War; Eisenhower, Dwight; World War II
Merkel, Angela 176; and Barack Obama 48; and China 194; and NATO 102; and US leadership 210; *see also* EU; EU-US relations; Germany; NATO; *and individual US presidents*
Mexico: and EU 167; and NAFTA 39, 45; and population movement 11–12, 20n4; *see also* US; *and individual trade agreements*
migration: and asylum system 150–51, 255, 257; Migration Crisis 151; and right-wing populism 254, 256; *see also* populism; public opinion; *and individual countries*
Mogherini, Federica 49, 67, 166–68; *see also* EU; European Commission
Monnet, Jean 33–34, 42; and ECSC 38; and transatlantic relations 34
Mulroney, Brian 46, 51
multilateralism 105–6; and Biden administration 154, 221, 240; and China 191, 194, 197; and defense 243; and environmental policy 80, 87, 90–92, 94, 172; and EU 41, 149, 172, 177, 208; failure of 91; and human rights 140, 142, 149; and Obama administration 221; and public opinion 215, 221; and trade 169, 171; and Trump administration 153–54, 188, 191, 222; US public opinion on 140, 148, 206, 221–22; US challenge to 148–49, 153, 172, 222–23; *see also* human rights; public opinion; unilateralism; *and individual countries, trade agreements, and US presidents*

NAFTA (North American Free Trade Agreement) 39, 45, 170; *see also* Canada; Mexico; Reagan, Ronald; trade
National Front *see* Front National
nationalism 151, 170, 204–5, 252, 256; and Donald J. Trump 59, 146, 153; *see also* authoritarianism; liberalism; populism
National Rally *see* Front National
NATO (North Atlantic Treaty Organization) 3, 5, 103, 110, 113; and Afghanistan 50; Article 5 17, 51, 146, 217; and Biden administration 50–51, 103, 168–69, 185, 240; and burden sharing 18, 69, 104–5, 175, 229; challenges to 101–2, 107–9, 111, 113; and China 113, 198; and defense cooperation 172; Donald J. Trump 18, 49, 71, 103, 105, 146, 172, 198, 217–18, 242, 252; history of 32, 35, 37, 39–48, 104, 110–11, 148, 174; and human rights 110, 142–43, 145; and Iraq War 18, 204; language of 36; and populism 9, 151; public opinion of 213, 218; and Russia 111–12, 115n14; and transatlantic relations 19, 30, 107, 185–86, 196; and US public opinion 218; *see also* foreign policy; *and individual countries, organizations, and leaders*
New Transatlantic Agenda 40, 49, 87, 174
9/11 *see* 11 September 2001
Nixon, Richard 44–45, 61; *see also* China; Cold War; Kissinger, Henry
North Atlantic Council 37, 47–48; *see also* NATO
North Atlantic Treaty *see* NATO

Obama, Barack 51; environment policy 84–85, 88–89, 91; and EU 48, 150; European public opinion of 209–11; foreign policy 18, 48, 107, 217, 221; and Iran 18, 48; and NATO 18, 69; and Paris Climate Agreement 48, 91; "pivot to Asia" 64–65, 67, 113, 114n8, 133, 187, 189, 195; and trade 65, 127, 188; and transatlantic relations 8; and War on Terror 18, 152; *see also* Biden, Joseph R., Jr.; NATO; *and individual countries, leaders, and trade agreements*
"One Belt, One Road" initiative *see* BRI
Orbán, Viktor 251, 256; 6 January insurrection **258–59**, 261; *see also* populism; public opinion; Trump, Donald J.; 2020 US presidential election

Organisation for Economic Co-operation and Development 32, 143–44; *see also* human rights; UN

Paris Climate Agreement 48–50, 88, 153, 169, 172, 221; and Canada 93; and China 91–93; and EU 86, 91–93; negotiation 91–93; and US 50, 88, 91–94, 169; US withdrawal 153, 172; *see also* climate change; environment; EU; *and individual US presidents*
Partij voor de Vrijheid 251, 255, **258–59**; *see also* populism; Wilders, Geert
Pearson, Lester B. 33–34, 43; *see also* NATO
Pence, Michael 190; *see also* China; Trump, Donald J.; US-China relations
Permanent Structured Cooperation 37, 166, 168, 176, 178; *see also* EU
"pivot to Asia" *see* Obama, Barack
Pompeo, Michael: and China 61–62; and 6 January insurrection 62; *see also* Cold War; Trump, Donald J.; US
populism: anti-EU 256–57; approaches to 250; in Europe 9, 151–52, 220, 249–50, 252, 254, 257, 260–62, **263**; in France 250–51, 253, **258–59**, **263**; in Germany 250–55, **258–59**, 261–62; in Hungary 9, 111, 151, 177, 250–52, 257, **258–59**; influence of 152; in Italy 151, 250–51, 255–57, **258–59**, 260–61, **263**; and migration policy 253–55; nationalist populism 204–5; in the Netherlands 250–51, 255–56, **258–59**, 260; in Poland 9, 151, 250–51, 257, **258–59**, 260–62; rise of 9, 150; and 6 January insurrection **259**; in Spain 151, 250–51, 254–55, **258–59**, 260–61, **263**; in UK 9, 250–51, 253–54, 257, **258–59**, 261–62; in US 9, 84, 153, 155, 261; *see also* authoritarianism; Euroskepticism; nationalism; Orbán, Viktor; Trump, Donald J.; 2020 US presidential election; *and individual political organizations and leaders*
power: hard power 2, 6–7, 18, 41, 62, 139, 149, 177; soft power 2, 6–7, 41, 80, 173, 175, 177
Prawo i Sprawiedliwość 251, 257, **258–59**, 260; *see also* Andrzej Duda; populism
public opinion 206; on China 154–55, 186, 207, 211–13, *214*, 218, 252; on EU 151–52, 177, 204, 208, 211; on EU-US relations 16, 81, 105, 146, 205, 207, 218; and Iraq War 204, 215; 6 January insurrection 249; and think tanks 234, 243; on trade 216–18; and transatlantic relations 146, 203, 206, 215, 218–19, 222–23; on US leadership 154, 207, 208, *209*, 210–13, 217; *see also* anti-Americanism; transatlantic relations; *and individual countries and leaders*
Putin, Vladimir 49, 51, 111, 215, 217; *see also* NATO; Russia; Trump, Donald J.

Quadrilateral Security Dialogue *see individual countries*

REACH (Registration, Evaluation, Authorisation and Restriction of Chemicals) regulations 86, 90; *see also* climate change; environment
Reagan, Ronald: Cold War 19; defense policy 45; and Donald J. Trump 9; environmental policy 84; and public opinion 207; nuclear policy 46; and think tanks 236; and trade 45; *see also* NAFTA
resilience 6, 108, 173; definition of 4–6, 51; environmental 89; and NATO 5, 19, 103, 112–13; and transatlantic relations 4, 7, 11, 17, 19, 51, 80, 89, 94, 122, 174, 223, 228; and US 15, 29–30, 63
Roosevelt, Franklin 33–35, 41; *see also* Atlanticism; Churchill, Winston; transatlantic relations; World War II
Russia 173, 186; and China 2, 194; and Crimea 167; and EU 63, 150–51, 153, 167, 173, 175–77; and human rights 145, 149; and NATO 19, 47, 110–12, 115n14, 169, 198, 217; and public opinion 212–13, *214*; and right-wing populism 255; and transatlantic relations 169–70, 178–79; and Trump administration 217; and Ukraine 49, 51, 111–12, 194; and US 14, 212–13; *see also* Cold War; Putin, Vladimir; Soviet Union

Salvini, Mateo 251, 255–57, **258–59**, 260–61, **263**; *see also* Lega Nord; populism
6 January insurrection 29, 62, 248–49, 261–62; right-wing European reaction to 249, 251–52, **258–59**, 260–62, **263**; *see also* authoritarianism; Biden, Joseph R., Jr.; populism; Trump, Donald J.; 2020 US presidential election
Southeast Asia 64; ASEAN 65, 123, 188; and US trade 64
Soviet Union 59, 63; and Cold War 34, 43–46, 61, 111, 187, 192; breakdown of

60, 104, 143, 173, 211; EU-Soviet Action Plan 174; former Soviet client states 111–12, 194; and human rights 140; and US 189, 193; *see also* Cold War; NATO; Russia; transatlantic relations
Stoltenberg, Jens 50; *see also* NATO

tariffs: EU 119, 122–23, 125, 131, 144, 170, 176; and China 65; and Trump administration 121–22, 131, 170, 195, 240; US 119, 121–22, 126, 168, 176, 195; and WTO 123; *see also* trade; WTO; *and individual trade agreements*
terrorism *see* War on Terror
think tanks 228, 245; advocacy 233, 236, 243–44; and Barack Obama 241; and Biden administration 240–42, 244; and China 229; definition of 230–31; and EU 230–32, 234; in Europe 229–31, 237, 239, 243, 245; and foreign policy 3, 235–36; and policymaking 229, 232, 242; and public opinion 192; scholarship on 229; supranational 231–32, 238, 240, 242–43; and transatlantic relations 15, 40, 228, 230, 237, 239–40, 242; and Trump administration 61, 240–41; in US 229–38, 240–41, 243; US-EU think tank collaboration 237, 240, 243–44; *see also* liberalism; resilience; transatlantic relations; *and individual US presidents*
Tillerson, Rex 14; *see also* Pompeo, Michael; Trump, Donald J.; US
Toxic Substances Control Act 86, 90; *see also* climate change; environment
TPP (Trans-Pacific Partnership) 64–65; and Biden administration 64–65, 67; and China 64–65, 67, 188; and Japan 64; and negotiations 133; and Obama administration 65, 67, 188; opposition to 216; and Trump administration 64–65, 153, 188; *see also* trade; *and individual countries and leaders*
trade: disputes 16–17, 59, 121, 126, 146, 170; and defense and security 3, 7, 217, 222; and EU 124–25; free trade 38–40, 45, 66, 105, 122–23, 131; most-favored-nation status 119, 142; protectionism 101, 188, 216, 240; sanctions 126, 142; trade wars 64, 190; transatlantic relations 7, 15, 17, 41, 119; transatlantic trade 17, 38–40, 120–21, 205, 216–17; as weapon 62; *see also* human rights; *and individual countries, leaders, organizations, and trade agreements*

Transatlantic Declarations 39–40; 1990 Declaration 14, 40–41, 87, 174; *see also* transatlantic relations
Transatlantic Dialogues 185; on China 194–95, 197, 199n2; examples of 40; TransAtlantic Business Dialogue 40, 174
Transatlantic Economic Council 14, 41, 195; *see also* EU-US relations; trade
Transatlantic Environmental Dialogue *see* environment
transatlantic partnership 2, 7–8, 31, 133, 177, 206, 215; and Biden administration 30; and China 185–86; and NATO 19; and trade 120, 125; and US-EU relations 14, 40, 49, 133; *see also* transatlantic relations
transatlantic relations 4, 14–16, 243–45; challenges to 1, 9–11, 16–17, 19, 206, 215, 223; and climate change 80, 89, 94, 219; consensus 30, 114n5; defense and security 17, 19; and Donald J. Trump 1–3, 17, 176, 196, 242, 245; history of 33–41; knowledge exchange 15; and populism 204; public opinion 205–6, 222; relevance of 4, 6; *see also* Atlanticism; NATO; public opinion; resilience; think tanks; trade; transatlantic trade; transatlantic values; *and individual countries, leaders, organizations, and trade agreements*
transatlantic security *see individual countries, leaders, and organizations*
transatlantic trade *see* trade
transatlantic values 7, 41, 147, 151, 155, 169, 178–79; and EU 80–81, 129–30, 143, 150; and transatlantic relations 9, 49, 80, 146–47, 151; and US 62, 80–81, 155; values gap 8–9, 147, 215; World Values Survey 8, 147; *see also* human rights; liberalism; public opinion; transatlantic relations; UN
Treaties of the European Union 143–44; *see also individual treaties*
Trudeau, Justin 49, 51
Trudeau, Pierre Elliott 46, 51; *see also* Canada; Cold War
Trump, Donald J. 49, 103; and Canada 179; and China 59, 64, 133, 186, 189–92, 195–96; and COVID-19 58–59, 69, 248; environmental policy 80, 84–85, 88, 90, 94, 219; foreign policy 9, 64, 146, 153–54, 221, 223, 240, 243; and EU 1, 14, 16, 121, 172–77, 196, 205, 212, 221–22; and human rights 153–54; and Iran 18, 49, 153; and NATO 18, 49,

71, 102–3, 105, 146, 172, 198, 217–18, 242, 252; Paris Climate Agreement 93, 219; and populism 9, 84, 155; and public opinion 210–11; and right-wing populism 153, 175, 204, 249–50, 252–53, 255–56, **258–59**, 260–62; and security 3, 49–51, 103–7, 109, 217, 242; and think tanks 233; and trade 3, 62, 64–65, 130–31, 133, 205, 215–16, 240; and transatlantic relations 1, 6, 17, 146, 176, 178, 240, 243; and US exceptionalism 141; *see also* "America First"; 2020 US presidential election; *and individual countries and trade agreements*

TTIP (Transatlantic Trade and Investment Partnership): and China 187–88; collapse of 120, 131–32, 174–75; and EU 119, 129–30, 188, 217; negotiations 15, 66, 119, 170, 216, 125–26, 130; opposition to 120, 125–29, 216; and US 67, 174; *see also* GMOs; trade; *and individual countries and leaders*

2020 US presidential election 103, 257, **258**; Donald J. Trump 2–3, 29, 58–59, 62, 248, 251–52, 260; Joseph R. Biden, Jr. 177, 212, 230, 240–41, 248–49, 251–52, 260; and right-wing populism **258–59**, 260–262, **263**; *see also* authoritarianism; Biden, Joseph R., Jr.; populism; 6 January insurrection; Trump, Donald J.

UK (United Kingdom): and Canada 170; and China 61, 165, 191, 194; and Donald J. Trump 205; environmental policy 91, 126, 128; and EU 49, 165, 232, 244; and "Five Eyes" 71; foreign policy 198, 244; and human rights 143, 148, 165; and NATO 43, 143; and population movement 12–13; and public opinion 206–7, 209, 213, *214*, 215, 218–19; and think tanks 233; and trade 16, 44, 120, 122, 171, 237, 240, 242; and US 10, 91, 184, 212; *see also* Brexit; EU; intelligence; populism; trade; transatlantic relations
UKIP (UK Independence Party) 254, 257, **258–59**; see also Brexit; Farage, Nigel; populism
Ukraine *see* Russia
UN (United Nations) 7, 13, 32, 41–47, 144, 153, 163, 221; and climate change 84, 91; and human rights 148–49; and Donald J. Trump 153
unilateralism 221–22; and Trump administration 133, 153, 196; and George W. Bush administration 9, 47, 148, 152–53, 203, 211, 220; US preference for 31, 139, 148–49, 215, 221; *see also* bilateralism; multilateralism
UNHRC (UN Human Rights Council) 145, 147, 153–54
UN Security Council 46–48
US (United States); and Asia-Pacific region 64–67, 113, 133, 187–88, 195; and COVID-19 12, 58, 205, 222, 248; and debt 69–70; defense and security 3, 18, 63, 70–71, 107, 150–51, 189, 190, 195, 139, 217–18; environmental policy 79–83, 84, 87–96, 222; history of 31–33, 44–45; and human rights 139, 140–42, 146–49, 152–55; and NATO 9, 32, 36–38, 43, 46–47, 49–50, 71, 101, 103, 105–7, 148, 172; leadership 3, 106–9, 140, 189, 154, 196, 206, *209*, 210–12, 217; nuclear policy 44–46, 70, 104; population movement 11–13; and public opinion 105–6, 177–78, 196, 205–6, 223, 261; public opinion on climate change 219–20; and trade 16, 119, 121, 125, 170, 176, 215–16, 240; and trade deficit 16, 70, 170, 215; and transatlantic relations 10, 31, 163, 168–70, 176, 196, 223; *see also* foreign policy; intelligence; multilateralism; transatlantic relations; unilateralism; *and individual countries, organizations, relationships, trade agreements, and US presidents*
US-China relations 65, 133, 197, 199n14; cold war between 112–13, 185, 190–91, 192; and currency manipulation 189; decoupling of 63, 190–91; history of 60, 187–89, 194–95; and Indo-Pacific region 66, 184, 198; and intellectual property 189; as rivals 58–65, 67, 71, 154, 190, 192–93; sanctions 166; and security 66, 155, 169, 190; and technology 63, 68, 71–72, 132; and trade 16, 61, 64, 67, 187–88, 190, 196; *see also* COVID-19; *and individual trade agreements and US presidents*

von der Leyen, Ursula 166, 168; and Biden administration 122, 177; and China 71; *see also* EU Commission; trade
Vox 251, 254, **258–59**, 260–61; *see also* Abascal, Santiago; populism

War on Terror 18, 140, 145, 150, 152, 199n2, 204, 220; al-Qaeda 47–48, 152;

ISIL/ISIS 150, 152; and public opinion 203; *see also* Iraq War; *and individual countries and US presidents*
Washington Treaty 36–37, 41, 105; *see also* NATO
Wilders, Geert 251, 255–56, **258–59**, 260; *see also* Partij voor de Vrijheid; populism
World Health Organization 58, 153
World War I 34, 217
World War II 42, 253; and Atlanticists 33; and EU-US relations 173–75; and human rights 143; and transatlantic relations 32, 34–35, 176, 179; and US leadership 3, 102; *see also* liberalism; NATO; *and individual leaders*
WTO (World Trade Organization) 119, 122; and Canada 122, 126, 172; and China 185, 187, 195; decline of 123; disputes 121–23, 126, 170; and EU 121–22, 126, 170, 172; General Agreement on Tariffs and Trade 122; and US 121–22, 126, 170, 172, 195; *see also* trade; *and individual countries and trade agreements*

Xi Jingping 63; *see also* China; *and individual countries, relationships, and trade agreements*